# WARSHIPBUILDING ON THE CLYDE

## Naval Orders and the Prosperity of the Clyde Shipbuilding Industry, 1889–1939

### HUGH B. PEEBLES

JOHN DC
EDINBU

D1341592

Published in 2000 by
John Donald, an imprint of
Birlinn Limited
8 Canongate Venture
5 New Street
Edinburgh
EH8 8BH

First published in 1987 by
John Donald Publishers Limited

ISBN  0 85976 530 X

British Library Cataloguing-in-Publication Data
A catalogue record for this book is available from the British Library

Cover design by Barrie Tullett
Cover image of HMS *Hood* and plate 9 by courtesy of
Glasgow University Archives & Business Records Centre

Printed and bound by Redwood Books, Trowbridge

# Contents

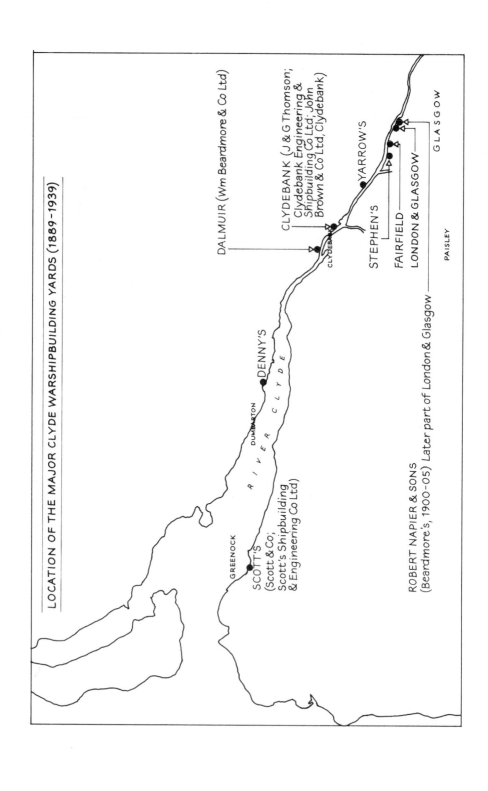

LOCATION OF THE MAJOR CLYDE WARSHIPBUILDING YARDS (1889–1939)

DALMUIR (Wm Beardmore & Co Ltd)

CLYDEBANK (J & G Thomson;
Clydebank Engineering &
Shipbuilding Co Ltd; John
Brown & Co Ltd, Clydebank)

YARROW'S

STEPHEN'S

FAIRFIELD

LONDON & GLASGOW

ROBERT NAPIER & SONS
(Beardmore's, 1900–05) Later part of London & Glasgow

GLASGOW

PAISLEY

CLYDEBANK

DENNY'S

DUMBARTON

RIVER CLYDE

SCOTT'S
(Scott & Co;
Scott's Shipbuilding
& Engineering Co Ltd)

GREENOCK

# Foreword

Through no fault of my own the original edition of this work omitted the acknowledgements which I had prepared. I am glad that this reprint affords me the opportunity, belatedly, to repair my publisher's omission.

This book is the product of research sponsored by the Social Science Research Council. Without their funding this book could never have been written and I am grateful to them and to the Department of Accountancy at the University of Stirling, which subsequently employed me, for their support.

I am indebted to the Keeper of the Records of Stirling and the staff of the Scottish Record Office; to Michael Moss and the staff of Glasgow University Archives; to Richard Dell and the staff of Strathclyde Regional Archives; and to the staff of the Mitchell Library for all their assistance in my researches.

While writing up my research and preparing the manuscript for this book I was fortunate to have as a colleague in the Department of Accountancy at Stirling Dr K. A. Ashford, who was prepared to give freely of his time in introducing me to the mysteries of the word-processor.

Above all I owe an enormous debt of gratitude to my supervisor, Professor R. H. Campbell, without whose encouragement and support my original thesis would never have been completed.

Hugh Peebles, May 2000

# 1
## Introduction

A number of writers have remarked upon the important part played by naval work in tiding the Clyde shipbuilding industry over the great depression of the 1930s. Dr. N. K. Buxton, in his comparative study of the Scottish shipbuilding industry in the inter-war period, has suggested that a high share of naval orders helped cushion the Clyde against the full impact of market forces with the result that it suffered less acutely from the slump than other shipbuilding districts in the United Kingdom and recovered more rapidly from it.[1] Professor R. H. Campbell, in an overview of the problems of the Scottish economy in the inter-war period, has noted the importance of naval work in providing a 'basis of activity' for Clyde shipyards in the mid and late 1930s when other work was in short supply.[2] In a later study, the same author has suggested that 'only demand for naval vessels kept the industry active'.[3] Professor A. Slaven, from the different perspective of a study of the experience of one of the leading Clyde firms in the inter-war period, has described naval orders as providing an 'infusion of profitable work' which played a major part in saving the ailing Clydebank yard of John Brown & Co. from extinction in the 1930s.[4]

For Clydebank, as for most of the Clyde firms which benefited from the revival in naval demand in the 1930s, warshipbuilding was not a new departure. It was rather a fresh opportunity to exercise skills and make use of expensive facilities acquired before the First World War.

The foundations of the Clyde warshipbuilding industry had been laid in the middle of the nineteenth century when Robert Napier, the 'Father' of the modern Clyde shipbuilding industry, built a succession of major warships, including one of the Royal Navy's first two 'ironclads' — HMS BLACK PRINCE. Up to 1889 the opportunities for private firms to build warships for the Royal Navy were limited as the Royal Dockyards had first call on Admiralty orders and extensive use was made of private yards only in an emergency. Nevertheless, a number of firms on the Clyde followed Napier's example in seeking Admiralty orders, and the experience gained in the thirty years following the introduction of the 'ironclad' in 1859 enabled these firms to take full advantage of the much more favourable conditions which prevailed from 1889 onwards when a massive expansion of the Royal Navy necessitated extensive use of private yards. In the twenty-five years between 1889 and the outbreak of the First World War in 1914 Clyde firms secured Admiralty orders for warships aggregating 793,481 tons, 44.56% of the total tonnage put out to contract by the Admiralty.[5] After the First World War, the British Government's decision to adopt a policy of arms limitation by international agreement denied Clyde firms the opportunity of continuing warshipbuilding on a large scale, but the experience gained before and during the war, when the Clyde's warshipbuilding capacity had been fully extended in meeting 43.08% of the Admiralty's wartime demand for warships,[6] stood them in good stead when the demand for warships revived with the beginnings of rearmament in the early 1930s. In the inter-war period, as before, the Clyde was, as Dr. Buxton remarks, 'the most important single private producer of naval tonnage for the Admiralty'.[7]

Until recently, this aspect of the Clyde shipbuilding industry has received little attention from historians. Warshipbuilding has long featured prominently in the histories of individual firms,[8] but, apart from a paper delivered by Sir John Biles in 1909,[9] nothing has been written of the importance of the Clyde as a warshipbuilding centre before the First World War, and Professor Campbell has broken new ground by making extensive reference to warshipbuilding in a recent study of the performance of the Clyde shipbuilding industry up to 1939.[10] Economic histories published before 1980 make little mention of warshipbuilding in dealing with this phase of the Clyde shipbuilding industry's development. Professor Campbell, writing in 1965, merely noted in passing that naval orders contributed to the industry's pre-war prosperity.[11] Some accounts of the industry's development up to 1914 make no mention of warshipbuilding at all.[12] Significantly, most references to the importance of naval work appear only in relation to the period after 1931 when the onset of the great depression brought merchant shipbuilding to a virtual standstill.

Viewed from the perspective of the Clyde shipbuilding industry as a whole, the importance of warshipbuilding is not immediately apparent. The Clyde owed its meteoric rise, from being a relatively unimportant provincial shipbuilding centre in the early nineteenth century to its pre-eminent position at the hub of the world's shipbuilding industry little more than half a century later, to the technical achievements of the local engineers and shipbuilders, who led the way in the application of steam power to marine propulsion and in the building of ships of iron and steel. Naval work made a minimal contribution to these developments. Success brought the Clyde to the attention of the Admiralty and paved the way for later naval orders, but it was the patronage of merchant shipowners which was largely responsible for the spectacular growth of the industry.[13] From 1889 onwards naval work was of more importance than it had been previously, and it is generally agreed that output figures which equate one displacement ton of warship with one gross ton of merchant ship understate the relative value of naval work.[14] Even so, warships still accounted for no more than a fraction of the total output of the Clyde shipbuilding industry in peacetime. In no year between 1889 and 1913 or between 1920 and 1938 did warships account for more than 14.5% of the total tonnage launched on the Clyde, and in both the five years before the First World War and the five years before the Second World War, when the demand for warships was at its height, merchant work accounted for over 91% of the tonnage launched.[15] More important, warshipbuilding in peacetime involved only a minority of the firms in the industry. Virtually all of the warships built on the

Clyde in peacetime between 1889 and 1939 were the work of one of only eight firms, and no more than seven of these firms were actively engaged in warshipbuilding at any one time.[16]

Warshipbuilding assumes greater significance when account is taken of the importance of these firms. They were the technical elite of the Clyde shipbuilding industry. All were able to combine warshipbuilding with the highest classes of merchant work and most of them did.[17] In consequence a large part of the total merchant output of the Clyde shipbuilding industry was produced in yards which combined naval and merchant work. Treating the firms involved in warshipbuilding before and after the First World War as separate groups, they accounted for 23.56% of the Clyde's total merchant output between 1894–1913 and for no less than 29.25% of its total merchant output in the inter-war period.[18] Given the value of their naval work and the higher quality and correspondingly greater value per ton of their merchant output compared with most merchant ships built on the Clyde, it is likely that the warshipbuilding firms were responsible for upwards of 40% of the total value of all the work undertaken by the Clyde shipbuilding industry between 1889 and 1939.[19] If, as Professor Campbell's recent study suggests, many of these firms depended on naval work for their prosperity in the years before the First World War, the case for a reassessment of the importance of warshipbuilding is compelling.[20]

This study explores the circumstances under which an important sector of the Clyde shipbuilding industry chose to specialise in naval work and tries to assess the extent to which the choice of warshipbuilding as a specialisation sustained them in the years before the First World War and put them at a disadvantage in the inter-war period when the demand for warships was less buoyant. It is based on an analysis of material extracted from the accounting records of the firms themselves. These records are of three main types. First, formal sets of annual financial statements designed for publication and produced to satisfy statutory requirements; second, informal accounts and working papers prepared for the information of management; third, the financial and cost records from which the first two were prepared. Complete sets of records covering the whole of the fifty-year period are rare and, in practice, relatively complete sets of accounting records survive for only three of the leading firms.[21] Further, even where they are available, such records need to be used with discretion. As Professor Marriner has pointed out, published annual financial statements are, at best, relatively uninformative and, at worst, positively misleading as historical documents:[22] informal accounts and working papers may be informative but, in the absence of the records from which they were prepared, they need to be interpreted with great care: the financial and cost records themselves are as likely to mislead as to inform anyone who lacks at least a thorough working knowledge of book-keeping if not a formal training in accountancy. Nevertheless, the records which have survived contain a wealth of information, and careful examination of them has yielded a mass of accounting and cost data.

Readers seeking full details of these data, the sources used and the methodology employed in collecting and collating it are referred to the volume of appendices attached to my unpublished thesis,[23] but it is appropriate here to make special mention of some of the terms used extensively in the text, as it is open to misrepresentation if these terms are not accorded the specific meaning given to them by the author for the purposes of this study. TRADING PROFIT, the standard measure of profitability used throughout the text, is defined as the operating profit excluding exceptional items and before deducting provisions for depreciation of fixed assets, bank and loan interest, debenture interest and taxation. In striking the trading profit before providing for depreciation of fixed assets, the author is aware that he is at odds with modern accounting practice but, at the time in question, provisions for depreciation were generally viewed as appropriations of profit and it was unusual for firms to include depreciation in overheads for costing purposes. The exclusion of exceptional items, which are defined as all amounts written off investments, all profits and losses on the sale of investments, and material items of a non-recurring nature whose inclusion in trading profits would give a distorted view of the trading results, is less controversial although the judgment as to whether specific items are 'non-recurring' is necessarily a subjective one.[24] NET ADDITIONS TO FIXED ASSETS are defined as fixed assets purchased less the book value of fixed assets sold or scrapped. This has been chosen as the standard measure of capital expenditure in preference to gross capital expenditure primarily because the book value of disposals is extremely difficult to determine without reference to detailed plant registers which are not always available.

As regards the profitability of contracts there are two distinct measures available. The first, NET PROFIT OR LOSS, is the net profit or loss on the contract as calculated by the managements of the firms themselves. The second, CONTRIBUTION TO OVERHEADS AND PROFIT, is defined as the balance remaining after deducting from invoice price, amounts reserved for agents and levies and the costs of materials and labour only. Both terms are used in the text, the former where it is appropriate to give an indication of management's perception of the outcome of a contract, the latter as the standard measure of the profitability of contracts for the purposes of both inter-firm and intra-firm comparison. This distinction is vital as the net profit or loss computed by management is struck after deducting overhead charges allocated to contracts on arbitrary bases which varied not only between different firms but within the same firm over time and even between one contract and another.[25]

The study is arranged in chronological order so that the actions of the warshipbuilders can be seen not only in the context of their own immediate situation but also in the wider contexts of fluctuations in the fortunes of the Clyde shipbuilding industry as a whole and the evolution of Admiralty policy in response to changing political, strategic and technical priorities.

The next two chapters examine the links which were forged between the Clyde shipbuilding industry and the Admiralty in the decades before 1889 when Admiralty orders were relatively scarce. Chapter 2 concentrates on the seminal role of Robert Napier as the founder of the Clyde warshipbuilding industry. Chapter 3 explores the interest shown by other Clyde shipbuilders in naval contracts at a time when conditions made Admiralty work less attractive than it subsequently became.

The three chapters which follow cover the period between 1889 and 1914. Chapter 4 deals with the response of Clyde firms to the opportunities which opened up as a result of the expansion of the Royal Navy in the 1890s with particular emphasis on the circumstances in which individual firms found themselves at the time. Chapter 5 traces the rapid growth of the Clyde warshipbuilding industry between 1899 and 1907 and the effect of the intervention of the great armaments manufacturers on its development. Chapter 6 examines the experience of the Clyde warshipbuilders between 1907 and 1914 when a short period of relatively low naval demand was followed by what proved to be a profitless boom as the naval arms race with Germany gathered momentum.

The following four chapters cover the period from 1914 to the outbreak of the Second World War in 1939. Chapter 7, which covers the First World War and its immediate aftermath, explores the extent to which the Clyde warshipbuilders' contribution to the war effort placed them at a disadvantage at the end of the war and assesses their situation in 1921 when the Washington Treaty heralded the beginning of an era of arms limitation. Chapters 8 and 9 deal with the problems created by arms limitation in the period between 1921 and 1934. Chapter 8, which deals with the period between 1921 and 1929, highlights the problems which the Clyde warshipbuilders faced in finding profitable employment for their facilities even when merchant work was relatively plentiful. Chapter 9, which deals with the crisis which ensued when a further reduction in naval programmes was followed by the total collapse of merchant demand in the early 1930s, highlights the extent to which the financial stability of some of the leading Clyde warshipbuilders had been compromised by the post-war disintegration of the armaments industry. Chapter 10 examines the extent to which rearmament had resolved the warshipbuilders' problems by the outbreak of war in 1939.

Finally, Chapter 11 reviews the salient features of the development of the Clyde warshipbuilding industry up to 1939 and argues that, although the achievements of the Clyde warshipbuilders should not be exaggerated and certain aspects of their performance are open to criticism, naval work was of critical importance not only in sustaining an important part of the Clyde shipbuilding industry before the First World War but also in enabling it to survive the inter-war period.

### NOTES

1. N. K. Buxton, 'The Scottish Shipbuilding Industry between the Wars: A Comparative Study', *Business History*, Vol. X (1968).

2. R. H. Campbell, *Scotland since 1707: The Rise of an Industrial Society* (Oxford 1965), 1971 edition, p. 261.

3. R. H. Campbell, *The Rise and Fall of Scottish Industry, 1707–1939* (Edinburgh 1980), p. 163.

4. A. Slaven, 'A Shipyard in Depression: John Brown's of Clydebank, 1919–1938', *Business History*, Vol. XIX (1977).

5. See Appendix D.

6. *Ibid.*

7. See Buxton, 'The Scottish Shipbuilding Industry between the Wars'. While the statement happens to be based on figures taken from the Statistical Abstract for the United Kingdom, which seriously overstates the Clyde's output of warships in the 1920s by wrongly crediting it with an output of 35,000 tons in 1925 rightly attributable to the Mersey, the substance of the claim is justified.

8. See especially Sir Allan Grant, *Steel and Ships: The History of John Brown's* (London 1950); *The Fairfield Shipbuilding & Engineering Works* (London 1909); C. R. V. More, The Fairfield Shipbuilding and Engineering Co. Ltd. 1889–1914, unpublished M.Litt. Thesis (London School of Economics 1976); J. R. Hume & M. S. Moss, *Beardmore: The History of a Scottish Industrial Giant* (London 1979); *Two Centuries of Shipbuilding by Scotts at Greenock* (London 1906); *Yarrow & Co. Ltd., 1865–1977* (Glasgow 1977); J. L. Carvel, *Stephens of Linthouse: A record of Two Hundred Years of Shipbuilding* (Glasgow 1951).

9. J. H. Biles, 'Fifty Years of Warshipbuilding on the Clyde', *North-East Coast Institute of Engineers and Shipbuilders Transactions*, Vol. XXVI (1908–09).

10. Campbell, *The Rise and Fall of Scottish Industry*, pp. 60–68 & 136–40.

11. Campbell, *Scotland since 1707*, p. 231.

12. Most notably H. Hamilton, *The Industrial Revolution in Scotland* (Oxford 1932: reissued London 1966); A. Slaven, *The Development of the West of Scotland, 1750–1960* (London 1975).

13. Up to 1859 the Clyde's output of warships was negligible. Between 1859 and 1878 it produced 73,341 tons of warships for the Admiralty and a further 27,189 tons of warships for foreign governments but, over the same period, the total output of the Clyde shipyards was 3,190,571 tons.

14. See F. C. Lane, 'Tonnage, Medieval and Modern', *Economic History Review*, Second Series Vol. XVII (1964) and S. Pollard & P. Robertson, *The British Shipbuilding Industry, 1870–1914* (Cambridge, Mass. 1979), pp. 237–8.

15. See Appendix A. The peak year was 1903. Warships accounted for 8.8% of the total tonnage produced in 1908–1913 and for 8.7% of the total tonnage produced in 1934–1938.

16. The eight firms were — 1) J. & G. Thomson, which became in turn J. & G. Thomson Ltd., the Clydebank Engineering and Shipbuilding Co. Ltd. and John Brown & Co. Clydebank; 2) The Fairfield Shipbuilding & Engineering Co. Ltd; 3) Robert Napier & Sons which was taken over by William Beardmore & Co. in 1900; 4) Scott's Shipbuilding & Engineering Co. Ltd., an amalgamation of Scott & Co. and the Greenock Foundry Co. Ltd; 5) The London & Glasgow Engineering & Iron Shipbuilding Co. Ltd; 6) Alexander Stephen & Sons Ltd; 7) Alfred Yarrow & Co. which subsequently became Yarrow & Co. Ltd; 8) William Denny Brothers Ltd., an amalgamation of William Denny & Co. and Denny Brothers. The London & Glasgow discontinued warshipbuilding after being taken over by Harland & Wolff in 1913. Stephen's did not commence warshipbuilding in peacetime until the 1930s.

17. Of the eight firms, only Yarrow's produced very little merchant work.

18. See Appendix B.

19. In the absence of details of the selling prices of all the ships built in Clyde yards this is necessarily a rough estimate but the relatively high value of the merchant output of the leading warshipbuilding yards is well illustrated by the value of Fairfield's merchant output in the years before the First World War. In the ten years to 1913 Fairfield launched merchant ships aggregating 206,911 tons. The invoice value of this output was £5,715,216. By comparison, the firm of Russell & Co., the leading tramp builder on the Clyde, which launched 677,593 tons of ships in the same period, had total sales of only £7,888,589 in the ten years to November 1914.

20. Campbell, *The Rise and Fall of Scottish Industry*, p. 61.

21. Clydebank, Fairfield and Scott's.

22. S. Marriner, 'Company Financial Statements as Source Material for Business Historians', *Business History*, Vol. XXII (1980).

23. H. B. Peebles, Warshipbuilding on the Clyde, 1889–1939: A Financial Study, unpublished Ph.D. thesis (University of Stirling 1986) (hereafter referred to simply as thesis), Volume II.

24. Ibid.

25. For a more detailed discussion of this problem, see R. H. Campbell, 'Overhead Costs and Profitability: A Note of Some Uses of Business Records', *Scottish Industrial History*, I (1977).

# 2

# Robert Napier and the Foundation of the Clyde Warshipbuilding Industry

The credit for laying the foundations of the Clyde warshipbuilding industry belongs to Robert Napier. Scott's of Greenock were the builders of a wooden sloop commissioned during the Napoleonic Wars[1] but, at that time, there was little to distinguish Clyde shipbuilders from the numerous small-scale enterprises which had come into existence during the eighteenth century to serve the local needs of other Scottish seaports[2] and Scott's had little claim to being more than one of many provincial shipyards capable of building wooden hulls which met Admiralty requirements in time of war. By contrast Robert Napier brought to naval work the reputation of one of the world's foremost experts on steam propulsion and his warships were built in one of the first of the great new iron shipyards which made the Clyde the world's leading shipbuilding district in the late nineteenth century.

Robert Napier, born in 1789, was the son of a blacksmith. Having followed his father's trade he set up in business on his own account in Glasgow in 1815 when marine engineering was still in its infancy.[3] In 1812 Robert Napier's cousin and brother-in-law David Napier had been responsible for the boilers of Henry Bell's COMET,[4] and, in 1818, the ROB ROY, for which David Napier designed the hull and provided the machinery, was the first steam-powered ship to operate a regular service on the open sea.[5] Robert Napier probably gained from his relationship with David Napier but in these early days it was not exceptional for mechanics with a working knowledge of factory machinery to be commissioned to supply the engines for a ship[6] and, although Robert Napier undertook to make the engines for his first steamship in 1823,[7] two years after moving to the works at Camlachie from which David Napier had supplied the machinery for the ROB ROY,[8] he established his personal reputation in 1827 when ships powered by his engines took the first two places in a race to determine the fastest steamer on the Clyde.[9]

Napier's achievement enabled him to exploit the opportunities which were opening up as a result of the pioneering of the new technology on the Clyde[10] and, having moved to more convenient premises in central Glasgow, he proceeded to equip them with heavy machine tools for manufacturing larger engines in 1830.[11] As a result his business prospered and during the 1830s he added to his growing personal reputation by undertaking the construction of the engines for some of the largest steamships of the time. The patronage of T. Assheton Smith, for whom he built a series of steam yachts, led to his being entrusted with the order for the engines of the East India Company's BERENICE in 1835[12] and, although he was initially unsuccessful in his bid to supply the engines of the BRITISH QUEEN, a transatlantic steamer of 1,862 tons then being built on the Thames, the work reverted to him when the successful bidder was unable to complete the contract.[13] Success in this venture further enhanced his reputation, and the experience gained in supplying the engines for the BRITISH QUEEN, together with the connection with the East India Company, led to an approach by Samuel Cunard, the Halifax agent of the East India Company, who sought Napier's advice on the design of steamships for a projected transatlantic mail service. Napier's contribution was crucial to the successful launching of Cunard's British and North American Royal Mail Steam Packet Company in the early 1840s. At a time when steamships were still notoriously unreliable, Napier designed the ships and provided the engines which fulfilled the exacting requirements of the mail contract. On his advice the ships were made larger and more powerful than Cunard had originally contemplated and he was instrumental in persuading wealthy shipowners to back his judgement by putting up the extra capital needed to finance the venture.[14] Not only did much of the credit for the success of the venture accrue to him, he also gained an important customer who was to favour him with prestigious contracts for the next twenty years.

Up to this time Napier had confined himself to designing the ships and providing the machinery, leaving it to others to build the hulls, but by the early 1840s it was becoming increasingly difficult to construct wooden hulls capable of withstanding the stresses imposed by the largest steam engines and Napier was having difficulty with the subcontractors to whom he entrusted the building of his hulls.[15] As a result Napier was one of the first of the Clyde engineers to take an active interest in building iron ships,[16] which opened the way for larger and more powerful vessels.[17] In 1841 he purchased the small iron shipyard founded by McArthur and Alexander[18] and began iron shipbuilding on his own account.[19] At first the output of the shipyard was modest by comparison with the capacity of Napier's engine and boiler shops, which were now centred on the Lancefield Works, first leased and then purchased from his cousin David after the latter's departure for London in 1836,[20] and Napier's first iron steamer — the VANGUARD — launched in 1843 amounted to only 681 tons,[21] but by the early 1850s the growing demand for iron ships[22] encouraged Napier to purchase more ground at Govan on which he laid out a new yard capable of building vessels up to 400 feet long.[23] Meanwhile, to secure a supply of forgings for his shipyard and engine works,[24] he had also acquired, nominally on behalf of his sons, the Parkhead Forge previously owned by his now bankrupt cousin David.[25]

The firm of Robert Napier & Sons therefore gradually assumed the character of a fully integrated shipbuilding and engineering business and, although there is no reason to suppose that Napier had any intention of doing more than fitting himself for the task of building the large iron steamers required by such customers as Cunard, for whom he built the 3,300 ton PERSIA in 1854,[26] the facilities he had created also enabled him to undertake the building of the great iron warships which were to absorb most of his energies in the closing years of his life.

Robert Napier had been cultivating a connection with the Admiralty since the

1830s when he had first sought to secure contracts for the engines of naval ships.[27] The Royal Navy's ships were not generally fitted with steam engines until after the Crimean War, by which time the development of screw propulsion removed the need for paddle-drive which obstructed a warship's broadside and the introduction of more compact upright engines allowed machinery to be housed below the waterline where it was less vulnerable in battle.[28] Nevertheless, the Navy had ordered its first steam tug as early as 1821[29] and, by the 1830s, the growing demand for engines for small naval ships made it worthwhile for an enterprising engine builder to seek a share of Admiralty business.

At first Napier's attempts to establish himself as an Admiralty contractor were frustrated by the tendency of the naval authorities to favour specialist firms in the London area with whom they had already established a good working relationship but, after he had successfully completed the engines for the BERENICE for the East India Company and started on the machinery for the BRITISH QUEEN, his claims could not be ignored and he was awarded the contracts for the engines of two naval ships in 1838.[30] Providing the engines for HMS VESUVIUS and HMS STROMBOLI did not end Napier's difficulties, and only when a friendly MP[31] forced the Admiralty to admit that Napier's engines were proving to be trouble-free and less costly to maintain than those of his competitors was he given further opportunities to undertake naval work.[32] However, once Napier had overcome the Admiralty's initial reluctance to grant him recognition, his position as an Admiralty contractor was assured. First, as Melville, the Secretary of the East India Company, pointed out to Samuel Cunard in advising him to take Napier's advice on the machinery required for his transatlantic steamers:

> He was the great authority on steam navigation and knew much more about the subject than the Admiralty.[33]

Second, his acknowledged mastery of steam propulsion, together with his possession of an iron shipyard in the early 1840s, made him a strong contender when the Admiralty was seeking contractors to undertake the building of iron warships.

In the age of wooden warships, warshipbuilding had been the jealously guarded prerogative of the Royal Dockyards. In time of war or great national emergency their resources were sometimes augmented by subcontracting work to private yards, as in refurbishing the fleet at the end of the American War and again during the protracted struggle with Napoleonic France,[34] but, under normal circumstances, there had been little reason for the Admiralty to look beyond the ample resources of its own establishments. When the essential characteristics of naval ships had changed little in two hundred years[35] and the maintenance of British seapower, resting as it did on her possession of a large fleet of wooden warships, called for little more than regular refits and the occasional replacement of ships nearing the end of what was normally a very long working life,[36] no private yard could hope to match the skill and expertise of dockyard craftsmen who could draw on the fund of experience which the Royal Dockyards possessed through having been engaged continuously in repairing and building the Navy's ships since Tudor times. This established order was overturned by the advent of iron shipbuilding and, although the Admiralty was understandably reluctant to pioneer a development which would render its existing fleet obsolete, it could not ignore the possibility that Britain's naval supremacy might be lost if another power took advantage of the new technology and gained a decisive advantage by building iron warships. Accordingly the Admiralty was forced to explore the feasibility of iron warships, and as iron shipbuilding called for a blend of skills which the Royal Dockyards did not as yet possess, it was necessary to subcontract the work to private firms.

Admiralty orders for some of the Royal Navy's earliest iron ships laid the foundations of Robert Napier's fame as a warshipbuilder. In 1843 he was commissioned to build the Navy's first three paddle-driven iron steamers[37] and the following year he received the more important order for HMS SIMOON, one of five experimental iron-hulled screw frigates ordered from private contractors in that year.[38] Napier's first experience of warshipbuilding was far from encouraging. HMS SIMOON, laid down in December 1845, was not launched until May 1849 because of repeated changes of mind on the part of the Admiralty[39] and, although Napier received some financial compensation for the delay, he apparently did not consider the amount sufficient to compensate for the inconvenience to which he had been put.[40] Nevertheless he was undeterred and the absence of further orders for iron warships until 1855 probably owed less to his unwillingness to undertake the work than to the Admiralty's temporary loss of interest in iron warships.

When the Admiralty had ordered the five iron frigates in 1844 it had been hoped that iron hulls would afford warships greater protection against gunfire. This proved not to be the case. Tests subsequently showed that damage caused by solid round shot was as serious in iron-hulled ships as in the existing wooden hulls.[41] As a result the Royal Navy dropped all thought of iron warships until the experience of the Crimean War reminded them of the vulnerability of wooden warships to shellfire.[42] The French led the way in demonstrating that specially thickened iron plates afforded an effective measure of protection for the floating batteries employed in the siege of Sebastapol and the Admiralty followed their example. Napier's HMS EREBUS and her sister ship, HMS TERROR, built by Palmer's on the Tyne, were designed as copies of the French vessels.[43] Launched in 1856, they were not completed in time to see service in the Crimea, and floating batteries had no place in the Royal Navy in peacetime. Nevertheless, they were the Navy's first armoured vessels and their builders, who had accepted contracts which involved a penalty of £1,000 per day for late delivery,[44] gained some useful insights into the technical problems associated with the manufacture of armoured plates[45] in advance of the building of the first 'ironclad' battleship which followed in 1859.

The introduction of armour plate into ships of the line was forced upon the Admiralty by France's action in ordering the world's first armoured wooden battleship — the GLOIRE — in 1858.[46] Till then the British naval authorities had resolutely declined to entertain any idea of building shot-proof warships on the grounds that:

B

It is not in the interest of Great Britain — possessing as she does so large a navy — to adopt any important change in the construction of ships of war which might have the effect of rendering necessary the introduction of a new class of very costly vessels.[47]

When the French announced their intention of building the GLOIRE, the Admiralty was actively engaged in refurbishing its existing fleet of wooden men of war by converting them to steam.[48] But, when it became necessary to respond to the French initiative, the naval authorities plumped for the revolutionary alternative of combining armour plating with an iron hull and powerful steam engines, thereby regaining the technical initiative at the expense of making all existing capital ships obsolete.[49] Tactically, this was a masterstroke, as no foreign power could match Britain's capacity to build iron steamships. Practically, it involved a huge programme of new construction which could be carried out only with the active assistance of private shipbuilders and engineers, and everything depended on the willingness of firms such as Robert Napier & Sons to undertake warshipbuilding on a greatly increased scale.

In the spring of 1859 Napier was invited to submit proposals for the new class of warship. The Admiralty specification was for

A shot proof frigate of 36 guns cased with 4½ inch armour plates from the upper deck to five feet below the waterline, to steam 13½ knots and to be capable of carrying weights amounting to 1,200 tons in addition to coal for at least seven days full steaming.[50]

It called for a ship much larger, heavier and more complicated than anything he or anyone else on the Clyde or elsewhere had ever attempted before. Napier responded positively to the technical challenge and, having taken steps to buy more ground at Govan for a further extension of the shipyard,[51] he instructed one of his senior employees to begin an exhaustive series of tests to prove Parkhead's fitness to supply the necessary iron forgings and armour plate.[52]

Napier's enterprise and enthusiasm were rewarded with the order for the Royal Navy's second 'ironclad' — HMS BLACK PRINCE — launched in February 1861 after the upper Clyde had been specially dredged to take a ship 420 feet long and displacing 9,250 tons.[53] As it transpired, Napier had seriously underestimated the difficulty of building a ship containing so many novel features and, despite his efforts to prepare for the task of manufacturing iron plates weighing four tons each,[54] Parkhead succeeded in producing plates of the required quality only after the ship had been launched.[55] In consequence Napier's tender of £283,000[56] proved to be woefully inadequate and, as costs mounted and the firm's liquidity became increasingly strained, the firm's financial resources were stretched to meet the demands made upon them. As early as April 1860 Napier took steps to reduce his commitments by divesting himself of control of the Parkhead Forge.[57] By October 1860 the creditworthiness of his main business was in question and the Bank of Scotland was hesitant about agreeing to finance the completion of the contract.[58] The firm survived the immediate crisis but, in the spring of 1861, Napier — bravely or foolhardily — accepted the contract for a second 'ironclad' — the 6,710 ton HMS HECTOR — and by 1863 the firm's loan from the Bank of

Scotland had grown to £130,000.[59] While Napier was eventually awarded grants of £35,000 each in respect of both HMS BLACK PRINCE and HMS HECTOR in compensation for the heavy losses which he had incurred in undertaking the two contracts — 'When there were very few firms which had built ironclad ships at all ... there were no firms in a position to make a satisfactory estimate'[60] — his fortunes never fully recovered from the débâcle. Following the building of the two ironclads for the Royal Navy, Napier was able to secure a number of orders for warships for foreign governments — a 1,320 ton armoured turret ship for Denmark, three 6,400 ton 'ironclad' frigates for Turkey, a 2,284 ton turret ram and a 1,427 ton monitor for Holland[61] — and in 1865 he built the two fast 3,227 ton screw steamers with which the Compagnie Générale Transatlantique wrested the 'blue riband' for the fastest crossing of the North Atlantic from British owners for the first time[62] but, in the last ten years of his life, Robert Napier's business was beset with problems.

Napier's difficulties were partly attributable to his refusal to compromise on the standard of his workmanship. As William Pearce remarked after leaving Napier's employ in 1870:

> Such questions as 'What time will this take?' or 'What will this cost?' were always subordinate to the crucial one 'Is this the best?'[63]

In the 1830s and 1840s these attitudes had been an asset. Early steam engines were notoriously unreliable and Napier had prospered by following his own advice that:

> I would have everything connected with machinery very strong and of the best materials, it being of the utmost importance to give confidence at first.[64]

By the 1860s steam propulsion and iron shipbuilding had both advanced beyond the stage where quality of workmanship alone commanded premium prices and, as the Clyde output of steam tonnage soared from 81,400 tons in 1841–50 to 798,400 tons in 1860–70,[65] Napier faced mounting competition from new yards, many of them founded by men who had imitated Napier's example in taking up shipbuilding after first making their names as marine engineers.[66]

More fundamentally, Napier's problems were symptomatic of a long-term decline in his ability to compete. By the 1860s he had lost any claim to being considered 'the great authority on steam navigation'. As early as the 1850s three other Clyde firms, Denny's, Thomson's and Caird's, had all been commissioned to build iron-hulled screw steamers for Napier's best customer, Cunard;[67] while he had gone on building the largest paddle steamers, John Elder was busy pioneering the development of the compound engine which, with the introduction of the surface condenser, led to fuel economies of as much as 50 per cent.[68] Napier's extensive experience of naval work still gave him some advantage in tendering for naval contracts, particularly in building the largest warships, but this experience was of limited value in winning contracts for fast passenger ships, and it was notable that, from 1860 onwards, the engines of many of the major warships built by Napier were supplied by other firms.[69]

Against this background warshipbuilding came to be the main support of

Napier's declining fortunes. During the last ten years of his life the output of his yard still contained a useful leavening of merchant work. Sir Donald Currie was a regular customer from 1863 onwards,[70] the Pacific Steam Navigation Company, with whom he had severed relations after a quarrel in the 1850s, eventually returned to him,[71] and in the early 1870s he had a number of orders from Dutch owners,[72] but Cunard favoured him with no further orders after 1863.[73] He produced no record-breaking transatlantic steamers after 1865 and efforts to take advantage of an upturn in the demand for merchant ships during the Franco-Prussian War in 1870-71 were frustrated by the unwillingness of his bankers to finance prospective contracts.[74] Warships therefore constituted the major part of his output.

In contrast to the period up to the mid-1860s warshipbuilding in the final phase of Napier's long career was noted less for its novelty than for its volume, but he retained the confidence of the naval authorities, and Admiralty orders were sufficiently numerous to keep the business reasonably well employed. Two 6,010 ton central battery ironclads — HMS AUDACIOUS and HMS INVINCIBLE — laid down in 1867 were followed by the order for the hull and machinery of the 4,331 ton turret ram HMS HOTSPUR in 1868, and, two years later, there were orders for the hull of the 3,480 ton monitor HMS HYDRA, the machinery for the dockyard-built turret ram HMS RUPERT and two small flatiron gunboats.[75] Thereafter Napier received only one more major Admiralty contract — the order for the 7,630 ton armoured cruiser HMS NORTHAMPTON laid down in 1874 — but his continued interest in warshipbuilding was reflected in a succession of smaller naval orders: the hull and machinery of two composite gun vessels in 1873;[76] the engines for a composite corvette in 1874;[77] the hulls of two composite sloops and the hulls and machinery of two small composite gunboats in 1875,[78] the year before Napier's death.

This final phase of Robert Napier's career may have done little to enhance his reputation but it did not detract from his earlier achievements as a warshipbuilder and, although there is no evidence that naval work ever became particularly profitable, neither had it proved entirely ruinous to a firm in straitened circumstances. In consequence Robert Napier's death was not fatal to the Clyde's interest in warshipbuilding. On the contrary, in this, as in much else, others followed where he led and his example was pervasive because many of the leading figures of the next generation of Clyde shipbuilders had learned their trade in his workshops and shipyard.[79]

## NOTES

1. F. M. Walker, *The Song of the Clyde: A History of Clyde Shipbuilding* (Glasgow 1984), p. 131 corrects earlier accounts which implied that this ship — the PRINCE OF WALES — was built as a warship. According to his account the PRINCE OF WALES, built as a revenue brig in 1894, was purchased by the Admiralty, rerigged as a full-rigged ship and renamed HMS THRUSH.
2. Hamilton, *The Industrial Revolution in Scotland*, pp. 213-15.

3. J. Napier, *Life of Robert Napier of West Shandon* (Edinburgh 1904), p. 32.

4. *Ibid.*, p. 13.

5. A. Slaven, *The Development of the West of Scotland*, pp. 127–8.

6. D. Pollock, *The Shipbuilding Industry: Its History, Practice, Science and Finance* (London 1905), p. 25.

7. Napier, *Life of Robert Napier*, p. 32.

8. *Ibid.*, p. 29

9. *Ibid.*, p. 37.

10. Between 1812 and 1820 the Clyde accounted for 60% of all the steam-powered tonnage built in Britain. See Slaven, *The Development of the West of Scotland*, p. 127.

11. Napier, *Life of Robert Napier*, p. 48.

12. *Ibid.*, p. 45.

13. *Ibid.*, pp. 114–15.

14. *Ibid.*, pp. 131–45.

15. *Ibid.*, p. 149.

16. The first shipyard on the Clyde designed exclusively for the building of iron ships was opened by Tod & McGregor in 1834. Their first iron ship — the LOCH GOIL — was launched in 1835. See Walker, *The Song of the Clyde*, p. 32.

17. The use of iron resolved the problem of stress which had limited the size of steam-powered wooden ships. See Slaven, *The Development of the West of Scotland*, p. 131.

18. Walker, *The Song of the Clyde*, p. 169.

19. Napier, *Life of Robert Napier*, p. 149.

20. Hume & Moss, *Beardmore*, pp. 14 & 18.

21. Napier, *Life of Robert Napier*, p. 151.

22. At the outset, iron shipbuilders had to contend with a number of technical difficulties, most notably variations in the quality of iron plates and the absence of established rules of construction. Lloyds began granting A1 certificates for iron-hulled ships in 1844 but formal rules governing iron shipbuilding were not established until 1854. See L. Jones, *Shipbuilding in Britain. Mainly between the Two Wars* (Cardiff 1957), pp. 12–13.

23. Napier, *Life of Robert Napier*, p. 192.

24. Hume & Moss, *Beardmore*, p. 18.

25. *Ibid.*, p. 15.

26. F. E. Hyde, *Cunard and the North Atlantic, 1840-1973: A History of Shipping and Financial Management* (London 1975), p. 327.

27. Napier, *Life of Robert Napier*, pp. 69–70.

28. C. White, *Victoria's Navy: the End of the Sailing Navy* (Ensworth, Hampshire 1981), pp. 14–27.

29. M. Lewis, *The History of the British Navy* (London 1957), p. 199.

30. Napier, *Life of Robert Napier*, pp. 69–70.

31. *Ibid.*, p. 72. The member in question, Robert Gore, served as MP for New Ross from 1841 to 1847.

32. *Ibid.*, p. 72.

33. *Ibid.*, pp. 137–8.

34. H. Richmond, *Statesmen and Seapower* (Oxford 1946), pp. 158–9.

35. Lewis, *The History of the British Navy*, p. 198.

36. E.g., HMS VICTORY, laid down at Chatham in 1759, was already more than forty years old when she served as Nelson's flagship at Trafalgar.

37. Napier, *Life of Robert Napier*, p. 154.

38. White, *The End of the Sailing Navy*, p. 34.

39. Napier, *Life of Robert Napier*, p. 155.

40. *Ibid.*, p. 156.

41. White, *The End of the Sailing Navy*, pp. 34–39.

42. *Ibid.*, pp. 39–40.

43. *Ibid.*, p. 40.

44. Napier, *Life of Robert Napier*, p. 198.

45. Hume & Moss, *Beardmore*, p. 19.

46. The GLOIRE, a wooden-hulled, steam-powered battleship protected by a belt of iron armour plate 4½ inches thick, was ordered in March 1858 and launched in November 1859. See White, *The End of the Sailing Navy*, p. 40.

47. Admiralty memo dated 28th June, 1859, quoted by O. Parkes, *British Battleships: 'Warrior' 1860 to 'Vanguard' 1950: A History of Design, Construction and Armament etc.* (London 1957: revised edition London 1966), p. 11.

48. The process of introducing steam engines into the Royal Navy accelerated following the Crimean War when experience taught the Admiralty that ships not equipped with steam engines ran the risk of being outmanoeuvred by those which were. See Lewis, *The History of the British Navy*, p. 200.

49. Seven wooden capital ships already under construction were completed as 'ironclads' and two more wooden-hulled 'ironclads' were ordered to use up existing stocks of seasoned timber and provide employment in the Dockyards but no further wooden capital ships were built for the Royal Navy. The last wooden battleship, HMS RODNEY, was paid-off in 1870. See White, *The End of the Sailing Navy*, pp. 45–46.

50. Napier, *Life of Robert Napier*, p. 209.

51. *Ibid.*, p. 212.

52. Hume & Moss, *Beardmore*, pp. 22–23.

53. Napier, *Life of Robert Napier*, p. 212.

54. Conway's *All the World's Fighting Ships, 1860*–1905 (London 1979), p. 7.

55. Hume & Moss, *Beardmore*, p. 24.

56. Napier, *Life of Robert Napier*, p. 210.

57. Hume & Moss, *Beardmore*, p. 23.

58. *Ibid.*, p. 23.

59. *Ibid.*, p. 25.

60. Report of the Committee appointed to inquire into the conditions under which contracts are invited for the building and repairing of ships of the Navy, including their engines and into the mode in which repairs and refits of ships are effected in dockyards with Evidence and Appendices, *Parliamentary Papers, 1884–85* [C4219] XIV 125, (hereafter referred to as the *Report of the Ravensworth Committee*), Q's. 765-6.

61. See Appendix EV.

62. Napier, *Life of Robert Napier*, p. 222.

63. *Ibid.*, p. 248.

64. *Ibid.*, p. 102.

65. Slaven, *The Development of the West of Scotland*, p. 127.

66. Most notably Randolph & Elder and J & G Thomson. See Chapter 3 below.

67. Hyde, *Cunard and the North Atlantic*, pp. 326-9.

68. Jones, *Shipbuilding in Britain*, p. 19.

69. Of the seven armoured ships built by Robert Napier & Sons between 1859 and 1876, only three — HMS HECTOR, HMS INVINCIBLE and HMS HOTSPUR — were fitted with engines supplied by their builder. See Appendix EI.

70. Napier, *Life of Robert Napier*, Appendix II.

71. *Ibid.*, pp. 183-5 & p. 224.

72. *Ibid.*, p. 224.

73. Hyde, *Cunard and the North Atlantic*, pp. 326-9.

74. Hume & Moss, *Beardmore*, p. 28.

75. HMS BUSTARD and HMS KITE

76. HMS ARAB and HMS LILY.

77. HMS OPAL.

78. HMS WILD SWAN, HMS PENGUIN, HMS MOORHEN and HMS SHELDRAKE.

79. Most notably, John Elder and William Pearce of John Elder & Co., James and George Thomson of J. & G. Thomson and William Denny of Denny Brothers. See Slaven, *The Development of the West of Scotland*, p. 129.

# 3

# Robert Napier's Successors and Warshipbuilding on the Clyde Prior to 1889

In the thirty years between the building of the first 'ironclad' in 1859 and the Navy Defence Act in 1889, the Clyde produced for the Royal Navy fifty warships and sixty-three sets of warship engines aggregating 124,164 tons and 135,644 horse-power respectively. As shown in Table 3.1, apart from Robert Napier himself, who was responsible for fifteen of the warships and seventeen of the sets of engines, most of this output came from three firms, Robert Napier & Sons, John Elder & Co., which became the Fairfield Shipbuilding and Engineering Co. Ltd. in 1886, and J. & G. Thomson:

**Table 3.1.** Admiralty Contracts Undertaken by Clyde Firms 1859–1889

|  | WARSHIPS | | ENGINES | |
|---|---|---|---|---|
|  | NO. | TONNAGE | NO. | H.P. |
| ROBERT NAPIER & SONS |  |  |  |  |
| ROBERT NAPIER | 15 | 48,339 | 17 | 31,936 |
| HIS SUCCESSORS | 5 | 24,100 | 6 | 28,520 |
| JOHN ELDER & CO./FAIRFIELD | 12 | 29,926 | 11 | 28,544 |
| J. & G. THOMSON | 12 | 18,863 | 14 | 34,280 |
| OTHERS | 6 | 2,936 | 15 | 12,354 |

(Source: Abstracted from Appendix EVI)

Two firms which were to become major warshipbuilders after 1889 — Scott's of Greenock and the London & Glasgow Engineering and Iron Shipbuilding Co Ltd. — were only minor contributors to the output of the period.

As the builders of the wooden sloop HMS THRUSH, which was commissioned into the Navy during the Napoleonic Wars,[1] and the owners of a foundry which produced its first engine in 1825,[2] Scott's of Greenock had rivalled Robert Napier as an Admiralty contractor in the early days of steam and iron. In 1838–39 Scott's Greenock Foundry supplied the engines for the paddle-driven sloops HMS HECATE and HMS HECLA, the first dockyard-built warships to be fitted with engines made on the Clyde,[3] and their 1875 ton iron screw frigate HMS GREENOCK was contemporaneous with Napier's HMS SIMOON launched in 1849.[4] By 1859, when Napier built his first ironclad, the shipyard of Scott & Co., which continued a family tradition of shipbuilding at Greenock dating back to 1711, was otherwise engaged in building tea clippers. Six years later, in 1865, the Scotts found an alternative outlet for their enterprise by building the hulls and supplying the compound engines for the AGAMEMNON, AJAX and ACHILLES with which Alfred Holt & Co. inaugurated a steam service to China,[5] but over the next thirty years the firm's total contribution to the Clyde's output of warships was two composite gunboats laid down in 1888–89.[6] In the interval, the family's engine works, the Greenock Foundry Co., which retained a separate identity until 1901, maintained the Admiralty connection by supplying the engines for six dockyard-built wooden sloops laid down between 1859 and 1861,[7] but it too undertook no further Admiralty contracts until 1887–88, when it supplied the machinery for two composite sloops.[8]

The London & Glasgow, which was to take advantage of the Navy Defence Act in 1889 to secure the first of a series of cruiser contracts which gave the yard a significant share of the warships built on the Clyde between 1889–1912, played little part in warshipbuilding prior to 1889. The firm's contribution amounted to a single composite gun vessel laid down in 1866–67,[9] two years after the company had been formed to take over the iron shipbuilding yard founded by Smith & Rodger in 1842.[10]

John Elder & Co. was the more successful of the two new firms which shared the bulk of the Admiralty orders with Robert Napier & Sons. Its origins were in the partnership of Randolph & Elder, formed in September 1852 when John Elder gave up his position as Robert Napier's drawing-office manager to join the well-established engine manufacturers, Randolph, Elliott & Co., founded by Charles Randolph in 1834.[11] As with Robert Napier some thirty years earlier, Randolph and Elder initially confined themselves to marine engineering. Up to 1860, when they commenced shipbuilding on a modest scale, their reputation rested largely on John Elder's work in developing the compound engine.[12] However, the partners' reputation as marine engineers, combined with their enterprise in acquiring a 'green field' site at Fairfield, where they began laying out a great new shipyard equipped with its own engine and boiler shops in 1864,[13] were the foundations of the firm's subsequent success. By the time the new shipyard was completed in 1871, John Elder, the last of the original partners, was dead, but on his death the property had passed to his wife, and, in July 1870, John Ure, her brother, J. L. Jamieson, the manager of the engine works, and William Pearce, formerly manager of Robert Napier & Sons shipyard, had gone into partnership to carry on the business.[14]

Endowed with splendid new facilities and with an unrivalled experience of designing and manufacturing compound engines, the new firm of John Elder & Co. prospered and the Admiralty was among its most important early customers. As in much else, John Elder & Co. owed its success as an Admiralty contractor to the enterprise of Randolph & Elder who had provided the Admiralty with a set of compound engines for experimental purposes in the early 1860s. In 1865, after extensive trials of the engines, which had been fitted in the wooden frigate HMS CONSTANCE, the naval authorities had concluded that compound engines were as yet insufficiently reliable and much too complicated for naval engine staffs to operate successfully,[15] but the greatly increased range of operation resulting from the use of engines which offered substantial economies in fuel consumption could not be ignored. The Admiralty returned to Elder's for one of three sets of compound engines fitted in dockyard-built corvettes completed between 1869 and 1872.[16] This experiment, like its predecessor, was only a qualified success but in the early 1870s the Admiralty fitted compound engines in a number of other new warships and John Elder and Co., which had displayed its mastery of the new technology by providing the most satisfactory of the three sets of engines fitted in the corvettes,[17] supplied two more sets of engines for the armoured monitors HMS CYCLOPS and HMS HYDRA laid down in 1870. This in turn paved the way for the prestigious contract to supply the machinery for the 11,880 ton dockyard-built turret ship HMS INFLEXIBLE, the heaviest man-of-war yet conceived when it was laid down in 1874.[18] Meanwhile, the adoption of compound engines had opened the way for the building of steam-powered cruisers with long-range endurance. In 1874, possibly at the prompting of William Pearce, who had acquired the requisite experience of warshipbuilding at Napier's,[19] the firm undertook the building of one of the Royal Navy's first armoured cruisers — the 7,473 ton HMS NELSON — designed to steam 7,500 miles at 7 knots.[20] Unlike her sister ship HMS NORTHAMPTON, built by Napier's, HMS NELSON was fitted with engines supplied by its builder and this contract, together with another for six Comus class timber-clad steel-framed frigates launched in 1876,[21] set John Elder & Co. well on the way to supplanting Robert Napier & Sons as the leading warshipbuilder on the Clyde.

Having established itself as a major Admiralty contractor, John Elder & Co. was regularly invited to tender for any naval work put out to contract. In 1884, it was the only Clyde firm, apart from Robert Napier & Sons, listed by the Admiralty both as being capable of building the largest warships and as 'always' being invited to tender for machinery.[22] Nevertheless, from 1876 to 1889 warshipbuilding made only a modest contribution to the firm's output. This was not for lack of interest on the part of management. William Pearce, who became sole partner on the retiral of Ure and Jamieson in 1878,[23] continued to take a keen interest in naval work up to his untimely death in 1888. As a parliamentary candidate at Govan in 1885 he made the need for a strong Navy one of the features of his election addresses[24] and, immediately prior to his election to Parliament in 1885, the firm was reconstituted as a private limited company so that it might continue to tender for Admiralty contracts.[25] Nor was the lack of warship orders because the firm was unable or unwilling to compete on price for the largest contracts. On the contrary, Elder's submitted the lowest price for two battleships put out to tender in April 1885 only to be denied the contract on other grounds. As was customary at this time, the Admiralty had invited firms to submit alternative designs for machinery and some of Elder's competitors had proposed more powerful engines than those originally specified. When the tenders were opened, and it became apparent that the Admiralty favoured these alternative proposals, Elder's made frantic efforts to retrieve the situation by submitting alternative designs of their own but it was all to no avail. Although the Admiralty was offered the choice of having, for the price quoted, either engines of comparable power with an increase in weight of one hundred tons or engines of slightly less power with no increase in weight, the contracts went elsewhere.[26]

On the other hand, Elder's were not always competitive on price and the tenders which the firm submitted for the machinery of a succession of dockyard-built warships in the early 1880s suggest that it was either hopelessly uncompetitive or, more probably, uninterested in this class of work.[27] Under the management of William Pearce the firm had been extraordinarily successful in building up the merchant side of the business and it could afford to be selective. Particularly between 1879 and 1884 when it was engaged in building a succession of fast passenger liners — most notably the 'Atlantic Greyhounds' ARIZONA, ALASKA and OREGON for the Guion line and the 19½ knot liners UMBRIA and ETRURIA for Cunard — there was little need of other work to keep both the shipyard and engine works busy. Failure to secure the order for one or both of the two battleships in 1885 was annoying, as it would have provided another major contract to follow on the building of the two Cunarders, but the lack of naval work did not halt the firm's growth. As shown in Table 3.2, while Elder's intake of Admiralty orders between 1876 and 1889 comprised only two small composite gun vessels laid down in 1879-80[28] and the hulls of the 2,950 ton second-class cruisers HMS MARATHON and HMS MAGICIENNE laid down in 1887-88, the firm's total output in the decade 1881-90 was higher than it had been in the decade 1871-80:

**Table 3.2.** John Elder & Co.'s Output 1861-1890

| DECADE | TONNAGE OF VESSELS LAUNCHED | HORSE POWER OF ENGINES COMPLETED | VALUE OF WORK COMPLETED £ |
|---|---|---|---|
| 1861-70 | 80,558 | 79,146 | 2,782,150 |
| 1871-80 | 219,230 | 189,284 | 7,093,190 |
| 1881-90 | 248,257 | 386,682 | 7,910,490 |

(Source: *The Fairfield Shipbuilding & Engineering Works*, p. 15)

In contrast to John Elder & Co., which made its major contribution to the Clyde's output of warships in the 1870s, J. & G. Thomson showed little interest in warshipbuilding until the 1880s. Along with Elder's and the London & Glasgow, the firm had been entrusted with the building of a composite gun vessel in 1866-67[29] but, up to 1884, its only other contributions to the Clyde's output of Admiralty work had been to build two small composite gunboats laid down in 1875-76[30] and to supply the engines for the dockyard-built composite corvette HMS EMERALD laid down in 1874-75. Technically, J. & G. Thomson's record as a shipbuilder bore comparison with that of any shipyard on the Clyde, but up to 1884 the bias of its interest was towards merchant shipbuilding.

Founded in 1847 by James Thomson, who had moved from Manchester to take up employment as one of Robert Napier's managers in 1828, and his brother

George Thomson, who had followed him into Robert Napier's employ some years later,[31] the firm of J. & G. Thomson had been engaged in shipbuilding since 1851. The firm's emergence as a shipbuilder of the first rank dated from the 1860s when it supplanted Robert Napier & Sons as the builder of Cunard's biggest and fastest ships. Having started with the advantage of being the brother of Robert Thomson, who had been Cunard's first superintendent engineer,[32] James and George Thomson had been regularly employed in building screw-driven steamers for Cunard since 1854,[33] but it was not until Cunard finally abandoned paddle-drive in the 1860s that they had the opportunity to try their hand at building its flagships. The 2,959 ton single-screw liner RUSSIA launched in 1867 was J. & G. Thomson's first 'blue riband' holder.[34] Thereafter the firm chose to specialise in building fast oceangoing ships. In 1871, when the brothers James R. Thomson and George P. Thomson, who had fallen heir to the business on the death of their father George in 1866, moved the shipyard downriver from Mavisbank to Clydebank it was with the avowed intention of facilitating the building of larger ships.[35] As they remarked:

> For years past . . . the only vessels that have been at all remunerative are the larger classes of screw steamers and especially those for mail services.[36]

In the 1870s the firm's enterprise was not particularly well-rewarded as there was not always sufficient work to keep the shipyard well-employed but the firm persevered and in the early 1880s it was rewarded with the orders for a number of notable ships including the 515 foot long 7,392 ton SERVIA, Cunard's first all-steel liner,[37] launched in 1881, and the 9,500 ton Cunard liner AURANIA and the record-breaking National Line's AMERICA, both launched in 1883. Up to this time, only the firm's shipyard had been sited at Clydebank but, in 1881, no doubt encouraged by the buoyant demand, the firm started the construction of new engine and boiler works at Clydebank, specifically designed to accommodate the building of the largest triple-expansion engines.[38]

Finding work for these expanded facilities between 1883 and 1889 proved to be extremely difficult. In 1883 the output of the Clyde shipbuilding industry had reached a peak of 419,664 tons, a level not to be surpassed until 1896, but the boom years of 1881–83 were followed by a severe slump which lasted until 1888. At its worst, in 1886, the output of all the Clyde yards was only 172,440 tons, a level which was low even by the standards of the 1870s,[39] and one which the Clyde shipbuilding industry was not to experience again until the 1930s. Even before the onset of this slump, J. & G. Thomson had suffered a major reverse at the hands of John Elder & Co. which had secured the contract for the Cunard liners UMBRIA and ETRURIA. For twenty years J. & G. Thomson had built all of Cunard's most important ships, and between 1863 and 1883 twenty-one of the twenty-eight ships added to the Cunard fleet had been built in their yard.[40] When demand for all types of merchant ships fell away, the situation became critical. While John Elder & Co. survived the crisis by building ships on their own account or accepting shares in part payment for the work done,[41] J. & G. Thomson appear to have been unable to unwilling to follow suit. Between January 1884 and December 1886 the firm's total intake of merchant work amounted to four small vessels.[42]

Understandably, against this background J. & G. Thomson was eager to tender for any naval work which became available but, in seeking Admiralty contracts to replenish its order book, the firm was handicapped by a lack of what the Admiralty considered to be relevant experience. While it was invited to tender for the largest contracts, the Admiralty had no intention of entrusting the firm with any order which involved the manufacture of large engines. Admiralty contractors were expected to start with small engines and work their way up and, while J. & G. Thomson was acknowledged to have built engines of up to 12,000 horse power for merchant customers, it was rated as being fit to build naval engines of up to only 4,000 horse power 'simply because they have not hitherto made large engines for the Navy'.[43] The contract for the 5,500 horsepower engines of the dockyard-built armoured cruiser HMS AURORA in February 1886 was a first step towards removing this disability but, at the same time, the Admiralty overlooked the firm's highly competitive tender for the engines of two battleships on the grounds that the design was 'unsatisfactory' and the firm 'had no experience of this type of machinery'.[44] In consequence J. & G. Thomson's share of warship orders placed by the Admiralty on the Clyde between 1884 and 1889 comprised only a succession of nine third-class cruisers ranging in size between 1,580 and 2,575 tons. While these contracts, and particularly those for the 1,580 ton torpedo cruiser HMS SCOUT laid down in January 1884 and six more 1,770 ton torpedo cruisers laid down in February 1885,[45] were invaluable in keeping the yard going when it had little other work on hand, they were a meagre return for a great deal of effort. Further, they did not prevent J. & G. Thomson's suffering trading losses from 1885 onwards.[46]

By 1889, Robert Napier & Sons, the third of the major Clyde warshipbuilders, was in even greater difficulties. The decline in the firm's affairs which had been apparent during Robert Napier's lifetime continued after his death. The brothers John and James Hamilton and A. C. Kirk, formerly engine ship manager of John Elder & Co., who took over in 1879, managed to keep the business going but from the outset their room for manoeuvre was limited by the need to borrow £160,000 from Robert Napier's trustees to finance the purchase of assets and goodwill valued at £270,000.[47] For a few years Kirk's work in developing the triple expansion engine helped to keep the yard reasonably well-employed,[48] but hopes of a sustained improvement in the firm's fortunes disappeared with the onset of the severe depression of the mid-1880s. In 1880, when temporarily short of work, the firm managed to secure an Admiralty contract for three 4,300 ton second-class cruisers[49] to keep it going and in 1885, despite the late delivery of the earlier ships, it won the contract for the 5,600 ton Orlando class armoured cruisers HMS AUSTRALIA and HMS GALATEA but neither contract was of much assistance. The first ran into difficulties on account of shortages of labour when the demand for merchant work revived;[50] the second was taken at a price which can have left little if any margin for profit as Napier's tender of £215,000 per ship was not only £15,000 below that of J. & G. Thomson and £20,000 below that of John Elder & Co. but also the lowest of all the tenders submitted.[51] Meanwhile, indicative of Robert Napier & Sons' declining capabilities, it was not invited to tender for any of the battleships put out to contract by the Admiralty in the 1880s.[52] Short of work, handicapped by ageing plant and facilities inconveniently split between the shipyard at Govan and engine works at Lancefield Street on the other side of the Clyde, and saddled with a burden of debt which made the firm uncomfortably highly geared and precluded the raising of new capital for much-needed modernisation, Robert Napier & Sons survived but by 1889 it was nearing the end of its tether. Five years later Kirk was dead and the surviving partners had to admit that they were no longer able to meet their obligations.[53]

In seeking Admiralty work to compensate for the dearth of merchant orders in the mid-1880s, J. & G. Thomson and Robert Napier & Sons were fortunate that public alarm at the prospect of war with Russia in 1884 had forced the Liberal Government of the day to authorise the Northbrook Programme which provided for the building of two battleships, five armoured cruisers and six torpedo cruisers in private shipyards. For most of the 1870s and 1880s Admiralty orders were in extremely short supply. In seven of the twenty years between 1869–70 and 1888–89 no 'major' warships were laid down by the Admiralty in private yards and, excluding the Northbrook Programme, the volume of such orders exceeded 20,000 tons in one year on only two occasions.[54] This shortage of naval work owed less to any reduction in the size of naval programmes than to the re-emergence of the Royal Dockyards as the Navy's primary source of supply. In 1859 when the Admiralty decided to build ironclads it had no alternative but to entrust the work to private shipyards as the Royal Dockyards were not equipped for iron shipbuilding. As soon as it was decided to introduce iron-hulled capital ships into the Royal Navy, urgent steps were taken to equip the Dockyards to build them. The first dockyard-built ironclad was laid down at Chatham as early as August 1861[55] and, although it was some years before other dockyards were ready to commence production, Pembroke and Portsmouth were considered fit to be entrusted with the building of large armoured ships by 1865 and 1869 respectively.[56] Table 3.3 shows the effect of the revival of the Dockyards on the allocation of major warship orders between them and private suppliers between 1859 and 1889:

**Table 3.3.** Allocation of Major Warship Orders 1859–1889[57]

| LAID DOWN | ROYAL DOCKYARDS | | | | PRIVATE YARDS | |
| | WOODEN | | OTHER | | ALL OTHER | |
| | NO. | TONNAGE | NO. | TONNAGE | NO. | TONNAGE |
|---|---|---|---|---|---|---|
| 1859–64 | 20 | 48,704 | 2 | 17,380 | 10 | 79,788 |
| 1864–69 | 15 | 26,072 | 7 | 47,461 | 15 | 63,117 |
| 1869–74 | 8 | 15,178 | 13 | 82,083 | 7 | 19,260 |
| 1874–79 | | | 23 | 69,185 | 14 | 40,123 |
| 1879–84 | | | 30 | 123,830 | 9 | 29,670 |
| NORTHBROOK | | | | | 13 | 60,560 |
| 1884–89 | | | 38 | 103,403 | 16 | 35,405 |

(Source: detail abstracted from Conway's *All the World's Fighting Ships 1860–1905*)

The traditionally-minded Royal Dockyards may not have been particularly efficient producers of iron ships. Up to the 1880s, when belated steps were taken to overhaul their management and weed out inefficient practices,[58] it is doubtful whether their performance would have stood comparison with that of the more efficient private yards. They did not need to be. As an integral part of the Admiralty establishment, the Royal Dockyards were not required to compete with private yards. The Admiralty was in a position to allocate them such orders as it saw fit. Further, as the Admiralty was quick to point out when pressed, the interests of economy did not require that they should be able to compete with private yards in terms of cost of production. It was sufficient that the *additional* costs they incurred in shipbuilding did not exceed the prices charged by outside suppliers. As the Navy's Chief Constructor, Sir Nathaniel Barnaby, pointed out to the Ravensworth Committee in 1884:

> The establishment exists, the staff exists and we therefore compare our actual outlay upon the work with that which we pay outside; although that outside payment includes profit and general expenditure for plant and supervision.[59]

The revival of the Dockyards did not enable the Admiralty to dispense with the services of private firms altogether. First, they were required to supply the engines for all dockyard-built warships as the Admiralty possessed neither the facilities nor the expertise to produce their own.[60] Second, Britain's naval supremacy could no longer be taken for granted and it was expedient to allow private shipyards a leavening of warship orders so that a nucleus of firms would be familiar with the work which they would be required to undertake if it became necessary to outbuild a rival power in an emergency. Nevertheless, the role ascribed to the private shipbuilder in the 1870s and 1880s was not a particularly attractive one. Supplying engines for dockyard-built warships had limited appeal for firms such as those on the Clyde which sought work for both shipyard and engine works, and the volume and character of warship orders allocated to private yards was inadequate to provide them with regular employment. Excluding the Northbrook Programme, the volume of major warship laid down in private yards averaged only 6,223 tons per annum between 1869 and 1889, compared with 14,290 tons per annum in the decade following the introduction of the ironclad[61] and only four armoured warships — one battleship and three armoured cruisers[62] — were built outside the Royal Dockyards between 1870 and 1889. To compound the private warship-builders' problems any orders which they did manage to obtain were liable to be subject to frequent changes in specification and time-consuming delays in production as the Admiralty insisted on trying to incorporate the latest developments in gunnery and appliances into every ship that was built.[63]

Despite these defects there was no shortage of firms willing to undertake the work. In 1885 when the Admiralty placed the orders for the five armoured cruisers authorised by the Northbrook Programme it received serious bids from nine of the eleven firms invited to tender.[64] This may have been an exceptional case as merchant work was in particularly short supply at this time and the large number of ships on offer aroused a great deal of interest, but Admiralty contracts were almost always subject to competitive tender and the competition to secure them was fierce. Whether, as Sir Nathanial Barnaby claimed in 1884, the competition was so intense that 'a Government contract for building a ship of war ... almost always results in a loss',[65] is dubious. William Laird, the senior partner of Laird Brothers, the Birkenhead warshipbuilders, who spoke from personal experience, was probably more accurate when he told the same Parliamentary Committee that:

> A very large proportion of the contracts given out in late years have not been very profitable to the contractors.[66]

Certainly no one suggested that losses were on a scale comparable to those incurred on the first ironclads when the builders had no previous experience to guide them in framing their estimates. Nevertheless, there was a grain of truth in the assertion of John Field, the general manager of Palmers of Jarrow, that by the early 1880s no builder would take Admiralty work when he could get merchant work 'upon anything like reasonable terms'.[67] A preference for merchant work was implicit in the behaviour not only of John Elder & Co. and J. & G. Thomson but also of other Clyde firms which played little or no part in warshipbuilding. Scott's of Greenock apparently found developing a new specialisation in steamers for the Far East trade more profitable than building on its Admiralty connection. Other firms may not have had the same opportunity but at least one Clyde firm, Caird & Co. of Greenock, which had been awarded the contract for a monitor in 1870 before begging to be excused,[68] expressed its lack of interest in naval work in 1885 by submitting an outrageously high price when invited to tender for the Orlando class cruisers.[69] Possibly John Elder & Co. was the only Clyde shipbuilder apart from Robert Napier to have taken Admiralty orders out of choice rather than necessity.

Whatever their motivation, the action of John Elder & Co. and J. & G. Thomson in taking up warshipbuilding prior to 1889 made a major contribution to the development of the Clyde warshipbuilding industry. Neither firm came close to matching the achievements of Robert Napier by 1889 but they brought new blood to the industry. Robert Napier had been pre-eminent among the generation of Clyde shipbuilders and engineers which had laid the foundations of the local shipbuilding industry's success by pioneering the use of steam and iron, but his achievements belonged increasingly to the past and his interest in warshipbuilding could be dismissed as a personal idiosyncracy. By contrast, John Elder & Co. and J. & G. Thomson were closely identified with the development of the compound engine and the building of steel ships[70] which consolidated the Clyde's position as the world's foremost shipbuilding centre. They possessed the largest and best-equipped shipyards and engine works on the river and, unlike Robert Napier & Sons, they had the potential to build the largest warships if the opportunity presented itself. Meanwhile they had demonstrated that they could compete on price, they had established themselves as reliable Admiralty contractors and they had acquired a useful experience of building cruisers, a new class of work for which there was to be high demand in the future. While warshipbuilding played a relatively modest part in the growth of the Clyde shipbuilding industry in the

1870s and 1880s, there was no discontinuity between Robert Napier's pioneering work and the emergence of the Clyde as a major warshipbuilding centre in the 1890s. On the contrary, as Table 3.4 shows, the Clyde's output of Admiralty contracts for warships and engines grew, and any decline in the importance of warshipbuilding between 1859 and 1889 was relative rather than absolute.

**Table 3.4.** Clydeside's Intake of Admiralty Contracts 1859–1889

| LAID DOWN | WARSHIPS | | ENGINES | |
|---|---|---|---|---|
| | NO. | TONNAGE | NO. | H.P. |
| 1859–1869 | 9 | 34,723 | 19 | 26,542 |
| 1869–1879 | 19 | 38,691 | 21 | 44,062 |
| 1879–1889 | 22 | 50,750 | 23 | 67,040 |

(Source: Abstracted from Appendix E1)

## NOTES

1. See Chapter 2 above.
2. *Two Centuries of Shipbuilding by Scotts at Greenock*, p. 22.
3. *Ibid.*, pp. 23 & 46.
4. *Ibid.*, pp. 24 & 46.
5. *Ibid.*, pp. 36–9.
6. HMS SPARROW and HMS THRUSH.
7. HMS ROSARIO, HMS RAPID, HMS PETEREL, HMS AFRICA, HMS COLUMBINE and HMS ROYALIST.
8. HMS NYMPHE and HMS DAPHNE.
9. HMS ROCKET.
10. Walker, *The Song of the Clyde*, p. 171.
11. *The Fairfield Shipbuilding and Engineering Works*, p. 2.
12. Randolph & Elder first came to prominence by supplying successful compound engines for the coastal steamer BRANDON in 1854. See Walker, *The Song of the Clyde*, p. 26.
13. From 1860 to 1864 Randolph & Elder occupied the Govan Old Yard where Robert Napier had commenced shipbuilding in 1839. Their engine works were then situated at Centre Street and their boiler works at Dale Street in Tradeston. Shipbuilding moved to Fairfield in 1864 but work on the building of new engine and boiler shops on the same site did not start until 1868. See *The Fairfield Shipbuilding and Engineering Works*, p. 9.
14. *Ibid.*, p. 11.
15. Conway's *All the World's Fighting Ships, 1860–1905*, p. 46.
16. HMS TENEDOS.
17. Conway's *All the World's Fighting Ships, 1860–1905*, p. 48.
18. The wrought-iron armour plate in HMS INFLEXIBLE was 24″ thick in places, 'the thickest armour plate ever put afloat'. *Ibid.*, p. 26.
19. John Elder & Co.'s only previous experience of warshipbuilding had been to build the composite gun vessel HMS MIDGE laid down in 1866–67. See Appendix EI.
20. Conway's *All the World's Fighting Ships, 1860–1905*, p. 64.
21. HMS COMUS, HMS CARYSFORT, HMS CHAMPION, HMS CLEOPATRA, HMS CONQUEST and HMS CURACAO.
22. *Report of the Ravensworth Committee*, Appendix 1.

23. *The Fairfield Shipbuilding and Engineering Works*, p. 11.

24. *The Glasgow Herald*, 1st December 1885.

25. *Ibid.*, November 25th, 1888.

26. Report of the Committee appointed by the Admiralty to inquire into the system of purchase and contract in the Navy, with Minute of Lord George Hamilton thereon; with Evidence and Appendix. *Parliamentary Papers, 1887 [C4987] XVI 531* (hereafter referred to simply as the *Report of the Forwood Committee*), pp. 21–22 and Appendix III.

27. *Ibid.*, Appendix IV. See particularly tenders for the machinery of HMS RODNEY, HMS HOWE and HMS CAMPERDOWN in March 1883 and for the machinery of HMS ANSON in February 1884. In both cases Elder's was by far the highest tender submitted.

28. HMS RAMBLER and HMS RANGER.

29. HMS HART.

30. HMS FIREBRAND and HMS FIREFLY.

31. Napier, *Life of Robert Napier*, pp. 86–87.

32. M. S. Moss & J. R. Hume, *Workshop of the British Empire: Engineering and Shipbuilding in the West of Scotland* (London 1977), p. 113.

33. Hyde, *Cunard and the North Atlantic*, pp. 326–7.

34. Moss & Hume, *Workshop of the British Empire*, p. 117.

35. *Ibid.*, p. 117.

36. Letter from J. R. Thomson to his father's trustees in sederunt book of G. Thomson, vol. 2, held by McGrigor, Donald & Co. Quoted by Moss & Hume, *Workshop of the British Empire*, p. 117.

37. Hyde, *Cunard and the North Atlantic*, pp. 328–9.

38. Moss & Hume, *Workshop of the British Empire*, p. 117.

39. The output of the Clyde shipyards averaged 210,567 tons per annum in the decade 1870–79, output being at its nadir in 1877 when launchings aggregated 169,710 tons.

40. Hyde, *Cunard and the North Atlantic*, pp. 326–9.

41. Moss & Hume, *Workshop of the British Empire*, p. 118.

42. Yard Nos. 224, 225, 232 and 237.

43. *Report of the Ravensworth Committee*, Q's. 582–3.

44. *Report of the Forwood Committee*, Appendix IV.

45. HMS ARCHER, HMS BRISK, HMS COSSACK, HMS MOHAWK, HMS PORPOISE, and HMS TARTAR.

46. *UCS 1/3/25*. Report by McClelland, Mackinnon & Blyth on the liquidation of J. & G. Thomson. See also Chapter 4 below.

47. Hume & Moss, *Beardmore*, p. 49.

48. According to its bankers, the firm was 'extremely well employed' between 1877 and 1885. *Ibid.*, p. 49, quoting report in the Archives at the Glasgow Head Office of the Bank of Scotland, 5/15/12, Report Book 1885.

49. HMS ARETHUSA, HMS LEANDER and HMS PHAETON.

50. *Report of the Forwood Committee*, Q's. 3508–12.

51. *Ibid.*, Appendix IV.

52. *Ibid.*, Appendix IV.

53. *G.U.A. 49.30*, Papers relating to Robert Napier & Sons, penes Moncrieff Warren & Paterson, 20.

54. No major warships were laid down for the Admiralty in private yards in 1869–70, 1871–72, 1873–74, 1877–78, 1878–79, 1879–80 and 1886–87. The volume of such orders only exceeded 220,000 tons in 1874–75 (23,583 tons) and 1888–89 (26,795 tons). Analysis based on Conway's *All the World's Fighting Ships, 1860–1905*.

55. HMS ACHILLES, a 9,829 ton broadside 'ironclad'.

56. HMS PENELOPE, a 4,470 ton central battery armoured corvette, was laid down at Pembroke in September 1865. HMS DEVASTATION, a 9,330 ton turret ship, was laid down at Portsmouth in November 1869. See Conway's *All the World's Fighting Ships, 1860–1905*, pp. 15 & 23.

57. Excluding warships purchased by the Admiralty while under construction for foreign powers.

58. The management of the Royal Dockyards was drastically reformed in the 1880s. See Pollard & Robertson, *The British Shipbuilding Industry, 1870–1914*, pp. 205–11. See also W. S. Churchill, *Lord Randolph Churchill* (London 1907), pp. 688–90, for a letter to the author from the then First Lord of the Admiralty, Lord George Hamilton, outlining the changes made at this time in response to criticisms of dockyard inefficiencies.

59. *Report of the Ravensworth Committee*, Q. 280.

60. By 1889 the Royal Dockyards were equipped to repair warship engines in an emergency. For a time, from the late 1880s onwards, these facilities were used to build a number of warship engines. The practice appeaars to have been discontinued around the turn of the century but, from the outset, the Admiralty had disavowed any intention of doing more than providing regular work for the men already.employed and 'keeping up the engineering establishment to a proper standard of numbers and efficiency'. See Statement explanatory of the Navy Estimates for 1891–92, *Parliamentary Papers, 1890–91*. [*C 6279*] *LI 331*, p. 8.

61. See Table 3.3 above.

62. The battleship HMS BENBOW in 1882, the cruisers HMS NELSON and HMS NORTHAMPTON in 1874 and the cruiser HMS BLENHEIM in 1888.

63. *Report of the Ravensworth Committee*, p. 2.

64. The exceptions were Caird & Co. and Harland & Wolff. See *Report of the Forwood Committee*, Appendix IV.

65. *Report of the Ravensworth Committee*, Q. 262.

66. *Ibid.*, Q. 1535.

67. *Ibid.*, Q. 1758.

68. P. Banbury, *Shipbuilders of the Thames and Medway* (Newton Abbot 1971), p. 270.

69. On this occasion Caird & Co.'s tender prices were £90,000 per hull and £300,000 per set of engines for two cruisers. The most expensive of the successful bidders, Palmers of Jarrow, had offered prices of £60,165 per hull and £224,422 per set of engines. See *Report of the Forwood Committee*, Appendix IV.

70. John Elder & Co. and J.. & G. Thomson were among the first Clyde yards to build steel ships. Elder's launched two steel paddle-steamers in 1877. Thomson's built its first steel steamer in 1878. By 1881, Thomson's had built and launched the all-steel liner SERVIA for Cunard. Denny's ROTOMAHANA, the first Clyde-built oceangoing steel steamer, had been built only two years earlier in 1879. See Slaven, *The Development of the West of Scotland*, p. 179.

# 4

# *1889–1899: The Navy Defence Act and its Consequences*

The private warshipbuilders' prospects were transformed by the Navy Defence Act of 1889 which made financial provision for the building in private shipyards of a total of four battleships, five protected cruisers, seventeen second-class cruisers and six torpedo gunboats. These ships were the private warshipbuilders' share of a massive five-year programme costing £21.5 millions, which called for the building of no less than seventy new warships aggregating 335,060 tons. More important, they were the product of renewed public and political interest in the Royal Navy which augured well for the future level of demand.

Pressure to increase spending on the Royal Navy had been building up since 1881 when a Royal Commission on the defence of British possessions and commerce abroad, appointed in the aftermath of the Balkan crisis of 1878, reported that 'the strength of the navy should be increased with as little delay as possible'.[1] At the time no action was taken and the report itself was suppressed, but the issue resurfaced in 1884 when information supplied by serving naval officers inspired a series of highly critical articles in *The Pallmall Gazette*.[2] On this occasion the combination of press agitation and renewed fears of war with Russia forced the then First Lord of the Admiralty, Lord Northbrook, to act, although the critics of naval policy were far from being satisfied with the scale of the Northbrook Programme which provided·for the building of only two battleships, five protected cruisers, six torpedo cruisers and fourteen torpedo boats at a cost of £3.1 millions.[3] In January 1888 Lord Charles Beresford, the Fourth Sea Lord, resigned his post to campaign for a larger and better organised Navy.[4] The previous year, the Jubilee Review had shown the fleet to be a motley collection of ships, many of them barely seaworthy, far less serviceable as effective fighting units.[5] The complacent tone of the evidence given by the Sea Lords to the House of Commons Select Committee on the 1888 Naval Estimates did nothing to allay mounting public concern and, in 1888, the London Chamber of Commerce added its influential voice to those demanding the strengthening of the Navy.[6] By 1889 the pressure had become irresistible. No one had ever denied the importance of maintaining Britain's naval supremacy, and the report on the 1888 Navy Manoeuvres contained the warning that the existing fleet was:

> altogether inadequate to take the offensive in a war with only one great power and, supposing a combination of two powers to be allied as her enemies, the balance of maritime strength would be against England.[7]

In parliament, party controversy on the Government's proposals centred on the unorthodox character of the financial arrangements rather than on the programme itself and a vital consensus emerged on the need to maintain a 'Two Power Standard'. The statement by the Unionist First Lord of the Admiralty, Lord George Hamilton, that

> our establishment should be on such a scale that it should at least be equal to the naval strength of any two other countries[8]

was explicitly accepted by the opposition spokesman, the future Liberal leader and Prime Minister, Henry Campbell-Bannerman.[9] Originally directed against a possible combination of France and Russia, the Two Power Standard was to be the basis of all naval provision for the next quarter of a century. In 1909, the then Prime Minister, Henry Asquith, deprecated the tendency

> to treat the Two-Power Standard as though it had a sort of sacred sacro-sanctity and immutable authority which sheltered it from all criticism[10]

and the formula was subsequently modified to deal with the situation created by the rise of the Imperial German Navy[11] but, up to 1914, no government dared admit publicly that the principle of a Two Power Standard had been compromised.

The adoption of a Two Power Standard had far-reaching consequences for the subsequent level of naval construction. Even before the 1889 programme was completed, fears of a Franco-Russian alliance had led to agitation for a further addition to naval strength. In December 1893, when the Liberal Government which had taken office in 1892 faced an opposition motion that 'a considerable addition should be at once made to the Navy', the Prime Minister, Mr Gladstone, was virtually the only member of the cabinet who believed further expenditure to be unnecessary.[12] By March 1894 he had retired and the incoming Rosebery administration had announced a major new five-year building programme — the Spencer Programme — which provided for the immediate commencement of seven more battleships and six more cruisers, with the implicit promise that further cruisers would follow in succeeding years.[13] The return of a Unionist Government at the 1895 election did nothing to lessen the commitment to a big navy. Year by year the Naval Estimates made provision for the building of further battleships and cruisers, and in both 1897 and 1898 there were supplementary estimates to cover the building of yet more warships to satisfy the requirements of the Two Power Standard, which demanded that Britain should respond in kind to the building plans of the French and Russian governments. In July 1897 a new French cruiser programme was countered by orders for four cruisers and three destroyers. Similarly, in July 1898 provision had to be made for the building of a further four battleships, four cruisers and nine destroyers following the announcement of Russia's future building plans.

The escalating arms race had a dramatic impact on the volume of warshipbuilding available to private shipyards. In 1889, and again under the Spencer Programme of 1894–95, the largest share of the work was allocated to the

Royal Dockyards but there was a limit to how much work they could handle. The larger the naval construction programmes became, the greater the volume of Admiralty work which had to be put out to contract. In 1898–99, when the original programme called for the building of eleven ships aggregating 104,120 tons, six of the ships aggregating 59,710 tons were allocated to the Royal Dockyards, but when it became necessary to provide for the building of another seventeen ships aggregating a further 101,230 tons, only two more ships aggregating 19,600 tons could be accommodated in the Navy's own establishments. Meanwhile the introduction of the torpedo boat destroyer in 1893–94 had created a class of work for which the dockyards were ill-suited and the Admiralty decided to leave the design and construction of these small fast ships to private firms.[14] Equally important, the conditions under which private firms were expected to undertake Admiralty work were much more favourable than they had been prior to 1889. Contracts were no longer subject to frustrating delays while the Admiralty sorted out changes in specification and made up its mind on matters of detail. The emphasis was now on speed of production, and steps were taken to prevent such delays from occurring:

> It was decided after careful consideration to give the Dockyard-built ships of each type a sensible start upon the contract-built ships of similar type in order that all details of fitting and equipment might be thoroughly worked out in the dockyards by naval and professional officers and thus be available for guidance in the construction of the contract ships.[15]

For some contractors the building of a number of ships to a common design may have been a mixed blessing as the Admiralty tightened up on matters of detail, leaving builders with less room for discretion,[16] but this was not a change which worried the more efficient of their number. Further, since contractors were no longer expected to submit alternative engine designs[17] and the Admiralty now provided the outline drawings for both ships and engines, tendering for Admiralty contracts became less of a lottery. This made the work much more attractive and, despite the Admiralty's insistence on the highest standard of workmanship, contractors who could compete on price prospered.

None of this was apparent to private firms at the outset. On the Clyde renewed interest in warshipbuilding in the 1890s probably owed more to the situation in which individual firms found themselves than to any conscious decision to exploit a favourable opportunity. Nevertheless, the Navy Defence Act of 1889 afforded Admiralty contractors an exceptional opportunity to tender successfully for a share of naval work. Apart from the warships specifically allotted to private firms under the terms of the Act, it was necessary to make extensive use of private firms to provide the engines for Dockyard-built ships. Seven sets of engines were manufactured in the Royal Dockyards, using manpower and machinery provided for the purpose of repairing naval engines in an emergency,[18] but private firms supplied the rest. As a result the Admiralty found itself having to place orders for thirty-one sets of machinery for Dockyard-built ships as well as for the simultaneous building of thirty-two warships totalling 157,510 tons, a situation which called for the participation of an exceptionally large number of private firms. As was customary, the distribution of orders was determined by competitive tender and none of the Admiralty's regular suppliers was assured of a share of the work but, in practice, virtually all of the Admiralty's most experienced contractors had some share of the orders and only one of the nineteen firms favoured with a contract appears to have been entirely new to naval work.[19]

On Clydeside, five firms participated in the five-year programme started in 1889. J. & G. Thomson, which became J. & G. Thomson Ltd. in 1890, and traded as the Clydebank Engineering & Shipbuilding Co. Ltd. from 1896 to 1899 before becoming the Clydebank division of John Brown & Co. Ltd. (hereafter referred to simply as Clydebank to avoid confusion); the Fairfield Shipbuilding & Engineering Co. Ltd. (hereafter referred to simply as Fairfield); Robert Napier & Sons (hereafter referred to simply as Napier's); the London & Glasgow Engineering & Iron Shipbuilding Co. Ltd. (hereafter referred to simply as the London & Glasgow); and the Greenock Foundry Co. which merged with Scott & Co. to form Scott's Shipbuilding & Engineering Co. Ltd. in 1901 (thereafter referred to simply as Scott's).

Of the five firms, the principal beneficiary was Clydebank which received orders worth £1,023,071 for the building of three 3,400 ton Apollo class second-class cruisers,[20] the 14,150 ton Royal Sovereign class battleship HMS RAMILLIES and the machinery of the Dockyard-built cruiser HMS HERMIONE. Of the four other Clyde firms which participated in the programme, the London & Glasgow, with an order for three 3,600 ton second-class cruisers,[21] did as well as could be expected of a relatively small firm with little previous experience of naval work, and an order for the engines of two Dockyard-built battleships[22] admitted Greenock Foundry to the select group of firms which the Admiralty considered fit to undertake the building of the largest naval engines. Napier's, nearing the end of its long career as an Admiralty contractor, declined the opportunity to build more than one 7,700 ton Edgar class protected cruiser[23] and Fairfield, which had expected an order for cruisers,[24] and might reasonably have hoped for more, succeeded only in securing contracts for the construction of the machinery for two Dockyard-built cruisers and one Dockyard-built torpedo gunboat.[25]

While the disparity between the volume of orders received by Clydebank and Fairfield under the 1889 programme may not have been intentional, it was an accurate reflection of the very different circumstances in which the two firms found themselves in 1889 when most of the contracts were put out to tender, differences which were apparent in the circumstances under which each of them became public companies — Fairfield in July 1889 and Clydebank in March 1890.

When Fairfield came to the market in 1889 it was still a thriving concern. The firm had suffered a major loss in the untimely death of Sir William Pearce in 1888 as neither his business partner, Richard Barnwell, who served as managing director until his death in 1898, nor Sir William George Pearce, who succeeded his father as chairman, possessed Sir William's extraordinary flair for business which had made Fairfield the most successful shipbuilder on the Clyde, but the change in management did not prevent Fairfield from being valued at £750,000 including an unspecified amount for goodwill in the value of £279,537 attached to land. It would appear that the decision to 'go public' was primarily intended to allow the Pearce family to realise part of their fortune without relinquishing control. In any event, all of the benefits of the public issue appear to have accrued to the vendors. The capital of the new company was divided into 25,000 ordinary shares of £10 each, £250,000 of 6% preference shares and £250,000 of 4% debentures, and the vendors, who were allocated all of the ordinary shares and £139,390 of debentures, also received £391,804 in cash.[26]

By contrast, when the firm of J. & G. Thomson was reconstituted as J. & G. Thomson Ltd. in March 1890, there was no comparable element of goodwill in its valuation at £400,000.[27] An issue of £150,000 of 5% debentures was needed to refinance the business and the vendors retained nominal control only by the grace of their bankers who advanced them £250,000 to take up all of the ordinary shares in the new company. Since 1885 J. & G. Thomson had suffered trading losses of £84,860.[28] By March 1890 there was no alternative to the winding-up of the partnership. The partners' capital accounts were overdrawn by £78,841, the Inman Line was withholding £100,000 pending the settlement of outstanding claims on the 12,950 ton liners CITY OF NEW YORK and CITY OF PARIS launched in 1888, and the firm was heavily in debt to its bankers. By March 1891, after a settlement with the Inman Line costing £45,000, the deficiency on the partners' capital accounts had increased to £112,556.[29] Although they continued to be employed as directors of the new company, the Thomson brothers never regained full control of the business. By 1896, when the company's name was changed to the Clydebank Engineering and Shipbuilding Co. Ltd., the family interest was negligible.[30]

By the winter of 1893–94, when major Admiralty orders were next put out to tender, Fairfield had as much need of the work as Clydebank. In part, this was due to a slump in merchant demand. In contrast to 1889, when the Navy Defence Act had coincided with a boom in merchant shipbuilding, the renewed demand for warships in the winter of 1893–94 occurred when merchant work was in short supply. The volume of steam-powered merchant ships launched in the United Kingdom had declined steadily from a peak of 717,582 tons in 1889 to 460,000 tons in 1893.[31] By December 1893 *The Glasgow Herald*, which a year earlier, had remarked on the fact that much of the 1892 output had been in an advanced state of completion in December 1891,[32] was in no doubt as to the outlook:

> The returns from every quarter tell of a depression which is slowly but surely settling on the industry and the decline in trade generally precludes the immediate possibility of anything like a genuine revival.[33]

The ineptitude of Fairfield's management made matters worse. Over the three years to 30th June 1892, Fairfield's merchant order book had kept the company profitably employed. Despite providing £35,338 for depreciation, £33,750 for debenture interest and £44,675 for preference dividends, the directors had been able to recommend the payment of annual dividends of 10% on the ordinary shares and the transfer of a total of £30,000 to reserve but, as early as September 1890, the auditors observed that the costs of the shipbuilding department in the year to 30th June 1890 had exceeded estimate by £20,687.[34] The board ought to have realised that something was amiss when the engine and boiler shops, under the management of Andrew Laing, earned profits of £135,014 in the three years to 30th June 1892 while the shipbuilding department, under the management of J. Sexton White, barely broke even,[35] but no action was taken until 1892–93, when it became apparent that the contract for the building of the 12,950 ton liners CAMPANIA and LUCANIA for Cunard was going badly wrong. By June 1893, when White was finally asked to resign, it was too late to prevent a major reverse. Profitability declined sharply in the year to 30th June 1893; the directors were obliged to pass the ordinary dividend and draw on reserves to cover the preference dividend. Thereafter the situation became increasingly bleak. By October 1893, when the directors revealed that the Cunard contract would result in a loss,[36] the company had received a claim for damages amounting to £165,000 in respect of deficiencies in the vessels' deadweight carrying capacity. The board considered this claim 'monstrous' as, in their view, the deficiency was 'in a great measure' due to the extra weight of the engines fitted in the ships in response to Cunard's request for more speed,[37] but, contractually, Fairfield was in a weak position. With Cunard withholding the balance of the purchase price, the amount of the company's indebtedness was assuming such worrying proportions that, in July 1893, its bankers asked for a personal guarantee from the chairman in respect of the company's overdraft.[38] Meanwhile, the yard was running short of work and Fairfield was experiencing the greatest difficulty in competing for any new merchant orders which became available. Richard Barnwell informed the board in June 1893 that a tender for Burrell & Sons was

> greatly in excess of other Clyde yards despite [his] having taken it upon himself to eliminate all profit and a proportion of charges.[39]

Faced with this situation, the Fairfield board took an active interest in the naval work which became available in the winter of 1893–94. A few months earlier, on the advice of Francis Elgar, late Director of the Royal Dockyards,[40] who had joined the Fairfield board in September 1891, Barnwell had halted preparations of a bid for destroyers[41] but, in December 1893, after tenders for the machinery of two Dockyard-built battleships based on 20% charges and no profit[42] and for a Powerful class cruiser had both proved abortive, the board decided to tender for destroyers on the prompting of the chairman, who urged them to 'use every endeavour' to secure such a contract.[43] In February 1894 Fairfield was rewarded with an order for three.[44] While most welcome, as the firm's order book for delivery after June 1894 comprised only the steam yacht GERULDA for Mr. H. B. L. McCalmont and the S.S. ARUNDEL CASTLE for Sir Donald Currie, this order did not resolve the company's problems. Despite the appointment of a new shipyard manager, and a determined effort to cut costs, new work continued to be hard to find. Eventually Fairfield succeeded in securing the order for the 5,600 ton Eclipse class cruisers HMS DIANA and HMS VENUS in April 1894 and, following a settlement with Cunard which limited the loss on the contract for the CAMPANIA and LUCANIA to £89,022, the company was able to continue trading with the assistance of the Pearce family who paid in £90,000 to cover the deficiency in the accounts at 30th June 1894, but the weakness of Fairfield's competitive situation was evident in the outcome of the tenders for a Majestic class battleship in February 1894. Having submitted a bid of £446,129, the board was sufficiently anxious to secure the work to reduce its price to £430,000 when the Admiralty inquired whether Fairfield was prepared to accept the order at a lower price, but it did not feel able to accept £417,000, the price the Admiralty apparently was willing to pay.[45] In consequence the orders were awarded to Laird's of Birkenhead and to Clydebank which had already beaten Fairfield in securing the order for the Powerful class cruiser HMS TERRIBLE in December 1893.

Clydebank's success in securing the orders for, both the 14,200 ton protected cruiser HMS TERRIBLE and the 14,725 ton battleship HMS JUPITER in the winter of 1893–94 was not achieved at the expense of accepting the work at what, for Clydebank, would have been unremunerative prices. The cruiser HMS TERRIBLE produced a contribution to overheads and profit of £144,056 on an invoiced price of £561,111 despite the problems associated with building engines to drive a 14,200 ton ship at 22 knots. The battleship HMS JUPITER which was priced at £435,855, £58,029 below the price received for the battleship HMS RAMILLIES ordered in 1889, still yielded a contribution to overheads and profit of £111,150. Nor was Clydebank successful in securing orders because it was better placed than Fairfield to take risks in tendering for major naval contracts. On the contrary, in the winter of 1893–94 it too was in financial difficulties and, unlike Fairfield, it did not have the Pearce family fortune to fall back on.

From the outset the fortunes of the new company had been heavily dependent on its success as a warshipbuilder. Unlike Fairfield, which had taken orders for 23,350 tons of merchant ships worth £756,576 between the death of Sir William Pearce in 1888 and July 1889,[46] Clydebank had derived little benefit from the buoyant demand for merchant ships in 1888–89. Its total intake of merchant work between the receipt of the Inman Line order in 1887 and the passing of the Navy Defence Act in 1889 comprised two ships aggregating 9,119 tons.[47] As a result Clydebank's order book had continued to be dominated by naval work and its success in securing a major share of the orders placed by the Admiralty under the Navy Defence Act had been of critical importance for the success of the capital reconstruction which followed. With warships accounting for seven of the eleven contracts taken over from the Thomson partnership, the works were described in the prospectus for the issue of debentures as being capable of producing either 30,000 tons of first-class steam ships or 20,000 tons of warships per annum.[48] In addition, the orders secured under the Navy Defence Act had provided the new company with three years of extremely profitable work. Profits of £49,571 on the three second class cruisers, HMS TERPSICHORE, HMS THETIS and HMS TRIBUNE, and £60,000 on account of a final profit of £93,767 on the battleship HMS RAMILLIES, resulted in trading profits totalling £137,961 before providing £38,621 for depreciation and £16,928 for debenture interest in the three years to 31st March 1893. By 1893-94 this period of prosperity appeared to be coming to an end. Clydebank had virtually exhausted its naval order book and the difficulty of finding a satisfactory substitute was underlined by the scale of the losses which the yard suffered in executing its first major merchant contracts since 1888. The 5,946 ton steamers NILE and DANUBE, built for the Royal Mail Steam Packet Co. at an average price of £126,405 each, failed to recover prime cost and resulted in losses of £23,143 and £20,565 respectively, while the 8,669 ton KENSINGTON built for the International Steam Navigation Co. at a price of £150,980 ended in a loss of £5,949. The directors were able to blame the resulting trading loss of £26,281 in the year to 31st March 1894 on a prolonged strike of the workforce in 1893 but, after distributing £50,000 in dividends to the ordinary shareholders over the previous three years, the company's profit and loss account was overdrawn by £10,027. Fortunately, by the time the extent of its difficulties became public knowledge, the company had been able to replenish its order book with Admiralty contracts but in the winter of 1893-94 it had come dangerously close to running out of work altogether. In March 1894 its entire order book consisted of naval orders taken since November 1893. Clydebank owed its prosperity over the next five years to these orders and to the further Admiralty orders which followed.

While none of the firms which undertook naval work in the winter of 1893-94 had any assurance that Admiralty orders would be more plentiful in the future than they had been in the past, and their availability continued to depend on the size of each year's naval programme, warship design was more stable than it had been prior to 1889, and the Admiralty was inclined to favour established contractors. These conditions favoured firms with previous experience of a particular class of work and, in practice, Clydebank, Fairfield and the London & Glasgow were all regularly employed on naval work from 1894 onwards.

Clydebank, which had received orders for three destroyers[49] as well as the 14,200 ton protected cruiser HMS TERRIBLE under the 1893-94 programme went on to undertake the building of the 14,750 ton battleship HMS JUPITER in 1894-95, the 11,000 ton protected cruiser HMS EUROPA, engines for the dockyard-built third-class cruiser HMS PELORUS and four destroyers[50] in 1895-96, another 11,000 ton protected cruiser — HMS ARIADNE — and two more destroyers[51] in 1896-97, the 12,000 ton armoured cruiser HMS SUTLEJ in 1897-98 and the 12,000 ton armoured cruiser HMS BACCHANTE, the 14,150 ton armoured cruiser HMS LEVIATHAN and the engines for the Dockyard-built cruiser HMS ESSEX in 1898-99. Similarly Fairfield, which started with the construction of its first three destroyers in 1893-94 and the 5,600 ton second-class cruisers HMS DIANA and HMS VENUS in 1894-95, received an order for the 11,000 ton protected cruiser HMS DIADEM in 1895-96, another 11,000 ton protected cruiser — HMS ARGONAUT — together with the 5,650 ton second-class cruisers HMS HERMES and HIGHFLYER and three destroyers[52] in 1896-97, the 12,000 ton armoured cruisers HMS CRESSY and HMS ABOUKIR and a destroyer[53] in 1897-98 and the 14,150 ton armoured cruiser HMS GOOD

HOPE and two more destroyers[54] in 1898–99. The third Clyde warshipbuilder, the London & Glasgow, received fewer orders but the 5,600 ton second-class cruisers HMS DIDO and HMS ISIS in 1894–95 were followed by the 5,650 ton second-class cruiser HMS HYACINTH in 1896–97 and two 710 ton gunboats[55] in 1897–98. This represented a significant volume of work for a relatively small yard, sufficient to ensure that at no time between 1894 and 1899 was it too without some naval work on hand.

In all, the three Clyde yards received orders for a total of thirty-nine warships aggregating 196,150 tons as a result of the naval programmes for the six years 1893–94 to 1898–99, an average of 32,692 tons per year. This amount of work represented a spectacular increase over the volume of naval work undertaken by Clyde yards at any time in the past, the district's share of the orders placed under the five-year programme authorised by the Navy Defence Act having amounted to only 42,850 tons in total. It also represented a significant volume of work in relation to the total output of the Clyde shipbuilding industry which averaged 329,025 tons per annum between 1890 and 1894 and 415,787 tons per annum between 1895 and 1899.[56] More important, from the point of view of the individual contractor, the work was generally profitable. Clydebank, which undertook seventeen contracts worth £4,067,477 between April 1893 and March 1899, eventually suffered losses on three of the destroyers[57] but all of the yard's major contracts yielded good profits, the net profit of £43,475 earned on the £438,668 contract for the protected cruiser HMS ARIADNE being the lowest net profit earned on any of its seven armoured or protected ships. Similarly, Fairfield, with nineteen contracts worth £4,006,552 in the same period, appears to have earned profits on seventeen of them, the exceptions being the second-class cruiser HMS HERMES and the engines for the Dockyard-built cruiser HMS PIONEER on which it appears to have suffered losses of £1,543 and £6,263 respectively.

The profitability of naval work may have owed something to collusion between contractors. In March 1896, Richard Barnwell of Fairfield had a meeting with his counterparts at Jarrow and Barrow at which they arranged to concert their bids for 30-knot destroyers by submitting tenders of £52,000, £51,900 and £51,800 respectively and to meet again before tendering for 33-knot boats.[58] There is no record of any further meetings having taken place but it is unlikely that this was an isolated occurrence. Common membership of bodies such as the Society of Naval Architects afforded leading warshipbuilders the opportunity to meet regularly on an informal basis and to exchange information and concert their bids if they had a mind to do so. Whether such arrangements were effective in raising prices is more questionable. As far as destroyers were concerned, effective price-fixing would have required an arrangement which satisfied most of the twelve firms which were actively involved in the business, and in July 1897 at least one leading warshipbuilder — Clydebank — refused to participate in an arrangement to compare prices and ballot for orders proposed by Mr Adamson of Barrow.[59] Further, if there was widespread collusion on prices, it did not prevent some Admiralty contractors from suffering heavy losses on naval contracts undertaken in the 1890s. Admittedly, Palmer's of Jarrow, which was forced to write down its capital in 1896, had encountered difficulties only as a result of having taken a contract for two battleships at uneconomic prices in 1889–90, when large naval contracts were still something of a novelty,[60] while Earle & Co. of Hull and Maudslay, Son & Field of London, which both went bankrupt in 1899–1900, were heavily involved in the manufacture of machinery for Dockyard-built warships,[61] a class of work which even the more efficient Clyde yards did not find particularly profitable. The positive evidence that the high profits earned by Clyde yards on major Admiralty contracts in the 1890s was the result of price fixing is thin. On two of the three occasions between April 1893 and March 1899, when Clydebank and Fairfield secured orders for large cruisers of the same class at the same time, their prices were remarkably similar but this may have been a coincidence and the high profits earned by these two yards on a succession of large cruiser contracts may simply have reflected their particular aptitude for this class of work. Significantly, while both firms were extraordinarily successful in earning large profits on the contracts for big cruisers, which had much in common with the building of fast passenger liners in terms of size and speed, Clydebank in particular had difficulty with destroyers, which called for a totally different blend of skills.[62]

Whatever the reasons for the profitability of their naval orders, regular and profitable Admiralty orders resulted in a dramatic improvement in the trading results of the two major Clyde warshipbuilders between 1894 and 1899. Clydebank's trading profit before depreciation, which had averaged £45,987 in the three years to 31st March 1893 before slumping into a loss of £26,281 in the following year, recovered to £31,587 in 1894–95, £86,491 in 1895–96 and an average of no less than £125,557 per annum in the three years to 31st March 1899. Fairfield too was consistently profitable. After suffering a trading loss before depreciation of £17,519 in the year to 30th June 1894, the company returned to profitability with a trading profit before depreciation of £35,625 in 1894–95. The following year, trading profits before depreciation of £75,245 exceeded those of any of the three relatively prosperous years at the beginning of the decade, and between 1896–97 and 1898–99 they averaged £89,893 per annum.

The revival in the fortunes of Fairfield and Clydebank owed little to merchant shipbuilding. The demand for first-class merchant ships recovered slowly from the depression of 1893–94. Apart from 1897, when the growth in output was checked by a prolonged lock-out of engineering workers, the total tonnage of ships launched on the Clyde increased steadily from 280,160 tons in 1893 to 491,074 tons in 1899, but, as *The Glasgow Herald* remarked in 1896, there was a notable shortage of first-class merchant work for much of the period.[63] In 1898, 'a year of great plenty',[64] and 1899, a year in which the resources of the British shipbuilding industry were described as being 'taxed to the full' to meet the demand,[65] high-class merchant work was in more plentiful supply and Clydebank, in particular, took advantage of the opportunity by taking orders for the 14,280 ton liner SAXONIA for Cunard, the 11,667 ton liners VADERLAND and ZEELAND for the Red Star Line, the 11,635 ton liner HAVERFORD for the International Navigation Co. and the 11,621 ton liner MERION for the Dominion Line, but these orders came too late to make a significant contribution to Clydebank's profitability up to March 1899 and they were untypical of the merchant ships produced by both Clydebank and Fairfield between 1894 and 1899. Apart from two steamers for the Russian Volunteer Fleet[66] and two 5,672 ton cargo ships built for Turnbull & Martin,[67] the merchant contracts completed by Clydebank in the five years to 31st March 1899 comprised only nine railway ferries and pleasure steamers, four yachts and twenty barges, and the total value of the yard's merchant output amounted only to £1,002,894. Fairfield produced a rather higher volume of merchant work in the five years to 30th June 1899 only because Sir Donald Currie had favoured the yard with five contracts worth £732,260.[68] The 8,291 ton liner OMRAH, built for the Orient Line at a price of £224,816, which failed to recover prime cost by £7,686, was the only other major merchant contract completed by Fairfield in this period. The remainder of the yard's merchant output comprised three small ships for the Scottish Oriental Co., six ferries and pleasure steamers and two yachts worth in all £507,444. As Table 4.1 shows, while the total value of Fairfield's output in the five years to 30th June 1899 differed little from that of the previous five years, the balance between merchant and naval work was strikingly different:

**Table 4.1.** Contracts Completed by Fairfield 1889–1899

|  | 1889–1894 | | 1894–1899 | |
|---|---|---|---|---|
|  | No. | £ | No. | £ |
| MERCHANT | 33 | 3,400,891 | 17 | 1,657,375 |
| NAVAL | 3 | 229,589 | 14 | 2,196,630 |
|  | 36 | 3,630,480 | 31 | 3,854,005 |

(Source: Author's figures based on detail abstracted from *UCS 2*. See Peebles, **thesis**, Appendix FII)

Overall, the value of Clydebank's output in the five years to 31st March 1899 was broadly similar to that of Fairfield since a succession of small warships built for the Spanish government helped to make up for the lower volume of merchant work but its dependence on warshipbuilding was all the greater. As Table 4.2 shows, 71.8% of sales and 83.1% of the contribution to overheads and profit derived from all the contracts completed between April 1894 and March 1899 were attributable to naval work:

**Table 4.2.** Contracts Completed by Clydebank 1894–1899

|  | No. | Sales £ | Contribution £ |
|---|---|---|---|
| ADMIRALTY | 9 | 2,103,108 | 500,184 |
| FOREIGN WARSHIPS | 13 | 449,450 | 174,266 |
| OTHER WORK | 37 | 1,002,894 | 137,304 |
|  | 59 | 3,555,452 | 811,754 |

(Source: author's figures based on detail abstracted from *UCS 1*. See Peebles, **thesis**, Appendix FIII)

Clydebank's directors were clearly concerned at this imbalance between naval and merchant work and, in December 1896, after discussing the desirability of getting orders for merchant ships, they decided in principle to entertain proposals which entailed extending credit to customers.[69] Although this did not produce immediate results, it signalled the beginning of a determined effort to revive the yard's merchant business. In 1897, having purchased additional land to the west of the existing yard, the board embarked on a major programme of building and re-equipment which put Clydebank in a better position to take advantage of the subsequent upturn in the demand for first-class passenger liners. The firm's ability to finance net additions to fixed assets, amounting to £246,676 in the three years to 31st March 1899, without having to resort to external funding testified both to the profitability of warshipbuilding and to the care with which the Clydebank directors husbanded their resources. After two years during which no dividend had been paid on the ordinary shares, payment was resumed at a rate of 10% in 1896 but distributions were limited to 20% in each of the two following years. By March 1899 reserves of £150,000 and a credit balance of £102,876 on the profit and loss account bore testimony to their prudence.

At Fairfield a different order of priorities prevailed. Here, distributions to ordinary shareholders took preference over everything else. A dividend of 3% in 1894-95 was followed by payments of 15%, 13%, 15% and 16% respectively in each of the next four years with the result that the total profits retained in the business in the five years to 30th June 1899 amounted to only £24,653. With provisions for depreciation of fixed assets restricted to £3,811 in 1894-95 and £10,000 per annum in each of the following four years and the company still in debt to its bankers, there was little scope for capital investment. In 1897-98, after four years during which additions to fixed assets amounted to a mere £21,566, a modest programme of essential extensions and improvements had to be financed by the issue of £100,000 of 5% second debentures. At least one director — Francis Elgar — had some misgivings about the company's policy. He wrote to the chairman in October 1898 advising against the payment of a dividend larger than 15% on the grounds that it would have a bad effect on both the future negotiation of prices with Sir Donald Currie and on the attitude of the workforce while the provision for depreciation was 'quite little enough' as

> We require now to make good as opportunities offer the encroachments upon depreciation and reserves during our bad years.[70]

However, the Pearce family, as the owners of most of the ordinary shares, had a decisive say in such matters. Their anxiety to recoup the £90,000 paid in to cover the deficiency in the company's accounts in June 1894 dictated that high distributions should continue until this was achieved.

Whether the failure to plough a larger proportion of Fairfield's profits back into the business in these years made any significant difference to the company's fortunes in the long run is debatable. Fairfield's lack of adequate facilities in the opening years of the new century was a factor in the re-emergence of Clydebank as the builder of Cunard's biggest and fastest liners but, following its unfortunate experience with the CAMPANIA and LUCANIA in the 1890s, Fairfield was understandably reluctant even to quote a fixed price for such orders.[71] Significantly, there is no evidence that lack of investment had an adverse effect on Fairfield's ability to secure major Admiralty contracts then or later. Further, while the high distribution policy left the company uncomfortably highly geared, this did not matter as long as the business continued to be profitable. In July 1899, when the company's bankers showed some unease over an overdraft of £243,000, Strachan, the company secretary, was able to reassure them by pointing out that the situation was temporary and that payments from customers would reduce the overdraft to less than £30,000 by the end of August.[72]

Meanwhile, Fairfield had fully recovered its competitiveness. Under the competent management of Edmund Sharer, who had succeeded White as manager of the shipbuilding department in 1893, and Alexander Gracie, who had become manager of the engine and boiler department after Andrew Laing had his service contract terminated in 1895,[73] both sides of the business were operating profitably. In March 1899 the board's primary concern was to secure further orders for completion by June 1900.[74] They were unsuccessful, and, apart from the liners KINFAUNS CASTLE and KILDONAN CASTLE for Sir Donald Currie, completions in the year to 30th June 1900 consisted only of the destroyers HMS FALCON and HMS OSTRICH, but the firm was far from being short of work. It already had orders on hand for the 12,000 ton armoured cruisers HMS CRESSY and HMS ABOUKIR, due for completion in 1900–01, and for the 14,150 ton armoured cruiser HMS GOOD HOPE, which was not due for completion until 1901–02. Further, in April 1899, Fairfield was able to add to its order book by securing the order for the 9,800 ton armoured cruiser HMS BEDFORD, one of only two such ships put out to contract at this time. In consequence, Fairfield's order book at 30th June 1899 comprised the two liners for Sir Donald Currie, which were worth £547,224, and six naval vessels worth £2,313,022, a total of £2,860,246.

Clydebank's order book at 31st March 1899 was even more impressive. Apart from the armoured cruisers HMS SUTLEJ, HMS BACCHANTE and HMS LEVIATHAN aggregating 38,150 tons, the yard had yet to complete six destroyers for the Admiralty and three more were being built 'on spec'.[75] In addition, Clydebank was building the 14,150 ton battleship ASAHI for the Japanese government and there were orders on hand for six merchant ships aggregating 61,487 tons.[76] In consequence Clydebank's order book was worth £4,518,843, comprising twelve orders destined for the Admiralty worth £2,190,035, the Japanese battleship worth £876,350, and six merchant ships worth £1,452,458.

After five years of regular Admiralty orders both Clydebank and Fairfield could face the future with confidence. Several years of profitable work lay behind them, their financial situation was fundamentally sound, and they already had enough orders on hand to suggest that they were likely to be profitably employed for two or three years ahead. The role of an Admiralty contractor had become for the first time a highly rewarding specialisation, and barring unforeseen developments there was no reason why they should not continue to prosper.

NOTES

1. The Report of the Royal Commission presided over by Lord Caernarvon was never published but extracts from it were included in the papers laid before the 1887 Colonial Conference. See Proceedings of the Colonial Conference in London with Appendix, *Parliamentary Papers, 1887 [C5091] LVI 1.*

2. C. White, *Victoria's Navy, the Heyday of Steam* (Ensworth, Hampshire 1985), p. 29.

3. Conway's *All the World's Fighting Ships, 1860-1905*, p. 1.

4. Parkes, *British Battleships*, p. 350.

5. White, *The Heyday of Steam*, p. 30.

6. A. J. Marder, *The Anatomy of British Seapower: A History of British Naval Policy in the Pre-Dreadnought Era, 1880-1905* (London 1941: reissued London 1964), pp. 131-2.

7. Extracts from the Report of the Committee on the Naval Manoeuvres, 1888 with the Narrative of the Operations and the rules laid down for conducting the same, *Parliamentary Papers, 1889 [C5632] L 735.*

8. House of Commons, 7th March 1889. *Hansard, 3rd series, CCCXXXIII. 1889.* col. 1171.

9. House of Commons, 1st April 1889. *Hansard, 3rd series, CCCXXXIV. 1889.* col. 1272.

10. House of Commons, 26th May 1909. *Hansard, 5th series, V. 1909.* col. 1298.

11. See Chapter 6 below.

12. P. Magnus, *Gladstone, a Biography* (London 1954), pp. 414-17.

13. Statement of the First Lord of the Admiralty, explanatory of the Navy Estimates, 1894-95. *Parliamentary Papers, 1894 [C7295] LIV 305,* p. 16.

14. E. J. March, *British Destroyers: A History of Development, 1892-1953* (London 1967), p. 24.

15. Statement of the First Lord of the Admiralty, explanatory of the Navy Estimates, 1890-91. *Parliamentary Papers, 1890 [C5958] XLIV 347,* p. 5.

16. Parkes, *British Battleships*, p. 383.

17. The practice of allowing contractors to submit alternative engine designs when tendering had been criticised by the Forwood Committee. 'When it is considered desirable to obtain from engine makers suggestions as to the construction of engines — competitive designs should be invited before sending out invitations to tender and a decision come to by the aid of such designs as to the type of engine best adapted for the purpose. This would enable tenders to be invited upon one common basis and allow the wholesome principle of accepting the lowest tender to prevail.' *Report of the Forwood Committee*, p. 18.

18. Statement of the First Lord of the Admiralty, explanatory of the Navy Estimates, 1891-92, *Parliamentary Papers, 1890-91 [C6279] LI 331* p. 8.

19. Apart from the five Clydeside firms mentioned in the text, fourteen firms received a share of the orders — Thames Iron Works, Samuda Bros., J. I. Thornycroft & Co., A. Yarrow & Co., Humphrey Tennant & Co., John Penn and Maudslay, Son & Field on the Thames, Armstrong, Mitchell & Co., Palmers Shipbuilding & Iron Co., Hawthorn Leslie & Co. and Geo. Stephenson & Co. on the Tyne, Earle & Co. of Hull, Laird Bros. of Birkenhead, and the Navy Construction & Armaments Co. of Barrow. All of these firms except Geo. Stephenson & Co. are listed in Conway's *All the World's Fighting Ships, 1860-1905* as having supplied the Admiralty with warships or engines prior to 1889.

20. HMS TERPSICHORE, HMS THETIS and HMS TRIBUNE.

21. HMS INDEFATIGABLE, HMS INTREPID and HMS IPHIGENIA.

22. HMS CENTURION and HMS BARFLEUR.

23. HMS GIBRALTAR. According to Arnold Hill, the Chairman of the Thames Iron Works Co., the Admiralty offered Napier's a contract for three cruisers at the price quoted but the firm declined to accept an order for more than one. See Evidence taken before the Fair Wages Committee, *Parliamentary Papers, 1908 [Cd4423] XXXIV 607,* Q. 4065.

24. *UCS 2/20/1*, letter to Mr Lyne dated 27th July 1889.

25. The protected cruisers HMS EDGAR and HMS HAWKE and the torpedo gunboat HMS HAZARD.

26. *UCS 2/31/1*, Vendors' Ledger Account.

27. On the formation of J. & G. Thomson Ltd. the fixed assets were revalued and the surplus credited to the partners' capital accounts but the surplus amounted to only £26,447 and it was partly offset by a debit of £10,423 in respect of a 'property difference'. See *UCS 1/3/25*, Report by McClelland Mackinnon & Blyth on the liquidation of James and George Thomson.

Interestingly, the details of the valuations of the Fairfield Shipbuilding & Engineering Co. Ltd. in July 1889 and of J. & G. Thomson Ltd. in March 1890 suggest that, apart from the element of goodwill, the fixed assets of the two firms were broadly similar:

|  | FAIRFIELD | CLYDEBANK |
|---|---|---|
| LAND & GOODWILL | 279,537 | 53,016 |
| BUILDINGS | 98,324 | 77,000 |
| HOUSES |  | 23,320 |
| YARD RAILWAY |  | 4,515 |
| DOCK | 68,172 | 34,000 |
| MACHINERY | 108,967 | 121,000 |
| LOOSE TOOLS | 45,000 | 33,474 |
|  | 600,000 | 346,325 |

(Sources: Fairfield, *UCS 2/31/1*; Clydebank, *UCS 1/3/10*).

28. Between June 1885 and March 1890 the partners' capital accounts were credited with profits of £6,082 and debited with losses of £83,194, a net trading loss of £77,182. These losses were struck after deducting partners' salaries of £17,346, reducing the trading loss to £59,776, but at March 1890 no account had been taken of losses of £48,300 on the liners CITY OF NEW YORK and CITY OF PARIS although these were partly offset by profits of £23,216 on other contracts. The total trading losses for the period from June 1885 to March 1890 could therefore be said to have amounted to £84,860. See *UCS 1/3/25*, Report by McClelland Mackinnon & Blyth on the liquidation of James and George Thomson.

29. Ibid.

30. Moss & Hume, *Workshop of the British Empire*, p. 122.

31. British and Foreign Trade and Industry, Statistical Tables and Charts, *Parliamentary Papers, 1909 [Cd4954] CII 693*, pp. 104–5.

32. *The Glasgow Herald*, 19th December 1892.

33. *Ibid.*, 18th December 1893.

34. *UCS 2/1/1*, Minutes of Board Meeting of 10th September 1890.

35. See *UCS 2/31/1*.

36. *UCS 2/1/1*, Minutes of Annual General Meeting, 23rd October 1893.

37. Ibid., Minutes of Board Meeting, 23rd October 1893.

38. *UCS 2/20/1*, Letter to Sir William G. Pearce, 21st July 1893.

39. *UCS 2/1/1*, Minutes of Board Meeting, 6th June 1893.

40. Francis Elgar, first Elder Professor of Naval architecture at Glasgow University, served as Director of Dockyards from 1886 to 1891. See Pollard & Robertson, *The British Shipbuilding Industry*, pp. 221–2.

41. *UCS 2/20/1*, Letter from R. Barnwell to F. Elgar, 25th September 1893.

42. *UCS 2/1/1*, Minutes of Board Meeting, 10th November 1893.

43. Ibid., Minutes of Board Meeting, 20th December, 1893.

44. HMS HANDY, HMS HART and HMS HUNTER.

45. *UCS 2/1/1*, Minutes of Board Meeting, 30th March 1894.

46. *UCS 2/20/1*, Letter to Mr Lyne, 27th July 1889.

47. The 7,116 ton FRIESLAND and the 2,003 ton BRAZIL.

48. *UCS 1/3/4*, Prospectus re issue of 5% Debenture.

49. HMS ROCKET, HMS SURLY and HMS SHARK.

50. HMS BRAZEN, HMS ELECTRA, HMS RECRUIT and HMS VULTURE.

51. HMS ARAB and HMS KESTREL.

52. HMS GYPSY, HMS FAIRY and HMS OSPREY.

53. HMS LEVEN.

54. HMS OSTRICH and HMS FALCON.

55. HMS DWARF and HMS THISTLE.

56. See Appendix A.

57. HMS BRAZEN, HMS VULTURE and HMS ARAB.

58. *UCS 2/20/1*, Letter from R. Barnwell to F. Elgar, 11th March 1896.

59. *UCS 1/1/12*, Minutes of Board Meeting, 1st July 1897.

60. For a fuller account of Palmer's difficulties, see D. Dougan, *The History of North East Shipbuilding* (London 1968), Chapter 4.

61. J. M. Bellamy attributes Earle's problems to losses incurred in building HMS ENDYMION and HMS ST. GEORGE, but both of these ships were completed in 1894 and the crucial provision of £30,000 against losses on Admiralty contracts was not made until 1897, the year in which the firm delivered the engines for the Dockyard-built cruisers HMS ARROGANT and HMS FURIOUS, the first second-class cruisers to be fitted with water-tube boilers. See J. M. Bellamy, 'A Hull Shipbuilding Firm', *Business History*, Volume VI, (1964).

62. See Chapter 5 below.

63. *The Glasgow Herald*, 18th December 1896.

64. *Ibid.*, 16th December 1898.

65. *Ibid.*, 18th December 1899.

66. Yard Nos. 279 and 307.

67. Yard Nos. 331 and 332.

68. ARUNDEL CASTLE, DUNVEGAN CASTLE, TINTAGEL CASTLE, ARMADALE CASTLE and CARISBROOK CASTLE.

69. *UCS 1/1/12*, Minutes of Board Meeting, 29th December 1896.

70. *UCS 2/20/1*, letter from F. Elgar to Sir William G. Pearce, 6th October 1898.

71. *UCS 2/1/3*, Minutes of Board Meetings, 18th November 1902 and 4th December 1903.

72. *UCS 2/20/1*, letter to W. M. Rhodes, 12th July 1899.

73. *UCS 2/5/2*, Directors' Report on Accounts for the year to 30th June 1895.

74. *UCS 2/20/1*, letter to W. M. Rhodes, 8th March 1899.

75. The three destroyers, allocated yard numbers 334–6, presumably in 1897–98, were eventually purchased by the Admiralty in 1900 and completed as HMS THORN, HMS TIGER and HMS VIGILANT respectively.

76. The 14,221 ton SAXONIA, the 443 ton DUCHESS OF FIFE, the 11,900 ton VADERLAND, the 11,667 ton ZEELAND, the 11,635 ton HAVERFORD and the 11,621 ton MERION.

# 5

# 1899–1907: The Intervention of the Armaments Manufacturers

Between 1899 and 1907 the character of the Clyde warshipbuilding industry underwent a fundamental change. Up to 1899 warshipbuilding on the Clyde had been the work of independent shipbuilders and engineers whose interest in naval work did not extend beyond the building of warships and the supply of warship engines. By 1907 the leading warshipbuilders on the river formed part of a complex, vertically integrated armaments industry geared not only to the building of warships but also to the manufacture of the armour plate, ordnance and gun mountings which went into them. John Brown & Co. Ltd., the Sheffield-based steel and armour plate manufacturer[1] which took over Clydebank in 1899, subsequently combined with its Sheffield neighbour and erstwhile rival Cammell Laird & Co. Ltd. to equip the latter's Coventry Ordnance Works[2] for the manufacture of the biggest naval guns and gun mountings. By 1907, when this project reached fruition, half of Cammell Laird's fifty percent share in it had passed to Fairfield as part of a deal which gave Cammell Laird a fifty percent interest in the ordinary shares of Fairfield itself. Meanwhile, William Beardmore & Co. Ltd., the Glasgow armour plate and ordnance manufacturer,[3] which purchased the shipbuilding business of Robert Napier & Sons in 1900, had built a great new naval yard at Dalmuir after merging with Vickers Sons & Maxim Ltd. which already ranked as one of the greatest private armaments manufacturers in the world.[4]

The origins of this vertically integrated armaments industry lay in the activities of a handful of ambitious armaments manufacturers. The expansion of the Royal Navy in the 1890s gave an enormous stimulus to the private armaments industry. Faced particularly with the problem of obtaining large quantities of all-steel armour plate[5] for its new armoured ships, the Admiralty had encouraged selected firms both to expand their capacity and to undertake costly research and development on their own account.[6] By 1897 the firms which had taken advantage of this opportunity were extremely prosperous concerns but the Admiralty was unable to guarantee its suppliers regular orders, and quasi-official arrangements to share out the available work among the firms did not extend to overseas business. Accordingly, when Vickers, Sons & Co. Ltd., which had been engaged in the manufacture of all-steel armour plate since 1889, took over both the Barrow shipyard of the Naval Construction and Armaments Co.[7] and the ordnance factories of the Maxim Nordenfeld Gun and Ammunition Co. in 1897, the other armour-plate manufacturers were not long in following their example, particularly when Sir William G. Armstrong & Co. Ltd., which had combined the manufacture of ordnance with warshipbuilding at Elswick on the Tyne since 1884,[8] also announced its intention of commencing the manufacture of armour plate following a merger with Sir Joseph Whitworth & Co., the Manchester gun makers and engineers,[9] in 1897.

The situation as it appeared to the directors of John Brown & Co. Ltd. was set out by Mr. J. D. Ellis in his speech to the shareholders' meeting which approved arrangements for the purchase of Clydebank in June 1899:

> The company's armour plate department was flourishing, the collieries were doing well and the general business was satisfactory ... If the directors had studied their own inclinations they would have remained as they were. But he could not help remembering that slack times came in coal and also in the armour plate trade and at these times those who were able to make ships were the people to get armour plate orders. He could remember times when John Brown & Co. had scarcely any orders for Her Majesty's Government and yet other firms received orders for ships carrying armour for foreign governments. Messrs. Vickers had bought a shipyard and Messrs. Armstrong & Co. were going to make armour plate. If they took no action they might find themselves without orders while their neighbours were full of work.[10]

In Clydebank, John Brown & Co. found a shipyard which was ideally suited to its purpose. Apart from being a major Admiralty contractor, the yard had extensive experience of building warships for foreign governments. J. & G. Thomson had first undertaken such work in 1884–85 when orders for the 166 ton Russian torpedo boat VIBORG, the 348 ton Spanish torpedo boat DESTRUCTOR and the 4,725 ton Spanish protected cruiser REINA REGENTE helped to keep Clydebank going at a time when it was desperately short of other work.[11] Orders for the 2,400 ton Japanese armoured cruiser CHIYODA and the 787 ton Dutch gunboat BORNEO followed in 1888 and 1891 respectively and, although warshipbuilding for foreign governments diminished in relative importance with the growth of the yard's Admiralty business in the 1890s, Clydebank continued to be a major contender for overseas naval contracts in general and Spanish and Japanese contracts in particular. At one stage in September 1896, with tenders out to the Spanish government for two large armoured cruisers, two smaller cruisers and a battleship,[12] there was so much work in prospect for this one customer that the Clydebank board, which had already offered to share the cruiser contracts with Barrow in exchange for a five percent commission,[13] decided to defer a final decision on the price of a battleship for Japan until the outcome of the Spanish tenders became known.[14] As it turned out, neither the Spanish tenders nor subsequent inquiries from China, Rumania and Costa Rica[15] bore fruit, but in the interval the firm had completed a further thirteen small warships for Spain.[16] These contracts, worth £449,450 net of penalties for late delivery, yielded a contribution to overheads and profit of £174,266 (38.7% of net invoice price) and, in 1899, the firm was in process of building its biggest foreign warship to date, the 15,200 ton Japanese battleship

ASAHI — an order for which John Brown & Co. had already contracted to supply armour plate costing £299,409.[17]

Equally important, Clydebank's owners were amenable to a takeover bid. At the time of John Brown's approach in 1899 they were apparently contemplating some alternative arrangement, most probably a public issue of shares.[18] Whether their intention was to raise additional funds for investment in the business or simply to enable existing shareholders to take advantage of the firm's prosperity to realise all or part of their holdings on favourable terms, they were receptive to a cash offer. In consequence John Brown & Co. was able to acquire the assets of a recently modernised warshipbuilding yard for £923,255, a price which was £191,921 more than their book value but not, it would seem, of their real worth.[19] Having acquired Clydebank, John Brown & Co. went on to join with Cammell Laird & Co. Ltd., itself the product of the merger in 1903 of Charles Cammell & Co.'s steel and armoured plate business with Laird Brothers' long-established Birkenhead shipyard,[20] in a project designed to turn Cammell Laird's Coventry Ordnance Works into a major armaments manufacturer capable of producing the largest naval guns and gun mountings.[21]

At one time most of the Royal Navy's guns and gun mountings had been supplied by Woolwich Arsenal but the War Office, which was responsible for the Royal Ordnance Works, was slow to develop breech-loading guns and by the 1890s the Admiralty was making increasing use of private firms to supply its special needs.[22] By the turn of the century Armstrong Whitworth's and Vickers had effectively supplanted the Royal Ordnance Works as the Admiralty's main suppliers not only of naval ordnance but also of gun mountings. In 1899–1900 Woolwich Arsenal's share of Admiralty orders for gun mountings amounted to only 10.7%.[23] The manufacture of naval guns and gun mountings was big business. By 1907–08, the year the Coventry Ordnance Works project reached fruition, Admiralty expenditure on gun mountings alone was estimated to amount to £1,825,239[24] and it cannot have escaped John Brown & Co.'s notice that Clydebank was likely to be at a disadvantage compared with Barrow and Elswick in tendering for overseas naval contracts as long as only Vickers and Armstrong's were able to supply the largest guns and gun mountings.[25]

Similar considerations may have been a factor in the decision of Fairfield's owners to sell Cammell Laird & Co. half of their ordinary shares in 1905 since the terms of the deal provided for Fairfield to acquire half of Cammell Laird's interest in the Coventry Ordnance Works for £212,500,[26] a move which resulted in the Coventry Ordnance Works being owned 50% by John Brown and 25% each by Cammell Laird and Fairfield. As far as Admiralty orders were concerned, access to supplies of guns, gun mountings and armour plate on preferential terms made little difference to a warshipbuilder's competitive situation. The chronic shortage of armour plate in the early 1890s had forced the Admiralty to abandon its pre-1889 practice of allowing contractors to make their own arrangements with suppliers as it was essential that

> The Admiralty ... should be in a position to allocate the available supply of armour to those vessels which most urgently needed it.[27]

In consequence, from 1889 onwards Admiralty orders for armour plate were almost always placed separately from orders for hulls and machinery,[28] the shipbuilders effectively receiving their supplies of armour plate from the Admiralty 'free of charge' as was invariably the case with supplies of guns and gun mountings for Royal Navy ships. Overseas warship orders were another matter. Although Fairfield, unlike Clydebank, had never built a warship for a foreign power, it aspired to do so and arrangements had already been made for Cammell Laird & Co. to supply any armour plate which might be needed in such an eventuality.[29]

On the other hand, Fairfield's investment in the Coventry Ordnance Works project may not have been so much an act of deliberate policy as the price which the company paid to enable the Pearce family to liquidate half of their investment in the company. Certainly the terms of the agreement between the Chairman, Sir William G. Pearce, and Cammell Laird & Co. Ltd., dated 31st October 1905, were not formally communicated to the other directors until a special board meeting held at Ralli Lodge, Newtonmore on 16th November 1905 at which time it was resolved

> That the clauses affecting the Fairfield Company be and are hereby adopted and approved and agreements on behalf of the Company to give effect to these clauses be prepared.[30]

Either way, the result was the same. Fairfield like Clydebank became part of the vertically integrated armaments industry. The deal made Fairfield the owner of twenty-five percent of a major ordnance works and effectively transferred control of Fairfield itself to Cammell Laird & Co., Sir William G. Pearce, who died without issue in 1907, being the last member of the Pearce family to play an active part in the yard's management.[31]

In the short run neither Clydebank nor Fairfield was greatly changed by the intervention of the armaments manufacturers. While Clydebank as the shipbuilding department of John Brown & Co. and Fairfield as part-owner of the ordnance works were necessarily more closely identified with the fortunes of the armaments industry than they had been previously, both were already heavily committed to warshipbuilding. Further, while John Brown & Co. gradually introduced new management at Clydebank[32] and representatives of Cammell Laird & Co. joined the Fairfield board,[33] there was no obvious discontinuity in policy. Both yards continued to combine naval work with merchant shipbuilding and there was no significant change in the scale or pattern of either yard's capital investment.

Under John Brown's management, net additions to fixed assets at Clydebank amounted to £356,383 in the eight years to 31st March 1907, compared with provisions for depreciation amounting to £228,669, but Clydebank was a thriving concern and there is no reason to suppose that other owners would have been unable to finance similar outlays if they had wished to do so. On the contrary Clydebank's previous owners had spent an average of £82,225 per annum on net additions to fixed assets in the three years preceding the takeover, compared with the average of £44,548 per annum spent by John Brown & Co. Similarly, while net additions to fixed assets at Fairfield rose from an average of £26,823 per annum in the six years to 30th June 1905 to £51,587 per annum in the two years following Cammell Laird & Co.'s intervention, arrangements for an issue of debentures had been made in June 1904 since

> It will be necessary in the immediate future to expend large sums on the improvement of the Dock, the electrification of the works and the provision of new machinery.[34]

In contrast to Clydebank and Fairfield, Dalmuir, the other Clyde warship-building yard controlled by the great armaments manufacturers, owed its very existence to their intervention. Completed in 1907 at a total cost of £923,036,[35] Dalmuir's facilities were expressly designed to give William Beardmore & Co. the capability to build the largest warships. A ninety-acre site with a river frontage nearly a mile long was served by its own power station and producer gas plant. The engine and boiler works, covering an area of five and a half acres, were equipped with the latest machine tools; contemporaries particularly noted the absence of belting and shafting as each machine tool was driven by its own motor. The largest of seven shipbuilding berths, designed to accommodate vessels of up to 830 feet in length and 100 feet in beam, was equipped with travelling cranes mounted on a gantry. The fitting-out basin, occupying an area of seven and a half acres in the middle of the yard and serviced by a crane capable of lifting 150 tons, was reckoned to be the largest in the world.[36]

Beardmore's decision to follow Armstrong's earlier example by building a completely new naval yard rather than taking over an existing warshipbuilding yard, as Vickers, John Brown and Cammell all did, was as much a matter of necessity as of choice. For obvious reasons it was desirable that Beardmore's shipyard should be situated on the Clyde rather than elsewhere, and John Brown & Co.'s coup in acquiring Clydebank effectively limited the options. Fairfield, the only other Clyde warshipbuilder of comparable size and experience, was beyond Beardmore's means and the Fairfield directors declined to entertain a proposal for 'an amalgamation of shipbuilding interests'.[37] Beardmore's, as the occupants of the Parkhead Forge once owned by Robert Napier, was able to resurrect famous associations by purchasing the goodwill of the shipbuilding business of Robert Napier & Sons in 1900, but outdated buildings and plant at Govan and Lancefield Street, valued at only £26,500 in July 1898,[38] were hopelessly inadequate for an ambitious armaments manufacturer's purpose. Although a short lease of these facilities enabled Beardmore's to start warshipbuilding on a modest scale, it was never intended to be more than an interim solution, the site for the new yard at Dalmuir having been bought in 1900.[39]

The building of Dalmuir necessitated a major reorganisation of Beardmore's affairs. Unlike the other leading armaments manufacturers, the firm was still a private concern in 1899 and William Beardmore's personal resources were already fully stretched to cover a major programme of capital investment at Parkhead begun in 1898.[40] In 1900 he was able to borrow £110,000 from the Bank of

Scotland to help finance the purchase of Robert Napier & Sons' business[41] but the construction of a great new naval yard was beyond his private means. Work on the new yard finally started in earnest in 1902. In the meantime Beardmore had reconstituted his business as a limited company in December 1901 and the project went ahead only with the powerful backing of Vickers, which had purchased half of the equity presumably with a view to gaining some control over an ambitious rival.[42]

From the outset Dalmuir was more heavily dependent on warshipbuilding than either of its major rivals on the Clyde. While naval work constituted by far the largest and most profitable element in the businesses of both Clydebank and Fairfield in the opening years of the new century, neither yard was totally dependent on warshipbuilding for its livelihood. Most of the profit Fairfield and Clydebank earned on merchant work between 1899 and 1906 was attributable to a handful of contracts. Apart from the 9,033 ton Orient liner ORONTES on which the firm earned a profit of £34,982, virtually all of Fairfield's merchant shipbuilding profits in the seven years to 30th June 1906 were attributable to six contracts which between them resulted in net profits of £134,841 — four ships built for Sir Donald Currie (£115,551)[43] and the liners EMPRESS OF BRITAIN and EMPRESS OF IRELAND built for Canadian Pacific (£19,289). Similarly, at Clydebank, the profitability of merchant work in the seven years to 31st March 1906 was entirely attributable to the profits earned on five contracts — four contracts dating back to 1898 which yielded net profits of £83,262,[44] and the contract for the Cunard liner CARONIA which resulted in a net profit of £100,222. Nevertheless both yards had this leavening of profitable merchant work and could boast of a substantial volume of merchant business on which to recover overheads — Clydebank completed merchant orders worth £3,195,672 in the seven years to 31st March 1906 and Fairfield completed merchant orders worth £3,262,501 in the seven years to 30th June 1906.

Despite the problems created for other shipbuilders by the involvement of William Pirrie, chairman of the Belfast shipbuilders Harland & Wolff, both in the rash of shipping mergers and amalgamations which accompanied the formation of the International Mercantile Marine Co. in 1902[45] and in the subsequent rise of the Royal Mail Group, which ultimately controlled fifteen percent of the entire British merchant fleet,[46] Fairfield and Clydebank both strengthened their merchant shipbuilding businesses in the opening years of the century. Fairfield, which found itself in conflict with Harland & Wolff over the division of work following the merger of its valued customer Sir Donald Currie's Castle Line with the Union Line in 1900,[47] gained an important new customer in Canadian Pacific, which was beginning to build up its liner fleet.[48] More important, Clydebank, under John Brown & Co.'s management, succeeded in re-establishing itself as the premier merchant shipbuilding yard on the Clyde by regaining the custom of Cunard, the principal transatlantic operator to stand aloof from the International Mercantile Marine combination.

Clydebank's previous owners had taken the first step towards re-establishing the yard's connection with Cunard by undertaking the building of the liner

SAXONIA in 1898, and the yard had gone on to take the order for the 9,851 ton PANNONIA in 1901, but it was John Brown & Co. which seized the opportunity presented by the decision of the Government to subsidise the building by Cunard of a pair of fast passenger liners expressly designed to recapture the 'blue riband' of the North Atlantic for Britain.[49] In contrast to Fairfield which, as already noted,[50] was understandably reluctant to quote Cunard a price for a 25-knot liner in 1902 after its disastrous experience with the liners CAMPANIA and LUCANIA in 1893-94, John Brown & Co. was not deterred by the risks involved in such an undertaking and was eventually rewarded with the contract for the 31,550 ton turbine-powered liner LUSITANIA ordered in April 1904. Following as it did earlier orders for a pair of slower intermediate liners — the 19,687 ton CARONIA, the largest ship yet built on the Clyde when she was launched in 1904, and her sister the CARMANIA, which differed in being turbine-powered[51] — the order for the LUSITANIA brought Clydebank's tally of orders from Cunard to over 80,000 tons in the space of four years. Work for Cunard was not particularly profitable. The CARONIA was exceptional in yielding Clydebank a large net profit. Although the contract for the LUSITANIA was profitable, a net profit of £50,972 was a poor return on a £1.6 millions contract, which had involved capital expenditure of at least £55,145.[52] More typically, the contracts for the SAXONIA, the PANNONIA and the CARMANIA all resulted in small net losses, the discrepancy between the net profit of £100,022 on the CARONIA and the net loss of £4,317 on the CARMANIA being only partly attributable to the latter's turbines which cost £70,279 more than the reciprocating machinery fitted in the CARONIA.[53] Nevertheless, big liner contracts which did not result in heavy losses were a welcome addition to any warshipbuilder's order book if only because no other merchant work was more compatible with the building of major warships and the biggest liners were the only merchant contracts comparable in value with a major naval contract.[54]

In contrast to Fairfield and Clydebank, Beardmore's merchant business was neither extensive nor profitable. Even allowing for the limitations of the facilities with which it had to work, the firm's record in the years leading up to the opening of Dalmuir was poor. The goodwill attached to Robert Napier & Sons' business proved to be virtually worthless. Between 1894, when the firm had been reconstituted as a limited company following the insolvency of the previous partnership, and 1900, when Beardmore's took over, Napier's yard at Govan had produced a respectable output of thirty merchant ships aggregating 76,773 tons, including seven ships for the Royal Mail Steam Packet Co.,[55] but Beardmore's inherited only an order for one 1,018 ton ship[56] and, more disappointing, only one of Napier's former customers — the Eastern and Australian Steamship Co. — subsequently placed an order with the new owners. Beardmore's had some initial success in attracting other business. In 1901 and 1902 the yard won orders from both the Nelson Line and the Union-Castle Line[57] but the success did not last. The total value of all the merchant contracts undertaken by the firm between 1900 and the end of 1905 amounted to only £560,436, only four of the ten contracts were reported to have yielded net profits, and one of these had not been charged with a share of overheads.[58] By 1905, when Dalmuir opened, the firm did not have a single merchant order on its books. Nevertheless, at the time Dalmuir was conceived, an ambitious armaments manufacturer might be excused for believing that a new yard could hope to prosper on warshipbuilding alone.

The extensive use of private yards to build the Navy's ships in the decade following the Navy Defence Act of 1889 had not been an unqualified success. By the end of 1900 the bankruptcy of Earle & Co. and Maudslay, Son & Field, the disruption caused by a prolonged lock-out of engineering workers in 1897–98, a chronic shortage of armour plate, and the difficulties experienced by many firms in achieving the design speed on 27-knot destroyers had all contributed to a situation where deliveries by contractors were falling seriously behind schedule.[59] Despite these shortcomings the outlook for the private warshipbuilder had never been better. Admiralty demand remained high and the Royal Dockyards were experiencing the greatest difficulty in meeting all the demands being made upon them. In the Dockyards progress on new construction was being adversely affected by the competing claims of other work associated with servicing a growing fleet. In 1900–01 the pressure was eased by having one of the battleships originally allocated to the Dockyards put out to contract,[60] but they were moving inexorably towards the position where a mounting backlog of repairs and refits would eventually force the Admiralty to take extraordinary measures to deal with the situation. Meanwhile an Admiralty committee, appointed to inquire into the arrears at 31st December 1900, was expressly asked not only to examine the reason for the arrears but also to report on

> Whether the private sources of the United Kingdom are utilised to the fullest possible extent for the purposes of production for naval shipbuilding and armament and if not, generally how this end can be obtained.[61]

Like many of the Admiralty's contractors, the Clyde warshipbuilders had experienced the greatest difficulty in building destroyers. Hannah, Donald & Wilson, a small Paisley firm which had successfully built torpedo boats for the Admiralty in 1879 and 1888, ruined itself in the attempt. Awarded a contract to build two destroyers in 1894, the firm had found the work to be beyond its capabilities. Neither HMS FERVENT nor HMS ZEPHYR came close to achieving her design speed. During construction their locomotive boilers had to be replaced with water-tube boilers at an additional cost of £10,560 each and, by the time the boats were finally completed in 1900–01,[62] their builder had been driven out of business.[63] Clydebank and Fairfield, which had undertaken the building of destroyers at the same time, were more successful but they too found the work uncongenial and Clydebank in particular ran into serious technical difficulties in building 30-knot boats. None of the five destroyers ordered in 1895–96 and 1896–97 had been delivered by 1900, one of them — HMS KESTREL — only achieved the design speed after ten attempts and two others — HMS BRAZEN and HMS ELECTRA — completely failed to do so.[64] Another destroyer — HMS ARAB — one of three 'specials' ordered from separate builders in 1896, was a technical fiasco. Designed to steam at 33 knots, her best speed was 30½ knots, and on most of her trials she achieved speeds of between 28 and 29 knots only.[65] Fortunately the Admiralty was prepared to make allowance for the technical difficulty of building small fast boats with the technology available and, apart from abatements in the price when boats failed to achieve the design speed after numerous trials, the contractors suffered no real penalties beyond the trouble and expense to which they were put in running the additional trials and modifying machinery.[66] More important, failure with destroyers did not debar contractors from tendering successfully for other Admiralty work and the Clyde's record with cruisers was not marred by comparable blemishes.[67]

In the opening years of the new century cruiser contracts were plentiful. The 1900–01 and 1901–02 programmes included an exceptionally large number of armoured cruisers and the Clyde warshipbuilding industry, which had built eight of the eleven armoured cruisers put out to contract up to 1900, repeated its success in the bidding for a further nine ordered from private firms in 1900 and 1901. Three of the four ships ordered under the 1900–01 programme and four of the five ships ordered under the 1901–02 programme went to Clydeside firms. These seven armoured cruisers together with two King Edward VII class battleships added no less than 104,295 tons of warships to Clyde order books in the space of two years, the intake of 59,010 tons from the 1901–02 programme being the largest tonnage of Admiralty orders yet placed on the Clyde in a single year.

Under these conditions even the smallest of the Clyde warshipbuilding yards flourished. Scott's of Greenock, which secured the contract for the 10,850 ton Devonshire class armoured cruiser HMS ARGYLL ordered under the 1901–02 programme, had been seeking such a contract since before the turn of the century. Although the firm was reported to have submitted the lowest of the unsuccessful tenders for Monmouth class cruisers in both August 1899 and October 1900,[68] success eluded it until 1901 when the exceptionally large number of ships on offer tipped the scales in its favour.[69] For Scott's the contract for a complete ship was a logical extension of the work of the Greenock Foundry Co. which had already supplied the engines for three Dockyard-built battleships — HMS BARFLEUR and HMS CENTURION, laid down in 1890, and HMS CANOPUS, laid down in 1897 — and was currently engaged in making those for a fourth — HMS PRINCE OF WALES. There is no evidence that the Greenock Foundry Co. had found naval work particularly profitable, 1895 being the only year between 1892 and 1900 when the firm's trading profits were sufficient to cover provisions for depreciation and interest paid to third parties,[70] but the record of the shipyard, which had confined itself to merchant shipbuilding since 1888, was even less satisfactory. Apart from 1895, when it earned a profit after depreciation of £28,958, and 1898, Scott & Co. had suffered a net loss in every year from 1893 to 1900. In the nine years to 31st December 1901 the firm had suffered an overall loss of £39,395 after providing for depreciation.[71]

Scott's fundamental problem was that by the turn of the century its business consisted almost entirely of orders from John Swire & Sons' China Navigation Co. and from Alfred Holt for whom Swires acted as agent. Excluding yachts and lighters, the number of ships completed for Alfred Holt, Holt's Ocean Steamship Co. and the China Navigation Co. increased from fifteen in 1890–1893 to sixteen in 1894–1897 and twenty in 1898–1901,[72] while the number of ships completed for other customers fell from twenty-one in 1890–1893 to nine in 1894–1897 and three in 1898–1901. Further, while contracts for the China Navigation Co., in which the Scott family were major shareholders, were invariably profitable, the outcome of contracts for Alfred Holt was not as dependable, all of those completed between 1896 and 1901 having resulted in losses. The underlying deterioration in the firm's trading situation during the 1890s is apparent from Table 5.1:

**Table 5.1.** Profitability of Contracts Completed by Scott & Co.

|  | 1890–1895 | | 1896–1901 | |
|---|---|---|---|---|
|  | No. | £ | No. | £ |
| ALFRED HOLT/OCEAN S.S. | 12 | 27,255 | 10 | (40,006) |
| CHINA NAVIGATION | 17 | 36,767 | 12 | 33,741 |
| OTHER CUSTOMERS | 23 | 15,985 | 10 | 3,222 |
| TOTAL | 52 | 80,007 | 32 | (3,043) |

(Source: *GD 319/7/1/1*)

Following the receipt of the order for HMS ARGYLL, Scott's Shipbuilding and Engineering Co. Ltd., the product of a merger of Scott & Co. and the Greenock Foundry Co. in December 1901,[73] had to embark on a major programme of capital expenditure involving the outlay of £169,454 in the four years to 31st December 1905. Building a major warship was beyond the shipyard's existing facilities. In particular, the public dock previously used by Scott & Co. for fitting-out was inadequate for fitting-out a major warship in accordance with Admiralty requirements and Scott's was obliged to build its own wet dock with 'sufficient depth of water to permit of the heaviest class of warships remaining afloat at all states of the tide'.[74] While the cost of equipping itself for warshipbuilding was high, the prospects were better than they had been in 1888 and Scott's, which had secured the contract for HMS ARGYLL at a most favourable price, had reason to hope that its enterprise would be rewarded with lucrative repeat orders.

In the short run Scott's had good reason to be satisfied with the outcome of its resumption of warshipbuilding. The £622,262 contract for the armoured cruiser HMS ARGYLL gave particular cause for satisfaction as it yielded a net profit of £152,039, allowing Scott's to write £50,000 off the cost of the new wet dock.[75] Up to 31st December 1905 the family shareholders had received little in the way of dividends, total distributions comprising a payment of 10% in respect of 1903 and one of 5% in respect of 1905, but, in the first four years of the company's existence £147,927 had been written off as depreciation of fixed assets and bank borrowings had been reduced to the manageable figure of £74,083. The addition of the order for HMS ARGYLL made all the difference to the firm's profitability. In the four years to 31st December 1905, the period during which the cruiser was under construction, both the shipyard and the engine works traded profitably. During these years the firm also completed fourteen more ships for the China Navigation Co. and fourteen other merchant ships, including the 9,160 ton NARRA-GANSETT, the largest oil-carrying vessel of its day, but, as shown in Table 5.2, the two Admiralty contracts accounted for 54.3% of the total contribution to overheads and profit from all the contracts completed:

**Table 5.2.** Contracts Completed by Scott's 1902–1905

|  | NO. | SALES PROCEEDS £ | CONTRIBUTION TO OVERHEADS AND PROFIT £ |
|---|---|---|---|
| ADMIRALTY | 2 | 820,164 | 228,774 |
| CHINA NAVIGATION | 14 | 527,845 | 134,453 |
| OTHERS | 14 | 672,034 | 57,870 |
|  | 30 | 2,020,043 | 421,097 |

(Source: Author's figures based on detail abstracted from *GD 319*. See Peebles, **thesis**, Appendix FV)

While nothing is known of the details of the trading performance of the London & Glasgow, whose facilities were if anything inferior to those of Scott's, the profitability of the yard's naval work can be inferred from the published accounts for the eight years to 30th June 1906. In the four years to 30th June 1902, a period during which the yard completed twelve ships aggregating 34,354 tons[76] but only one major naval contract — that for the 5,600 ton second-class cruiser HMS HYACINTH — its trading profits before depreciation averaged only £18,600 per annum. In the four years following after 30th June 1902, during which it completed six ships aggregating 42,924 tons[77] including three major Admiralty contracts — those for the 9,800 ton Monmouth class armoured cruisers HMS MONMOUTH and HMS CUMBERLAND and for the 10,850 ton Devonshire class armoured cruiser HMS ROXBURGH ordered in 1899, 1900 and 1901 respectively — trading profits before depreciation averaged £71,454 per annum. Since the London & Glasgow's HMS ROXBURGH cost the Admiralty £46,035 less than Scott's HMS ARGYLL,[78] it is possible that the firm did not earn as large a profit as Scott's on the Devonshire class ship, but it is unlikely that any part of the London & Glasgow's £1.6 millions of Admiralty business was unprofitable. Certainly it was achieved with a minimum of capital expenditure. Net additions to fixed assets in the eight years to 30th June 1906 amounted to only £49,724. Meanwhile the directors were at pains to build up the company's finances. In the eight years to 30th June 1906 the directors distributed £157,800 to ordinary shareholders but they also realised £65,395 by calling up the unpaid balances on the ordinary shares. In consequence they were able to repay mortgages of £40,000 and accumulate substantial liquid assets, the balance sheet at 30th June 1906 showing cash balances of £141,403 and investments in British government securities, debentures and preference shares with a market value of £83,988.[79]

Beardmore's did not share fully in this period of prosperity. Handicapped by Robert Napier & Sons' inadequate facilities, it prudently tendered on the basis of subcontracting the manufacture of machinery to other firms.[80] Subcontracting necessarily affected the profitability of the 9,800 ton Monmouth class armoured cruiser HMS BERWICK and the 10,850 ton Devonshire class armoured cruiser HMS CARNARVON. Nevertheless, net profits of £47,146 and £63,939 respectively were encouraging in light of the limited facilities at the firm's disposal and, by the spring of 1905, when Dalmuir opened to build the hull of the 15,925 ton Lord Nelson class battleship HMS AGAMEMNON, Beardmore's was poised to join Clydebank and Fairfield as one of the three leading warshipbuilders on the Clyde.

For Clydebank and Fairfield the opening years of the century had been a period of unprecedented prosperity. Fairfield, with £2,313,022 worth of Admiralty work on hand in the summer of 1899, had gone on to secure the contracts for the 9,800 ton Monmouth class cruiser HMS DONEGAL in 1900–01, the 15,610 ton King Edward VII class battleship HMS COMMONWEALTH in 1901–02, the 2,860 ton Scout class light cruisers HMS FORWARD and HMS FORESIGHT in 1902–03 and the 13,550 ton Warrior class armoured cruiser HMS COCHRANE in 1903–04. Clydebank, with £2,190,035 worth of Admiralty work on hand at the time of John Brown & Co.'s takeover, had been excluded from tendering for cruisers in 1900–01 on account of the late delivery of other work and the problems with destroyers,[81] but the yard's return to favour had been marked by the order for the 10,850 ton Devonshire class armoured cruiser HMS ANTRIM in 1901–02 and it had gone on to take orders for the 15,885 ton King Edward VII class battleship HMS HINDUSTAN in 1902–03 and the engines for the Dockyard-built battleship HMS AFRICA in 1903–04. In addition both Fairfield and Clydebank had a share of the naval repairs and refits put out to private firms on a 'cost-plus' basis in 1902 and 1903, the former having undertaken the refit of three torpedo boats at a cost to the Admiralty of £129,006[82] and the latter the refit of three cruisers at a cost to the Admiralty of £290,353.[83]

As in the 1890s, major Admiralty contracts invariably proved to be very profitable to the two big yards. Fairfield's five contracts eventually yielded net profits of £505,188 on a total invoiced price of £2,334,783, contributions to overheads and profit ranging between an average of 30.51% of invoice price on the two light cruisers and 26.68% of invoice price on the battleship HMS COMMONWEALTH. Similarly Clydebank's three contracts eventually yielded net profits of £348,390 on a total invoiced price of £1,485,836, contributions to overheads and profit on the contracts for the cruiser HMS ANTRIM and the battleship HMS HINDUSTAN working out at 41.97% of invoice price and 32.34% of invoice price respectively.

Since neither yard normally took credit for the profits on contracts until they were completed, the outcome of these contracts was not fully reflected in their accounts until 1906-07 when Fairfield completed HMS COCHRANE and Clydebank finished HMS HINDUSTAN and the engines for HMS AFRICA, but, as a corollary, the profitability of both yards in the seven years to 1906 benefited from the completion of all the Admiralty contracts on hand in 1899. Fairfield, which completed Admiralty contracts worth £4,200,183 in the seven years to 30th June 1906, was able to report trading profits before depreciation amounting to £909,147, an average of £129,878 per year. Clydebank, which completed the £874,983 contract for the Japanese battleship ASAHI as well as Admiralty contracts worth £3,064,565 in the seven years to 31st March 1906, earned trading profits before depreciation amounting to £661,542, the yard's lower average profits of £94,506 per year being partly explained by the £50,877 of profit on uncompleted contracts taken by the previous owners in 1899[84] and partly by the lower volume of naval work.

As has already been noted, merchant shipbuilding contributed to the profitability of both yards but the critical importance of warshipbuilding is apparent from the analysis of the net profits earned on all contracts completed in the seven years to 1906 in Table 5.3:

**Table 5.3.** Net Profits on Contracts Completed 1899–1906

|  | FAIRFIELD £ | CLYDEBANK £ |
|---|---|---|
| NAVAL WORK | 701,216 | 576,498 |
| MERCHANT WORK | 173,367 | 174,946 |

(Source: Author's figures based on details abstracted from *UCS 1 and UCS 2*. See Peebles, **thesis**, Appendices FII and FIII)

The record of Fairfield, the only one of the two yards to retain a separate corporate identity, was indicative of the strength of the warshipbuilders' position. In contrast to the 1890s, when the size of distributions to ordinary shareholders had been dictated primarily by the desire of the Pearce family to recoup the capital paid in to meet the deficiency in the company's accounts at 30th June 1894, payments of 8% in respect of 1899–1900 and 1900–01, 12% in respect of 1901–02, 20% in respect of 1902–03, 1903–04 and 1904–05 and 30% in respect of 1905–06 were fully justified by the firm's trading performance. Over these seven years provisions for depreciation of fixed assets had amounted to £273,500 and the company had managed to finance net additions to fixed assets amounting to £210,857 and an initial investment of £187,500 in the Coventry Ordnance Works without as yet having issued the new debenture authorised in 1904. It had also turned a bank overdraft of £215,220 at 30th June 1899 into cash on hand of £57,129 at 30th June 1906.

This period of extraordinary prosperity was drawing to a close by the time Dalmuir opened but this was not apparent at the time. The total volume of new warship orders placed with private firms had declined steadily from a peak of 91,125 tons in 1901-02 to 34,815 tons in 1904-05,[85] largely because the elimination of the backlog of repairs and refits allowed the Royal Dockyards to undertake more new construction but circumstances still appeared to favour the private warshipbuilder. In 1902-03, at the height of the Dockyard crisis, the Admiralty decided to allow private contractors to undertake work which heretofore had remained the jealously guarded prerogative of their own establishments:

> It has been arranged ... that the vessels in course of construction at the contractors premises will be completed in all respects ready for immediate passing into the Fleet Reserve on delivery instead of as heretofore leaving the carrying out of the trials, installation of the armament and completion of certain details till after delivery at one of His Majesty's Dockyards.[86]

Meanwhile the committee set up to inquire into the arrears in shipbuilding programmes at 31st December 1900 had produced a report which was extremely favourable to the interests of the private warshipbuilder. While it acknowledged that the Admiralty was in no position to 'follow the practice of private firms by guaranteeing a continuance of orders to any particular firm', it pointedly remarked that

> Those shipowners of the mercantile marine are best served who are able to give constant employment to a particular firm or firms.[87]

In 1904 the Admiralty decided against discontinuing shipbuilding in the Royal Dockyards altogether on the grounds that it was desirable to have both a check on prices and an insurance against strikes,[88] but the statement accompanying the 1905-06 Naval Estimates, which reported that it was no longer necessary to provide for repairs in private yards, emphasised that

> Henceforth it should be borne in mind that the first business of the Royal Dockyards is to keep the Fleet in repair and accordingly the amount of new construction allocated to those dockyards should be subordinated to this consideration.[89]

Most important of all, the Admiralty, under the leadership of Admiral Fisher who became First Sea Lord in 1904, was about to give a further stimulus to the demand for warships by introducing a revolutionary new generation of capital ship.

The 17,900 ton battleship HMS DREADNOUGHT, laid down at Portsmouth in October 1905 and completed less than a year later, set a new standard for capital ships. The design of the new ship, about which Fisher had taken the advice of both Admiralty officials and civilian experts,[90] was a logical progression from earlier battleships, which had grown steadily from the 14,150 ton 17½-knot Royal Sovereign class of 1889 to the 16,350 ton 19-knot King Edward VII class of 1903, but it incorporated two revolutionary features. First, to facilitate gun control and shot sighting, the Admiralty abandoned the mixture of four twelve-inch, four nine-inch and ten six-inch guns of the King Edward VII class in favour of ten twelve-inch guns and, in some respects the most revolutionary aspect of the whole design, the disposition of these guns was such that eight could be brought to bear on either broadside or six ahead or astern.[91] Second, to take maximum advantage of the ship's ability to engage the enemy at long range without any loss of tactical mobility, the new ship was designed to be faster than any previous battleship, and to secure the design speed of 21 knots without an unacceptable increase in engine weight it was necessary to use steam turbines.[92]

The Admiralty's decision to take the lead in building a battleship which was bigger, faster and more powerfully armed than any other battleship in existence and, more controversially, to build faster but less heavily armoured battlecruisers of a similar size to act in concert with it, was widely criticised as a break with Britain's traditional policy of leaving innovation to others. Fisher and his supporters believed the developments to be inevitable and they were determined to ensure that the Royal Navy had a lead over its rivals.[93] Accordingly, the 1905–06 Navy Estimates provided for the building of HMS DREADNOUGHT and three battlecruisers and, since none of the Royal Dockyards could accommodate the building of such ships without extensive modification,[94] all three battlecruisers had to be built in private yards. The result was that the total tonnage of warships put out to contract under the 1905–06 programme rose to 64,762 tons.

In a significant departure from normal Admiralty practice the contracts for the three battlecruisers were placed with carefully selected firms rather than being put out to tender.[95] Clydebank and Fairfield were two of the three firms selected for the work, Clydebank having the order for the 17,290 ton HMS INFLEXIBLE and Fairfield the order for the 17,410 ton HMS INDOMITABLE. As experienced warshipbuilders which had previously built the largest battleships and armoured cruisers, the two firms were natural choices to undertake this type of work and it was fitting that they should have been chosen to build these particular ships. Clydebank's earlier orders for the Cunard liners CARMANIA and LUSITANIA set it apart as the only major warshipbuilding yard with previous experience of building a big turbine-powered ship.[96] Sir Alexander Gracie, Fairfield's engineering director, had been one of the experts consulted by Fisher in developing the idea of the dreadnought.[97] While Gracie was consulted as a private individual rather than as a director of Fairfield, there can be little doubt that Fairfield's decision to undertake a major programme of capital investment in 1904 was made in the knowledge that the dreadnought was in the offing, and it was no coincidence that, by the time the order arrived, the firm had been at pains to acquire some experience of manufacturing turbines, first by building the yacht NARCISSUS for Colonel Moseley, one of the firm's directors, and then by undertaking the building of the channel ferry DIEPPE for the London, Brighton & South Coast Railway Co. and the Irish ferry VIPER for G. & J. Burns.

With the receipt of the orders for the two battlecruisers in the autumn of 1905 Clydebank and Fairfield were better placed than other warshipbuilders on the Clyde. The London & Glasgow was exceptional in having no Admiralty orders to follow the completion of HMS ROXBURGH, but by the end of 1905 Scott's had only the machinery for the Dockyard-built cruiser HMS DEFENCE on hand and, prior to the commencement of the battlecruisers, Dalmuir was unique in having a warship on the stocks, all of the Admiralty work on hand at Clydebank and Fairfield being in an advanced state of completion. Compared with the situation in 1902 and 1903 when, as *The Glasgow Herald* remarked, the exceptional number of warships on the stocks and fitting-out explained 'to a very large extent' the way in which employment continued to be fairly plentiful in spite of a falling away of merchant demand,[98] Admiralty work was in relatively short supply.

However, as far as the three big yards in particular were concerned the outlook was far from discouraging. The private warshipbuilding industry had enjoyed a period of unprecedented prosperity; there was no indication that the Clyde was uncompetitive on cost; Clydebank and Fairfield had each received an order for one of the new generation of capital ships; Dalmuir was well on the way to acquiring the capability to do the same; all three yards had established links with a powerful armaments industry which appeared to augur well for their chances of securing foreign warship orders. All three yards could therefore look to the future with confidence, comfortable in the knowledge that they ranked with Armstrong Whitworth's Elswick yard, Vickers' Barrow yard and Cammell Laird's Birkenhead yard among the six or seven biggest, best-equipped and, at least as far as Clydebank and Fairfield were concerned, most successful private warship-building yards in Britain.[99]

## NOTES

1. John Brown's had been engaged in the manufacture of armour plate since the 1850s. By 1867 the firm, which had become a limited company capitalised at £1,000,000 in 1864, was reported to have supplied the wrought-iron armoured plates for three-quarters of the ironclads in the Royal Navy. See Grant, *Steel and Ships: The History of John Brown's*, pp. 21-22.

2. The Coventry Ordnance Works Co. had its origins in the Birmingham firm of Mulliner & Wigley which manufactured scientific measuring equipment and tools for producing the most complicated parts of ordnance. Following a move to Coventry, the firm began manufacturing ordnance for the Army on its own account, and an amalgamation with Charles Cammell & Co. had been arranged to ensure the supply of the high-quality steel needed for this purpose. For a fuller description of the firm and its history, see *The Times*, June 9th 1909.

3. William Beardmore, who had become sole partner in the Parkhead Forge once owned by Robert Napier in 1887, started experimenting with the manufacture of all-steel armour plate in 1889. By 1898-99, Beardmore's armour plate business was thriving and a massive expansion of the facilities at Parkhead included provision for the manufacture of guns. See Hume & Moss, *Beardmore*, pp. 37 & 47-48.

4. Vickers Sons & Co., the Sheffield steelmakers, had installed equipment for the manufacture of guns and all-steel armour plate in 1888. By the early 1900s, following the acquisition of Maxim Nordenfelt's artillery and ammunition works and the Barrow shipyard of the Naval Construction and Armaments Co., the firm of Vickers, Maxim & Co. Ltd. ranked alongside Armstrong-Whitworth's and Krupps as one of the three greatest armaments manufacturers in the world. See C. L. Trebilcock, *The Vickers Brothers. Armaments and Enterprise, 1854-1914* (London 1977), p. 31 and *The Times*, 2nd June 1909.

5. All-steel armour plate superseded compound armour plate after tests at Shoeburyness

in 1888 had shown that the best compound armour plate manufactured in Britain was shattered by gunfire which did not even penetrate all-steel armour plate of the same thickness. See Hume & Moss, *Beardmore*, pp. 35–36.

6. In 1889, when the specification of a single battleship of the Royal Sovereign class called for 4,560 tons of all-steel armour plate, only John Brown & Co. and Charles Cammell & Co. had started production and total output amounted to 8,000 tons per annum. By the time the programme authorised by the Navy Defence Act of 1889 was completed, five firms were in production and output had grown to 50,000 tons per annum. See *The Times*, 12th May 1909.

7. Built to the design of Robert Duncan of Port Glasgow in 1869, the yard had traded as the Barrow Shipbuilding Co. until 1888 when it was taken over by the Naval Construction & Armaments Co. which made a particular specialisation of warshipbuilding including work on Nordenfelt submarines. See Pollard & Robertson, *The British Shipbuilding Industry*, pp. 111–12.

8. Sir William Armstrong, who had made his name by inventing a rifled breech-loading gun during the Crimean War, commenced the manufacture of ordnance at Elswick in 1863. In 1867 he began building warships in Charles Mitchell's Walker shipyard and in 1884, following a merger of the two firms, a new warshipbuilding yard was laid out at Elswick alongside the existing ordnance works. See Dougan, *The History of North East Shipbuilding*, Chapters 2 & 3.

9. In 1888 Sir Joseph Whitworth & Co. and Armstrong's were the only private firms in Britain capable of producing the largest guns. See Trebilcock, *The Vickers Brothers*, p. 54.

10. *The Times*, 24th June 1899.

11. See Chapter 3 above.

12. *UCS 1/1/12*, Minutes of Board Meetings, 31st July 1896 and 4th September 1896.

13. Ibid., Minutes of Board Meeting, 31st July 1896.

14. Ibid., Minutes of Board Meeting, 4th September 1896.

15. Ibid., Minutes of Board Meetings, 6th October 1896 and 2nd November 1896.

16. See Appendix EV.

17. *UCS 1/1/12*, Minutes of Board Meeting, 7th September 1897. The total cost of the armour plate is given in the Contract Cost Book (*UCS 1/86/1*).

18. *The Times*, 24th June 1899, quotes Mr. J. D. Ellis as having told the John Brown & Co. shareholders' meeting that Clydebank was 'about to be converted into a limited company' but this is clearly wrong. Either he had chosen his words without sufficient care or he was misreported.

19. Clydebank's fixed assets and tools and utensils were revalued by John Brown & Co. after the takeover:

|  | BOOK VALUE 31.3.1899 £ | VALUATION 1.4.1899 £ |
|---|---|---|
| GROUND | 92,234 | 112,790 |
| BUILDINGS | 175,423 | 208,460 |
| WORKS IMPROVEMENTS | 13,899 |  |
| HOUSES | 24,677 | 38,774 |
| YARD RAILWAY | 13,629 | 15,500 |
| DOCK | 34,000 | 55,000 |
| MACHINERY | 209,053 | 297,220 |
| TOOLS & UTENSILS | 76,578 | 103,670 |
| OTHER ASSETS | 91,841 | 91,841 |
|  | 731,334 | 923,255 |

(SOURCE: *UCS 1/3/6*).

20. The Birkenhead firm of Laird Brothers Ltd., founded in 1824 by William Laird, had extensive experience of building warships for both the Admiralty and foreign powers. At the time of the merger with Charles Cammell & Co. Ltd. in October 1903, it was in process of constructing a new shipyard and two graving docks at Tranmere Bay immediately south of its existing yard. For a fuller description of the yard and its history, see *The Times*, 9th June 1909.

21. Preparations for the manufacture of the largest naval guns and gun mountings involved the extensive rebuilding and re-equipment of the firm's Coventry works and the development of a new site at Scotstoun on the Clyde for the erection and fitting of the gun mountings. A quarter of a million pounds was spent in building and equipping the shops on the Scotstoun site alone. See *The Times*, 9th June 1909.

22. H. Lyons, 'The Admiralty and Private Industry', in *Technical Change and British Naval Policy, 1860–1939* (London 1977), ed. B. Ranft, pp. 49–50.

23. Report of the Conference appointed to examine the Shops and Machinery at Woolwich arsenal, other than in the Danger Buildings and Torpedo Factory, in order to consider whether any article not now made in the Ordnance Factories can appropriately be made there with this machinery: with proceedings of the Conference, Minutes of Evidence and appendices, *Parliamentary Papers 1907 [Cd3514] XLIX 449*, p. 8.

24. *Ibid.*, p. 9.

25. As early as 1897, when there was an abortive proposal that Clydebank and Vickers should combine forces to tender for a battleship order in China, the Clydebank board was particularly anxious to know how Clydebank would be safeguarded against abnormal profits being put on armour and armament by Vickers 'with a view to cutting down our figures for hull and machinery'. Ironically Clydebank had earlier decided against establishing its own gun factory. See *UCS 1/1/12*, Minutes of Board Meetings, 12th July 1897 and 10th March 1896.

26. *UCS 2/1/3*, Minutes of Board Meeting, 16th November 1905. Fairfield paid £187,500 for 125,000 £1 ordinary shares, sixteen shillings paid, and £25,000 for 25,000 5% Preference Stock.

27. Report of the Committee appointed to inquire into the arrears of shipbuilding, *Parliamentary Papers, 1902 [Cd1055] LX 1* (hereafter referred to simply as *The Report of the Foster Committee*), p. 10.

28. The costs of the hulls of the battlecruisers HMS INFLEXIBLE (Clydebank Yard No. 374) and HMS INDOMITABLE (Fairfield Yard No. 445) suggest that these contracts included armour plate, but this was exceptional. Under normal circumstances the Admiralty went out of its way to place the contracts for armour plate separately from those for hulls to the extent that the armaments manufacturers rarely supplied the armour plate for British warships built in their own shipyards. See Lyons, *The Admiralty and Private Industry*, p. 41.

29. *UCS 2/1/3*, Minutes of Board Meeting, 27th January 1903.

30. Ibid., Minutes of Board Meeting, 16th November 1905.

31. Links with the Pearce family were not finally severed until the death, in 1918, of the dowager Lady Pearce, the late Sir William Pearce's widow. As a major shareholder, the dowager Lady Pearce was asked to guarantee the company's overdraft in 1909 and she was consulted on a proposal to borrow £250,000 in 1912 (see *UCS 2/1/4*, Minutes of Board Meetings, 22nd May 1909 and 12th September 1912), but she was never actively involved in the running of the company. On Sir William G. Pearce's death, the chairmanship of the company passed to Francis Elgar.

32. Most notably Thomas (later Sir Thomas) Bell, who was appointed a director in 1907 and succeeded J. G. Dunlop as Managing Director of Clydebank on the latter's retirement in 1908. See Grant, *Steel and Ships*, p. 59.

33. J. M. Laird and R. R. Bevis joined the Fairfield board in December 1905. See *UCS 2/3/1*.

34. *UCS 2/1/3*, Minutes of Extraordinary General Meeting, 17th June 1904.

35. This figure represents the valuation of Dalmuir at 1st January 1902 plus net additions to fixed assets between then and 31st December 1907 excluding transfers from Govan and Lancefield Street.

36. A full description of the facilities at Dalmuir is given in a special article in *The Times*, 7th July 1909. See also Hume & Moss, *Beardmore*, pp. 72–73.

37. *UCS 2/1/3*, Minutes of Board Meeting, 29th November 1901.

38. *GU 4935*, Robert Napier & Sons Papers, No. 25. Valuation of Govan Shipbuilding Yard and Lancefield Engine Works by Thomas W. Smillie & Fraser dated 20th July 1898.

39. Hume & Moss, *Beardmore*, p. 50.

40. *Ibid.*, pp. 47–48.

41. National Bank of Scotland Minute Books (held at the Head Office of the Royal Bank of Scotland, Edinburgh), Vol. 36, p. 549, 29th November 1900. Quoted by Hume & Moss, *Beardmore*, p. 51.

42. Trebilcock, *The Vickers Brothers*, p. 91.

43. KINFAUNS CASTLE, KILDONAN CASTLE, ARMADALE CASTLE and DURHAM CASTLE.

44. VADERLAND, ZEELAND, HAVERFORD and MERION.

45. E. Green & M. Moss, *A Business of National Importance: The Royal Mail Shipping Group, 1902-1937* (London 1982), p. 17.

46. By 1928, Lord Kylsant, the chairman of the Royal Mail Group, effectively controlled 140 companies including the Royal Mail Steam Packet Co., Elder Dempster & Co., the Union-Castle Mail Steamship Co. and the White Star line. See *ibid.*, p. 80 & pp. 223-6.

47. *UCS 2/20/1*, letter from Francis Elgar to Alexander Gracie, dated 15th January 1903.

48. Walker, *The Song of the Clyde*, p. 108.

49. *Ibid.*, pp. 110-11. The building of these ships was made possible by the Admiralty agreeing to lend Cunard £2,600,000 at $2\frac{3}{4}$% to help finance the building of the ships and to pay an annual operating subsidy of £150,000. In exchange the Admiralty had the right to have these ships built in accordance with its requirements for war service and to amend the design of any other new Cunard liner capable of more than 17 knots. See Pollard & Robertson, *The British Shipbuilding Industry*, p. 225.

50. See Chapter 4 above.

51. The decision to fit steam turbines in the 19-knot CARMANIA was taken following the recommendation of a committee of experts that the 25-knot liners should be powered by turbines. See Walker, *The Song of the Clyde*, p. 111.

52. *UCS 1/1/13*, Minutes of Board Meeting, 18th May 1904.

53. The invoice price of the CARMANIA was £43,253 less than that of the CARONIA. See Peebles, thesis, Appendix FIII.

54. It is interesting to compare the labour costs of the battleship HMS HINDUSTAN with those of the liner CARONIA built by Clydebank at approximately the same time. The labour expended on the £647,711 contract for the hull and machinery of the battleship totalled £179,301 compared with only £163,836 expended on the £630,467 contract for the hull and machinery of the liner, most of the difference arising from the lower labour cost of constructing and fitting out the liner's hull — £123,842 compared with £137,260 for the battleship. Breakdowns of the labour costs of the two ships are to be found in *UCS 1/85/2*.

55. LA PLATA, LUNHO, EBRO, NILE, TAGUS, TRENT and TYNE (Yard Nos. 449, 450, 451, 454, 466, 467 and 470).

56. The TALCA built for the Pacific Steam Navigation Co.

57. The 5,662 ton HIGHLAND BRIGADE and the 3,750 ton HIGHLAND LADDIE for the Nelson Line and the 5,893 ton ALNWICK CASTLE and the 5,883 ton BERWICK CASTLE for the Union-Castle Line.

58. See Peebles, thesis, Appendix FIV.

59. *Report of the Foster Committee*, pp. 4–7.

60. Statement of the First Lord of the Admiralty explanatory of the Navy Estimates for 1902-1903, *Parliamentary Papers, 1902 [Cd950] LIX 307*, p. 13.

61. *Report of the Foster Committee*, p. 2.

62. March, *British Destroyers*, p. 35.

63. Walker, *The Song of the Clyde*, p. 75.

64. March, *British Destroyers*, p. 47.

65. *Ibid.*, p. 54.

66. Clydebank suffered abatements of price of £750 on HMS BRAZEN, £500 on HMS ELECTRA and £3,000 on HMS ARAB in respect of shortfalls in their design speed but the Admiralty did not exact additional penalties for late delivery. See *UCS 1/75/4*.

67. Fairfield, in particular, could boast of a good record on the delivery of cruisers. HMS VENUS, HMS DIANA and HMS DIADEM had been delivered 37 days early, 44 days early and 27 days early respectively. Despite a fire HMS ARGONAUT had been delivered only 14 days late and, although HMS HERMES had been delivered one month late because of a strike, her sister ship HMS HIGHFLYER had been delivered one month early. Only HMS ABOUKIR was seriously late but this was attributed to the want of armour 'which was a separate Government order with which they had nothing whatever to do'. See report of speech by Sir William G. Pearce at the launching of HMS BEDFORD in *Fairplay*, 5th September 1901.

68. *Fairplay*, 1st November 1900.

69. Figures abstracted from papers accompanying later Navy estimates suggest that HMS ARGYLL was the most expensive of the five Devonshire class armoured cruisers put out to contract in 1901-1902. Excluding dockyard incidental charges, her first cost was £860,740. By comparison, the first cost of Clydebank's HMS ANTRIM was given as £858,778, the next most expensive ship — Beardmore's HMS CARNARVON — cost only £840,932, and HMS ROXBURGH, built by the London & Glasgow, and HMS HAMPSHIRE, built by Armstrong Whitworth's, appear to have cost the Admiralty only £814,705 and £818,105 respectively.

70. The net profits/losses of the Greenock Foundry Co. for the years 1890 to 1900 inclusive are taken from *GD 319/7/2/5-6*. Similarly the net profits/losses of Scott & Co. for the years 1889 to 1901 inclusive are taken from *GD 319/7/1/1*. In both cases interest on partners' capital accounts has been added back in computing the figures:

*NET PROFITS/LOSSES OF THE GREENOCK FOUNDRY CO.*
*AND SCOTT & CO. 1889-1901*

| YEAR TO 31st DECEMBER | GREENOCK FOUNDRY CO. £ | SCOTT & CO. £ |
|---|---|---|
| 1889 | ? | 4,570 |
| 1890 | 5,906 | 19,891 |
| 1891 | 10,077 | 19,273 |
| 1892 | 36 | 7,643 |
| 1893 | −250 | −5,322 |
| 1894 | −3,862 | −4,498 |
| 1895 | 17,688 | 28,958 |
| 1896 | −1,441 | −4,653 |
| 1897 | −2,954 | −1,650 |
| 1898 | −4,345 | 1,081 |
| 1899 | −3,491 | −18,513 |
| 1900 | 4,490 | −44,714 |
| 1901 | ? | 11,916 |

71. See note 70 above.

72. Analysis of contracts abstracted from *GD 319/7/1/1*.

73. Although the new company nominally dates its existence from 1st January 1902, there is some doubt whether the decision to form it was made then or later. The accounts for the two years to 31 December, 1903 appear to have been prepared retrospectively and the estate of John Scott, who died in May 1903, lists his interests as being in Scott & Co. and the Greenock Foundry Co. rather than in Scott's Shipbuilding and Engineering Co. Ltd. See *Fairplay*, 7th January 1904.

74. *Fairplay*, 13th November 1902, quoting report in the *Greenock Telegraph* of the previous week.

75. In the company's books the £50,000 was debited direct to the contract for HMS ARGYLL. The author has treated it as a provision for depreciation and the cost of the ship has been amended accordingly.

76. Yard Nos. 292, 294–297, 300–302, 308, and 310–312.

77. Yard Nos. 304, 313–314, 317, 320 and 322.

78. See Note 69 above.

79. The market value is given as a note on the published accounts for the year to 30th June 1906.

80. In 1900, Beardmore's tendered for Monmouth class cruisers with engines supplied by either Hawthorn Leslie or Humphrey Tennant, and while the former tender was the cheaper, the Admiralty preferred the latter. See *Fairplay*, 1st November 1900. Humphrey Tennant also supplied the engines for HMS CARNARVON although Hawthorn Leslie later provided those for HMS AGAMEMNON.

81. This was a rare instance of firms being penalised for late delivery. The firms involved were reported to be 'complaining bitterly' about being excluded and the Admiralty was said to have promised that they would be allowed to participate in the bidding for battleships and cruisers due to be put out to tender in a few months' time. See *Fairplay*, 1st November 1900.

82. HMS JASON, HMS CIRCE and HMS LEDA.

83. HMS TERRIBLE, HMS AURORA and HMS PELORUS. In contrast to Fairfield, Clydebank treated these contracts as miscellaneous sales and they were not ascribed a ship number.

84. *UCS 1/3/6*, working papers on accounts for year to 30th June 1899.

85. Excluding warships purchased while under construction for foreign powers.

86. Statement of the First lord of the Admiralty explanatory of the Navy estimates for 1903–1904, *Parliamentary Papers 1903 [Cd1478] XXXIX 305*, p. 14.

87. *Report of the Foster Committee*, p. 14.

88. Marder, *The Anatomy of British Seapower*, p. 42.

89. Statement of the First Lord of the Admiralty explanatory of the Navy Estimates for 1905–1906, *Parliamentary Papers 1905 [Cd2402] XLVII 293*, p. 7.

90. A. J. Marder, *From the Dreadnought to Scapa Flow: The Royal Navy in the Fisher Era, 1904–1919* (five volumes: London 1961–1970), Vol. 1, pp. 67–68.

91. Marder, *The Anatomy of British Seapower*, p. 533.

92. Conway's *All the World's Fighting Ships, 1906–1921*, p. 21.

93. Marder, *From the Dreadnought to Scapa Flow*, Vol. 1, pp. 56–70.

94. After the introduction of the dreadnought only Portsmouth and Devonport Dockyards were equipped to build the largest warships. Pembroke Dockyard was relegated to building nothing larger than cruisers and Chatham Dockyard was primarily used to build submarines.

95. Although the contract was not signed until 30th January 1906, Clydebank was approached regarding the building of HMS INFLEXIBLE in August 1905. See *UCS 1/1/3*, Minutes of Board Meeting, 16th August 1905.

96. Swan Hunter's, the builders of the LUSITANIA's sister ship MAURETANIA, did not become involved in warshipbuilding until later. The destroyer HMS HOPE laid down in 1909 appears to have been their first warship contract. See *Conway's All the World's Fighting Ships, 1906–1921*.

97. The civilian members of the committee also included Professor J. H. Biles who served Clydebank and later Denny's as a naval architect.

98. *The Glasgow Herald*, Shipbuilding & Engineering Supplement, 21st December 1904.

99. Apart from these five firms, only Palmer's of Jarrow and the Thames Iron Works had recent experience of building the largest warships and the latter, which was forced into liquidation in 1911, was already in financial difficulties. It had suffered a loss in building the battleship HMS ALBION, completed in 1902, and it was reported that it had been awarded the contract for the armoured cruiser HMS BLACK PRINCE in 1902–03 only for political reasons. See *Fairplay*, 4th December 1902 and 1st January 1903.

# 6
# 1907–1914: Pre-War Problems

The years immediately following the introduction of the dreadnought in 1905 were lean years for the private warshipbuilder. While the resignation of the Unionist Government in December 1905 did not result in any fundamental change in naval policy and the incoming Liberal administration made no attempt to reverse the controversial decision to proceed with the building of dreadnoughts, the Liberals were pledged to reduce expenditure on armaments. They inherited a situation which permitted some reduction in the planned rate of new construction without jeopardising Britain's naval supremacy. The Anglo-Japanese Alliance of 1902, which assured the Royal Navy of a powerful ally in the Far East in the event of war with any two other powers, had recently been renewed; the United States was already regarded more as a kindred power than a potential enemy and, in 1904, the Entente Cordiale with France together with the crushing defeat inflicted on Russia by Japan had effectively neutralised the hostile combination against which all of Britain's naval preparations had previously been directed. Germany, once seen as a potential ally, was increasingly identified as Britain's most likely enemy in the event of war but in 1906, with the bulk of the British battlefleet in process of being concentrated in home waters and the first of the new dreadnoughts in the offing, there was no immediate danger. Britain enjoyed an overwhelming naval superiority and the Admiralty's original intention of laying down four new dreadnoughts a year was difficult to justify. In consequence the number of capital ships included in the 1906–07 and 1907–08 programmes was reduced from four to three[1] and, although the outcome of the 1907 Hague Peace Conference dispelled any illusion that the other powers would be willing to agree to any plan for the limitation of armaments which would perpetuate Britain's existing naval supremacy,[2] the Admiralty was able to persuade a reluctant Cabinet to agree to the inclusion of a battleship as well as a battlecruiser in the 1908–09 programme only on the grounds that the omission of a battleship would bring the heavy armaments industry to a standstill at an inopportune moment:

> Although it is quite true that our preponderance in battleships at the present moment might justify the omission of the solitary battleship proposed, yet with the full knowledge and absolute certainty (now afforded by the German programme just issued) of having to commence a large battleship programme in 1909–10, it would be most unbusiness like and indeed disastrous, to close down the armour plate industry of this country by the entire cessation of battleship building. It would be similarly disastrous to abruptly stop the manufacture of heavy gun mountings which the omission of the battleship would also involve.[3]

The private warshipbuilding industry was accorded less consideration. The Admiralty professed to be favourably disposed towards an industry which had served the Royal Navy well since 1889, and Lord Tweedmouth, the newly appointed Liberal First Lord of the Admiralty, told a delegation of dockyard workers from Chatham in 1906 that

> He could not accept in its fullest sense the proposition that the nation's work should be carried on in the national shipbuilding establishments.[4]

Nevertheless the Admiralty's earlier decision not to abandon shipbuilding in the Royal Dockyards meant that in practice it was still the private shipbuilders who bore the brunt of any contraction in demand. While Portsmouth and Devonport, the only dockyards equipped to build 'dreadnoughts', were allocated six of the eight capital ships laid down in the three years 1906–07 to 1908–09, private contractors were starved of major warship orders. Apart from destroyers, torpedo boats and submarines, their total share comprised one battleship in each of 1906–07 and 1907–08 and five 4,800 ton protected cruisers in 1908–09.[5]

The contraction in Admiralty demand had an adverse effect on the fortunes of the Clyde warshipbuilders. Denny's of Dumbarton, which, as an unincorporated family concern, had been debarred from tendering for Admiralty contracts between 1895 and 1905 when one of its partners served as a Member of Parliament,[6] was able to turn its pioneering work on turbine-powered steamers[7] to advantage by securing orders for four torpedo boats and a destroyer,[8] but the bigger warshipbuilding yards were less successful. The battleships on offer in 1906–07 and 1907–08 went to Armstrong's and Vickers respectively, despite a determined effort by Clydebank to secure the second order by taking 'a considerable amount' off charges in its tender.[9] Clydebank and Fairfield, the only Clydeside yards judged fit to build large turbine-powered warships in 1905, both managed to secure an order for the machinery of a dockyard-built ship[10] and Scott's was encouraged to equip itself for the manufacture of turbines by the award of the contract for the machinery of the Dockyard-built battleship HMS ST. VINCENT in 1907, but neither Scott's not Dalmuir, admitted to the list of firms invited to tender for complete dreadnoughts after representations by Beardmore's in 1906,[11] succeeded in securing a single warship order between 1905 and the end of 1908. Further, unlike Alfred Yarrow & Co. the destroyer specialist, which transferred its business from Poplar to a new yard at Scotstoun on the Clyde in 1907,[12] none of them had naval work for foreign governments to keep them going.[13] Consequently, the Clyde yards were progressively denuded of naval work. By December 1907, following the launching of the 17,290 ton battlecruiser HMS INFLEXIBLE at Clydebank and the 17,410 ton battlecruiser HMS INDOMI-TABLE at Fairfield, the only naval work on the stocks on the Clyde was the destroyers building at Denny's and Yarrow's. As *The Glasgow Herald* remarked, this was 'a condition of affairs quite unprecedented within recent years'.[14]

All of the erstwhile warshipbuilders were running short of work of any kind. The London & Glasgow had no orders to follow the launching of a 5,180 ton merchantman in 1907.[15] In December of the same year it was reported that Scott's and Dalmuir each had only one merchant vessel on hand, at Fairfield only two small steamers were on the stocks, and all of Clydebank's berths stood empty.[16] While the plight of the warshipbuilders was no worse than that of the majority of Clyde yards, which were all beginning to feel the effects of the onset of the abnormally severe slump in merchant demand which was to reduce the district's total output of ships from an all-time high of 619,919 tons in 1907 to 355,886 tons in 1908, they had particular cause for concern. All of them had experienced difficulty in securing worthwhile merchant orders even when demand was relatively buoyant between 1904 and 1907.

Two yards had indeed experienced difficulty in securing work of any kind. Since opening Dalmuir to build the battleship HMS AGAMEMNON in the spring of 1905, Beardmore's total intake of new work had consisted of five ships for the Pacific Steam Navigation Co. worth £533,789,[17] all of them taken at prices which failed to cover prime cost, while the London & Glasgow had built only six merchant ships aggregating 27,099 tons since the beginning of 1904.[18] Clydebank's record was little better. Since April 1904, when the yard had received the order for the LUSITANIA, it had managed to secure only thirteen merchant orders worth £1,043,808.[19] Six of these thirteen orders had resulted in losses, three of them failing to cover even prime cost, and all thirteen contracts together had yielded a contribution to overheads and profit of only £83,311. Even those warshipbuilding yards which had managed to secure a volume of merchant orders commensurate with their capacity had run into difficulties. Scott's, which had taken orders for thirty-two ships worth £1,167,763 in the three years to December 1907,[20] suffered net losses on ten, and the total contribution to overheads and profit from all thirty-two contracts amounted to only £132,947, compared with the contribution of £184,963 from the building of the armed cruiser HMS ARGYLL alone. Fairfield, which had taken fifteen merchant contracts worth £2,187,738 since February 1904,[21] had most cause for satisfaction, not least because the intake included four orders for large passenger liners each worth more than £300,000 — the 14,190 ton EMPRESS OF BRITAIN and EMPRESS OF IRELAND for Canadian Pacific and the 10,897 ton HELIOPOLIS and CAIRO for the Egyptian Mail Steamship Co. — but even Fairfield's record was seriously flawed. Four of the orders, including both the HELIOPOLIS and the CAIRO, resulted in losses, and, more seriously, both the Egyptian Mail Steamship Co., which had bought its two liners on credit, and Italian owners, who had bought the steamer VOLTURNO on similar terms, failed to meet their contractual obligations. Fairfield was obliged to repossess all three ships, the VOLTURNO in August 1907[22] and the others in October 1908,[23] leaving the company with the problem of disposing of second-hand ships in a depressed market. Eventually a Canadian buyer took all three ships off Fairfield's hands in November 1909.[24] In the meantime the company had to borrow to cover the dishonoured bills. The transaction resulted in further losses of £22,960,[25] and only £100,000 of the resale price of £415,000 was paid in cash, the balance being settled by promissory notes for £90,000 and £225,000 of debenture stock in the Canadian Northern Railway which, under the terms of the deal, could not be sold for less than £95 per £100 of stock[26] — a price which was still not obtainable in the open market four years later.[27]

In the depressed conditions of 1908 the outlook for merchant shipbuilding became even bleaker. The London & Glasgow, which had been at a complete standstill for most of the year to 30th June 1908 due to the fact that

> Orders could not be obtained at prices which the Directors would have been justified in accepting,[28]

reopened to build the 12,129 ton mailship OSTERLEY for the Orient Line. Clydebank and Fairfield both had similar orders for the same owners but other merchant work was in desperately short supply. Apart from the liner ORSOVA which was worth £365,837, Clydebank took only two other merchant orders, the £107,000 rail ferry MUNICH and a contract worth £32,397 on which it suffered a net loss of £9,219.[29] Fairfield with orders for three ferries for the Zeeland Steamship Co. worth £306,766[30] in addition to the £324,800 order for the liner OTWAY fared rather better but it was barely enough to keep the yard going. Scott's, which took orders for only six small merchant ships worth £290,626 between December 1907 and the spring of 1909,[31] was in a similar position., Dalmuir had no work at all to follow the completion of the last of the five ships for Pacific Steam Navigation.

Fortunately the 1908-09 naval programme afforded the big yards their best chance of securing a major warship order since 1905-06. Apart from sixteen destroyers and twelve submarines, the programme provided for the building of five 4,800 ton protected cruisers in private yards, the Admiralty having revised its earlier opinion that there was no place for small cruisers in the post-dreadnought fleet.[32] The major Clyde yards made the most of their opportunity. While the contracts for two of the five ships went to Vickers and Armstrong's, the other three orders went to Clyde yards — HMS GLOUCESTER to Dalmuir, HMS GLASGOW to Fairfield, and HMS BRISTOL, the lead ship of the class, to Clydebank. Fairfield and Clydebank also had the contracts for the machinery of two more Dockyard-built warships, the former for the unarmoured cruiser HMS BELLONA and the latter for the battlecruiser HMS INDEFATIGABLE. Meanwhile Fairfield, Clydebank, Denny's and the London & Glasgow between them took orders for eight of the sixteen destroyers on offer, Fairfield and Clydebank having been awarded the contracts for three vessels each as a reward for having submitted the lowest tenders.[33]

Not all of these orders were remunerative. Despite Fairfield and Clydebank receiving average prices of only £100,407 and £102,210 respectively on each of their Beagle class destroyers compared with £115,771 paid to Denny's for HMS PINCHER, they reported average net profits of £21,471 per vessel and £20,090 per vessel respectively. The larger and more prestigious contracts for cruisers were much less profitable. HMS GLASGOW gave Fairfield a net profit of only £9,434 on a price of £302,806 and Clydebank suffered a net loss of £1,024 on the £312,950 contract for HMS BRISTOL. The outcomes of the two cruiser contracts were adversely affected by the practice followed by both firms of allocating all their overheads to work in progress irrespective of how little work they had on hand, and it is notable that Beardmore's, which apparently took the view that the low level of throughput at Dalmuir obliged it to distinguish between the charges which contracts could be expected to bear and the balance which had to be written off as irrecoverable, reported a net profit of £30,143 on the £301,537 contract to build HMS GLOUCESTER. Nevertheless, as Table 6.1 shows, disparities in the treatment of overheads do not account for the low contributions to overhead and profit earned on all of these contracts.

**Table 6.1.** Outcome of Cruiser Contracts Taken in 1908/09

| YARD | SHIP | INVOICE PRICE | CONTRIBUTION TO OVERHEADS AND PROFIT | |
|------|------|------|------|------|
| | | £ | £ | % |
| CLYDEBANK | BRISTOL | 312,950 | 57,769 | 18.46 |
| DALMUIR | GLOUCESTER | 301,537 | 55,791 | 18.50 |
| FAIRFIELD | GLASGOW | 302,806 | 44,287 | 14.63 |

(Source: Author's figures based on detail abstracted from *UCS 1*, *UCS 2* and *UGD 100*. See Peebles, **thesis**, Appendices FII, FIII and FIV)

The contributions earned by Clydebank and Fairfield on their two contracts were both less than half the average contributions of 37.06% and 29.82% respectively earned by the two yards on all the warships undertaken by them between the turn of the century and the advent of the dreadnought. However, in the conditions which prevailed in the winter of 1908–09, depressed prices did not lessen the attractions of Admiralty orders. Work of any kind was in short supply and warship contracts which did not result in serious losses were most welcome, particularly as pressure was already building up for a more substantial programme of naval construction to begin in 1909–10.

For a government pledged to peace abroad and social reform at home it was a bitter blow to have to sanction any increase in naval expenditure, especially at a time when it was already committed to finding the money to pay for a state-funded old-age pension scheme.[34] By the spring of 1909 the Cabinet had no choice. Up to 1908 it had been possible to resist pressure for increased naval expenditure by pointing to the absence of any immediate threat to Britain's naval supremacy. By the end of 1908 Germany had started laying down dreadnoughts at the rate of four a year: she possessed the industrial capacity to sustain this level of output, and, crucially, she was credited with being able to match or even better Britain's speed of construction.[35] If no action was taken it was feared that Germany would possess more dreadnoughts than Britain by 1912. The issue was no longer whether Britain's own building programme should be increased but how many dreadnoughts needed to be laid down in 1909–10. The Admiralty asked for six, the Opposition, supported by the pro-navy press and the armaments manufacturers, demanded eight and the Cabinet, which baulked at the cost of laying down more than four, gave an undertaking that preparations would be put in hand to permit the laying down of a further four before April 1910 if this should prove necessary.[36]

The publication of the 1909-10 Naval Estimates marked the beginning of another period of naval expansion. With Britain's prestige committed to the maintenance of her naval supremacy and Germany bent on acquiring a navy appropriate to her status as the leading power on the continent of Europe, the scene was set for a protracted naval arms race which continued until the outbreak of war in 1914. By 1912 the Government had explicitly redefined Britain's naval supremacy in terms of a sixty percent margin of superiority in dreadnoughts over Germany alone[37] and the eight dreadnoughts of the 1909-10 programme were followed by twenty more, the programmes for each of the next four years providing for the building of a further five. At the same time provision had to be made for a host of smaller warships whose number tended to increase in proportion to the size of the main battlefleet, with the result that, in addition to twenty-four battleships and six battlecruisers,[38] no less than twelve protected cruisers, twenty-one unarmoured cruisers, one hundred and three destroyers, fifty submarines, two depot ships and two depot-ship tenders were laid down by the Admiralty in British yards between April 1909 and the outbreak of war in August 1914.[39] The services of private warshipbuilders were in growing demand and, as shown in Table 6.2, the total tonnage of British warships under construction in Clyde yards rose steadily year by year from 1,276 tons in December 1908 to 167,286 tons in December 1913:

**Table 6.2.** Admiralty Work in progress in Clyde Yards

| YEAR END | ON STOCKS (TONS) | FITTING-OUT (TONS) | TOTAL (TONS) |
|---|---|---|---|
| 1908 | 1,026 | 250 | 1,276 |
| 1909 | 30,303 | 13,378 | 43,681 |
| 1910 | 71,442 | 29,285 | 100,727 |
| 1911 | 38,067 | 75,047 | 113,114 |
| 1912 | 74,924 | 56,615 | 131,539 |
| 1913 | 104,018 | 63,268 | 167,286 |

(Source: Abstracted from Appendix EII) 40

The renewed demand for warships, together with a later revival in the demand for merchant ships, raised the output of the Clyde shipbuilding industry to record levels in the years preceding the First World War. By December 1911 *The Glasgow Herald* was speaking of 'A period of unexampled prosperity'[41] and in 1913 the volume of ships launched on the river reached an all-time high of 756,976 tons, more than double the output of 355,586 tons achieved at the depths of the preceding slump in 1908. Unfortunately, as *The Glasgow Herald* also remarked, the boom was accompanied by increases in the costs of materials and labour and in 1913 shipbuilders' profits were reported to be 'far lower than they were when less money was passing through their hands'.[42]

As in previous periods of high naval demand, warshipbuilding was confined to a relatively small number of firms. The distribution of orders is given in Table 6.3. Apart from A. & J. Inglis, which built a single destroyer, and Yarrow's and Denny's, which likewise confined themselves to building destroyers, all of the Clyde's share of Admiralty orders was attributable to the efforts of the same five yards which had been actively engaged in warshipbuilding prior to the introduction of the dreadnought in 1905:

**Table 6.3.** Distribution of Admiralty Orders 1909–1914

| YARD | WARSHIPS | | ENGINES | |
|------|------|------|------|------|
|  | NO. | TONS | NO. | H.P. |
| DALMUIR | 11 | 96,852 | 12 | 343,500 |
| CLYDEBANK | 16 | 90,035 | 17 | 555,500 |
| FAIRFIELD | 13 | 58,169 | 15 | 408,000 |
| SCOTT'S | 7 | 48,552 | 8 | 100,350 |
| LONDON & GLASGOW | 6 | 16,835 | 6 | 123,100 |
| YARROW'S | 12 | 10,478 | 12 | 259,000 |
| DENNY'S | 11 | 9,923 | 9 | 175,225 |
| INGLIS | 1 | 760 | 1 | 13,500 |

(Source: Abstracted from Appendix EII)

Of the five firms, Scott's and the London & Glasgow both laboured under the disadvantage that, at the outset, neither was properly equipped to take full advantage of the renewed demand for large turbine-powered warships. By 1909, both Scott's, which had been awarded the contract for the machinery of the Dockyard-built battleship HMS ST. VINCENT in December 1907, and the London & Glasgow, which had secured the order for a Beagle class destroyer at the end of 1908,[43] had taken the vital first steps towards proving their capability to produce turbine-powered ships. The upturn in naval demand encouraged both to proceed with more costly schemes of reconstruction designed to enable them to build the largest warships. The amounts spent by the two firms in re-equipping themselves were relatively modest by comparison with the sum which had been expended by Beardmore's in building Dalmuir, but the sums of £139,998, expended by Scott's on net additions to fixed assets between December 1908 and December 1914, and £117,631, expended by the London & Glasgow on net additions to fixed assets between June 1909 and June 1911, were significant outlays for the firms involved.

Of the two firms the London & Glasgow was the more fortunate in being able to finance most of this capital expenditure from its own resources. While the company had paid a dividend of 30s. per share in respect of the year to 30th June 1907, when the trading results did not justify it, the directors had been careful to husband the company's cash resources by passing the dividend on the ordinary shares in each of the two years following, and in June 1909 they had a cash balance of £106,632 and short-term investments worth £60,292[44] on which to draw when the need arose. By contrast, Scott's had been undercapitalised since the formation of the company and, although the directors had pursued an extremely conservative depreciation policy which resulted in the book value of fixed assets falling from a peak of £475,065 at 31st December 1904 to £376,525 at 31st December 1908, and distributions to ordinary shareholders had amounted to only £48,125 in total since the company's formation, it still owed its bankers £106,726 at 31st December 1908.

Any misgivings which Scott's might have had about borrowing more money for further capital expenditure did not prevent them from doing so when the firm succeeded in winning the Clyde's first order for a dreadnought battleship — the 20,000 ton Colossus class battleship HMS COLOSSUS laid down in July 1909. While there was some surprise that Scott's rather than one of the bigger yards was favoured with such an important contract[45] and, at the time, the firm could offer little proof of its fitness for the work beyond having undertaken the, as yet unfinished, contract for the machinery of HMS ST. VINCENT, the appeal of a large naval contract to the management was understandable. Three years had elapsed since completing the cruiser HMS Argyll in 1905, during which time the firm had no major warship orders on hand. While the company had managed to earn trading profits before depreciation amounting to £78,958, the directors must have been well aware that virtually all of the profit was attributable to the net profit of £62,369 earned by the engine works in manufacturing the machinery for the Dockyard-built armoured cruiser HMS DEFENCE and that the shipyard had suffered a loss before providing for depreciation in all three years.[46]

Scott's expansion programme resulted in the building of a new shop equipped with overhead cranes to service the new boring, blading and planing machines needed to manufacture turbines.[47] Over the next four years

> Practically the whole of the buildings embraced in the shipyard and the engine shop and boiler shop department were reconstructed and equipped with modern and in many cases new classes of machinery and tools.[48]

Such a comprehensive reconstruction imposed heavy strains on the company's liquidity. By December 1912 bank borrowings amounted to £310,397 but, at the outset, the prospects seemed favourable. Apart from the firm's happy experience with HMS ARGYLL when a similar initiative had been quickly rewarded, the chances of repeat orders were good and the development of the naval business was made more attractive by the depressed state of merchant demand which made profitable merchant work increasingly difficult to obtain.

The London & Glasgow's programme of capital investment was necessarily more speculative. The directors embarked on it with only the order for the Beagle class destroyer HMS RATTLESNAKE on hand. Here, too, there was nothing in the firm's recent trading performance to encourage optimism should the firm fail to preserve its position as a credible contender for major Admiralty contracts. The company had not earned satisfactory profits in any year since completing the cruiser HMS Roxburgh in 1905–06. Total trading profits before depreciation in the three years to 30th June 1909 amounted to only £18,609 and the yard had no merchant work to follow the 12,029 ton mail liner OSTERLEY launched in 1909. The board's hand may have been forced by the need to find alternative fitting-out facilities to replace a deep berth on the river which was no longer available,[49] but the need for facilities capable of building the largest warships was clearly uppermost in the directors' minds when they came to determine the layout of an expanded yard incorporating the ground formerly occupied by Robert Napier & Sons' yard. A slipway set at an angle to the river and a new wet basin were both designed to accommodate ships of up to 700 feet in length and 100 feet in beam. As *The Times* commented:

> While mercantile ships, as in the past, will probably form a major portion of the work being provided for, the immediate object of the extension and dock formation is the provision of adequate facilities for building and outfitting naval ships including the largest class of battleships.[50]

To complement the improvements in the shipyard more ground was purchased adjoining the existing engine works on the other side of the river so that new shops could be erected to permit, as the directors themselves said, 'the construction of turbines of the great power now required by the Admiralty'.[51]

The London & Glasgow's enterprise was not particularly well rewarded. Hopes that the reconstruction of the shipyard would result in an order for a 'dreadnought' had not been realised by the winter of 1911–12. Although the firm had apparently been tendering for the machinery of Dockyard-built battleships since 1910,[52] and its aspirations were implicit in the appointment as general manager in 1911 of Mr. J. R. Bond, who had previously been employed in supervising the building of dreadnoughts at Portsmouth Dockyard,[53] the yard's share of the 1909–10 and 1910–11 naval programmes consisted of only two small cruisers — the 5,250 ton HMS YARMOUTH and the 5,400 ton HMS SYDNEY. These orders, together with a 5,750 ton merchantman,[54] were apparently not sufficient to keep the firm profitably employed. By June 1911 trading results, which had recovered from a trading loss before depreciation of £8,319 in 1907–08 to a trading profit before depreciation of £13,545 in 1908–09, were again deteriorating. A trading profit before depreciation of £6,472 in 1909–10 was followed by a trading profit before depreciation of only £1,779 in 1910–11 when the ordinary dividend had to be passed for the third time in four years. By the end of 1911, with no signs of any improvement in the trading situation and an order intake from the 1911–12 naval programme comprising only three destroyers[55] and the 3,380 ton destroyer depot-ship HMS WOOLWICH, the directors apparently decided that the prospects were not sufficiently encouraging for the firm to continue unchanged. In any event they approached Harland & Wolff, which was then looking for additional capacity to augment the resources of its busy Belfast yard, and in February 1912 they advised the shareholders to accept Harland & Wolff's offer of nine pounds, three shillings for each nine-pound share.[56]

Following the takeover the firm's engine works were turned over to Harland & Wolff's associates Burmeister & Wain for conversion to the manufacture of diesel engines. After informing the Admiralty that it no longer wished to be considered for machinery of its own manufacture,[57] the yard was entrusted with no further naval work before the outbreak of war in 1914, but under Harland & Wolff's management the yard was well supplied with merchant work. Output was 30,468 tons in 1913 alone.[58]

Unlike the London & Glasgow, Scott's persevered with warshipbuilding but it had little to show for a great deal of effort up to the outbreak of war. The contract for HMS COLOSSUS was followed by orders for the 3,600 ton submarine depot-ship HMS MAIDSTONE and the 23,000 ton King George V class battleship HMS AJAX in 1910–11 but the outcome of all these contracts was adversely affected by the disruption involved in the reconstruction of the yard.[59] Of the three contracts, only HMS MAIDSTONE, on which the firm failed to recover prime costs of £22,983, actually resulted in a loss, but, as Table 6.4 shows, neither of the two battleship contracts came close to matching the profitability of the firm's earlier contract for HMS ARGYLL:

**Table 6.4.** Profitability of Scott's Major Admiralty Contracts

| SHIP | INVOICE PRICE | CONTRIBUTION TO OVERHEADS & PROFIT | | |
| --- | --- | --- | --- | --- |
| | | HULL | ENGINES | TOTAL |
| | £ | £ | £ | £ |
| HMS ARGYLL | 622,262 | 124,832 | 60,131 | 184,963 |
| HMS COLOSSUS | 717,597 | 57,399 | 30,437 | 87,836 |
| HMS AJAX | 847,578 | 100,597 | 20,964 | 121,561 |

(Source: Author's figures based on detail abstracted from *GD 319*. See Peebles, **thesis**, Appendix FV)

Since all of the nine contracts for merchant ships[60] taken by Scott's between 1909 and 1912 resulted in losses — £806,599 worth of work yielded a contribution to overheads and profit of only £13,575 — the firm was unquestionably better off with the naval contracts than it would have been without them but trading profits before depreciation of £164,410 over the next two years, but by the outbreak of December 1912. Scott's survived this crisis and went on to earn trading profits before depreciation of £164,410 over the next two years, but by the outbreak of war in 1914 there were two main reasons for questioning whether the improvement could be sustained.

First, the profitability of the firm in 1913 and 1914 was attributable largely to the profits earned in building three liners for Cunard's Canadian service. The contracts for the 13,405 ton liners ALAUNIA and ANDONIA and for the 14,500 ton liner TRANSYLVANIA, the first transatlantic liner fitted with geared turbines, yielded Scott's contributions to overheads and profit totalling £130,378, but the firm had no comparable merchant work to follow them in 1914. Apart from the Cunard contracts, Scott's total intake of merchant work since 1912 amounted to only ten ships worth £957,971,[61] all but three of them for the firm's regular customers Alfred Holt and the China Navigation Co.

Second, after receiving the order for the battleship HMS AJAX the firm's total intake of conventional Admiralty work comprised a single contract for the manufacture of the machinery for the Dockyard-built light cruiser HMS CONQUEST. In 1909 Scott's had shown commendable enterprise in arranging to build Fiat-designed submarines under licence in Britain[62] and, although it remained to be seen whether the Admiralty, which had placed orders for three of this type of vessel by 1914,[63] would return for more, the firm had gone on to accept an order for HMS SWORDFISH, a revolutionary Admiralty-designed, steam-powered submarine displacing 932 tons afloat. If all went well, these two ventures promised to make Scott's name as a submarine builder and to open up a potentially lucrative market, as the Admiralty was anxious to reduce its dependence on Vickers for this class of work.[64] In the meantime the firm had suffered a loss of £11,623 in building its first Fiat submarine, the contract price of £53,044 having failed to cover prime cost by £7,340.

In consequence Scott's, like the London & Glasgow, could not claim to have had more than limited success in exploiting the opportunities presented by the revival in naval demand from 1909 onwards. In December 1914 the company still owed its bankers £215,177 and, apart from emergency orders placed by the Admiralty after the start of the war, its order book comprised only two merchant ships,[65] the three remaining submarines and the machinery of the Dockyard-built cruiser.

The performance of the bigger Clyde warshipbuilding yards was in some respects even more disappointing than that of their smaller neighbours. Of the four major warshipbuilding yards which remained in the business at the outbreak of war in 1914, Scott's was exceptional in failing to add substantially to its tally of Admiralty orders after 1911. Dalmuir, Clydebank and Fairfield all secured further major Admiralty orders in 1912 and 1913. In the six years preceding the outbreak of war in 1914, Clydebank had orders for one battleship, two battlecruisers, two light cruisers and fifteen destroyers as well as the machinery for the battlecruiser HMS QUEEN MARY built by Palmers of Jarrow; Dalmuir had orders for three battleships, six light cruisers, three destroyers and the machinery for a Dockyard-built light cruiser; Fairfield had orders for one battleship, one battlecruiser, two light cruisers, thirteen destroyers and the machinery for two Dockyard-built light cruisers.[66] Between them the three firms had received Admiralty orders worth £16,618,400, an average of £923,244 per yard per year. Fairfield, the least successful, took orders worth £4,376,113, nearly double the value of all Admiralty contracts taken by Scott's (£2,265,092). It was a measure of the capacity of the three major yards that they were able to undertake the huge volume of Admiralty work without having to spend large sums on additional capital investment. Total net additions to fixed assets in all three yards in the six years prior to the outbreak of war amounted to only £387,473, nearly half of which (£187,609) was incurred at

Clydebank in the two years to 31st March 1912 when the yard had to be extensively modified to accommodate the building of the mammoth 45,647 ton Cunard liner AQUITANIA.[67] Nevertheless, none of the three enjoyed a measure of prosperity commensurate with the high volume of Admiralty work passing through their hands.

Dalmuir's record was abysmal. After suffering a trading loss before depreciation of £4,276 in the year to 31st December 1905, the yard incurred further trading losses before depreciation totalling £207,006 over the following three years, partly because of the heavy losses incurred on the Pacific Steam Navigation Co. contracts but primarily because the yard's facilities were chronically underutilised. Even in 1908, when both the shipyard and engine works were at a virtual standstill, overheads amounted to £54,705, including £8,339 for gas, electricity, light and power,[68] and over the two years to 31st December 1908 overheads totalling £136,419 had to be written off as irrecoverable.[69] Following the upturn in the demand for warships in the winter of 1908-09, the situation began to improve and, after suffering a further trading loss before depreciation of £48,457 in 1909, the yard managed to earn small trading profits before depreciation in each of the next two years but the improvement was not sustained. Despite increasing activity, Dalmuir suffered trading losses before depreciation of £170,927 in 1912 and £163,347 in 1913. Even in 1914, with two battleships and three light cruisers under construction, it still reported a trading loss before depreciation of £22,768.

A number of factors contributed to Dalmuir's dismal record. Some were peculiar to Beardmore's. First, the firm had not made significant progress in building up its merchant business. In 1911 it secured orders for three 7,700 ton ships for the Adelaide Steamship Co. and for the more prestigious 18,500 ton liner ALSATIAN for the Allan Line, but the yard's only other merchant orders in the six years to 31st December 1913 were for a sludge boat and a lighthouse tender.[70] The total value of Dalmuir's merchant business in these years amounted to only £999,994. Second, Dalmuir started with the disadvantage of having no previous experience of manufacturing turbine-powered machinery and of having been unable to offer regular employment to skilled workers prior to 1909. Third, there is some evidence that prime costs at Dalmuir compared unfavourably with those at both Clydebank and Fairfield. Certainly the prime costs of both the liner ALSATIAN and the cruiser HMS DUBLIN were significantly higher than those of sister ships built in the other two yards at the same time, the prime cost of the ALSATIAN being £543,569 compared with £480,714 for the CALGARIAN built by Fairfield, and the prime cost of HMS DUBLIN being £282,036 compared with £260,438 for HMS SOUTHAMPTON built by Clydebank.

Two facets of Dalmuir's performance — losses on merchant contracts and the declining profitability of Admiralty work — were common to the experience of all three major warshipbuilding yards. Neither Fairfield nor Clydebank suffered losses on merchant contracts comparable with those suffered by Dalmuir in building the three ships for the Adelaide Steamship Co. and the liner ALSATIAN, which together resulted in net losses of £302,564, but few of the merchant contracts undertaken by either yard between 1909 and 1911 ended profitably.

Demand for merchant tonnage revived in 1909 and 1910 when naval work was still in relatively short supply. Clydebank and Fairfield both took advantage of the opportunity to replenish their order books with major merchant orders by the end of 1911. Between the beginning of 1909 and the end of 1911 Clydebank took orders for twelve merchant ships worth £3,031,740.[71] None of these ships was designed for great speed, but the 45,647 ton Cunard liner AQUITANIA was the biggest merchant ship yet built in Britain and both the 13,000 ton liner ORAMA, built for the Orient Line, and the 13,415 ton liner NIAGARA, built for the Union Steamship Co., were notable ships in their own right. Similarly, Fairfield's intake of thirteen merchant orders worth £2,408,007[72] included the 13,300 ton Union Castle liner BALMORAL CASTLE, the 16,850 ton Canadian Pacific liners EMPRESS OF RUSSIA and EMPRESS OF ASIA and the 18,500 ton Allan liner CALGARIAN, all of which ranked among the biggest liners of their day.

Unhappily, ten of the twelve merchant contracts undertaken by Clydebank and nine of the thirteen merchant contracts undertaken by Fairfield resulted in net losses, three of the Fairfield contracts and no less than seven of the Clydebank contracts having been taken at prices which proved to be insufficient to cover prime cost. The large volume of merchant work made only a modest contribution to overheads and profit. The total contribution to overheads and profit from Fairfield's twelve contracts was £214,453 (8.9% of sales value) but only £109,446 (3.6% of sales value) from the thirteen contracts undertaken by Clydebank.

Warshipbuilding was more profitable, but here too Dalmuir was typical in experiencing a progressive decline in the profitability of Admiralty contracts undertaken between 1908 and 1912. The cruisers HMS GLOUCESTER, HMS FALMOUTH and HMS DUBLIN, completed at Dalmuir in 1911, 1912 and 1913 respectively, yielded progressively lower contributions to overheads and profit of £55,791, £37,186 and £13,207, the contract for HMS DUBLIN resulting in a net loss of £20,087. Similarly, the contribution to overheads and profit from destroyer contracts fell from £9,521 on HMS GOSHAWK completed in 1912 to an average of £5,835 each on HMS LLEWELYN and HMS LENNOX completed in 1914. Most ominous of all, in December 1914 the management at Dalmuir was anticipating a loss of £44,750 on the contract for the 25,000 ton Iron Duke class battleship HMS BENBOW ordered in 1912,[73] whereas the 22,200 ton Orion class battleship HMS CONQUEROR, ordered in 1910 and completed in 1913, had yielded a net profit of £44,149.

Unlike Dalmuir, Clydebank and Fairfield were largely spared the embarrassment of suffering losses on Admiralty contracts completed before the war: the cruiser HMS BRISTOL at Clydebank and the small survey ship HMS ENDEAVOUR at Fairfield were the only Admiralty contracts on which either yard failed to report a net profit, but an underlying decline in the profitability of naval work was apparent in the outcome of the most important of the naval contracts undertaken by the two yards between 1909 and 1911, those for the battlecruisers HMAS AUSTRALIA and HMS NEW ZEALAND. In both cases the contracts yielded their builders profits, but the net profit of £32,040 earned by Clydebank in building HMAS AUSTRALIA and the net profit of £50,454 earned by Fairfield in building HMS NEW ZEALAND were both more than £90,000 lower than the net profits earned by the same yards in building the battlecruisers HMS INFLEXIBLE and HMS INDOMITABLE some four years earlier. At both Clydebank and Fairfield the decline in profitability as measured by the average percentage contributions to overheads and profit was as marked in the case of Admiralty contracts as it was on merchant work. The detail is in Table 6.5:

**Table 6.5.** Average Percentage Contributions to Overheads & Profit

| CONTRACTS | CLYDEBANK | | FAIRFIELD | |
| COMPLETED | NAVAL | MERCHANT | NAVAL | MERCHANT |
| | (% SALES) | (% SALES) | (% SALES) | (% SALES) |
| 1905–10 | 25.43 | 13.35 | 24.40 | 15.18 |
| 1910–15 | 17.68 | 4.57 | 17.87 | 8.20 |

(Source: Author's figures based on details abstracted from *UCS 1* and *UCS 2*. See Peebles, **thesis**, Appendices FI and FIII)

In retrospect, contemporary commentators were perhaps too ready to accept that the contracting profit margins which characterised the period were attributable wholly to factors beyond the shipbuilders' control. While both the depressed prices which prevailed when work was in generally short supply and the sharp rise in costs of materials and labour which accompanied the ensuing boom necessarily had an adverse effect on the warshipbuilders' profitability, at least one of their number — Fairfield — placed some of the blame on the shortcomings of its own management. Mr. Sampson, the firm's shipbuilding director, tendered his resignation in May 1914 after a board meeting at which reference was made

> to the repeated losses in the shipbuilding department on contracts completed between 1911 and 1914, also to the fact that notwithstanding repeated references by the management no changes had been made in any section of the Shipbuilding Department with a view of improving matters.[74]

Whatever the cause, the problems had not been completely resolved by the outbreak of war in 1914. As the volume of naval work on hand built up, both Clydebank and Fairfield could afford to be more selective in their choice of merchant work and the orders for two steamers for the Russian Steam Navigation Company[75] and for the Union Castle liner LLANSTEPHEN CASTLE, taken by Clydebank and Fairfield respectively in 1912, all yielded their builders contributions to overheads and profit in excess of 15% of selling price, but the improvement in profit margins was achieved at the expense of drastically curtailing the volume of merchant business. Neither yard secured any other merchant orders in 1912 and Clydebank's order for the Orient liner ORMONDE was the only merchant work booked by either yard in 1913. More important, there was no evidence of a corresponding improvement in the profitability of Admiralty contracts. On the contrary, as shown in Table 6.6, the outcome of successive batches of destroyers built at Clydebank suggests that profit margins had not recovered to previous levels by the outbreak of war:

**Table 6.6.** Destroyer Contracts Undertaken by Clydebank

| YEAR LAID DOWN | TYPE | NO. IN BATCH | AVERAGE SELLING PRICE £ | CONTRIBUTION TO OVERHEADS AND PROFIT | |
|---|---|---|---|---|---|
| | | | | £ | % |
| 1908–09 | 'G'Class | 3 | 101,876 | 37,323 | 36.6 |
| 1909–10 | 'H'Class | 3 | 93,524 | 27,826 | 29.8 |
| 1910–11 | 'I'Class | 3 | 85,927 | 18,107 | 21.1 |
| 1911–12 | 'K'Class | 3 | 97,678 | 21,651 | 22.2 |
| 1913–14 | 'M'Class | 3 | 122,872 | 26,951 | 21.9 |

(Source: Author's figures based on detail abstracted from *UCS 1*. See Peebles, **thesis**, Appendix FIII)

Meanwhile, the combination of the unprofitable merchant contracts taken before 1912 and the lower profit margins on Admiralty work necessarily had an adverse effect on the warshipbuilders' profitability. Neither Clydebank nor Fairfield was as profitable in the four years to 1914 as it had been in the previous four years. Fairfield, which had earned trading profits before depreciation averaging £115,872 per annum in the four years to 30th June 1910, reported average trading profits before depreciation of only £68,406 per annum over the following four years, the year to 30th June 1912 resulting in a trading loss before depreciation of £4,013. There is no reason to suppose that Clydebank's experience was different. John Brown & Co.'s shareholders were told that the yard had earned little profit in the year to 31st March 1911[76] and the surviving records show that profits taken on contracts which had totalled £306,172 in the four years to 31st March 1910, when trading profits before depreciation and losses on demolitions etc. are known to have aggregated £350,422, amounted to only £45,860 over the following four years.

To add to their disappointing trading results, neither Clydebank nor Fairfield had much success in securing warship orders from foreign governments. Following an agreement to pool resources with Cammell Laird & Co.,[77] Fairfield was finally rewarded with its first overseas warship orders in 1913–14 but the contracts, on hand at the outbreak of war in 1914, for two Greek destroyers and a Turkish despatch vessel,[78] represented the sum total of the yard's intake of foreign naval work. Under John Brown & Co.'s management Clydebank's record was little better. As with Fairfield, the yard received orders for two destroyers for Greece[79] as a member of the Coventry Ordnance Works Syndicate, but its only other successes were orders for the engines of two Russian battleships completed in 1914-15 and the machinery of a battleship for Chile subcontracted to Clydebank by Armstrong-Whitworth's.[80]

To some extent Clydebank's lack of success could be attributed to a change of policy on the part of major overseas customers. The massive naval expansion programme of which the battleship ASAHI formed part was the last occasion on which the Japanese government made extensive use of British shipyards. By the turn of the century smaller warships were already being built in Japanese yards, the first Japanese-built capital ship followed in 1905, and the battlecruiser KONGO delivered by Vickers in 1913 was the last major Japanese warship built abroad.[81] Similarly, in 1908, when the Spanish government started to make good the heavy losses suffered by the Spanish Navy in the Spanish–American War of 1898, it did so through the agency of its own armaments company, the Sociedad Espanola da Construcion. John Brown & Co. as the heir to Clydebank's connection had a minority share in the new venture but the role of the British participants was to supply equipment and technical expertise.[82] There was little profit for Clydebank in supervising the re-equipment and re-organisation of Spanish dockyards at Cartagena and Ferrol.

More worrying, the dearth of overseas orders for both Clydebank and Fairfield was a reflection of the failure of the Coventry Ordnance Works to overcome opposition from Vickers and Armstrong-Whitworth's. Between them these two firms contrived to prevent the Coventry Ordnance Works from obtaining major Admiralty contracts until 1910,[83] thereby denying the enterprise both the domestic orders which it needed and the official recognition without which it had little hope of securing major overseas naval orders. The participants in the Coventry Ordnance Works Syndicate therefore found themselves in the unfortunate position of deriving little advantage from their investment and of having to support a loss-making enterprise which absorbed upwards of £2 millions of their capital before it became self-supporting.

The problems of the Coventry Ordnance Works bore particularly heavily on Fairfield. Clydebank, as the shipbuilding department of John Brown & Co., was not directly involved but Fairfield, as one of the principals, was faced with the problem of finding the cash to finance its share of the mounting cost. By 1910, after the failure of an attempted issue of debentures by the Coventry Ordnance Works Company Ltd., Fairfield was left in the position of having to subscribe for its share of the unwanted stock.[84] The Fairfield board became alarmed at the strain which the enterprise was imposing on their liquidity but could do little about it. An attempt to dispose of part of Fairfield's holding to Cammell Laird & Co. in 1911[85] came to nothing and the problem of a profitless investment, which accounted for approximately one-third of all the funds employed in the business, remained unresolved in 1914.

Despite the setbacks, neither Fairfield nor Clydebank was in serious difficulties on the eve of the First World War. Unlike Dalmuir, which was becoming a persistent drain on Beardmore's resources,[86] Clydebank's record was a matter of disappointment rather than serious concern to its parent. The yard had not been stinted for funds. Apart from net additions to fixed assets amounting to £571,895, John Brown & Co. had spent more than £90,000 on demolitions and disposals of old plant to make way for improvements and £193,646 in additions to stocks of tools and raw materials in the fifteen years to 31st March 1914.[87] The business was essentially self-supporting as cumulative trading profits before depreciation and losses on demolitions etc. amounted to £1,054,538 by 31st March 1910. At worst, Clydebank was an investment from which John Brown & Co. was deriving prestige more than profit.

Similarly, while Fairfield's decision to pay no dividends on its ordinary shares in respect of 1911-12, 1912-13 and 1913-14 and the omission of any provision for depreciation of Fixed Assets in 1911-12 and 1913-14, together with only nominal provisions of £17,500 in 1910-11 and £7,500 in 1912-13, were symptomatic of the firm's unsatisfactory trading performance, the company was not at risk as long it could meet its obligations to preference shareholders and debenture holders. Following the death of Sir William G. Pearce in 1907, the directors were under less pressure to pay large dividends on the ordinary shares, and distributions had been limited to payments of 2½ percent per annum from 1907-08 to 1910-11. The need for a further issue of debentures, mooted in 1912,[88] had been avoided by the Bank of Scotland's willingness to grant the company a loan on the security of its investments. By June 1914 Fairfield owed its bankers £413,000 but the company's investments amounted to £735,085 and there was no immediate problem so long as the Coventry Ordnance Works situation did not deteriorate to the point where a significant part of Fairfield's total investment of £516,609 in the enterprise became irrecoverable.

Nevertheless, Clydebank and Fairfield had as much reason as any of the Clyde warshipbuilders to be concerned at the situation in which they found themselves in the summer of 1914. Membership of the Coventry Ordnance Works Syndicate had not resulted in a significant number of overseas naval orders, a large volume of first-class merchant work had produced very little profit, and Admiralty work, which had been the backbone of their businesses for twenty years, was no longer yielding the phenomenal returns which had characterised the decade preceding the introduction of the dreadnought. Clydebank and Fairfield were better off than Dalmuir, which had yet to prove that it was capable of operating at a profit, or Scott's, which had yet to prove that a specialisation in submarines was an alternative to conventional warshipbuilding. They still had plenty of naval work on hand, but it was worrying that even the most successful of the Clyde warshipbuilders had not profited greatly from the boom conditions of 1911-1913 as merchant demand was already falling away.[89] If, as seemed probable in the summer of 1914, the Clyde shipbuilding industry was facing another period of depression, then the warshipbuilders might still hope to be kept better employed than most of their neighbours, but they could no longer take prosperity for granted. Twenty years of sustained growth had resulted in the creation of as much warshipbuilding capacity as would ever be needed in peacetime, and it was becoming increasingly difficult to find profitable employment for it all.

NOTES

1. Marder, *From the Dreadnought to Scapa Flow*, Vol. 1, p. 126.

2. *Ibid.*, p. 129.

3. *Ibid.*, p. 137, quoting Lennoxgrove MSS, 'Report to the First Lord on the Navy Estimates 1908–1909' dated 3rd December 1907.

4. *The Times*, 5th May 1906.

5. See Appendix EII.

6. Col. J. M. Denny, MP for Kilmarnock District, 1895–1906.

7. Denny's KING EDWARD, built for Turbine Steamers in 1901 and powered by turbines supplied by Parsons Marine Turbine Co., was the world's first turbine-powered merchant ship. See *The Denny List* (London 1975), compiled by D. J. Lyon, Ship No. 651.

8. Torpedo Boats No. 17, No. 18, No. 29 and No. 30 and the destroyer HMS MAORI.

9. *UCS 1/1/13*, Minutes of Board Meeting, 26th November 1907.

10. The machinery of the light cruiser HMS BOADICEA for Clydebank and the machinery of the battleship HMS BELLEROPHON for Fairfield.

11. Hume & Moss, *Beardmore*, pp. 78–79.

12. Alfred Yarrow, who had been engaged in shipbuilding at Poplar since 1868, had decided that rising costs on the Thames made it necessary for him to move his business elsewhere:

> It is evident that shipbuilding on the Thames is a waning industry and if we imagine that we are cleverer than other people in overcoming adverse conditions we make a mistake; we must move while we still can to some district where shipbuilding is growing and thriving.

In 1906 the firm found a suitable twelve-acre site at Scotstoun on the Clyde and proceeded to lay out a new yard with eight building berths, a covered wet dock and modern machine shops. These facilities compared favourably with those which Yarrow's possessed at Poplar and they had the advantage of being situated in a shipbuilding district where supplies of materials and skilled labour were more readily available than on the Thames. Further they were conveniently sited for speed trials in the deep and sheltered waters of the Firth of Clyde. See E. C. Barnes (Lady Yarrow), *Alfred Yarrow, His Life and Work* (London 1923), pp. 193–4.

Interestingly, after the move, Alfred Yarrow estimated that his costs of production were 12.5% lower on the Clyde than they had been in London. See *Fairplay*, 14th May 1908.

13. Over the years Yarrow's had acquired an international reputation as the builders of the fastest torpedo boats and destroyers. By the time of its move to the Clyde the firm had already supplied over one hundred torpedo boats and destroyers to foreign powers and between 1908 and 1911 the Scotstoun yard produced ten destroyers for Brazil and a gunboat for Portugal (see Appendix EV).

14. *The Glasgow Herald*, Shipbuilding & Engineering Supplement, 31st December 1907.

15. PLATA (Yard No. 329).

16. *The Glasgow Herald*, Shipbuilding & Engineering Supplement, 31st December 1907.

17. QUILLOTA, QUILPAC, HUANCHO, JUNIN and ORCOMA.

18. See Peebles, thesis, Appendix D2.

19. Yard Nos. 368–73, 375–80 and 382.

20. Yard Nos. 392–423.

21. Yard Nos. 438–44, 446–53 and 457–8.

22. *UCS 2/1/3*, Minutes of Board Meeting, 1st August 1907.

23. *UCS 2/1/4*, Minutes of Board Meeting, 15th October 1908.

24. *UCS 2/1/4*, Minutes of Board Meeting, 19th November 1909.

25. See Peebles, thesis, Appendix EIId, 1906–1907 to 1911–1912.

26. Agreement dated 5th October 1909. See *UCS 2/1/4*, Minutes of Board Meeting, 14th May 1913.

27. *UCS 2/1/4*, Minutes of Board Meeting, 24th June 1913.

28. Directors' Report on the Accounts for the Year to 30th June 1908. See *Fairplay*, 10th September 1908.

29. GOLDEN EAGLE.

30. PRINSES JULIANA, ORANGE NASSAU and MECKLENBURG.

31. Yard Nos. 424–9.

32. Conway's *All the World's Fighting Ships, 1906–1921* (London 1985), p. 2.

33. March, *British Destroyers*, p. 103.

34. Some financial provision for the cost of a state-financed old-age pension scheme had already been made in the 1908 Budget. See R. Jenkins, *Asquith* (London 1964), pp. 166–7.

35. Marder, *From the Dreadnought to Scapa Flow*, Vol. 1, pp. 159–69.

36. Statement by the First Lord of the Admiralty explanatory of the Navy Estimates for 1909–1910, *Parliamentary Papers 1909 [Cd4553] LIII 285*, pp. 3–4.

37. Speech of the First Lord of the Admiralty, Mr Churchill, introducing the 1912–1913 Navy Estimates to the House of Commons, 18th March, 1912. *Hansard, 5th series, Vol. XXXV 1912* Col. 1535–7.

38. In addition to the dreadnoughts mentioned above, the battlecruisers HMAS AUSTRALIA and HMS NEW ZEALAND had been laid down at the expense of the Australian and New Zealand governments. See Peebles, thesis, Appendix AI note 3.

39. See Peebles, thesis, Appendix AIIIb.

40. Work 'on the stocks' comprises warships laid down but not launched. Work 'fitting-out' comprises warships launched but not completed. The calendar years in which individual warships were laid down, launched and completed are given in Appendix EII.

41. *The Glasgow Herald*, Shipbuilding & Engineering Supplement, 29th December 1911.

42. *Ibid.*, 30th December 1913.

43. HMS RATTLESNAKE.

44. The market value of investments is taken from a note on the published accounts for the year to 30th June 1909.

45. *The Times*, 15th September 1909.

46. See Peebles, thesis, Appendix EVc.

47. *The Times*, 15th September 1909.

48. *GD 319/5/2/26*, General Statement in support of Proposed New Standard Profits, (c.1915).

49. Directors' Report on the Accounts for the year to 30th June 1910. See *Fairplay*, 22nd September 1910.

50. *The Times*, 3rd August 1910.

51. Directors' Report on the Accounts for the year to 30th June 1910. See *Fairplay*, 22nd September 1910.

52. *Ibid.*

53. 'The London & Glasgow Engineering and Iron Shipbuilding Co. Ltd.', *Fairplay*, 15th June 1911, one of a series of special articles on 'British Shipbuilders'.

54. INDRAGHIRA.

55. HMS LYNX, HMS MIDGE and HMS OWL.

56. *The Times*, 28th February 1912.

57. March, *British Destroyers*, p. 145.

58. *The Glasgow Herald*, Shipbuilding & Engineering Supplement, 30th December 1913.

59. *GD 319/5/2/6*, General statement in support of Proposed New Standard Profits (c.1915). The management appears to have seriously underestimated the impact of the disruption on profitability. In the year to 31st December, 1910 the company took credit for £30,000 on account of the expected profit on the hull of the battleship HMS COLOSSUS. In the event the final profit on the hull was only £11,572.

60. Yard Nos. 431–4, 436–7 and 442–4.

61. Yard Nos. 448–50, 452, 455 and 457–61.

62. Conway's *All the World's Fighting Ships, 1906–1921*, p. 89.

63. S1 (September 1911) and S2 and S3 (June 1913).

64. In 1902 the Admiralty granted Vickers what was tantamount to a commercial monopoly of submarines for the Royal Navy in exchange for its agreeing not to sell submarines to third parties. The Admiralty started building submarines at Chatham Dockyard in 1907 but Vickers' monopoly of contract-built submarines lasted until 1911 when delays in delivery and criticisms of Vickers' designs led to Scotts and Armstrong-Whitworth's being awarded contracts to build submarines of Italian and French design respectively. See Trebilcock, *The Vickers Brothers*, pp. 106–8 and Conway's *All the World's Fighting Ships 1906–1921*, p. 2.

65. Yard Nos. 460 and 461.

66. Full details of all these warships are to be found in Appendix EII.

67. *Engineering*, 18th April 1913.

68. Details abstracted from UGD *100/1/8/8*.

69. See Peebles, thesis, Appendix EIVb.

70. Yard Nos. 496 and 497.

71. Yard Nos. 392, 396–8, 400–1, 403, 408–9, 411, 415 and 417.

72. Yard Nos. 468, 474–6, 478–82 and 484–6.

73. *UGD 100/1/8/14*, Dalmuir Profit and Loss Account for the Year to 31st December 1914.

74. *UCS 2/1/4*, Minutes of Board Meeting, 6th May 1914.

75. Yard Nos. 419 and 420.

76. Directors' Report on the Accounts of John Brown & Co. Ltd. for the Year to 31st March 1911. See *Fairplay*, 6th July 1911.

77. *UCS 2/1/4*, Minutes of Board Meeting, 16th May 1911.

78. The destroyers CHIOS and SAMOS and the despatch vessel RACHID PASHA (Yard Nos. 500, 501 and 502), on the stocks at the outbreak of war in 1914, were taken over by the Admiralty and completed as HMS MELAMPUS, HMS MELPOMENE and HMS WATERWITCH respectively.

79. The destroyers KRITI and LESVOS (Yard Nos 429 and 430), on the stocks at the outbreak of war in 1914, were taken over by the Admiralty and completed as HMS MEDEA and HMS MEDUSA.

80. Yard Nos. 421, 422 and 423. The Russian battleship engines appear to have been delivered in 1915. The Chilean battleship was taken over by the Admiralty and eventually completed as the aircraft carrier HMS EAGLE.

81. Conway's *All the World's Fighting Ships 1906–1921*, p. 234.

82. Conway's *All the World's Fighting Ships 1922–1946* (London 1981), p. 398.

83. Trebilcock, *The Vickers Brothers*, pp. 93–95.

84. *UCS 2/1/4*, Minutes of Board Meeting, 17th February 1910.

85. Ibid., Minutes of Board Meeting, 15th September 1911.

86. By 31st December, 1914 Beardmore's had suffered a cumulative trading loss of £638,088 on shipbuilding since 1900. In addition Dalmuir's net fixed assets totalled £937,281 and a further £453,320 was tied up in stocks and work in progress (all figures abstracted from *UGD 100/1/8/* series).

87. The figure for stocks of tools and materials at 31st March 1914 (£472,885) is given in *UCS 1/38/1*. At 31st March 1899 stocks of tools and materials had been valued at £279,239. See Chapter 5 note 19 above.

88. *UCS 2/1/4*, Minutes of Board Meeting, 11th October 1912.

89. W. R. Scott & J. Cunnison, *The Industries of the Clyde Valley during the War* (Oxford 1924) (part of a series on the Economic and Social History of the First World War), p. 76.

# 7

# The First World War and its Aftermath

The shadow of overcapacity which hung over the Clyde shipbuilding industry in the summer of 1914 was dispelled by the outbreak of the First World War. Although normal trade was disrupted and the United Kingdom's output of merchant ships, which had reached a peak of 1,932,153 gross tons in 1913, slumped to 650,919 gross tons in 1915,[1] the Admiralty needed ships to prosecute the war. It soon became apparent that the Admiralty had made insufficient provision for the large number of small ships required to maintain a distant blockade of Germany and keep the sea lanes round Britain clear of mines. Later the U-boat added an unwelcome new dimension to sea warfare and the Admiralty had to provide for the building of further escort vessels to counter the menace and also for the replacement of heavy losses of merchant shipping. As a result the Admiralty had to augment its normal resources of supply by designing new types of warship which could be built under the supervision of Lloyd's surveyors in yards with no previous experience of naval work.[2] The entire shipbuilding industry was mobilised progressively from 1915 onwards to meet the insatiable demand. By 1917 its resources were stretched to the limit. The mounting losses of merchantmen forced the government to modify its priorities to allow merchant shipbuilding a larger share of the available resources and merchant output recovered from 608,235 gross tons in 1916 to 1,348,120 gross tons in 1918,[3] but the manpower required for warshipbuilding was still rising in the fourth year of the war and yards which had been earmarked for merchant shipbuilding in 1917 were still engaged in warshipbuilding at the end of the war.[4]

Situated as they were on the west side of the country, away from the danger of attack by enemy surface raiders and outside the range of German air attack, the Clyde shipyards were ideally suited for wartime construction and the Admiralty made extensive use of their facilities. According to statistics published by *The Glasgow Herald* in 1918, the district's contribution to the war effort included an output of 481 naval vessels aggregating 759,407 tons in the five years 1914–18,[5] and a further twenty-six warships and fifty naval auxiliaries were launched in 1919.[6] Much of this wartime output was attributable to the six firms which had been involved in warshipbuilding before the war. Although as many as thirty separate firms were listed as having made some contribution to the output, only eight firms produced more than 17,500 tons of naval vessels. One of these — Barclay Curle — credited with thirty-nine naval ships aggregating 47,246 tons, produced only sloops and minesweepers. Another, Harland & Wolff, credited with twelve naval vessels totalling 27,405 tons, had resumed warshipbuilding in the London & Glasgow's Govan yard to produce six destroyers and three monitors in 1915–16, only to return to merchant shipbuilding as soon as the opportunity presented itself.

The remaining six — Clydebank, Fairfield, Dalmuir, Scott's, Denny's and Yarrow's — were the pre-war warshipbuilders. Indeed, apart from the warships built by Harland & Wolff and eighteen destroyers ordered from Alexander Stephen & Son, these six yards were responsible for virtually all of the conventional warships[7] built on the Clyde during the war. In the five years 1914–18 they were credited with 70.5% of the tonnage of all naval vessels launched on the Clyde and 86.6% of the horsepower attributed to them, a record which was only partly attributable to the inclusion of warships ordered before the war.[8] As shown in Table 7.1, the six firms had been the recipients of Admiralty orders for a total of 248 warships aggregating 469,526 tons during the war itself:

**Table 7.1.** Wartime Admiralty Orders for Conventional Warships

|  | HULLS | | ENGINES | |
| --- | --- | --- | --- | --- |
|  | NO. | TONNAGE | NO. | H.P. |
| CLYDEBANK | 47 | 144,205 | 48 | 1,442,950 |
| FAIRFIELD | 49 | 137,615 | 49 | 1,295,800 |
| DALMUIR | 35 | 60,750 | 35 | 606,380 |
| SCOTT'S | 31 | 48,662 | 31 | 645,780 |
| DENNY'S | 39 | 45,340 | 37 | 774,430 |
| YARROW'S | 47 | 32,854 | 47 | 705,200 |
| ALL OTHERS | 37 | 62,445 | 28 | 495,500 |
|  | 285 | 531,971 | 275 | 5,966,040 |

(Source: Abstracted from Appendix EIII)

Clydebank's share comprised two battlecruisers, one aircraft carrier, three light cruisers, thirty-seven destroyers, three submarines and a depot ship. Fairfield had orders for two battlecruisers, five light cruisers, twenty-nine destroyers and thirteen submarines. Dalmuir had an aircraft carrier, two light cruisers, nineteen destroyers, and thirteen submarines. Scott's were entrusted with three light cruisers, nineteen destroyers, eight submarines and a monitor. Denny's were asked to build a small aircraft carrier, three flotilla leaders, twenty-seven destroyers and eight submarines. Yarrow's accounted for twenty-nine destroyers, one submarine, sixteen river gunboats and a small depot ship.[9]

None of the six yards was a free agent during the war. Fairfield, Clydebank and Dalmuir all became Admiralty-controlled dockyards on the outbreak of war and the other three yards were subject to Admiralty direction from the passing of the Munitions of War Act in 1915 if not sooner.[10] In consequence they were allowed to undertake very little merchant shipbuilding. A few merchant ships, which were at an advanced stage of completion when the Admiralty took over, were finished during the war, most notably the 14,850 ton Orient Liner ORMONDE at

Clydebank, but other merchant ships under construction were taken over on the stocks and converted to naval use. The Lloyd Sabaudo liner CONTE ROSSO, on the stocks at Dalmuir at the outbreak of war, finished up as the aircraft carrier HMS ARGUS; at Fairfield the 15,300 ton AVENGER was completed as an armed merchant cruiser. Further, apart from a few 'standard' cargo ships laid down in 1918,[11] no new merchant ships were laid down in the three big naval yards during the war. By 1918 a number of yards, including Alexander Stephen & Son on the Clyde, which were still engaged in warshipbuilding, were designated to be turned over to merchant shipbuilding as part of planned division of capacity between the Admiralty and the Ministry of Shipping, but the six Clyde yards were numbered among the eleven firms which were to continue to be wholly at the Admiralty's disposal.[12] This did not necessarily mean warshipbuilding, as Dalmuir in particular had been denied a larger share of warship orders to leave room for the production of armaments, tanks and aircraft,[13] but it precluded their undertaking any work of which the Admiralty did not approve.

Being an Admiralty-controlled establishment was not without its advantages. Throughout the war years the warshipbuilders had the highest priority in the allocation of scarce supplies of manpower and materials. At the start of the war workmen were transferred to them from merchant yards[14] and, as late as 1918, Sir James Lithgow, the Deputy Controller of Merchant Shipbuilding, was still complaining that, despite the fact that additional manpower had only been made available to the shipbuilding industry in consideration of the urgency of merchant work, the Admiralty had secured the services of two-thirds of the additional 18,300 men employed in the construction of hulls in the six months to 31st July 1918:

> It is not for me to criticise the policy of the Government in regard to construction for the Navy, but I am entitled to draw attention to the fact that although the Naval authorities had for three years the entire run of the shipbuilding resources of the country they have still considered it necessary to augment the manpower so engaged throughout the whole of the fourth year of the war.[15]

While many of the merchant yards were poorly supplied with work until 1916, the naval yards were assured of a steady flow of work which kept them fully occupied throughout the war. The average numbers employed during the war at Scott's (2,345 in the shipyard and 1,974 in the engine works) and in Denny's shipyard (2,266) were lower than the numbers employed by these firms at the height of the pre-war boom in 1913 when Scott's employed 5,687 workmen in total and Denny's shipyard 2,622,[16] but the reverse was true of the three major yards. At Clydebank the numbers employed averaged 9,693 over the four years 1915–1918 compared with a pre-war peak of 9,715 in January 1913 and an average of 8,910 for the two years 1912 and 1913;[17] at Fairfield the wartime workforce averaged 9,640 compared with 7,632 in December 1913;[18] at Dalmuir the payroll increased from 5,854 in 1914 to 10,855 in 1917,[19] although in this case most of the increase was probably attributable primarily to the expansion of other activities. During the war Beardmore's had spent £67,181 in laying down fuse-making plant at Dalmuir.

1. HMS *Black Prince* (1860): The revolutionary ironclad which posed major technical and financial problems for her builder, Robert Napier & Sons.

2. HMS *Ramillies* (1892): The battleship built at Clydebank under the terms of the Navy Defence Act of 1889. Note the absence of armament which at this date was invariably added in one of the Royal Dockyards.

3. *Asahi* (1899): The biggest warship ever built on the Clyde for a foreign government. Built at Clydebank, the armour plate was supplied by John Brown & Co., which took over the yard while the ship was under construction.

4. HMS *Arab* (1901): The early destroyer designed and built at Clydebank which never achieved its design speed despite numerous speed trials.

5. HMS *Leviathan* (1901): One of the succession of fast armoured cruisers which provided Clyde yards with a plentiful supply of profitable naval work between 1896 and 1907.

6. HMS *Carnarvon* (1903): The last warship built in Robert Napier & Sons' old yard at Govan, which had been leased by William Beardmore & Co. pending construction of a new yard at Dalmuir.

7. HMS *Inflexible* (1907): This battlecruiser was the first of the new dreadnoughts to be laid down on the Clyde.

8. HMS *Repulse* (1916): One of the pair of battlecruisers ordered from Clyde yards after the outbreak of war in 1914 and delivered in less than two years.

9. HMS *Hood* (1918): Perhaps the most famous warship ever built on the Clyde. Seen here leaving John Brown's Clydebank yard. The only one of four new battlecruisers ordered by the Admiralty in 1916 to be completed, she proved to be the last battlecruiser ever to be built for the Royal Navy.

10. HMS *Berwick* (1926): The first of seven cruisers built in Clyde yards in the late 1920s, when new naval construction, now limited by the terms of the Washington Treaty, finally resumed after the war.

11. HMS *Galatea* (1934): Built by Scott's of Greenock. The first cruiser to be laid down on the Clyde in six years.

12. HMS *Mallard* (1936): One of the smaller warships which provided much needed work for a number of Clyde yards recovering from the Depression of the early 1930s.

13. HMS *Ashanti* (1937): An artist's impression of one of eight Tribal class destroyers built on the Clyde under the naval rearmament programmes which started in 1935.

14. HMS *Ceylon* (1942): The last cruiser to be laid down on the Clyde before the outbreak of war in 1939.

15. HMS *Implacable* (1942): When laid down at Fairfield in 1939, she was the first purpose-built aircraft carrier to be constructed on the Clyde.

This work was subsequently transferred to Anniesland but, up to 1917, the Admiralty used part of Dalmuir's facilities to manufacture aircraft and airships, and the Ministry of Munitions spent £261,196 equipping Dalmuir for the manufacture of howitzers and field guns.[20] As shown in Table 7.2, nearly 40% of Dalmuir's total overhead recovery was imputed to these activities by 1917 although the proportion dropped to 30% in 1918, following the transfer of the manufacture of aircraft and airships to Inchinnan:

**Table 7.2.** Overhead Recovery at Dalmuir 1915–1918

| YEAR | TOTAL OVERHEAD £ | AIRCRAFT ETC. £ | MUNITIONS £ | TOTAL NON-SHIPBUILDING £ | % |
|------|------|------|------|------|------|
| 1915 | 248,251 | 43,048 | 11,576 | 54,624 | 22.0 |
| 1916 | 382,682 | 50,944 | 59,437 | 110,381 | 28.8 |
| 1917 | 494,383 | 46,654 | 144,178 | 190,832 | 38.6 |
| 1918 | 650,749 | Nil | 195,621 | 195,621 | 30.1 |

(Source: Detail abstracted from *UGD 100/1/8/15*–18)

Most important of all, the high level of war work was extremely profitable. From the beginning of the war the Admiralty had abandoned its peacetime system of competitive tender and, apart from a brief period in 1916 when, at the insistence of the Public Accounts Committee of the House of Commons, some contracts were placed at a fixed price,[21] all wartime naval contracts were on a 'time and line' basis. In the long run, the use of what was effectively a cost-plus system may not have been in the best interests of the firms concerned, as it necessarily encouraged wasteful and inefficient practices which were not conducive to economical production after the war, but in the short run it eliminated any possibility of unprofitable contracts. None of the four big yards lost money on a single order taken after the outbreak of war and most contracts yielded a contribution of between twenty and thirty percent of the invoice price.

The combination of high output and profitable contracts made the war years a period of great prosperity. Provisions for Excess Profits Tax, introduced in 1915 to prevent firms from profiting unduly from the national emergency,[22] absorbed a large proportion of the profits but, even so, the warshipbuilders earned high profits in the five years to 1919. In the five years to 30th June 1919, Fairfield's trading profits before depreciation amounted to £1,910,555. In the five year to 31st December 1919, Scott's reported trading profits before depreciation totalled £975,288. There is no record of the profit earned by Clydebank in these years but the records which are available show that profits taken on contracts in the five years to 31st March 1919 amounted to £1,105,495 and, at that stage, John Brown & Co., which had always been more conservative than Fairfield or Scott's in anticipating profits on uncompleted contracts, had not yet taken credit for any part of the profit earned in building the battlecruiser HMS HOOD (£214,108), the light cruiser HMS ENTERPRISE (£44,046), three destroyers (£19,642) and two sets of warship engines (£9,044).[23] Even Dalmuir, which had never managed to earn a satisfactory profit in peacetime, was profitable under wartime conditions. Despite the fact that some of the munitions work had been transferred to Parkhead at cost, Dalmuir was credited with having earned trading profits before depreciation amounting to £1,569,177 in the five years to 31st December 1919.

The high profits were not accompanied by further large expenditure on the expansion of shipbuilding capacity. Fairfield was exceptional in spending £384,334 on net additions to fixed assets in the five years to 30th June 1919. At Dalmuir, much of the expenditure of £398,443 nominally attributed to the shipyard and engine works in the five years to 31st December 1918 appears to have been associated with the production of aircraft, airships and tanks.[24] At Clydebank and Scott's, where net additions to fixed assets other than houses amounted to £79,379 and £87,967 respectively in the five years to 1918–19, expenditure was lower than in the five years preceding the outbreak of war. The modest level of capital expenditure required was partly a reflection of the extent to which the major yards had equipped themselves for warshipbuilding before 1914. It also partly reflected the character of wartime demand. Unlike the pre-war period when the demand for big armoured ships required heavy expenditure on large berths, on heavy lifting equipment and on capacious wet docks, wartime programmes were dominated by the demand for large numbers of relatively small warships. While some of the yards, most notably Fairfield and Dalmuir, had to be equipped to build submarines (a specialisation which had previously been confined to Scott's on the Clyde), and while, in the last year of the war, Clydebank, Fairfield and Dalmuir all received sanction for extensions and improvements including measures to expedite production in inclement weather,[25] the Admiralty's needs were largely served by making intensive use of existing facilities. When regard is had to the heavy wear and tear to which plant and machinery was subjected during the war, it is possible to maintain that the rates of depreciation allowed by the authorities were less than generous and that the war years may have witnessed an erosion of the warshipbuilders' real fixed capital stock. As a corollory they were spared the cost of adding substantially to their capacity with corresponding advantage to their liquidity.

The impact of high profits and relatively modest capital expenditure on the financial situation of the warshipbuilders is apparent from the balance sheets of the two major yards — Fairfield and Scott's — which were independent corporate entities. Even after providing £1,106,000 for taxation and paying dividends of 7.5% in 1915 and 1916 and 10% in each of the following three years, Fairfield's retained profits, including transfers to reserve, amounted to £170,296 in the five years to 30th June 1919. Allowing for provisions for depreciation and amounts written off pre-war investments, total retentions amounted to £531,073. The full benefits of these retentions were not reflected in the company's balance sheet at 30th June 1919. The Admiralty was slow in settling its accounts and bank loans net of cash on hand had only fallen from £408,467 in June 1914 to £269,792 in June 1919, but the underlying financial situation had been improved out of all recognition. The high wartime demand for armaments had solved the liquidity problems of the Coventry Ordnance Works, and by 1916 Fairfield had been repaid all of its loans which had amounted to £157,450 in June 1914.[26] Meanwhile the company had financed an outlay of £384,334 in additions to fixed assets and there had been a qualititive improvement in its investments as the holding of Canadian Northern Railway's debentures, which had stood in the books at £222,750 in June 1914, had been sold off and investments at 30th June 1919 consisted principally of a holding of £190,000 of 5% of War Loan purchased in 1917. The transformation which the war had created in the warshipbuilders' finances was even more apparent from the balance sheet of Scott's. Bank borrowings had all been repaid by 1917. By 31st December 1919 there was cash on hand of £104,321, the company had an investment of £50,625 in War Loan and, including wartime provisions which would never be needed, reserves and retained profits amounted to £528,373.

That the strength of the warshipbuilders' balance sheets at the end of the war was to be of critical importance in enabling them to survive the depressed conditions which prevailed in the shipbuilding industry for much of the inter-war period did not become apparent until some years after hostilities had ended. In the immediate aftermath of the war the warshipbuilders were more concerned to deploy their resources to take advantage of the post-war boom in merchant shipbuilding. By comparison with other yards which had been turned over to merchant production during the war, the warshipbuilders were at a disadvantage in still being almost totally committed to naval work when the war ended, but most of them were able to face the prospect of having to resume merchant shipbuilding with relative equanimity.

During the war it had been impossible to provide for the replacement of all the merchant tonnage which had been lost. Such capacity as could be spared for merchant shipbuilding had been reserved for the production of cargo ships. The heavy wartime losses of passenger liners still remained to be made good at the end of the war and owners had taken the precaution of reserving capacity on the understanding that work would begin as soon as circumstances permitted. All three major warshipbuilding yards on the Clyde emerged from the war with big passenger liners on order. Clydebank had orders on hand for the 19,800 ton Union Castle liner WINDSOR CASTLE and for the 16,000 ton Canadian Pacific liners MONTCALM and MONTCLARE. Shortly afterwards, Cunard, which had booked a large berth for ten years and a smaller berth for five years,[27] exercised its option by placing orders for the 20,000 ton FRANCONIA and the smaller ALAUNIA. Fairfield, with firm orders for six big passenger liners,[28] two each for Canadian Pacific, the Anchor Line and the Anchor Donaldson Line, was even better placed. With more than 100,000 tons of merchant orders on hand, the firm's merchant order book was larger than it had been at any time for more than thirty years. Dalmuir was in an equally happy position. Apart from the order to replace the liner CONTE ROSSO, taken over by the Admiralty for conversion to an aircraft carrier in 1915, the firm had a further order to build the 18,765 ton liner CONTE VERDE for the Lloyd Sabaudo Line. In addition Cunard had placed an order for the 16,243 ton liner TYRRHENIA, the Anchor Line had booked space for the 16,297 ton CAMERONIA and there were also orders on hand for two 14,000 ton refrigerated cargo liners for the Commonwealth Dominion Line.[29]

Downriver at Scott's and Denny's, the size and quality of the order books were less impressive but here too there was no shortage of work and both firms could look forward with confidence to the resumption of long-established merchant connections which had been interrupted by the war. Only Yarrow's, with no tradition of merchant shipbuilding and faced with the problem of finding suitable merchant work for a yard specifically designed to build destroyers, was put at a serious disadvantage by the absence of naval work. Although Yarrow's suffered no more than other Clyde warshipbuilding yards from the cancellation of naval orders after the Armistice,[30] it was the only one where the announcement of the cancellations was reported to have met with protests from the workforce.[31] For the rest it was a matter of disengaging themselves from war work as quickly as possible.

As soon as the Armistice was signed the Admiralty moved quickly to suspend work on all warships under construction 'to permit of increasing the production of merchant shipping'.[32] The first cancellations followed in December 1918 but it was some months before decisions were reached on how to proceed with all of the contracts on hand at the end of the war, and some of the warshipbuilders chafed at the delay. In January 1919 the Fairfield board decided to communicate with the Admiralty,

> protesting against the war ships now on hand being dealt with as stand-by jobs thus delaying the laying down of merchant ships

and asking in particular for a decision on the battlecruiser RODNEY.[33] Ordered in 1916 as one of four ships intended to make good the losses suffered at Jutland, the RODNEY had been standing idle in Fairfield's biggest berth since 1917, when work had been halted to free resources for small warships and merchantmen which were more urgently required. Eventually, in February 1919, the Admiralty decided to scrap the RODNEY[34] and it became one of forty-three Clydeside orders for conventional warships cancelled by the Admiralty after the war.[35] Work on other orders, including the RODNEY's sister ship HMS HOOD at Clydebank, carried on without much sense of urgency and the warshipbuilders were not entirely clear of Admiralty work until 1920. In the long run the resulting delay in resuming merchant work probably worked to the warshipbuilders' advantage, but in 1919 they were more concerned to be free of Admiralty control so that they might devote themselves wholeheartedly to the task of post-war reconstruction.

Faced with the prospect that naval work would be in relatively short supply for some years to come, the warshipbuilders prepared themselves as best they could to expand their merchant output. Beardmore's, which had most reason to doubt its ability to attract a sufficient volume of first-class merchant work under normal conditions, sought to augment Dalmuir's product range by securing a share of the promising market for tankers and diesel engines. After first acquiring a licence to use the Isherwood system of longitudinal framing employed in the building of tankers[36] and entering into an agreement with the Italian Tosti Company for the joint development of a heavy diesel engine,[37] the Beardmore board formally authorised the expenditure of £260,000 on the construction of four new berths, specifically designed for the building of tankers and cargo vessels.[38] Fairfield, which had embarked on the development of a similar new West Yard in January 1919, moved in the same direction, its membership of the Northumberland Group providing access to Doxford's proven diesel-engine technology.[39] On the other hand, expenditure on additions to fixed assets was on a relatively modest scale when account is taken of the inflationary conditions of the time. Excluding expenditure on non-shipbuilding activities at Dalmuir, the net outlay on additions to fixed assets in the four big naval yards amounted to only £1,165,638 in the five years to 1924.[40] Much of the money which was spent was devoted either to changes made necessary by the switch to peacetime production, such as the widening of berths designed for narrow-beamed destroyers to accommodate broader-beamed merchantmen, or to replacing worn-out plant, improving material handling and generally rearranging the layout of yards with a view to more efficient production. As Sir Thomas Bell reminded the John Brown board, in recommending a programme of capital investment at Clydebank estimated to cost £174,000 in October 1919:

> It is only too apparent that when in the course of another eighteen months prices for ships and engines are once more only obtainable after severe competition only those firms equipped with every type of labour saving appliance and the most advantageous arrangements for transport of materials can hope to hold its own.[41]

The situation in 1921 was to be much worse than Bell or anyone else could have envisaged in 1919. All of the warshipbuilders' post-war attempts to make a success of merchant shipbuilding were doomed to fail, but until 1920 there was no reason to take a pessimistic view of the prospects. To have failed to have made any provision for capital investment would have left them open to the charge that they had missed out on a favourable opportunity to exploit the situation.

As in the rest of the shipbuilding industry, the warshipbuilders suffered their share of the interminable labour disputes and the chronic shortages of manpower and materials which hampered post-war production. In September 1921 Bell remarked on the difficulties which Clydebank had encountered in building the Canadian Pacific liner MONTCALM:

> We have experienced every conceivable form of trouble during the construction of this vessel. To begin with shortage of men, then shortage of steel, then a strike of shipyard platers for a couple of months followed by a rail strike which again completely upset our steel and coal deliveries and finally the joiners' strike which lasted within a week of nine months.[42]

Faced with these problems, many managements made costly mistakes, particularly in acting on the assumption that steel would continue to be in short supply. Fairfield paid a heavy price for having entered into onerous long-term contracts for the supply of steel at the height of the post-war boom;[43] Beardmore's,

Denny's and Yarrow's all had reason to regret their decision to buy out the existing owners of steelworks at premium prices when in due course demand turned down and steelmaking ceased to be a profitable business.[44] None of this was apparent in 1919–20. Even John Brown was buying steel from America to overcome the shortage.[45] The demand for ships was buoyant, cost was no obstacle as long as owners were happy to place orders at cost-plus prices, and securing access to supplies of a scarce commodity was essential if firms were to honour their existing commitments.

By May 1919 John Brown's connection with Lord Pirrie had resulted in Clydebank receiving contracts for the hull of the 9,500 ton LOCH KATRINE for the Royal Mail Line and for four 7,000 ton vessels for the Elder Dempster Line.[46] In consequence it was reported that there were ships under construction in all of the yard's eight berths, 'a condition of matters which has never existed before in the history of the yard'.[47] By 1920 Fairfield's order book had been topped up with orders from its new associates in the Northumberland Group including four tankers for the Globe Shipping Co;[48] Dalmuir had secured orders for five tankers and two small diesel-powered cargo ships;[49] Scott's, which had emerged from the war with relatively few merchant orders on hand, had booked two 10,000 ton passenger and cargo liners for Lloyds Royal Belge, three more large ships for Donaldson Brothers, two 7,000 ton merchantmen for South American owners and no less than five orders each for Alfred Holt and the China Navigation Co;[50] Denny's, which had also secured the contracts for two 10,000 ton liners for Lloyds Royal Belge,[51] was well supplied with work and even Yarrow's was having some success in securing merchant orders with contracts for two small cargo boats, four coastal vessels and a number of shallow-draught river boats.[52]

Success came easily in the boom conditions of 1919–20 when berths were at a premium and owners were prepared to pay any price to renew their fleets and make good wartime losses as quickly as possible so that they might share in the post-war boom in trade. The outlook for merchant shipbuilding began to look much less promising once the wartime losses had been replaced, a condition which was broadly satisfied within two years of the end of the war. By the end of 1920, when it was reported that there was insufficient work for all the ships in existence,[53] there was little demand for new ships and such orders as were still available looked increasingly unattractive in relation to costs of production which had been on the increase since the outbreak of war in 1914. After six years, during which inflation had raised costs of production to more than four times the level of 1914,[54] the downturn in demand, coupled with the deflationary policies adopted by the government in the spring of 1920,[55] made the shipbuilding industry's existing cost structure untenable. A reduction of costs became a matter of necessity, but all costs were not equally responsive. While the price of steel ship-plates, which had reached a peak of £26 per ton in May 1920, fell to £10.10/- per ton by November 1921 and the price of steel sections, which had reached a peak of £25.10/- per ton in May 1920, likewise fell to £10 per ton by November 1921,[56] reductions in the industry's wage rates were the subject of protracted negotiations between managements and unions and the first round of cuts in wages was not implemented until the autumn of 1921.[57] With the open-market price of a new 7,500 ton deadweight cargo steamer slumping from an all-time high of £258,750 in March 1920 to £82,500 a year later,[58] tenders for new work became hopelessly uneconomic and there was no alternative but to lay off men as existing order books ran out. By the autumn of 1921 Yarrow's, which required a continuing flow of new work to keep going, had been forced to close its yard altogether until such times as 'conditions enable business to be carried on with some chance of success',[59] and even those yards which had large orders on hand were running into serious difficulties.

Under normal circumstances the big yards which specialised in building liners would have been less vulnerable to any downturn in demand if only because it took time before they felt the effect of the shortage of new work; in 1920–21 conditions were far from normal. Once the inflationary expectations which had fuelled the post-war boom began to evaporate, owners not only declined to place new orders but also became reluctant to proceed with cost-plus contracts for ships for which there was no prospect of finding profitable employment in the foreseeable future. In consequence the major Clyde warshipbuilders, in common with other liner builders, faced a spate of cancellations and stoppages of work in the winter of 1920–21. Several important contracts had been suspended or cancelled by the end of 1920. In September Fairfield was negotiating with the Houlder Line on its suspension of an order for two ships;[60] in December both Scott's and Denny's suffered from Lloyd Royal Belge's decision to cancel all its outstanding orders.[61] More seriously, by the spring of 1921 stoppages of work had reached epidemic proportions as some owners were running out of money and the most dependable of customers realised that it was to their advantage to defer the completion of cost-plus contracts until such times as the intense deflationary pressures were reflected in lower costs of production. By May 1921 Lloyd Sabaudo had halted work on the liner CONTE VERDE at Dalmuir,[62] the Anchor Line had ordered the suspension of work on its two liners at Fairfield,[63] Anchor Donaldson having already indicated that it was unable to proceed with one of its two ships,[64] and at Clydebank, where Cunard had first threatened to stop work on its orders 'in view of the high costs of shipbuilding and the disappointingly slow delivery' in the spring of 1920,[65] work on both the Cunard liners had been stopped.[66]

The stoppage of work on so many major contracts caused their builders acute embarrassment but there was very little they could do as they were powerless to force customers to honour their contractual obligations without running the risk of outright cancellation and a probable loss of goodwill. Temporary stoppages were preferable to outright cancellations. It was always possible that work might be resumed at a later date, and in any event there was nothing to be gained by releasing berths for which there was no other work. In consequence the leading warshipbuilders found themselves in the unusual situation that, although they had plenty of work on hand, very little of it was proceeding normally. Scott's and Denny's managed to keep going on the strength of the loyalty of their regular customers, but the situation facing Clydebank in May 1921 was typical of the state of affairs which prevailed in the three big yards in the spring of 1921. Lord Pirrie had stopped work altogether on the hull of the LOCH KATRINE and slowed down the completion of the last two ships for Elder Dempster;[67] it was feared that work would shortly be suspended on the tanker INVERGORDON, ordered in May 1920;[68] meanwhile, work was at a standstill on the two Cunarders and the management could only hope that Canadian Pacific would agree to continuing with their two liners which were at a relatively advanced stage of completion.[69]

Under these circumstances managements had little room for manoeuvre and, barely two years after the end of the war, the warshipbuilders found themselves laying off men and struggling with the painful task of cutting overheads to a level compatible with the greatly reduced volume of output. Doing so was extremely difficult. At Clydebank, where charges had been cut by one-third by May 1921 with a further seven or eight percent to follow when reductions in wages became effective,[70] management found that by October 1921 labour on contracts was down to £18,000 per week, less than half of what it had been a year earlier and only 75% of the amount required to support even this reduced level of charges.[71]

Against this background the success of Clydebank, Fairfield and Dalmuir in winning the contracts for three of the four new battlecruisers ordered by the Admiralty in October 1921[72] was a most welcome development. While there was, as yet, no reason to suppose that the demand for merchant ships would not revive once the necessary action had been taken to reduce costs of production, the receipt of major naval contracts appeared to herald a decisive turn for the better. Apart from providing immediate relief, it appeared that the major warshipbuilders would have less need for merchant work in future since the orders for the battlecruisers promised to be only the beginning of many post-war naval contracts. In 1920 the Government had formally abandoned its commitment to maintaining a Two Power Standard,[73] but its avowed purpose was that the Royal Navy should remain the equal of any other navy in the world and, with both the United States and Japan in process of building modern battle fleets,[74] the replacement of Britain's ageing fleet of battleships and battlecruisers was becoming unavoidable. While a large number of modern light cruisers, destroyers and submarines had been built during the war, the light battlecruisers HMS REPULSE and HMS RENOWN and the 41,200 ton battlecruiser HMS HOOD were the only capital ships to have been added to the fleet as a result of wartime building programmes, and the Admiralty had yet to make good the battlecruisers lost at the Battle of Jutland let alone begin to modernise its existing fleet of capital ships.

Unfortunately, from the point of view of the warshipbuilders, the need to provide for the building of a large number of new capital ships was obviated by the Washington Naval Treaty of 1921. It secured parity with the United States and a margin of superiority over Japan in terms of both capital ships and cruisers without the need for the expenditure of large sums on new construction. Indeed, the treaty expressly provided for the cancellation of the four battlecruisers already on order and limited Britain to building no more than two battleships of up to 35,000 tons standard displacement over the next decade.[75] At a stroke of the pen all prospect of naval programmes containing a large number of new capital ships had disappeared. What remained of the pre-war armaments industry, which had prospered by supplying armour plate, heavy ordnance and large gun mountings, suffered a crippling blow and special subsidies had to be paid to a nucleus of firms to keep any of the capacity in existence.[76] Meanwhile thc warshipbuilders had to adjust to a long-term contraction in the demand for warships which they had never envisaged.

A policy of arms limitation suited Britain's straitened economic circumstances. The war had left a crippling national debt, the success of deflationary policies demanded that there should be drastic cuts in government spending, and a renewed arms race was something which Britain could ill afford. In 1921 the government had given in to the Admiralty's request for the resumption of naval construction with great reluctance. Since the end of the war the emphasis had been on reducing naval expenditure. To this end the Admiralty had first been instructed to plan on the basis that they would not be required to fight a war with another major power for at least ten years[77] and then persuaded to accept a one-power standard with a corresponding reduction in the size of the fleet,[78] but the naval estimates had continued to run at levels which the politicians considered to be unacceptable in peacetime. The Geddes Committee on National Expenditure, set up to make recommendations to cut government spending in the light of the 'present and prospective position of the Revenue', agreed with them. In its first report, published in December 1921 while the Washington Conference was still in progress, it pointed out that:

> The estimates provide that in the year 1923, the fifth year after the Armistice was signed, with a broken and exhausted Europe and with no German menace, we are to have far greater fighting power, with a larger personnel, and a greater preparation for war than ever before in our history. ... the Admiralty have clearly given the deepest thought to the production of a thoroughly equipped force to meet immediately any possible naval contingencies. Their plans seem to us to take too little account of the period of peace which they have been instructed to anticipate and of the present serious financial condition of this country.[79]

In fact the Cabinet had only agreed to provide £2 millions for the replacement of 'obsolete ships' after members of a Cabinet committee, set up in December 1921 to examine the Admiralty's case, had concluded that to delay laying down new capital ships would not only adversely affect Britain's prestige but would also mean that Britain would be at a disadvantage in any negotiations with the United States on arms limitation.[80]

For Clydeside, which suffered the loss of contracts which would have provided employment for some 18,000 men in the months ahead, the timing of the Washington Treaty could hardly have been worse, and news of the cancellation of the contracts was reported to have caused 'something approaching consternation'.[81] While no-one rejoiced at a decision

> which will probably mean a spell of continued idleness for many thousands of men who would otherwise have found employment,[82]

the principle of arms limitation met with general approval. The views of the local business community were reflected in an editorial in *The Glasgow Herald* which saw

> the real interest of the country and of the working population in particular being better served by the general stimulus in trade ensuing on reduced naval estimates than by transitory and unproductive employment created by a naval building programme.[83]

Politically the use of warshipbuilding to provide relief commanded little support. In contrast to the pre-war period, when large naval programmes had enjoyed bipartisan support and a Conservative opposition had used unemployment as an additional justification for building more warships,[84] the opposition Labour Party now regarded any expenditure on armaments as wasteful. A 'Scottish Labour Manifesto' published on November 22nd 1921, three days after the news of the cancellation, pointed out that the decision spelled 'economic distress and starvation to thousands of working men' but it also dismissed the building of battleships as 'waste and folly' and implied that the government was remiss only in having failed to provide 'alternative and socially necessary employment'.[85]

Both the armaments manufacturers and the warshipbuilders were placed in a difficult situation. While arms limitation was inimical to their interests and even a popular newspaper such as *The Daily Record* remarked on the particular problem facing the shipbuilding industry when 'the proportion of warshipbuilding upon which the shipyards relied in former times will no longer be available',[86] there was no prospect of reversing the decision. Raising the issue merely drew attention to their predicament. William Beardmore, now Lord Invernairn,[87] in his speech to the Annual General Meeting of William Beardmore & Co. Ltd. on 13th December 1921, was careful to balance a criticism of government policy in general with reassurances that the company's prospects did not depend on armaments alone:

> I think the Government would be well advised to consider economies and greater economies which could be effected on other items of expenditure, which do not by their very nature give anything like the employment which would be afforded by a naval programme ... I do not desire to see a continuance of the exhausting policy of competition in armaments between nations, but I do think we cannot afford to allow our naval supremacy to be lowered to any degree. ... In the present depressed state of trade, the suspension of these orders is naturally a matter of serious importance to this company but I should point out that the spirit of economy underlying the suspension of these orders — if extended to other items of national expenditure — will release funds for expenditure on ordinary commercial products for the manufacture of which the resources of this company are even more suited, as our principal business is that of steel manufacturers, forgemasters, shipbuilders and engineers. I think it desirable to draw attention to this fact as the impression appears to be current that the manufacturing facilities of this company are mainly for the production of armaments.[88]

Under the circumstances there was little else an armaments manufacturer could say, but acceptance of the inevitable could not disguise the fact that the armaments industry had suffered a major blow. For warshipbuilders in general the outlook was not quite as bleak, as the Washington Treaty did not forbid the construction of cruisers of less than 10,000 tons or the replacement of smaller warships but, without capital ships, the larger warshipbuilding yards in particular faced an uncertain future and it remained to be seen whether they could survive and prosper on the limited amount of naval work which would be available. At best, their past history suggested that it would be an uphill struggle, and the conditions which they were to face in merchant shipbuilding were to be worse than the most pessimistic could have anticipated. In 1921 there was still room for hope; it was not until the experience of the 1920s had shown that merchant shipbuilding could not compensate for the lack of naval orders that there was a belated acceptance of the fact that arms limitation was incompatible with the preservation of all of the warshipbuilders' capacity.

## NOTES

1. *Report of the Committee on Industry and Trade, Vol IV, Survey of Metal industries* (H.M.S.O. 1928), p. 402.
2. E. T. d'Eyncourt, *A Shipbuilder's Yarn: The Record of a Naval Constructor* (London 1948) pp. 198–9.
3. *Report of the Committee on Industry and Trade*, Vol. IV, p. 402.
4. *UGD 49/35/71*, List of Yards designated for Merchant Shipbuilding.
5. *The Glasgow Herald*, Annual Trade Review, 28th December 1918.
6. See Appendix A.
7. I.e. excluding types of warship expressly designed to be built in yards with no previous experience of warshipbuilding.
8. The Clyde's output of warships during the First World War was made up as follows:

| YARD | NO. | TONS | H.P. |
|------|-----|------|------|
| CLYDEBANK | 47 | 155,153 | 1,563,500 |
| FAIRFIELD | 43 | 136,270 | 1,157,570 |
| DALMUIR | 69 | 118,080 | 634,290 |
| SCOTT'S | 33 | 52,099 | 651,350 |
| YARROW'S | 48 | 37,554 | 613,900 |
| DENNY'S | 46 | 36,456 | 666,900 |
| | 286 | 535,612 | 5,287,510 |
| OTHERS | 195 | 223,795 | 814,820 |
| | 481 | 759,407 | 6,102,330 |

(Source: *The Glasgow Herald*, 28th December 1918).

9. See Appendix EIII for details.
10. Scott & Cunnison, *The Industries of the Clyde Valley during the War*, p. 76.
11. Fairfield Yard Nos. 536–7, 541 and 542–3 and Clydebank Yard Nos. 468–71.
12. *UGD 49/35/71*, List of Yards reserved for Naval Work.
13. Hume & Moss, *Beardmore*, pp. 132–3.
14. Scott & Cunnison, *The Industries of the Clyde Valley during the War*, p. 86.

15. *UGD 49/35/71*, Draft Letter from James Lithgow to Lord Pirrie dated September 1918.

16. The figures for Scott's are given in *The Glasgow Herald*, Annual Trade Review, 28th December 1918. Those for Denny's are taken from figures abstracted from *UGD 3/12/6* and kindly made available to me by Prof. R. H. Campbell.

17. Taken from figures abstracted from *UCS 1/52/1-6* and kindly made available to me by Prof. R. H. Campbell.

18. *The Glasgow Herald*, 28th December 1918.

19. *Ibid.*, p. 8.

20. See Peebles, thesis, Appendix EIVd.

21. J. D. Scott, *Vickers: A History* (London 1962), pp. 128-9.

22. Excess Profits Duty applied to all profits in excess of a notional pre-war 'standard'. Levied initially at a rate of 50%, the duty was raised to 80% in 1917, cut to 40% at the end of the war and raised again to 60% in 1920 before being finally abolished in 1921. See S. Pollard, *The Development of the British Economy, 1914-1967* (London 1962: revised edition London 1969), p. 64. Owing to protracted arguments over the computation of 'standard' profits and the allowances to be made for depreciation, the amount of some firms' liabilities was not finally determined until long after the war, and provisions made in company accounts during and after the war were not always required in full. In 1928-29 the final settlement of Fairfield's tax liabilities released provisions amounting to £333,796. See Peebles, thesis, Appendix EIIa.

23. HMS VENOMOUS, HMS VERITY and HMS VETERAN and the engines for HMS SESAME and HMS EAGLE.

24. See details of additions to fixed assets in *UGD 100/1/1/15-18*.

25. Fairfield received approval for the expenditure of £78,700 on a new berth, a new ironworkers' shed, a new sawmill and sundry other improvements in December 1917; Beardmore's received approval for the expenditure of £92,500 on buildings 'to cover shipyard workers in wet weather' in January 1918; Clydebank received approval for the expenditure of £49,223 on the extension of a berth-covering gantry in February 1918. See *UGD 49/35/71*.

26. *UCS 2/31/8*, Coventry Ordnance Works Loan Account.

27. *UCS 1/21/138*.

28. EMPRESS OF CANADA and MONTROSE; TUSCANIA and TRANSYL-VANIA; ATHENIA and LETITIA.

29. LARGS BAY and ESPERANCE BAY.

30. See Peebles, thesis, Appendix CIIIa.

31. *The Glasgow Herald*, 31st March 1919.

32. *UCS 2/1/5*, Minutes of Board Meeting, 27th November 1918.

33. Ibid., 22nd January 1918.

34. Ibid., 5th March 1918.

35. See Appendix D.

36. *UGD 100/1/5/2*, Minutes of Board Meeting, 11th February 1920.

37. *UGD 100/1/8/19*.

38. *UGD 100/1/5/2*, Minutes of Board Meeting, 11th February 1920.

39. William Doxford & Co., the Sunderland shipbuilders, had successfully developed an oil engine before the war. In the post-war period, the firm was described as 'the most successful oil engine manufacturers in this country and the only company really able to compete with continental Engineers'. See Dougan, *The History of North East Shipbuilding*, p. 115.

40. Fairfield £320,221; Clydebank £322,229; Dalmuir £357,789; and Scott's £165,399. See Peebles, thesis, Appendices EII, EIII, EIV and EV.

41. *UCS 1/5/18*, Board Paper, 25th October 1919.

42. *UCS 1/5/20*, Board Paper, 29th September 1921.

43. See Chapter 9 below.

44. In 1920 Beardmore's joined with Swan Hunter's to purchase the Glasgow Iron & Steel Co. for £1,500,000. Denny's and Yarrow's (along with Alexander Stephen & Son and the Campbeltown Shipbuilding Co.) were members of the syndicate which took over the Steel Company of Scotland in the same year. See Hume & Moss, *Beardmore*, pp. 171-2. For the losses incurred by Stephen's on its part of the investment in the Steel Company of Scotland, see Chapter 10, note 31 below.

45. *UCS 1/5/19*, Board Paper, 19th September 1920.

46. *UCS 1/5/18*, Board Paper, 29th May 1919.

47. Ibid., Board Paper, 25th October 1919.

48. Yard Nos. 602, 604 and 609-10.

49. Yard Nos. 621-5 and 618-19.

50. Yard Nos. 503-19.

51. Yard Nos. 1135-6.

52. *Yarrow & Co. Ltd., 1865-1977*, p. 49.

53. *The Glasgow Herald*, Annual Trade Review, 30th December 1920.

54. *UCS 1/5/19*, Board Paper, 29th June 1920.

55. Pollard, *The Development of the British Economy*, p. 215.

56. P. L. Payne, *Colvilles and the Scottish Steel Industry* (Oxford 1979), p. 148.

57. Jones, *Shipbuilding in Britain*, p. 182.

58. *Report of the Committee on Industry and Trade*, Vol. IV, p. 406.

59. *The Glasgow Herald*, 13th August 1921.

60. *UCS 2/1/5*, Minutes of Board Meeting, 7th September 1920.

61. *The Glasgow Herald*, 7th December 1920.

62. *Ibid.*, 22nd October 1922.

63. *UCS 2/1/5*, Minutes of Board Meeting, 24th May 1921.

64. Ibid., Minutes of Board Meeting, 12th April 1921.

65. *UCS 1/5/19*, Board Paper, 29th June 1920.

66. *UCS 1/5/20*, Board Paper, 5th May 1921.

67. Ibid., Board Paper, 6th April 1921.

68. *UCS 1/5/19*, Board Paper, 29th June 1920.

69. *UCS 1/5/20*, Board Paper, 5th May 1921.

70. Ibid., Board Paper, 4th May 1921.

71. Ibid., Board Paper, 28th October 1921.

72. The Fourth battlecruiser was to be built by Swan Hunter with machinery subcontracted to Parsons.

73. The announcement that 'The Navy was to be maintained in sufficient strength to ensure the safety of the British Empire and its sea communications against any one other Naval Power' was made by the First Lord of the Admiralty, W. H. Long, in a speech opening the debate on the 1920–21 Navy Estimates. House of Commons, 17th March 1920, *Hansard 5th series Vol. 126*, cols. 2300–01.

74. At the end of the war the United States had sixteen dreadnoughts in commission and three more nearing completion, another sixteen remained to be built under the 1916 building programme and a new building programme, announced in 1919, provided for the building of sixteen more. When all of these ships were completed the United States would possess a larger and more modern battle fleet than Britain, thirteen of whose forty-two dreadnoughts were already considered obsolescent. Marder, *From the Dreadnought to Scapa Flow*, Vol. V, p. 225.

75. The Washington Treaty allowed Britain to build two new capital ships of not more than 35,000 tons 'standard' displacement on condition that four King George V class battleships were scrapped when the new ships were completed. S. W. Roskill, *Naval Policy between the Wars* (2 Volumes: London 1968 & 1976), Vol. 1, p. 331.

76. In November 1923, following representations by the armaments manufacturers, the Admiralty agreed that all armour-plate manufacturers should receive a maintenance allowance, but the total amount paid was limited to the sum necessary for maintaining three

firms only. Hume & Moss, *Beardmore*, p. 194 (quoting PRO ADM/116/3351).

77. The 'Ten Year Rule', promulgated by the War Cabinet in August 1919, directed the three fighting services to prepare their estimates on the assumption that no great war was to be anticipated within the next ten years although provision was to be made for the possible expansion of trained units in case of an emergency arising. Roskill, *Naval Policy between the Wars*, Vol. 1, p. 213 (quoting PRO ADM/167/56).

78. See Note 73 above.

79. First Interim Report of Committee on National Expenditure, *Parliamentary Papers 1922 [Cmd1581] IX 1*, p. 7.

80. Roskill, *Naval Policy between the Wars*, Vol. 1, p. 340.

81. *The Glasgow Herald*, 19th November 1921.

82. *Ibid.*

83. *Ibid.* 21st November 1921.

84. Marder, *From the Dreadnought to Scapa Flow*, Vol. V, p. 156.

85. *The Glasgow Herald*, 22nd November 1921.

86. *The Daily Record*, 19th November 1921.

87. William Beardmore, created a baronet in 1914, took the title Baron Invernairn of Strathnairn on his elevation to the peerage in 1921.

88. *The Glasgow Herald*, 14th December 1921.

# 8

# *1921–1929: Arms Limitation*

While the slump in demand which began in 1920 appeared to have reached bottom at the end of 1922, when there were under construction in the whole of the United Kingdom only 331 ships aggregating 1,617,045 tons,[1] the anticipated recovery was slow to materialise. In 1923 production was severely disrupted by a prolonged dispute with the boilermakers.[2] Although there were some signs of recovery in 1924, prices were reported to be 'poor' and much of the output on the Clyde consisted of arrears of work carried forward from 1922 and 1923.[3] Trade continued to be depressed in 1925 and recovery was further delayed by the coal strike in 1926. Thereafter the situation improved and 1927, 'a year of absolute shipyard peace',[4] and 1928 were years of relative prosperity for the shipbuilding industry, but even in 1928 the Clyde's output of 604,611 tons was below the levels achieved in the boom years of 1911–1913 and 1919–1920, and a rise in the proportion of the industry's workforce unemployed from 20.6% in January 1928 to 32.6% in November 1928 heralded the beginning of another downturn in demand.[5] Against this background the warshipbuilders had little chance of finding sufficient merchant work to compensate for the contraction in demand for naval ships but, at least in the beginning, it was possible to believe that the problem was only temporary and that, given time, all would be well. Periods of depression were to be expected in a highly cyclical business; sooner or later the demand for warships would revive, and it was unthinkable that large and well-equipped yards should be closed down on account of some temporary difficulties when years of prosperity had given them the means to survive a prolonged period of unprofitable trading.

Ironically the commitment to naval work, which had delayed the warship-builders' resumption of merchant work at the end of the war, now worked to their advantage. Despite the fact that deflationary policies were only partly successful and costs failed to return to pre-war levels,[6] the unions were forced to accept drastic reductions in wage rates which were sufficient to persuade owners to resume work on contracts which had been suspended in 1921. At Dalmuir, work on the liner CONTE VERDE restarted in February 1922 with the assistance of loans of £600,000 guaranteed under the Trade Facilities Act;[7] in June 1922 work recommenced on the hull of the FRANCONIA at Clydebank, the resumption being attributed to

> the recent reduction in shipyard wages and the consequent decrease in the costs of construction.[8]

Although, at that time, work was still suspended on the ALAUNIA at Clydebank, and on both the TRANSYLVANIA and LETITIA at Fairfield, all of these liners too were eventually completed. The big post-war order books were not exhausted until 1925, and most of the warshipbuilders were able to maintain a semblance of prosperity for some time after the reality had disappeared.

Dalmuir was exceptional in recording a trading loss before depreciation as early as 1920. In part this reflected provisions for losses on fixed-price contracts and on the need to write down ships being used for development purposes in consequence of the collapse in the market value of second-hand ships, but it also reflected the extraordinary measure of freedom which Beardmore's enjoyed in the preparation of their 1920 accounts. Pending the resolution of the many complex issues arising from wartime contracts with the Ministry of Munitions, the company had not submitted accounts to its shareholders for five years and, as long as average annual profits for the five years to 31st December 1920 were higher than those achieved in 1915, provisions made in 1920 were not going to cause the management any serious embarrassment. Dalmuir's loss of £352,822 before depreciation in 1920 was therefore probably as much a matter of convenience as of strict necessity. There was a spectacular recovery in the profits reported by Dalmuir in each of the two years following, and it was not until 1923 that the yard's fortunes took a permanent turn for the worse. More typically, Scott's accounts showed no signs of any downturn until 1923 and Fairfield's profits held up until 1923–24.

The years immediately following the war had been extremely profitable for Fairfield. Excluding provisions for damages arising from the cancellation of steel contracts, trading profits before depreciation had averaged £250,492 per annum in the three years to June 1922 despite losses on the cancellation of Globe tankers in 1921.[9] The trading profit before depreciation fell to £132,661 in 1922–23 but the year's results were boosted by a credit of £103,161 arising from the final settlement of outstanding Admiralty claims, and the Chairman was able to reflect on the 'satisfactory' nature of the Company's position given the 'unprecedented industrial depression' of the last two and a half years and 'the difficulties which they in common with other shipbuilding concerns had had to face'.[10] Nevertheless the Company had to provide for the loss of its investment in the Northumberland Shipbuilding Co. and the dividend which had been cut to 5% in 1921 was passed for the first time since 1914. A year later the trading profit before depreciation was down to £19,088, and after providing for interest and tax there was a deficit of £21,461.

The key to Fairfield's prosperity in the immediate post-war years was the large merchant orders carried over from the end of the war. Although the Houlder Line had cancelled its order for two ships before work on them had proceeded very far[11] and the Orient Line had not taken up its option on a berth booked during the war,[12] the six big liners which had been on order at the end of the war were all completed. The liners EMPRESS OF CANADA and MONTROSE for Canadian Pacific were completed in 1921–22 and, although work was suspended for a time on three of the four ships being built for the Anchor Line and the Anchor-Donaldson Line and the latter considered cancelling one of its orders altogether,[13] all four were eventually finished, the last of them, the 16,293 ton

TRANSYLVANIA, in 1925–26. Moreover, despite at least two of these contracts being renegotiated on a fixed price basis[14] and a claim for damages on the Canadian Pacific contracts which was settled for £52,049 in 1924–25, all six liners yielded high profits. The details are given in Table 8.1:

**Table 8.1.** Profitability of Fairfield's Post-War Liner Contracts

| WORKS ORDER | VESSEL | INVOICE PRICE | CONTRIBUTION TO OVERHEADS AND PROFIT | |
|---|---|---|---|---|
| | | £ | £ | % |
| 528 | EMPRESS OF CANADA | 2,052,535 | 430,838 | 21.0 |
| 529 | MONTROSE | 1,668,455 | 340,522 | 20.4 |
| 595 | TUSCANIA | 1,449,839 | 307,661 | 21.2 |
| 596 | ATHENIA | 1,043,848 | 236,198 | 22.6 |
| 600 | TRANSYLVANIA | 1,358,696 | 373,992 | 27.5 |
| 601 | LETITIA | 812,305 | 203,202 | 25.0 |

(Source: Author's figures based on detail abstracted from *UCS 2*. See Peebles, **thesis**, Appendix FII)

When these contracts were completed there was no new business to take their place. Apart from relatively small orders from other members of the Northumberland Group, the only new merchant order booked by Fairfield in the five years from the end of the war to the spring of 1924 was the 17,491 ton AORANGI for the United Steamship Company of New Zealand. This ship was technically interesting in being an exceptionally large motorship powered by four sets of Sulzer two-cycle single-acting six-cylinder engines specifically modified to ensure maximum reliability on long voyages,[15] but it yielded a net profit of only £855 and resulted in no repeat business.

Scott's fared better by virtue of its longstanding connections with Alfred Holt and China Navigation, both of whom placed further orders in this period; but Beardmore's, which had no such advantage, succeeded only in attracting orders for one sludge boat and two sets of engines in 1922–23, with the result that by September 1923 the naval yard was completely empty of work and there were only two small ships on the stocks in the new East Yard.[16] Thereafter Beardmore's situation was improved by the receipt of the order for the 24,416 ton liner CONTE BIANCAMANO for the Lloyd Sabaudo Line, and in the course of 1924 the firm was also able to secure orders for three 2,700 ton tankers and a 3,272 ton cargo ship.[17] The improvement did not last and, in 1925, the total order intake again consisted of a single sludge boat.

The difficulties which the warshipbuilders faced in this period are all too apparent from Clydebank's experience. Table 8.2 shows that it too earned high profits on the big liners on order from the end of the war:

**Table 8.2.** Profitability of Clydebank's Post-War Liner Contracts

| WORKS ORDER | VESSEL | INVOICE PRICE | CONTRIBUTION TO OVERHEADS AND PROFIT | |
|---|---|---|---|---|
| | | £ | £ | % |
| 456 | WINDSOR CASTLE | 1,767,380 | 329,085 | 18.6 |
| 464 | MONTCALM | 1,714,064 | 338,845 | 19.8 |
| 465 | MONTCLARE | 1,632,494 | 338,671 | 20.8 |
| 492 | FRANCONIA | 1,559,910 | 296,273 | 19.0 |
| 495 | ALAUNIA | 907,752 | 165,746 | 18.3 |

(Source: Author's figures based on detail abstracted from *UCS 1*. See Peebles, **thesis**, Appendix FIII)

Finding new work to take their place proved to be extremely difficult. During 1922 there were some new orders — a yacht in April, two cable steamers in July 'to provide work for the nucleus of our best and oldest established men'[18] and, towards the end of the year, the long-awaited order for the Orient Line's 19,800 ton liner ORONSAY — but by the spring of 1923 the situation was again desperate. In the hope of securing more work Bell approached Lord Pirrie who had given them to understand that he would require four of Clydebank's eight berths for five or six years after the war.[19] With Harland & Wolff's own yards under-employed and ships lying idle — two of the Elder Dempster ships completed in March 1923 having gone straight to Dartmouth 'to be laid up for an indefinite time'[20] — Pirrie was able to offer no assistance beyond promising to keep Clydebank in mind 'if anything turns up'.[21] With his death in 1924 the personal connection was severed and any hope of relief from that quarter disappeared.[22]

Under these circumstances Clydebank which, until then, had avoided taking hopelessly uneconomic contracts, was forced to consider any opportunity. Even so the options were limited. In December 1923 Bell pointed out that whereas pre-war it had been possible to compete for ordinary cargo ships,

> the difference between our price and that of cheap cargo building firms being constituted by their obtaining in addition to their actual expenditure probably one-third to one-half charges,[23]

these same firms were now quoting for vessels at the bare cost of their labour and material and:

> Firms like John Brown and Company are at a hopeless disadvantage for in the same shop we cannot do the rough type of work that they do and yet maintain the standard of workmanship required for the turbines and gearings for high class passenger vessels and warships and also for diesel machinery.[24]

Clydebank therefore gave up any idea of tendering for ordinary cargo boats with steam reciprocating machinery and concentrated on turbine-driven and diesel-powered ships. Little such work was on offer and, since Clydebank was not successful in securing any of the limited number of naval contracts which were put out to tender between 1921 and 1925, the only new business secured by the yard from the end of 1922 to the spring of 1925 consisted of a yacht, a tanker for H. E. Moss, two 6,100 ton ships for Canadian Pacific, two cross-channel ferries for Great Western Railways, and three sets of engines.[25] Worse still, apart from the yacht on which Clydebank earned a reasonable profit, none of the business taken in this period was profitable and the price of seven of the other eight contracts failed to cover prime cost. The progressive deterioration in the situation is obvious from the analysis in Table 8.3 of the outcome of all the contracts begun by Clydebank from the end of the war to the spring of 1925:

**Table 8.3.** Profitability of Orders Taken by Clydebank 1919–1925

| PERIOD | NO. | INVOICE VALUE £ | CONTRIBUTION TO OVERHEADS AND PROFIT £ | % |
|---|---|---|---|---|
| UP TO MAY 1920 | 16 | 11,576,628 | 2,231,043 | 19.3 |
| JUNE 1920 TO NOVEMBER 1922 | 4 | 1,107,015 | 80,393 | 7.3 |
| NOVEMBER 1922 TO MARCH 1925 | 10 | 1,341,704 | (121,504) | LOSS |

(Source: Author's figures based on detail abstracted from *UCS 1*. See Peebles, **thesis**, Appendix FIII)[26]

In Clydebank's trading accounts the deteriorating profit margin was reflected in the trading profit before depreciation and cost of demolitions etc. which declined steadily from £368,134 in 1919–20 to £76,616 in 1924–25. But for the delays in the completion of the Cunarders and the building of the ORONSAY, it is difficult to see how Clydebank could have recovered any significant part of its overheads in the two years to 31st March 1925. As it was, by the winter of 1924–25 Clydebank was nearing the end of its tether. As early as the summer of 1920 it had been reported that the engine and boiler works were only being kept going by 'a large number of outside orders', including a quarter of a million pounds' worth of work for Kawasaki Dockyard, as

> The present shipbuilding output of Clydebank would not suffice to keep 50% of our engine and boiler capacity going.[27]

By November 1924 the yard's principal ironworks squad had been disbanded as there was no work for heavy frame setters and platers:

> The best of our men are now working in Beardmore's on their new Lloyd Sabaudo Atlantic liner but whenever that work is finished it will be necessary for us to do something to prevent them from drifting out of the district.[28]

In the winter of 1924–25 a decision to lay down a second tanker 'on spec.' saw the yard through the immediate crisis.[29] Hopes of securing an order for two mail steamers were repeatedly deferred. It was not until the spring of 1925, when an order arrived for two 10,000 ton cruisers for the Australian government, that Clydebank's prospects took a turn for the better.

The order for the two cruisers was followed by another for two passenger and refrigerated cargo ships for the Blue Star Line's London and South American service.[30] These ships, on which work started at once, had the more immediate effect on employment in the yard, but, both here and at Fairfield, where an Admiralty order had been received under similar circumstances in the spring of 1924, the resumption of warshipbuilding could not have been more timely. Quite apart from the welcome boost to morale, contracts for big naval ships guaranteed regular work for at least some of the skilled men in the shipyard and engine works for two or three years ahead. More important, the work was profitable. The Australian cruisers yielded Clydebank a contribution to overheads and profit of 16.7% of invoice value (£369,211), and Fairfield, which obtained a contribution of 16.7% from HMS BERWICK, earned 27.5% (£314,367) on a second 10,000 ton cruiser HMS NORFOLK laid down in 1927. Unhappily, such contracts continued to be in short supply. The only other major warship built on the Clyde in the 1920s was the 10,000 ton London class cruiser HMS SHROPSHIRE which was awarded to Beardmore's in 1926, although Dalmuir also had the contract for the machinery of the Dockyard-built cruiser HMS CORNWALL in 1924 and Fairfield supplied the machinery for the cruiser HMS LONDON laid down in Devonport Dockyard in 1926.

Sir Alexander Kennedy, the Chairman of Fairfield's, warned the public of the danger that vital defence capacity would be lost for want of orders:

> It had to be borne in mind that the shipbuilding industry and in particular many shipbuilding firms had been built up on warshipbuilding as well as merchant shipbuilding . . . one of our greatest national assets in the past had been our capacity for adequately meeting all the requirements of our national defence . . . today private firms were finding themselves burdened with equipment and resources capable of meeting naval requirements far beyond any programme of naval shipbuilding that was now or might be for some years to come — if not for ever — likely to be laid down. The scrapping of all that naval capacity would be of most serious moment to the country and yet the deadweight burden of it was a very serious matter indeed to their industry. He did not believe it was unreasonable to ask that the country should view their interest from the point of view of wise insurance.[31]

This was a forlorn hope. There was nothing in the international situation to warrant bigger naval programmes, and as long as governments of both parties remained committed to a policy of arms limitation there was little hope of persuading the public of the need to insure against some remote contingency. The warshipbuilders had an ally in the Admiralty, which shared their interest in preserving naval capacity, but the naval authorities were powerless to do more than distribute the available work as equitably as possible. Even then the Admiralty's room for manoeuvre was strictly limited. While it was able to arrange for the contracts for two destroyers which ought to have gone to Beardmore's on price considerations alone to be switched to Hawthorn Leslie's on the Tyne on account of the higher level of unemployment in that district in 1929,[32] the Controller of the Navy could only note with regret that differences in price ruled out the possibility of awarding any of the destroyer contracts to Yarrow's in 1928 and 1929.[33]

Against this background the warshipbuilders' response to the revival in warshipbuilding was instinctively defensive and an unofficial rota, drawn up with the Admiralty's assistance in November 1926, was the first step towards the formation of the Warshipbuilders' Committee which became the forum for co-ordinating bids and sharing out the work among member firms in the 1930s.[34] In consequence, the shortage of work did not result in ruinous competition for warship orders and, at least in the short run, all warshipbuilding yards were able to stay in business. On the other hand it did not add to the volume of demand and, apart from the five cruisers, the Clyde's share of naval work in the 1920s comprised only two 1,475 ton Odin class submarines laid down at Dalmuir in 1927,[35] four river gunboats aggregating 1,144 tons built at Yarrow's in 1926-27[36] and a total of seven destroyers — Yarrow's 1,173 ton HMS AMBUSCADE, one of two prototypes ordered by the Admiralty in 1924, four 'A' class ships of 1,350 tons each laid down in 1928 (two each by Clydebank and Scott's)[37] and two 1,360 ton 'B' class ships laid down at Clydebank in 1929.[38] Further, the operation of the rota was not entirely successful in raising prices to an economical level. Fairfield lost £1,375 on the contract for the machinery for the cruiser HMS LONDON, Beardmore's thought it necessary to provide £35,252 for losses on the two submarines in 1928 and 1929,[39] and neither Clydebank nor Scott's did well out of their destroyer contracts. Clydebank, which had quoted a price 'as low as prudence would permit', to provide work for its machine shop,[40] suffered a net loss of £9,537 on the contract for the two 'A' class ships. The outcome of the order for Clydebank's two 'B' class ships was rather better, but the contribution to overheads and profit was still only 11.8% (compared with 7.1% on the earlier order) and, although Scott's earned a contribution to overheads and profit of 13.5% on its two 'B' class ships, the result was a net loss of £516.

Under these circumstances no firm could hope to prosper on warshipbuilding alone. Yarrow's, which had reopened its shipyard in 1922, survived by applying its expertise to the manufacture of land boilers. In the 1920s these often represented more than half the firm's production.[41] Beardmore's attempt to find a substitute for munitions work at Dalmuir was less successful, and £241,499 spent on setting up a locomotive department in 1919-21 only added to Dalmuir's problems.

Conceptually Beardmore's locomotive project could not be faulted. Although the firm had no previous experience of the business, Parkhead had made wheels, axles and steel tyres for other manufacturers before the war,[42] the product suited the firm's expertise in heavy engineering and it was hoped to gain some competitive advantage by applying techniques of interchangeability of parts developed in the manufacture of munitions during the war.[43] Unfortunately locomotives, unlike land boilers, suffered from the fatal flaw that demand collapsed once railway companies had replaced their wartime losses and renewed run-down rolling stock and, from 1920 onwards, the industry faced the same combination of depressed demand and excess capacity which plagued the shipbuilding industry. Subventions from a 'locomotive pool' organised to share out the benefits of such contracts as were available brought Dalmuir credits of £34,973 in 1924, £26,104 in 1925 and £30,308 in 1927,[44] but locomotive manufacturing was not a success. Even in 1920-22 there had been losses of £77,389 on locomotive contracts, apparently because two of the first four contracts had been taken at fixed prices to gain a foothold in the market,[45] and according to figures prepared for Securities Management Trust in 1930, the department suffered a trading loss in every year bar one from 1923 onwards.[46]

This failure was all the more serious because, apart from Yarrow's, Beardmore's was the yard which was most vulnerable to the lack of demand for naval vessels. For Dalmuir the order for a single cruiser in 1926 was too little and too late. As Table 8.4 shows, Beardmore's output of merchant ships was broadly comparable with that of the other three big naval yards on the Clyde down to 1927:

Table 8.4. Output of Merchant Ships 1920-27 Inclusive

|  | NO. | HULLS TONNAGE | ENGINES H.P. |
|---|---|---|---|
| BEARDMORE | 28 | 196,955 | 217,595 |
| CLYDEBANK | 27 | 223,251 | 200,900 |
| FAIRFIELD | 17 | 181,090 | 199,700 |
| SCOTT'S | 30 | 176,758 | 126,400 |

(Source: *The Glasgow Herald*, Annual Trade Reviews)

Nevertheless, in the absence of a major warship order, the shipyard remained hopelessly uneconomic. Excluding Head Office charges, trading losses before depreciation amounted to £545,598 in the four years to December 1927. The engine department did rather better with the help of the contract for the machinery of the cruiser HMS LONDON but, here too, there were trading losses in two years out of four and an overall loss of £151,826 in these four years.[47] Losses on this scale could not be sustained indefinitely. Although there was some improvement in 1928, and both the shipyard and the engine department reported trading profits before depreciation in 1929, the year in which the cruiser HMS SHROPSHIRE was completed, Dalmuir's chances of being able to take advantage of the upturn in merchant shipbuilding were not improved by the uncertainties which surrounded the financial stability of Beardmore's even before the appointment of a Committee of Investigation in March 1927.[48]

In some respects Dalmuir was a special case. First, it was said to be at a particular disadvantage in lacking 'co-operative arrangements with lines such as other naval yards have had'.[49] The formal link with Lloyd Sabaudo in which

Beardmore invested £209,375 was of limited value. Judging by the modest profit of £28,057 on the £1,516,378 contract for the CONTE ROSSO, completed in 1922, any business was taken at prices which allowed Dalmuir little if any profit and there were no further orders after the CONTE BIANCAMANO as Mussolini insisted that Italian shipping lines should place their business with Italian shipyards.[50] In addition Beardmore's appears to have lacked the informal links which resulted in other yards being treated as preferred suppliers. Second, Beardmore's commitment to a policy of technical innovation after the war was expensive. While the 1,250 h.p. six-cylinder four-stroke single-acting Beardmore-Tosi diesel engines fitted in the PINZON and PIZARRO in 1922-23 and a modified version supplied to the Blythswood Shipbuilding Company for the SILURIAN in 1924, and also fitted in three 5,000 ton cargo ships built at Dalmuir for Brazilian owners in 1927-28,[51] all appear to have been technically successful, they did not result in repeat orders and Dalmuir's trading results were adversely affected by the losses incurred in their development. In 1920 Beardmore's had taken the opportunity of providing £32,220 against possible losses on the PINZON and PIZARRO, the contracts having been taken at fixed prices,[52] presumably as a means of winning acceptance for new and untried products. Eight years later the contracts for the three Brazilian ships required provisions of at least £75,339 against losses incurred up to August 1928 with the likelihood that a further £20-£25,000 would be needed by the time the ships were completed[53] and, judging by provisions in the 1923 accounts, some £16,000 had been lost on the contract for the engines of the SILURIAN.[54] Third, there is some evidence that Dalmuir remained fundamentally uncompetitive. Despite the opening of the East Yard to facilitate the building of smaller ships, Beardmore's was unable to secure a single tanker order after 1924, and it was indicative of the costs in the big naval yard that the contract for the 20,119 ton Canadian Pacific liner DUCHESS OF ATHOLL, the only major merchant order taken in competition with other Clyde yards after the end of the post-war boom, was reported to have resulted in a loss of £138,000 in December 1928.[55]

Dalmuir was not the only warshipbuilding yard on the Clyde to be plagued with persistent losses once post-war order books were exhausted. Scott's, which had been kept reasonably well employed throughout the post-war slump with a succession of orders from Alfred Holt and China Navigation, finally ran out of profitable work in 1926. In nine successive years from 1925 the Company was to report a trading loss before depreciation and interest. After 1925 Scott's still had first refusal of any business that Holt's and China Navigation had to offer but the work was not plentiful, and as Table 8.5 shows, any orders which were forthcoming were much less profitable:

Scott's also experimented with new forms of propulsion in the hope of augmenting its product range, but with little success. The development of a Scott-still oil engine was abandoned after a prototype had been fitted in Alfred Holt & Co.'s DOLIUS, the engine works having lost £22,287 on the contract.[56] Later, Scott's pioneered the building of diesel–electric powered ships on the Clyde. The tanker BRUNSWICK, completed at Greenock in 1928, was the

**Table 8.5.** Profitability of Selected Contracts Completed by Scott's 1919–1929

| | | 1919–24 | | | 1925–29 | |
|---|---|---|---|---|---|---|
| | NO. | INVOICE VALUE | CONTRIBUTION TO OVERHEADS AND PROFIT | NO. | INVOICE VALUE | CONTRIBUTION TO OVERHEADS AND PROFIT |
| | | £ | £ % | | £ | £ % |
| ALFRED HOLT | 13 | 4,442,185 | 954,773 21.5 | 5 | 1,246,899 | 108,617 8.7 |
| CHINA NAV. | 9 | 1,183,764 | 258,110 24.3 | 1 | 141,778 | 21,173 14.9 |

(Source: Author's figures based on detail abstracted from *GD 319*.

See Peebles, **thesis**, Appendix FV)

largest such vessel yet built anywhere[57] and Scott's subsequently built two more diesel–electric tankers[58] for the same owner — the Atlantic Refining Company — but three tankers made only a marginal difference to the yard's order book.

Apart from the orders from Alfred Holt and China Navigation, the three tankers and the single destroyer order, Scott's orders in the five years 1925–29 were for a succession of modest cargo boats which provided little work and made only a modest contribution to overheads and profit. Unlike some other yards, Scott's appears to have been unwilling to accept orders which made no contribution to overheads. Only one contract failed to cover prime cost, but only six out of twenty-three merchantmen ordered in the five years 1925–29 recovered their full share of overheads, and three of these were for Alfred Holt and China Navigation.[59]

Clydebank and Fairfield were better placed, if only because they had the lion's share of the naval orders placed on the Clyde. Major Admiralty orders came their way when most needed, but, even when the demand for merchant ships revived, they still experienced great difficulty in obtaining sufficient merchant work at remunerative prices. Their difficulties were partly attributable to the lack of demand for the big passenger liners which alone were comparable in work content to a large warship. Since most liner companies had replaced their fleets at the end of the war, and the transatlantic passenger business was adversely affected by the restriction of immigration into the United States,[60] few owners were in the market for additional tonnage. But for Canadian Pacific, the Clyde yards would have been wholly devoid of major passenger liners from the launching of the CONTE BIANCAMANO at Dalmuir in 1924 until the laying down of the QUEEN MARY at Clydebank in 1930.

Canadian Pacific favoured the Clyde yards with a large amount of work. Apart from the 25,800 ton EMPRESS OF JAPAN built by Fairfield and the 42,500 ton EMPRESS OF BRITAIN built by Clydebank, they placed orders for three 18,000 ton passenger and cargo liners and a ferry with Clydebank,[61] three more ferries[62] and the reconstruction of the EMPRESS OF AUSTRALIA and the EMPRESS OF CANADA with Fairfield, an 18,000 ton passenger and cargo liner with Beardmore's,[63] and a 4,000 ton ferry with Denny's,[64] all within the space of five years. Denny's also built one of three 10,000 ton cargo liners ordered from Clyde yards in the same period.[65] Canadian Pacific contracts were, however, subject to competitive tender. As many as nine firms were reported to have been invited to tender for the four 18,000 ton liners in 1926.[66] In consequence, profit margins were at best slight, and in the case of the more prestigious contracts they were non-existent. The contract for the EMPRESS OF BRITAIN yielded Clydebank a contribution to overheads and profit of only £63,485 on an invoice price of £2,130,723, and the £1,268,647 EMPRESS OF JAPAN failed to recover Fairfield's prime costs by £84,395.

The demand for slower liners of the passenger and refrigerated cargo variety was more buoyant and this was the only segment of the market which offered large yards any prospect of obtaining a substantial volume of work at reasonable prices. Here, too, orders were not plentiful and prices were poor. Fairfield, which was reported to have the advantage of receiving all of Bibby Brothers' work without competition,[67] showed a net profit on only the last of the four contracts received in this period,[68] the first three ships yielding an average contribution to overheads and profit of only 8.67% on invoice price. Clydebank, whose definition of 'profit' was less exacting, showed the three 18,000 ton liners for Canadian Pacific as having been profitable although the average contribution to overheads and profit had been only 8.9%. Even in the years 1925-28, when the demand for merchant ships was at its best, Clydebank was able to secure 'profitable' work from only a handful of customers — the Blue Star Line, L.N.E.R., and Canadian Pacific. Additional business could be obtained only at prices which, at best, made little if any contribution to overheads and could end in disastrous losses if anything went wrong, as Clydebank found out when it accepted such a contract from the New Zealand Shipping Company. This contract, in which they had first become interested when the owner's intention had been to build two large 'mail steamers' costing £1.8 millions,[69] eventually turned into an order for three 17,000 tons refrigerated cargo and passenger liners.[70] A combination of a loosely worded contract, confusion over the specification and 'rapacious agents', compounded by a serious miscalculation on the part of Brown's own employees, which resulted in instability and a shortfall of 25% in the specified draught,[71] produced a nightmare contract on which Clydebank failed to recover prime cost by £235,014.

Fairfield's experience was similar, and in this case the company's costing system, which provided for all contracts to be charged with overheads at a predetermined fixed rate proportionate to their direct labour cost, helps to define the problem. First, contracts were costed on a consistent basis and it was easy to identify orders which did not recover their fair share of overheads. Apart from the fourth ship for Bibby Brothers, the only profitable merchant orders taken by the firm in the six years to June 1929 were two 8,000 ton refrigerated cargo liners for the Shaw Savill Line and another of 9,500 tons for the British and Argentine Steam Navigation Co.,[72] all ordered in February 1927. All of the other twelve merchant ships ordered between February 1924 and June 1929[73] resulted in losses, three of the four contracts for Canadian Pacific taken towards the end of the period being accepted at prices which failed to recover prime cost.[74] Second, the use of a fixed rate of overhead recovery resulted in some balance of overhead being left over to be written off to departmental trading accounts at the end of a year, and in every year from 1923-24 to 1928-29 output consistently failed to match up to management's perception of 'normality', leaving overheads under-recovered by a substantial amount:

**Table 8.6.** Overhead Recovery at Fairfield

| YEAR | OVERHEADS £ | RECOVERED £ | % |
|------|------|------|------|
| 1923–24 | 160,296 | 70,529 | 44.0 |
| 1924–25 | 193,842 | 165,018 | 85.1 |
| 1925–26 | 206,942 | 142,588 | 68.9 |
| 1926–27 | 230,023 | 193,509 | 84.1 |
| 1927–28 | 244,267 | 171,258 | 70.1 |
| 1928–29 | 218,309 | 199,757 | 91.5 |

(Source: Details abstracted from *UCS 2/31/10*–11)

While Clydebank and Fairfield were the most successful of the Clydeside warshipbuilders in the 1920s, even they had little reason to feel confident about a future which depended primarily on their success as merchant shipbuilders. It was therefore a matter of serious concern when, in the summer of 1929, the incoming Labour government announced its intention of curtailing naval programmes still further in advance of summoning a conference to negotiate another round of naval disarmament.[75] This move was not entirely unexpected. Clydebank, which had obtained the contract for two 'B' class destroyers in March 1929, had taken the precaution of ordering 'as much material as possible . . . to preclude the possibility of any cancellation of these contracts'.[76] Beardmore's had the misfortune of having work on the submarine HMS ROYALIST suspended and then cancelled and, with the government pledged to do something to ameliorate the situation of the Royal Dockyards which bore the immediate brunt of the cuts,[77] it was all too apparent that the prospects of the private sector obtaining any significant volume of naval orders in the future had taken a marked turn for the worse. This would have been an unappealing prospect at the best of times. Coming as it did at a time when the industry was already experiencing the beginnings of what was to become the worst slump in the industry's history, it was a potentially crippling blow.

By the late 1920s it was generally acknowledged that the shipbuilding industry was suffering from chronic over-capacity. The Committee on Industry and Trade had remarked in January 1928:

> Since the end of 1921 the shipyards of the United Kingdom could have produced the whole of the new tonnage constructed in each year in the world and still not have exhausted their capacity.[78]

By 1929 a Shipbuilding Conference, set up in 1928 to pool tenders and reimburse shipbuilders with the cost of preparing unsuccessful bids, was already contemplating the elimination of surplus capacity, and a sub-committee chaired by Sir James Lithgow was considering how the industry might finance the purchase of any shipyards which went out of business to prevent their being reopened under new management.[79] This scheme, which was to reach fruition with the formation of National Shipbuilders Securities Limited in the spring of 1930, had been conceived as a means of effecting a gradual and orderly reduction in capacity over a number of years. It was powerless to prevent the widespread distress which followed when the industry had to deal with a catastrophic slump in demand and an international financial crisis which destabilised the banking system and brought trade to a virtual standstill.

Under these circumstances the closure of large and well-equipped yards, which would have been unthinkable only a few years before, become unavoidable. It was no longer a question of whether some part of the industry should be sacrificed in the interest of the remainder but how much of it might be saved when, after a decade during which the combination of adverse trading conditions, costly investments and abortive attempts at diversification had taken their toll of their financial resources, few firms in the industry were in any condition to bear the strain of the further losses unaided.

## NOTES

1. *The Glasgow Herald*, Annual Trade Review, 29th December 1922.
2. *Ibid.*, Annual Trade Review, 29th December 1923.
3. *Ibid.*, Annual Trade Review, 30th December 1924.
4. *Ibid.*, Annual Trade Review, 30th December 1927.
5. *Ibid.*, Annual Trade Review, 29th December 1928.
6. In December 1923, when post-war hourly wage rates in the shipbuilding industry were at their lowest, they were still appreciably higher than they had been in July, 1914. In July 1914 the hourly rates for skilled and unskilled men had been 41/4 and 22/10 respectively. In December 1923 the hourly rates for skilled and unskilled men were 48/10 and 38/6 respectively. See Jones, *Shipbuilding in Britain*, p. 181.
7. *The Glasgow Herald*, 12th April 1922. The Trade Facilities Act, designed 'To guarantee the payment of loans to be applied towards the carrying out of capital undertakings or in the purchase of articles manufactured in the United Kingdom', was one of a series of reflationary measures introduced in October 1921 to relieve unemployment, particularly in the shipbuilding and engineering industries. See Green & Moss, *A Business of National Importance*, p. 54.
8. *The Glasgow Herald*, 14th June 1922.
9. See Chapter 9 below.
10. *UCS 2/1/5*, Minutes of Annual General Meeting, 29th October 1923.
11. See Chapter 7, note 60.
12. *UCS 2/1/5*, Minutes of Board Meeting, 20th March 1918.
13. Yard Nos. 595–6.
14. *UCS 2/1/5*, Minutes of Board Meetings, 18th October 1921 and 29th March 1922.
15. *The Glasgow Herald*, Annual Trade Review, 29th December 1923.
16. *Ibid.*, 19th September 1923.

17. Yard Nos. 638 and 641–2 and 637 respectively.

18. *UCS 1/5/21*, Board Paper, 26th July 1922.

19. *UCS 1/5/22*, Board Paper, 10th May 1923.

20. Ibid., Board Paper, 27th March 1923.

21. Ibid., Board Paper, 18th May 1923.

22. Lord Pirrie became a director of John Brown & Co. Ltd. in June 1907 when the latter took a 50% interest in Pirrie's Belfast shipbuilding business Harland & Wolff Ltd. in exchange for 100,000 £1 ordinary shares and 6,000 £10 preference shares in John Brown & Co. Ltd. together with £219,000 in cash. John Brown & Co.'s interest in Harland & Wolff declined after the war but Pirrie remained a director and major shareholder in John Brown & Co. Ltd. until his death. As originally conceived, the union of John Brown's and Harland & Wolff had been designed to provide mutual benefits in the shape of an outlet for the heavy forgings of John Brown's Sheffield works and a secure source of supply of steel and forgings for the Belfast shipyard rather than to provide work for Clydebank but, in the immediate post-war period, Lord Pirrie as head of the rapidly expanding Royal Mail Group found it convenient to use Clydebank's capacity to augment Harland & Wolff's own shipbuilding resources. By 1924, when Pirrie died, this was no longer necessary. Harland & Wolff, which had taken over the London & Glasgow's Govan shipyard before the war, had gone on to acquire five other Clyde shipyards — Caird & Co. (1916), A. Macmillan & Son (1918), A. & J. Inglis (1919), D. W. Henderson Ltd. (1919) and the Ardrossan Dry Dock and Shipbuilding Co. (1920) — and once the post-war boom had ended there was insufficient work to keep them all employed, far less provide work for Clydebank. By the time of Pirrie's death his personal finances were in a chaotic state and Harland & Wolff was in financial difficulties. Pirrie's personal holding of John Brown & Co.'s shares had to be sold off to pay his debts and Lord Kylsant, who succeeded him as Chairman of the Royal Mail Group, had to take personal control of Harland & Wolff in an effort to avert the collapse of the Royal Mail Group itself. See Green & Moss, *A Business of National Importance*, pp. 28, 48, 51 and 62–63.

23. *UCS 1/5/22*, Board Paper, 20th December, 1923.

24. Ibid.

25. Yard Nos. 501–6 and 509–11. (Yard No. 508, the hull of the motorship LOCH KATRINE, was completed in 1922 and is out of sequence, Yard No. 507, the tanker BRITISH DIPLOMAT, was built 'on spec'.)

26. The orders are made up as follows: up to May 1920, Yard Nos. 456, 464–5, 491–6, 508, 519, 596–9 and 644; from June 1920 to November 1922, Yard Nos. 497–500; from November 1922 to May 1925, Yard Nos. 501–7 and 509–11.

27. *UCS 1/5/19*, Board Paper, 28th October 1920.

28. *UCS 1/5/23*, Board Paper, 29th November 1924.

29. *UCS 1/1/2*, Minutes of Board Meeting, 27th February 1925.

30. AVILA and AVELONA.

31. Speech at the launching of the motor vessel TARANAKI on 10th December 1927. *The Glasgow Herald*, 12th December 1927.

32. March, *British Destroyers*, p. 261.

33. *Ibid.*, pp. 253 & 261.

34. See Slaven, 'A Shipyard in Depression: John Brown's of Clydebank. 1919–1938'.

35. HMS OLYMPUS and HMS ORPHEUS.

36. HMS GANNET, HMS PETREL, HMS SEAMEW and HMS TERN.

37. HMS ACASTA and HMS ACHATES by Clydebank and HMS ANTHONY and HMS ARDENT by Scott's.

38. HMS BASILISK and HMS BEAGLE.

39. *UGD 100/1/8/27 & 28*, Dalmuir Profit & Loss Accounts.

40. *UCS 1/5/26*, Board Paper, 19th December 1927.

41. *Yarrow & Co. Ltd. 1865–1977*, p. 52.

42. Hume & Moss, *Beardmore*, p. 63.

43. *Ibid.*, p. 157.

44. *UGD 100/1/8/24, 25 & 27*, Dalmuir Profit & Loss Accounts.

45. L1 and L3. See note in UGD 100/1/8/20, Dalmuir Profit & Loss Account.

46. See Peebles, thesis, Appendix EIVb.

47. Ibid.

48. In June 1926 the Admiralty required Lord Invernairn and Vickers Ltd. to guarantee jointly and severally the due performance of Beardmore's contract for HMS SHROP-SHIRE. See *UGD 100/1/1/3*, Minutes of Board Meeting, 29th June 1926.

49. *The Times*, 9th September 1930.

50. Hume & Moss, *Beardmore*, p. 180.

51. ITAPE, ITAQUICE and ITANAGE.

52. *UGD 100/1/8/20*, Note on Dalmuir Work in Progress.

53. *UGD 100/1/1/3*, Minutes of Board Meeting, 21st August 1928.

54. *UGD 100/1/8/23*, Dalmuir Profit & Loss Account.

55. *UGD 100/1/1/3*, Minutes of Board Meeting, 5th December 1928.

56. In Peebles, thesis, Appendix FV the loss on the engine is included in the outcome of Yard No. 520, but in Scott's accounts it was written off direct to Profit & Loss Account.

57. Walker, *The Song of the Clyde*, p. 54.

58. WINKLER and PERMIAM.

59. Out of Yard Nos. 528-37 and 540-552 which were ordered in this period, only Yard No. 535 failed to recover prime cost but Yard Nos. 529, 531, 548-9 and 551-2 were the only contracts to yield net profits. See Peebles, thesis, Appendix FV.

60. An Emergency Quota Bill, restricting annual immigration from each country to 3% of the number resident in the United States in 1910, was passed by Congress in 1921. As a result of the new statute, total immigration in 1920-21 was reduced from an expected 1,500,000 to 309,556. See D. R. McCoy, *Coming of Age: The United States during the 1920's and 1930's* (Harmondsworth 1973), p. 55.

61. The liners DUCHESS OF BEDFORD, DUCHESS OF RICHMOND and DUCHESS OF YORK and the ferry PRINCESS ELAINE.

62. PRINCESS NORAH, PRINCESS ELIZABETH and PRINCESS JOAN.

63. DUCHESS OF ATHOLL.

64. PRINCESS HELENE.

65. BEAVERBURN. (The other two ships were built by Barclay Curle.)

66. *The Glasgow Herald*, 18th June 1926.

67. *UGD 4/18/59*, Memorandum on the controlling interest held by P. & O. in Alexander Stephen & Sons dated March 1935.

68. SHROPSHIRE, CHESHIRE, STAFFORDSHIRE and WORCESTERSHIRE. Only the WORCESTERSHIRE, completed in 1930-31, yielded a net profit. See Peebles, thesis, Appendix FII.

69. *UCS 1/5/26*, Board Paper, 28th January 1927.

70. RANGITIKI, RANGITATA and RANGITANE.

71. *UCS 1/5/28*, Board Paper, 21st February 1929.

72. Yard Nos. 625, 626 and 629.

73. Yard Nos. 617-20, 622, 630-2, 634, 636 and 638-9.

74. Yard Nos. 632, 634 and 638.

75. On July 24th 1929, as a first step towards further naval disarmament, the incoming Labour government announced that it was slowing down work on the two 10,000 ton cruisers in the 1928-29 building programme. See D. Marquand, *Ramsay Macdonald* (London 1977), p. 503.

76. *UCS 1/5/28*, Board Paper, 21st July 1929.

77. The Labour government had cancelled the 10,000 ton cruisers HMS NORTH-UMBERLAND and HMS SURREY originally allocated to Devonport and Portsmouth Dockyards under the 1928-29 building programme. In the ordinary course this would have involved considerable discharges of dockyard workmen but ministers were anxious to avoid

compulsory discharges and, as an extraordinary measure, orders for two of the five 'C' class destroyers included in the 1929–30 building programme were given to the Dockyards, the first destroyers ever to have built in the Royal Dockyards. See Statement of the First Lord of the Admiralty explanatory of the 1930–31 Navy Estimates, *Parliamentary Papers, 1929–30 [Cmd3506] XX 575*, p. 10.

78. *Report of the Committee on Industry and Trade*, Vol. IV, p. 383.
79. Hume & Moss, *Beardmore*, p. 180.

# 9
## 1929–1934: Financial Crisis

Any lingering hope that the cuts in naval expenditure announced in 1929 would prove to be temporary was dispelled by the outcome of the London Naval Conference in 1930. With the ban on the construction of capital ships extended for another five years and further limitations imposed on the size of other warships,[1] a review of Britain's future naval requirements published in July 1930 spelled out the implications for the future level of demand.[2] A projected five-year building programme containing only three or four cruisers and a maximum of three submarines was barely sufficient to keep the Royal Dockyards employed and, at best, the private warshipbuilders could expect little more than token orders for these types of ship. Destroyer orders promised to be more plentiful, as the building of two flotillas of nine destroyers each per annum was admitted to be necessary to replace the large numbers of destroyers nearing the end of their working lives, but there was no sense of urgency and the 1930–31 programme provided for the building of only one flotilla.[3] In these circumstances the future of the private warshipbuilding industry looked increasingly bleak. The industry could not be sure of receiving orders for more than the machinery of Dockyard-built cruisers and an indeterminate and possibly modest number of destroyers, a volume of work which was hopelessly inadequate in relation to the capacity available. Armstrong's Walker yard[4] had already been put on a care and maintenance basis following the amalgamation of Vickers and Armstrong-Whitworth's armament interests in 1927, but, in the absence of any demand for the larger types of warship, further casualties among the major warshipbuilding yards seemed inevitable. The announcement by Beardmore's of the closure of their Dalmuir yard in September 1930 occasioned little surprise.

William Beardmore & Co. had been in financial difficulties for some time. In retrospect, the company's financial stability had been compromised by its attempt to reduce its dependence on armaments. Embarking on an ambitious programme of expansion and diversification at the end of the war had involved a high level of investment, when costs were at their highest. Together with the outlay involved in honouring contractual obligations to take over armaments plants erected at the expense of the Ministry of Munitions during the war,[5] the post-war expansion imposed intolerable strains on the company's liquidity. When an attempt to raise additional long-term capital failed in 1920, Beardmore's was saddled with a crippling burden of short-term debt which left insufficient room for manoeuvre when trading conditions deteriorated.[6] To compound the difficulties, arms limitation deprived the company of what remained of its most lucrative business and Vickers, which had seen Beardmore's through difficult periods before the war, was no longer in any condition to help.[7] After relations with Vickers were finally severed in 1926,[8] the company kept going for a time with the assistance of its bankers, but a committee of inquiry appointed in 1927 at their insistence was unable to devise a workable scheme of capital reconstruction.[9] By 1929, with the company's bankers refusing to extend it any more credit, Beardmore's was only saved from insolvency by the intervention of the Bank of England.[10]

With the involvement of the Bank of England in June 1929, Dalmuir's fate was effectively sealed. The primary purpose of the Bank of England's intervention was to save Beardmore's main business at Parkhead, and Montagu Norman, the Governor of the Bank of England, had insisted on being given a free hand to dispose of any of the company's other assets before he would agree to provide the capital which enabled Beardmore's to continue trading.[11] Dalmuir, whose abysmal trading record had contributed to Beardmore's plight, was expendable. A report subsequently prepared for the Bank of England's Securities Management Trust showed that on the most favourable interpretation none of Dalmuir's three departments had a satisfactory trading record in the six years to 31st December 1928.[12] Even excluding the costs of operating and selling the WULSTY CASTLE, Dalmuir's share of head-office expenses, and any provision for depreciation, the shipbuilding department had not earned a profit since 1923, the locomotive department had lost money in every year since 1924 and even the engine department, the most successful of the three, had suffered a loss in four years out of six. In all, the losses had amounted to £765,367 and the shipbuilding department alone had cost Beardmore's £526,524 in the space of six years. Following Lewis Ord's appointment as joint managing director in 1928,[13] there was some improvement in the situation, and both the shipbuilding department and the engine works reported trading profits in 1929. The improvement coincided with the building of the cruiser HMS SHROPSHIRE, completed in 1929, and it was unlikely that the improvement could be sustained. There was no prospect of another major Admiralty contract being awarded to the shipyard in the foreseeable future, the demand for merchant ships was again falling, and Beardmore's chances of securing a share of the limited amount of work available could not have been improved by the publicity surrounding its financial difficulties.[14] The engine department with its investment in diesel-engine technology stood a chance of paying its way, particularly if it secured a share of Admiralty contracts for the engines of Dockyard-built cruisers, but the outlook for the shipbuilding department was bleak. In the circumstances, the decision to retain the engine works and close down the shipyard was the only one possible.

Some aspects of the decision to close the shipyard down permanently rather than put it on a care and maintenance basis might have aroused controversy if all the facts had been known at the time. Norman, who had come to believe that the revival of the depressed industries depended on the ruthless elimination of surplus capacity, used Dalmuir to promote the rationalisation of the shipbuilding industry. Anxious to ensure the success of a scheme devised by the shipbuilding industry itself for the retirement of surplus capacity, he had agreed in principle to the sale of the Dalmuir shipyard in November 1929, before all the details of the industry's proposals had been fully worked out.[15] The Bank of England provided National Shipbuilders Securities Ltd. with £300,000 to purchase Dalmuir, pending the raising of a levy on the members of the Shipbuilding Conference.[16] Contemporaries were only in a position to judge the ends and not the means and the permanent closure of Dalmuir aroused little controversy at the time. Newspapers took their cue from Beardmore's press release which blamed the closure on

> the postwar curtailment of warship work and the absence of an adequate volume of the high class mercantile work for which the yard was suitable.[17]

Typically, *The Glasgow Herald* described Dalmuir as 'the victim of changing circumstances' and concentrated on the particular difficulties faced by a yard 'chiefly created for the construction of ships of war':

> Before the war warship work represented twenty-five per cent of the entire British output. Warship work on hand today is little more than one-twentieth of the prewar amount. It is only a fifth of what it was at the end of 1928.[18]

While it was to be regretted that a famous firm was closing down, its closure was in accord with economic realities. No one anticipated that Dalmuir's warship-building capacity would ever be needed again. The permanent closure of unwanted capacity was to be welcomed as a step towards correcting a chronic inbalance between supply and demand which was seen as being the fundamental cause of the shipbuilding industry's problems.

Although Dalmuir was in many ways a special case and none of the other Clyde warshipbuilders had as unenviable a record, neither Clydebank nor Fairfield had reason to be complacent about their own chances of survival if they too should find themselves in similar difficulties. By 1930 both were suffering from the effects of the decline in the demand for warships and both of them were wrestling with problems created by the disintegration of the prosperous pre-war armaments industry.

As at Dalmuir, Clydebank's affairs were inextricably linked with those of a parent whose own fortunes were adversely affected by the decline in the demand for armaments. Although John Brown & Co. had been more circumspect than William Beardmore & Co. in its approach to post-war reconstruction, involvement in the troubled coal and steel industries, coupled with the depressed demand for armour plate, had sapped its financial strength and, by the winter of 1929–30, with the holders of £481,000 of short-term notes unwilling to renew them, it faced a major financial crisis.[19] To overcome its difficulties it was proposed to write down the ordinary share capital by £2,375,000, to raise new capital by the issue of a debenture,[20] and to merge the company's steel interests with those of its Sheffield neighbour Thomas Firth. There was no guarantee that the scheme would succeed; it if should fail, the consequences for both John Brown and Clydebank were incalculable.

Unlike Dalmuir, Clydebank had not drained its parent company's resources.

On the contrary, figures prepared for Sir Thomas Bell, Clydebank's managing director, showed that the yard had generated a positive cash flow of £1,468,163 since April 1919.[21] Further, although on Bell's own figures trading profits before depreciation and losses on demolitions etc. had averaged only £30,515 per annum in the five years to 31st March 1929 compared with an average of £132,686 per annum in the previous five years, the business had consistently produced trading surpluses rather than trading losses. Nevertheless, by the spring of 1930 the mere 125 skilled ironworkers on the payroll was indicative of the state of the yard's order book,[22] and it was an enormous relief when Clydebank secured the contract for the 73,000 ton Cunard liner QUEEN MARY. During the previous winter there was some concern that Clydebank would suffer from John Brown's financial situation, and Bell was worried by the behaviour of Vickers, which seemed intent on competitive underpricing in the hope of securing enough first-class work to justify re-opening Armstrong's Walker yard.[23] In the event, Clydebank's longstanding connection with Cunard and its recent experience of building the EMPRESS OF BRITAIN, the largest passenger liner built in Britain since 1913, told in its favour.[24] Apart from providing Clydebank with much-needed work, the Cunard contract contributed to the success of John Brown's reconstruction which was carried through in the summer of 1930. During the winter of 1929–30 it was suggested that Clydebank's assets ought to be written down to reflect their current earning power. The proposal raised the spectre that the reconstruction of John Brown would fail, as it was pointed out that John Brown's ordinary share capital 'would have to be wiped out completely'.[25] With the timely arrival of the order for the QUEEN MARY, Clydebank's prospects appeared to take a decisive turn for the better. The proposed scheme of reconstruction proceeded according to plan and with its success Clydebank's position became more secure. Thereafter the yard enjoyed a greater measure of autonomy and Bell, who complained that John Brown's had failed to honour a post-war undertaking to put aside a sum, equal to two years' profits at Clydebank, which could be 'drawn on' in future years if the need arose,[26] arranged an overdraft facility of £200,000 with the Union Bank of Scotland.[27] This, together with advanced payments on the Cunard contract, spared Clydebank further financial embarrassment in the difficult years ahead.

While Clydebank's point of maximum danger passed with the reconstruction of John Brown & Co., Fairfield's was yet to come. Paradoxically, its difficulties originated in the post-war resolution of the problem of its investment in the Coventry Ordnance Works. By itself, the decision to discontinue the manufacture of armaments and turn Coventry's facilities over to peacetime production was wholly beneficial, and a merger with Dick, Kerr & Co. and the Phoenix Dynamo Co. to form the English Electric Co. Ltd. in 1919 left Fairfield with £195,000 of ordinary shares in the new company and £96,159 of 4½% debentures in Coventry Ordnance Works Ltd.[28] Although the nominal value of Fairfield's shares in the English Electric Co. was £67,500 less than the amount of its investment in the ordinary shares of the Coventry Ordnance Works, and the reconstruction led to £36,250 being written off in Fairfield's 1918–19 accounts (£31,250 having already been written off in 1914–15), it relieved Fairfield of an investment from which it had derived little benefit over the years. In the absence of major warship orders for foreign governments, part ownership of a major armaments company served little useful purpose. All Fairfield had to show for an investment which had caused it acute financial embarrassment before the war was ordinary dividends of £720 in 1905, £5,937 in 1906 and 1907 and £19,000 in 1918. On the other hand, a mutual interest in the Coventry Ordnance Works had been the bond holding Cammell Laird and Fairfield together, and the dissolution of their joint venture opened the way for Cammell Laird to dispose of its 50% holding in Fairfield. In June 1919 Cammell Laird proceeded to do so. Since the Dowager Lady Pearce's death in 1918 had already released a large parcel of Fairfield shares on the market[29] and the other major shareholder, Trinity College Cambridge, which had fallen heir to Sir William George Pearce's fortune, had begun to dispose of its holding in December 1918,[30] Cammell Laird's action was decisive in giving control of Fairfield to the Northumberland Shipbuilding Co., which emerged as the owners of more than 80% of Fairfield's ordinary shares in December 1919.[31]

In the short run the change of ownership appeared to be in Fairfield's best interest. The company stood to gain little from the maintenance of the connection with Cammell Laird. There was a potential conflict of interest as both firms were likely to be involved in tendering for the same classes of work, including any Admiralty contracts which became available. By contrast, there was no obvious conflict of interest in a group which initially comprised only Northumberland itself, Fairfield and William Doxford & Co.[32] Even after the group was expanded to incorporate Workman Clark & Co., the Belfast shipbuilders, the former national shipyard at Chepstow, which became the Monmouthshire Shipbuilding Co., and the Blythswood Shipbuilding Co., the Clydeside tanker specialists,[33] Fairfield could expect a clear run in tendering for the highest classes of work. Economies of scale in the purchase of supplies of steel were in prospect when contracts covering group requirements were negotiated in March 1920.[34] Other companies in the group also provided Fairfield with work: four sets of engines for Doxford's, the machinery for an oil tanker and for three barges being built at Chepstow and, most important, four tankers for the group's Globe Shipping Company.[35] Four new directors joined the Fairfield board and Robert A. Workman replaced Sir Alexander Gracie as chairman,[36] but there was no indication that the new owners intended to make any significant changes in company policy. The new board authorised the completion of the West Yard extension and the modification of building berths at a cost of £50,171,[37] there was no increase in the dividend paid on the ordinary shares in 1919–20, and the firm continued to accumulate cash. By June 1920, following the sale of the company's holdings of War Loan and Cammell Laird's decision to exercise an option to buy out Fairfield's interests in the English Electric Co. and the Coventry Ordnance Works,[38] the company had no bank borrowings and cash on hand amounted to £310,331.

The flaw in the new arrangements was that the combine was a highly speculative venture whose success depended on a continuation of the post-war boom. The series of deals whereby, in the space of less than a year, Messrs. Sperling & Co.

turned a relatively modest Tyneside firm, the Northumberland Shipbuilding Co., into the lynchpin of a vast shipbuilding combine resulted in the creation of an under-financed and highly geared group, ill-equipped to tackle any reversal in the industry's fortunes.[39] The prolonged slump which followed the ending of the post-war boom was fatal to its chances of success. Of all the members of the group, only Fairfield survived the ensuing débâcle with its credit relatively unimpaired. Northumberland itself ended in the hands of a receiver in 1926.[40] When a new concern, the Shipbuilding Investment Co. Ltd., purchased Northumberland's assets in May 1927, Sir Alexander Kennedy, who had been Chairman of Fairfield since 1923 and was now the designated chairman of the new company, stressed that the prospects of success depended largely on Fairfield and on a new company being formed to operate Northumberland's yard at Howden, since 'the shares of Workman Clark & Co and William Doxford & Co are considered to have no present saleable value'.[41] While Fairfield remained solvent, the Sperling Combine had taken a heavy toll of its financial resources. First, there were the claims arising from the cancellation of the group's orders for steel. These liabilities, which largely arose from contracts with Dorman, Long & Co. Ltd., the Cargo Fleet Iron Co. Ltd. and the South Durham Steel and Iron Co. Ltd., obliged Fairfield to provide £190,000 in the accounts for the year to 30th June 1920 and to make further provisions of £133,740 in the following year. The size of these provisions was discreetly glossed over in the company's published accounts, and payments were spread over a number of years, the profit and loss account being credited with £63,343 on a final settlement in 1928, but, by 1929, when the company quietly wrote off a balance of £22,937 owing by Sperling & Co. in respect of payments made to it for 'guaranteeing' the performance of these contracts,[42] Fairfield was the poorer by £283,334 in total.

Second, there were the losses arising from the cancellation of two of the Globe Shipping Co.'s tankers in 1921. When work on the two tankers was suspended at Globe's request in March–April 1921,[43] the Fairfield board's first concern was to recover the amount Globe already owed,[44] but, since the ships could not be sold and Globe was unable to pay its bills, Fairfield was eventually forced to agree to the outright cancellation of the orders and to allow Globe to settle its outstanding account with six-month bills.[45] Cancellations were common at the time as the most reputable shipping companies were obliged to review their plans in the light of the slump in trade, but these cancellations were unusual in causing losses to the builder. One of the tankers was subsequently completed and sold at a known loss of £17,858 in 1925,[46] and it is probable that total losses were much greater.[47]

Third, there was the difficulty in obtaining payment for the work done for the Monmouthshire Shipbuilding Co. In October 1922 the customer returned a bill for £32,765 in respect of work done on the engines for the oil tanker 'on the grounds that the vessel was unsold',[48] and in January 1923 it was reported that £53,375 was outstanding on the machinery for the three barges built at Chepstow for the Port of London Authority.[49] In this case Fairfield avoided a book loss by taking over the Chepstow yard for £25,000 and writing up its value by £66,349 to cover the outstanding debt. Superficially the deal was good, as the Chepstow yard was valued at £178,750,[50] but Fairfield already possessed more shipbuilding capacity than it could use. Chepstow had no future as a shipyard and its shipbuilding rights were eventually sold in 1937 to National Shipbuilders Securities for £7,500.[51] Although the site was given over to general engineering including the manufacture of railway wagons, Fairfield suffered a trading loss on its operation in every year until 1935.

Finally and most onerous of all, there were the losses suffered in supporting Northumberland itself. In October 1921 Fairfield had been required to subscribe £400,000 to a £5,000,000 issue of 6% non-cumulative preference shares in its parent company.[52] By 1923 the affairs of the Northumberland Group were so precarious that it was deemed necessary to provide in full against its loss.[53] Although a temporary loan of a further £100,000 in April 1922, and part of a further advance of £28,000 in June 1923, were subsequently applied to the settlement of part of Fairfield's share of the Group's steel contracts, a balance of £21,179 had to be written off as irrecoverable when the receiver was appointed at Northumberland in 1926.[54] While Fairfield's management contrived to minimise the damage by offsetting the loss of £400,000 on the Northumberland investment against a surplus provided by revaluing Fairfield's fixed assets which had not been revalued since 1889,[55] the damage was irreparable. Although there was no immediate liquidity crisis, Fairfield had been stripped of all the cash which it had accumulated in its years of prosperity.

One consequence of the Northumberland débâcle was that it became essential for Fairfield to foster an image of stability. With the judicious use of a 'contingency fund', created out of provisions for taxation no longer required, the public had no grounds for thinking that all was not well. Apart from 1923-24, when work was seriously disrupted by the boilermakers' strike, the company's published profit after depreciation and before meeting debenture interest and dividends ranged from £31,724 to £59,105 between 1921-22 and 1928-29.[56] Further, after a four-year period during which the company had only once paid a dividend on the ordinary shares, the directors recommended the payment of a dividend of 5% in each of the three years to 30th June 1929. This was not an accurate reflection of the company's true situation. Profits in the three years to 30th June 1926 had been struck without making any provision for depreciation on the grounds that the company had already made adequate provision by not taking full credit for the surplus arising on the revaluation of fixed assets in 1923.[57] In addition, items which otherwise would have been charged to the profit and loss account were charged to the 'contingency fund', and in the year to 30th June 1929 profits were boosted by drawing on the 'contingency fund' itself. In reality the company's underlying situation was far from satisfactory. Trading profits before depreciation had fallen from £132,661 in 1922-23 to £19,088 in 1923-24, recovered to £100,944 in 1924-25 and then averaged only £49,624 per annum in the four years to 30th June 1929. With debenture interest and preference dividends absorbing £38,750 per annum, this left no room for manoeuvre, and in the year to 30th June 1930 the scale of the losses suffered on the Canadian Pacific contracts made the situation unmanageable. Despite drawing a further £150,000 from the secret 'contingency fund', and omitting any provision for depreciation, the ordinary dividend had to be passed and shareholders' approval sought to borrow up to £500,000.[58] Armed with the requisite authority, the Fairfield board negotiated a cash credit of £300,000 from the Bank of Scotland in March 1931,[59] which enabled it to keep going for the time being, but the outlook became increasingly bleak as Fairfield, like the other Clyde warshipbuilders, faced the worst slump in the shipbuilding industry's history.

The downturn in demand for merchant ships, which had been apparent in 1929, gathered momentum in 1930. The new tonnage launched in the year was only half of what it had been in 1929, the tonnage commenced was only half of the tonnage completed, and unemployment almost doubled, leaving nearly one out of every two shipyard workers on the Clyde out of work.[60] Worse was to follow. In 1931 the tonnage laid down in British yards amounted to a sixth of the tonnage laid down in the previous year[61] and, by December 1931, it was reported that, apart from the great Cunarder on the stocks at Clydebank, the total tonnage under construction on the upper Clyde amounted to only 15,000 tons.[62] At the end of a further year, during which there had been little sign of any improvement in the situation, work was in progress in only 5% of the shipbuilding berths in Britain.[63] Demand began to recover in 1933 but, even in 1934, when output included the QUEEN MARY, the total tonnage of ships launched on the Clyde was still less than half of what it had been in 1929.[64]

Under these circumstances merchant work was virtually unobtainable. Fairfield, which managed to secure orders for only four small pleasure steamers between the summer of 1929 and the spring of 1931,[65] did not obtain any further merchant orders until the autumn of 1934 when it received the contracts for two more pleasure steamers and the 11,660 ton motor vessel DERBYSHIRE for Bibby Brothers. Denny's likewise had only a number of small ferries and pleasure steamers on its books. Scott's total output in 1932 and 1933 was two small vessels for the China Navigation Company.[66] Clydebank, which had received the order for the QUEEN MARY in the summer of 1930, had to wait until February 1934 before obtaining its next merchant order for the Commonwealth and Dominion Line's 8,800 ton refrigerated cargo liner PORT WYNDHAM. Meanwhile work on the great Cunarder itself was at a standstill for two years from December 1931 after Lloyds Bank had refused to join in a guarantee that Cunard would be able to discount three million pounds worth of bills while the liner was under construction.[67]

Up to 1933 the demand for warships was little better. In the three years 1930–32, the Clyde's share of Admiralty work was a single gunboat of 372 tons and two sets of engines for Dockyard-built sloops at Yarrow's,[68] two 1,375 ton 'D' class destroyers at Fairfield[69] and the machinery of the Dockyard-built destroyer leader HMS DUNCAN supplied by Beardmore's. In the autumn of 1930, when Fairfield's work on hand consisted of only three merchant ships aggregating 14,000 tons,[70] its chairman suggested that the government should 'anticipate rather than delay their necessary replacement programme'.[71] His appeal fell on deaf ears. Naval programmes continued to provide for the building of only one flotilla of destroyers each year, and as a result of the financial crisis of 1931, no orders were placed under the 1931-32 programme until the autumn of 1932.[72]

Faced with such exceptionally adverse conditions, the managements of individual firms responded by laying off workers and cutting overheads to the bone, but even the most frugal managements were unable to run their businesses profitably. At Fairfield, where spending on overheads other than depreciation and interest was cut from £244,231 in 1927-28 to £81,877 in 1932-33,[73] the board reported a breakeven situation in the year to 30th June 1931 but only by omitting any provision for depreciation and by drawing a further £15,720 from the 'contingency fund'. Such action could not continue, and in two of the three following years the company was forced to report heavy trading losses. Scott's, which had been operating at a loss since 1924, continued to do so up to 31st December 1933. Clydebank's trading situation deteriorated steadily; trading profits before depreciation of £38,948 in 1931-32 and of £16,187 in 1932-33 were followed by a trading loss of £44,394 in 1933-34. Only Yarrow's, which was kept relatively well employed by destroyer orders for Yugoslavia and Portugal[74] throughout the period, managed to stay in profit.

Falling profits took a heavy toll of what remained of the warshipbuilders' reserves. Denny's had to draw £35,000 from reserve in 1934 alone to keep its profit and loss account in credit.[75] In the same year Clydebank was reduced to the expedient of covering its loss by taking credit for a 'surplus' of £53,000 on its workmen's compensation account, which had stood at £65,748 since 1921. By the winter of 1933-34 some of the leading firms appeared to be heading towards bankruptcy. Scott's, which had used up reserves and retained profits totalling £480,650 in twelve years, had only £15,000 left in reserve in addition to a balance of £3,269 on its profit and loss account at 31st December 1933. At 30th June 1934, Fairfield still had a general reserve of £200,000 dating back to 1920 but, including the surplus on the revaluation of fixed assets in 1923, the company had depleted its resources by £829,370 since 1920 and, apart from the general reserve and a balance of £5,041 on the profit and loss account, all that remained was an amount of £33,237 in the 'contingency fund' which was now a matter of public record.[76]

Illiquidity added to the shipbuilders' problems. Over the years Clydeside firms had evolved a system whereby their working capital requirements were not only kept to a minimum but in some cases trade creditors also provided part of the fixed capital employed in the business. Since it was customary for work-in-progress to be subject to regular payments on account of the work done, and contracts generally provided for debts to be covered by bills which could be discounted, work-in-progress was virtually self-financing and debtors were minimal. In consequence, the amount owing to trade creditors for materials and services tended to be greatly in excess of the amount tied up in current assets which, apart from work-in-progress and debtors, consisted principally of modest stocks of raw materials and loose tools. These arrangements invariably caused problems when trade was depressed. Any reduction in the intake of materials resulting from the contraction in the volume of work in hand was not balanced by a corresponding decrease in the amount tied up in either work-in-progress or in debtors, and any reduction in the stocks of raw materials and loose tools was insufficient to balance the fall in the amount owing to trade creditors. In a period such as the early 1930s, when an exceptionally severe downturn in trade was accompanied by trading losses, the cash outflow assumed astronomical proportions. Fairfield suffered a net cash outflow of £443,351 in the two years to 30th June 1931.[77]

Faced with this situation, the Clyde shipbuilders had customarily been able to rely on their bankers to see them through their difficulties. On this occasion credit was not so readily available. Shipbuilders were no longer good risks, their recovery could no longer be taken for granted, the banks were already over-committed to the depressed industries, and confidence had been badly shaken by the international financial crisis of 1931. Fairfield in particular experienced the greatest difficulty in raising the cash it needed to keep going. After being granted a cash credit of £300,000 by the Bank of Scotland in March 1931, the company met with a frosty response to an attempt to borrow a further £200,000 two years later. 'Owing to their limited resources' the Bank of Scotland felt unable to accede to the request for more credit and Fairfield had to turn to the Bank of England for assistance. It was forthcoming but, before Fairfield was given an advance of £150,000, the Bank of England required the security of a prior charge over the company's heritable property.[78] To meet this condition Fairfield was obliged to repay existing debenture holders a proportion of their investment to gain their agreement to forego their prior claim. The only way the company could raise the necessary £40,000 to do so was to sell to National Shipbuilders Securities the building rights to the West Yard for £30,000.[79] Although Fairfield had escaped being closed down altogether, it had only secured the finance it needed to survive by closing down part of its capacity. It was not an exercise which could be repeated and Fairfield was close to exhausting its credit. It was not alone. Scott's had an overdraft of £87,387 in December 1933 after realising its only marketable security — a holding of War Loan. Clydebank, which had the advantage of Cunard's prepayments to see it through, was spared comparable difficulties. Few shipyards could feel entirely safe.

Against this sombre background, the resumption of naval construction by the Admiralty in the winter of 1932–33 provided all of the Clyde warshipbuilders with a welcome measure of relief. Under the 1931–32 and 1932–33 programmes, Scott's had orders for two 'E' class destroyers[80] and for the 5,220 ton Arethusa class cruiser HMS GALATEA; Clydebank for two minesweepers and two 'F' class destroyers;[81] Beardmore's for the machinery for two Dockyard-built Apollo class cruisers;[82] Fairfield for the 8,750 ton destroyer depot-ship HMS WOOLICH and the machinery for a Dockyard-built destroyer;[83] Denny's for two 'E' class destroyers;[84] and Yarrow's for a gunboat and a destroyer leader.[85] Clydebank, which had been virtually closed down by the suspension of work on the QUEEN MARY in December 1931, was able to reopen its West Yard following the receipt of the order for the two minesweepers in September 1932, and during the winter of 1932–33 their ironwork gave employment to foremen and chargehands for whom the firm had no other work.[86] Most of the others were in a similar situation. Fairfield and Beardmore had no work to follow the naval orders taken in 1931, and for two years running Scott's total output had consisted of a single ship for the China Navigation Co.

Perhaps surprisingly, in view of the state of demand, the naval work was profitable. Despite the intensity of the competition for the two minesweepers, no less than twenty-nine firms being invited to tender for them,[87] Clydebank earned a contribution to overheads and profit of 16.2% on the contract, and no other Admiralty contract undertaken by Clydebank, Fairfield or Scott's at this time yielded a contribution to overheads and profit of less than twenty percent. The success may have owed something to the quality of the labour used and to the attention which could be lavished on these contracts in the absence of other work, but was also a testimony to the growing effectiveness of the unofficial Warshipbuilders Committee in preventing cut-throat competition.[88] Clydebank, which had tendered 'as low as prudence would permit' to secure the order for two 'A' class destroyers in 1927, was paid 10.9% more for two 'F' class destroyers in 1933. In so far as the later ships incorporated an improved hull design and three boiler rooms instead of two, some increase in price could be justified but, in substance, the later ships were little more than enlarged versions of their predecessors and, as shown in Table 9.1, Clydebank's costs were lower than those on two 'B' class boats which had all the advantages of being repeat orders:

**Table 9.1.** Destroyer Prices and Costs at Clydebank

| NO. | CLASS | ORDERED | INVOICE VALUE | MATERIALS | LABOUR | CONTRIBUTION TO OVERHEADS AND PROFIT |
|-----|-------|---------|---------------|-----------|--------|--------------------------------------|
|     |       |         | £             | £         | £      | £                                    |
| 2   | 'A'   | MARCH 1928 | 441,690    | 244,789   | 164,151 | 32,810                              |
| 2   | 'B'   | MARCH 1929 | 437,619    | 245,594   | 138,202 | 54,023                              |
| 2   | 'F'   | MARCH 1933 | 489,996    | 245,194   | 124,852 | 119,950                             |

(Source: Author's figures based on detail abstracted from *UCS 1*.

See Peebles, **thesis**, Appendix FIII)

The problem which faced the warshipbuilders in 1933 and 1934 was that, while the resumption of naval construction was encouraging, the level of demand was insufficient to provide them with more than a leavening of profitable work. During 1933 the volume of naval work on hand in Clyde yards was higher than it had been at any time since the end of the war[89] but the warships laid down as a result of two years' naval programmes still amounted to only 25,716 tons. The 1933–34 programme added a further 21,865 tons to Clyde order books but the work was again shared among six firms. Clydebank had the 9,100 ton cruiser HMS SOUTHAMPTON and a sloop;[90] Fairfield had two 'G' class destroyers and a patrol vessel;[91] Yarrow's had the 1,465 ton destroyer leader HMS GRENVILLE and a netlayer;[92] and Scott's had the 670 ton Shark class submarine HMS SEAWOLF. Alexander Stephen & Sons, with an order for two 'G' class destroyers,[93] and William Hamilton & Sons, with an order for a minesweeper,[94] joined the number of Clyde firms among which the available work had to be shared. In consequence the resumption of naval construction did little more than afford the warshipbuilders a measure of relief. Typically, the chairman of Fairfield's, which had taken orders for the patrol vessel in December 1933 and two 'G' class destroyers in April 1934, had to report a trading loss before depreciation of £16,982 for the year to 30th June 1934. The results had not benefited from the orders received in the latter part of the year and he could only say that the prospects for the current year were 'better'.[95]

Meanwhile firms which found themselves in financial difficulties were still being closed down. Palmer's of Jarrow, which had been in financial difficulties for some time,[96] was finally closed down in the summer of 1934. William Beardmore's engine works which had survived the closure of the Dalmuir shipyard in 1930 suffered the same fate. Although the works had succeeded in securing orders for the machinery of four warships (the destroyer leader HMS DUNCAN and the Apollo class cruisers HMS AMPHION and HMS APOLLO, all built in the Royal Dockyards, and the minesweeper HMS SPEEDWELL, built by Hamilton's), they had attracted no other work. A proposal to merge with Fairfield had been blocked by the other engine manufacturers who objected to the engine works being kept in existence when their interests demanded the elimination of 'suicidal competition.' Accordingly they were closed down under the terms of an agreement whereby a consortium of other Admiralty contractors acting through the agency of National Shipbuilders Securities paid £200,000 for the residual rights.[97]

A surprisingly high proportion of private warshipbuilding capacity survived the years of arms limitation but, without a major change in government policy, further closures appeared inevitable. There was still insufficient Admiralty work to provide employment for all of the warshipbuilding capacity which remained in existence, and by 1934 Admiralty orders on hand were all that stood between several of the leading Clyde yards and insolvency.

## NOTES

1. Apart from extending the ban on the building of capital ships until 1936 and providing for the scrapping of another five dreadnoughts, the London Naval Treaty imposed new quantitative and qualitative limits on cruisers, destroyers and submarines. Numerically Britain's quota of cruisers was reduced from seventy to fifty, their total displacement was not to exceed 339,000 standard tons, and cruisers with guns of over 6.1-inch calibre were limited to a maximum of 146,800 standard tons. Similarly, Britain's quotas for destroyers and submarines, set at 150,000 standard tons and 52,700 standard tons respectively, were subject to added limitations with regard to the sizes of individual ships. No destroyer was to have a displacement greater than 1,850 standard tons and no more than one-sixth of the total displacement tonnage was to consist of ships with standard displacements of more than 1,500 tons: apart from three submarines of up to 2,800 tons, no submarine was to have a standard displacement of 2,000 tons. See Conway's *All the World's Fighting Ships 1921–1946*, p. 3.

2. Statement by the First Lord of the Admiralty explanatory of the Naval Construction Programme for 1930, *Parliamentary Papers 1929-30 [Cmd3620] XX 697*, p. 2.

3. *Ibid.*, p. 4.

4. Armstrong Whitworth's moved its naval yard from Elswick to a new site at Walker-on-Tyne on the eve of the First World War. See Pollard & Robertson, *The British Shipbuilding Industry*, p. 115.

5. In 1920, additions to fixed assets at Dalmuir alone included £252,910 for buildings, plant & machinery taken over from the Ministry of Munitions. See Peebles, thesis, Appendix EIVd.

6. Hume & Moss, *Beardmore*, p. 174.

7. Vickers' own share capital was written down by two-thirds in December 1926. See Scott, *Vickers*, 156-8.

8. Hume & Moss, *Beardmore*, p. 198.

9. *Ibid.*, pp. 202-6.

10. *Ibid.*, p. 210.

11. *Ibid.*, p. 211.

12. See Peebles, thesis, Appendix EIVb.

13. Hume & Moss , *Beardmore*, p. 203.

14. See Chapter 8, note 48 above.

15. Hune & Moss, *Beardmore*, pp. 215-16.

16. *Ibid.*, p. 216.

17. *The Times*, 9th September 1930.

18. *The Glasgow Herald*, 11th September 1930.

19. Grant, *Steel and Ships*, p. 73.

20. *Ibid.*, p. 74.

21. *UCS 1/2/1*, Statement attached to Report dated 23rd March 1931.

22. Ibid., Board Paper, 30th May 1930.

23. Ibid., Board Paper, 28th March 1930.

24. Ibid., Board Paper, 28th March 1930.

25. Ibid., Board Paper, 22nd January 1930.

26. Ibid., Statement attached to Report dated 23rd March 1931.

27. Ibid., Letter from Norman L. Hird, Chairman & General Manager of the Union Bank of Scotland Ltd., dated 29th May 1930.

28. As at 30th June 1919. See Peebles, thesis, Appendix EIIb.

29. *UCS 2/1/5*, Minutes of Board Meeting, 27th November 1918.

30. Ibid., Minutes of Board Meeting, 17th December 1918.

31. Ibid., Minutes of Board Meeting, 9th December 1919.

32. Northumberland was rumoured to have acquired a controlling interest in Doxford's in January 1919. See *Fairplay*, 30th January 1919. On 12th June 1919 the same source reported that Northumberland had 'practically acquired control of Fairfield'.

33. Northumberland owned a majority interest in Workman Clark & Co. by January 1920. Chepstow was purchased from the government on 23rd December 1919. See *Fairplay*, 8th January 1920 and 12th February 1920.

34. *UCS 2/1/5*, Minutes of Board Meeting, 1st July 1920.

35. Yard Nos. 602 and 604-14.

36. *UCS 2/1/5*, Minutes of Board Meeting, 9th December 1919.

37. Ibid., Minutes of Board Meeting, 10th June 1920.

38. Ibid., Minutes of Board Meeting, 12th December 1919.

39. The Balance Sheet of the Northumberland Shipbuilding Co. Ltd. at 30th June 1920 showed that while equity capital amounted to £2,001,346 (£400,000 of cumulative preference stock, £1,500,000 of ordinary shares and a balance of £101,346 on profit & loss account), there were outstanding debentures totalling £2,972,500 and the company owed its bankers £499,752. In addition net loans from associated companies amounted to £3,432,597.

40. *UCS 2/1/5*, Minutes of Board Meeting, 19th October 1926.

41. *The Times*, 21st May 1927.

42. See Peebles, thesis, Appendix EIId.

43. *UCS 2/1/5*, Minutes of Board Meetings, 22nd March 1921 and 12th April 1921.

44. Ibid., Minutes of Board Meeting, 12th April 1921.

45. Ibid., Minutes of Board Meeting, 19th May 1921.

46. *UCS 2/31/10*, Details of Profit & Loss Account for Year to 30th June 1925.

47. Amounts received from Globe and credited to the Shipyard, Engine Works and Boiler Shop Trading Accounts in respect of the two tankers totalled £106,424. In addition, a further £81,926 was received from the Argentinian Naval Commission in respect of the one completed on its account (Yard No. 604). It is difficult to see how these receipts together with the amount written off — a total of £206,208 — could have covered the total cost of the 6,950 ton tanker completed, let alone the costs incurred on the one scrapped. Two *3,900 ton* tankers laid down at approximately the same time (Yard Nos 602 and 609) cost £189,870 and £204,122 respectively in respect of materials and labour only. Including overheads their total finished cost averaged £221,996.

48. *UCS 2/1/5*, Minutes of Board Meeting, 27th October 1922.

49. Ibid., Minutes of Board Meeting, 24th January 1923.

50. Ibid., Minutes of Board Meeting, 3rd September 1925.

51. *UCS 2/1/6*, Minutes of Board Meeting, 11th March 1937.

52. *UCS 2/1/5*, Minutes of Board Meeting, 18th October 1921.

53. The caution was justified. Northumberland's accounts for the three years to 30th June 1923, published in September 1923, showed a debit balance of £390,850 on profit and loss account. Apart from investments in associate companies totalling £8,819,703, net tangible assets of the company amounted to only £259,945 and mortgages and debentures totalling £2,102,341, net loans from associates totalling £267,166 and cumulative preference shares of £400,000 all ranked before 'B' preference shareholders in the event of liquidation. Further, while the auditors were unable to form a definite opinion as to the value of the investments, none of which had an official market quotation, they remarked that given 'the extreme depression in the shipbuilding industry and the fact that in several of the companies there are large issues of debentures ranking before the shares, it would appear that the value of the shares is negligible at the present time'. See *Fairplay*, 25th September 1923.

54. *UCS 2/1/5*, Minutes of Board Meeting, 19th October 1926.

55. The revaluation threw up a total surplus of £583,272 but £35,237 was set aside as a special depreciation account and no credit was taken for £148,035 out of a total surplus of £164,645 on the revaluation of land and goodwill. The amount by which each category of fixed asset was revalued is given in the relevant accounts contained in *UCS 2/31/10*.

56. *UCS 2/5/2*, Published Accounts for the seven years to 30th June 1929.

57. See Note 55 above.

58. *UCS 2/1/5*, Minutes of Extraordinary Annual General Meeting, 10th December 1930.

59. Ibid., Minutes of Board Meetings, 4th March 1931 and 20th March 1931.

60. *The Glasgow Herald*, Annual Trade Review, 30th December 1930.

61. *Ibid.*, article by R. H. Green, President of the Shipbuilders and Engineering Federation, in Annual Trade Review, 31st December 1931.

62. *Ibid.*, Annual Trade Review, 31st December 1931.

63. *Ibid.*, article by J. B. Hutchison, President of the Shipbuilders and Engineering Federation, in Annual Trade Review, 31st December 1932.

64. Excluding the QUEEN MARY, the Clyde's output of 195,121 tons was barely one-third of the level of 565,798 tons achieved in 1929.

65. Yard Nos. 641-4.

66. Yard Nos. 555 and 558.

67. Green & Moss, *A Business of National Importance*, pp. 145-6.

68. HMS FALCON and the engines for HMS MILFORD and HMS WESTON.
69. HMS DAINTY and HMS DELIGHT.
70. Yard Nos. 640 and 643-4.
71. *UCS 2/1/5*, Minutes of Annual General Meeting, 4th November 1930.
72. Roskill, *Navy Policy between the Wars*, Vol. 2, p. 146.
73. The details of Fairfield's overheads in 1927-28 and 1932-33 were as follows:

|  | £ | £ |
|---|---:|---:|
| General Management | 21,682 | 25,358 |
| Wages & Salaries | 54,277 | 13,498 |
| Cleaning, Stocktaking, etc. | 3,829 | 1,048 |
| Heat, Light & Power | 31,253 | 5,416 |
| Moveable Tools | 11,941 | 3,950 |
| Maintenance | 60,984 | 6,755 |
| Carriage | 1,857 | 93 |
| Sundry Stores | 4,523 | 1,357 |
| Trade Subscriptions | 1,524 | 895 |
| Insurance | 25,909 | 5,664 |
| Rates & Taxes | 15,563 | 8,728 |
| Other | 8,799 | 8,629 |
|  | 244,231 | 81,877 |

(Source: *UCS 2/31/11*).

74. Between 1930 and 1933, Yarrow's built three small gunboats for Columbia, the destroyer DUBROVNIK for Yugoslavia and the destroyers LIMA and VOUGA for Portugal. See Appendix EV.

75. See Peebles, thesis, Appendix EVIId.

76. The Chairman revealed the existence of a 'Contingency Fund' at the Annual General Meeting in 1929 but the amount was not stated and the Contingency Reserve was not shown as a separate item in the company's published balance sheet until 1931. See *UCS 2/1/5*, Minutes of Annual General Meeting, 31st October 1929 and company's published accounts for 1928-29, 1929-30 and 1930-31 (*UCS 2/5/2*).

77. In conventional accounting terms, the company's cash flow for the two years to 30th June 1931 was made up as follows:

|  | £ .000 |
|---|---:|
| Trading Loss | -124.9 |
| less: Depreciation | nil |
| Chepstow Loss | —30.3 |
|  | -155.2 |
| Debenture Interest Paid | -47.6 |
| Net Dividends Paid | -34.7 |
| Capital Investment | -7.1 |
| *Net Retentions* | -244.6 |
| Working Capital | -198.7 |
| *Total Cash Flow* | -443.3 |

78. *UCS 2/1/5*, Minutes of Board Meeting, 22nd March 1933.
79. *UCS 2/1/6*, Minutes of Board Meeting, 28th June 1933.
80. HMS ESCAPADE and HMS ESCORT.
81. HMS FOXHOUND and HMS FORTUNE.
82. HMS AMPHION and HMS APOLLO.
83. HMS EXMOUTH.
84. HMS ECHO and HMS ECLIPSE.

85. HMS ROBIN and HMS FAULKNOR.

86. *UCS 1/5/31*, Board Paper, 28th April 1933.

87. *UCS 1/5/30*, Board Paper, 30th September 1932.

88. The unofficial Warshipbuilders Committee was an extension of the Shipbuilders Conference which arranged for the confidential exchange of information on merchant tenders and the imposition of levies to recompense unsuccessful bidders for the cost of preparing tenders. The Warshipbuilders Committee had no official status and, as its activities were politically sensitive, its operations were shrouded in secrecy but there is no reason to suppose that the naval authorities were unaware of its existence. On the contrary it seems likely that the Warshipbuilders Committee was set up with the tacit blessing of the Admiralty which, as has been noted in Chapter 8 above, was party to the earlier rota system introduced in 1926. See Slaven, 'A Shipyard in Depression: John Browns of Clydebank, 1919-1938'.

89. See Chapter 10, Table 10.1, below.

90. HMS ENCHANTRESS.

91. HMS GARLAND, HMS GIPSY, and HMS KINGFISHER.

92. HMS PROTECTOR.

93. HMS GALLANT and HMS GRENADE.

94. HMS SPEEDWELL.

95. *UCS 2/1/6*, Minutes of Annual General Meeting, 30th October 1934.

96. For an account of Palmer's post-war problems, see Dougan, *The History of North East Shipbuilding*, pp. 147-8.

97. Hume & Moss, *Beardmore*, pp. 218 & 235.

# 10
# *1934–1939: Rearmament and Recovery*

In the years leading to the outbreak of the Second World War in 1939 the fortunes of the private warshipbuilding industry took a marked turn for the better as the worsening international situation forced the government to abandon its pursuit of arms limitation and to set about rebuilding Britain's defences by embarking on a programme of rearmament. While the highest priority was accorded to re-equipping the Air Force, which had become Britain's first line of defence, and naval rearmament did not begin in earnest until 1936–37, the decisive turning point came in March 1935 with the publication of a White Paper announcing the National Government's decision to increase spending on defence.

Behind the scenes, the state of Britain's defences had been under review since October 1933 when Germany had announced its withdrawal from both the Geneva Disarmament Conference and the League of Nations. Up to October 1933 the National Government, in common with its Labour predecessor, had been prepared to turn a blind eye to deficiencies in Britain's defences in the mistaken belief that civilised nations would never again resort to war as an instrument of national policy. The uncomfortable example of Japan's invasion of Manchuria in September 1931 was largely ignored. Following that event the Cabinet had reluctantly acceded to the Chiefs of Staff's request for the cancellation of the 'Ten-Year Rule',[1] but this was never intended to be more than a gesture. In 1932, when the Admiralty produced a comprehensive 'Review of the Present Condition of the Navy and General Remarks on Future Policy' incorporating a ten-year building programme for the years 1933–1942, its efforts were not well received.[2] The Cabinet had only agreed to the cancellation of the Ten-Year Rule on the strict understanding that:

> This must not be taken to justify an expanding expenditure by the Defence Services without regard to the very serious financial and economic situation which still obtains.[3]

Britain's straitened financial circumstances ruled out the assumption of responsibility for maintaining the peace of the world single-handed and, in the absence of any direct threat to Britain's vital interests in the Far East, the National Government was not prepared to entertain the possibility of war with Japan.

The threat to the peace of Europe which was implicit in Hitler's rise to power in Germany in 1933 was not so easily ignored, and when Germany withdrew from both the League of Nations and the Geneva Disarmament Conference in October 1933 the Cabinet was sufficiently alarmed to set up a Defence Review Committee to examine the state of Britain's defences with a view to making good the worst of the deficiences.[4] This committee, which reported in February 1934, recommended the expenditure of an extra £76 millions on defence over the next five years, but the government had not given up hope that peace could be secured by diplomatic means and, in the absence of any immediate threat of war, Neville Chamberlain, the Chancellor of the Exchequer, was instrumental in reducing the proposed expenditure to £50 millions and no action was taken until 1935.[5] However, the tone of the Defence White Paper which was finally published over the initials of the Prime Minister Ramsay MacDonald in March 1935, reflected the fundamental change in the government's attitude to defence:

> Notwithstanding their confidence in the ultimate triumph of peaceful methods, in the present troubled state of the world, they realised that armaments cannot be dispensed with. They are required to preserve peace, to maintain security and to deter aggression. . . . His Majesty's Government felt that they would be failing in their responsibilities if . . . they delayed the initiation of steps to put our armaments on a footing to safeguard us against potential danger.[6]

From 1935 until the outbreak of war in 1939 the level of defence spending mounted inexorably in the face of a progressive deterioration in the international situation. By March 1936 a futile attempt to halt Italian aggression in Abyssinia by means of economic sanctions added Italy to the ranks of Britain's potential enemies; Hitler had not been appeased by the signature of an Anglo-German Naval Treaty in June 1935; and all hopes of continuing naval arms limitation after December 1936 disappeared when Japan walked out of a second London Naval Conference in January 1936. Accordingly, the National Government, which had been re-elected in October 1935 on a platform which committed it 'to do what is necessary to repair the gaps in our defences',[7] found itself issuing a second Defence White Paper outlining further measures of rearmament:

> We have really no alternative in the present state of the world but to review our defences and to provide the necessary means both of safeguarding ourselves and of playing our part in the enforcement of international obligations.[8]

Up to December 1936 the government insisted on observing the terms of the Washington Treaty and the London Naval Treaty to the letter,[9] with the result that no new capital ships could be laid down until January 1937 but, from 1936–37 onwards, the pace of rearmament quickened and, in February 1937, the government took powers to borrow £400 millions to finance a rearmament programme estimated to cost £1,500 millions over the next five years.[10]

Despite the steadily worsening international situation spending on defence continued to be subject to financial constraints right up to the outbreak of war in 1939.[11] Since there was never enough money to satisfy the demands of all three services, the Admiralty was not able to build all the warships which it considered necessary. Two battleships and two cruisers had to be left out of the 1938–39 programme to help keep expenditure within the limit of £410 millions allocated to the Royal Navy for the three years 1938–39 to 1940–41.[12] Nevertheless, from 1936–37 onwards warshipbuilding was on a massive scale. In 1934–35 and 1935–

36 programmes of new construction amounted to only 148,237 tons in total but, in 1936-37 the inclusion of two battleships and two aircraft carriers in the programme resulted in 214,935 tons of warships being laid down, and in 1937-38 provision for the building of another three battleships and another two aircraft carriers resulted in a building programme of 267,020 tons. In all, the building programmes for the five years 1934-35 to 1938-39 made provision for the building of five battleships, six aircraft carriers, twenty-eight cruisers, fifty-nine destroyers, twenty-four submarines, six sloops, one survey vessel, two escort vessels, eight patrol vessels, four minelayers, sixteen minesweepers, five depot ships and five river gunboats: a grand total of one hundred and sixty-nine warships aggregating 754,332 tons.

With Rosyth and Pembroke Dockyards closed down[13] and Portsmouth and Plymouth heavily committed to modernising old capital ships,[14] this programme necessarily entailed extensive use of private shipyards, and over the five-year period one hundred and fifty warships aggregating 698,922 tons and one hundred and sixty-four sets of warships engines aggregating 5,988,425 horse power were awarded to private firms.[15] Forty-nine warships aggregating 357,118 tons were laid down in private yards in 1937 alone.

The revival in the demand for warships was reflected in the growing volume of Admiralty work in Clyde yards. As shown in table 10.1, the tonnage on hand, which had been rising steadily since 1932, exceeded the previous post-war peak of 52,555 tons during 1936. By the end of 1938 it was approaching the record peacetime level achieved in 1913:

**Table 10.1.** Admiralty Work on Hand in Clyde Yards

| YEAR -END | ON THE STOCKS TONS | FITTING -OUT TONS | TOTAL TONS |
|---|---|---|---|
| 1923 | nil | nil | nil |
| 1924 | 10,923 | nil | 10,923 |
| 1925 | 30,663 | nil | 30,663 |
| 1926 | 20,884 | 9,750 | 30,634 |
| 1927 | 23,065 | 29,490 | 52,555 |
| 1928 | 6,823 | 21,280 | 28,103 |
| 1929 | 2,720 | 18,273 | 20,993 |
| 1930 | 372 | 2,720 | 3,092 |
| 1931 | 2,750 | nil | 2,750 |
| 1932 | nil | 1,375 | 1,375 |
| 1933 | 24,901 | 815 | 25,716 |
| 1934 | 17,960 | 19,325 | 37,285 |
| 1935 | 28,590 | 7,535 | 36,125 |
| 1936 | 39,523 | 22,280 | 61,803 |
| 1937 | 107,349 | 46,987 | 154,336 |
| 1938 | 139,279 | 25,632 | 164,911 |

(Source: Abstracted from Appendix EIV)[16]

K

On Clydeside, Fairfield and Clydebank (which ranked alongside Vickers-Armstrong's Barrow and Elswick yards, Cammell Laird's Birkenhead yard and Harland & Wolff's Belfast yard as the only private shipyards capable of building the largest warships following the closure of Dalmuir and Palmer's) had the largest share of these orders. Apart from Fairfield which received orders for one battleship, one aircraft carrier, two cruisers and four destroyers and Clydebank which received orders for one battleship, one cruiser, three depot ships and four destroyers, four other Clyde firms each received orders for more than 10,000 tons of warships over the five-year period — Scott's, Stephen's, Denny's and Yarrow's.[17] The distribution of Admiralty orders was as follows:

**Table 10.2.** Clyde's Share of Admiralty Contracts 1934-1939

| FIRM | HULLS | | ENGINES | |
| --- | --- | --- | --- | --- |
| | No. | TONNAGE | No. | H.P. |
| FAIRFIELD | 8 | 82,615 | 8 | 570,500 |
| CLYDEBANK | 9 | 80,467 | 10 | 427,000 |
| SCOTT'S | 14 | 46,528 | 16 | 608,980 |
| STEPHEN'S | 8 | 30,248 | 8 | 374,200 |
| DENNY'S | 11 | 14,523 | 11 | 251,500 |
| YARROW'S | 11 | 14,480 | 11 | 263,800 |
| OTHERS | 5 | 4,075 | 5 | 8,750 |
| | 66 | 272,936 | 69 | 2,504,730 |

(Source: Abstracted from Appendix EIV)

The early stages of rearmament were accompanied by an upturn in merchant demand and, as in the years before the First World War, the combination of a revival in merchant shipbuilding with a boom in naval demand resulted in a sharp rise in costs of production. Typically, the time rates paid to skilled and unskilled shipyard workers increased from sixty shillings per week and forty-one shillings per week respectively at the end of 1935 to sixty-eight shillings per week and forty-nine shillings per week at the end of 1938,[18] and the average wages per man per week at Clydebank increased by 18.0% between 1935 and 1938.[19] Percentage increase in the costs of materials and overheads appear to have been of a similar order. The cost of a new 9,000 ton deadweight tramp steamer was reckoned to have risen from £83,500 in February 1936 to £101,000 in February 1939 — an increase of 20.96%.[20]

The upturn in demand resulted in shortages of vital raw materials and components. As early as September 1937 Stephen Piggott, who succeeded Sir Thomas Bell as Clydebank's managing director, spoke of a general shortage of steel plates,[21] and the warshipbuilders faced the particular problem that the dismemberment of the armaments industry during the years of arms limitation had left Britain short of capacity to produce armour plate, guns and gun mountings. In consequence the rearmament programme soon ran into difficulties.

In February 1938, following consultations with John Brown's armour-plate department in Sheffield on the delivery of armour plate, the Clydebank board was advised that the new battleship under construction in the yard could not be completed until June 1940, some five months after the contract date and four-and-a-half years after the ship was laid down.[22] Two months later the Admiralty was forced to extend the time allowed to build a destroyer from twenty-seven months to thirty months[23] — the time taken to build a Queen Elizabeth class battleship a quarter of a century earlier. By June 1938, a chronic shortage of gun mountings for Tribal class destroyers forced the Admiralty to issue detailed instructions dealing with the maintenance of completed ships pending the delivery of the missing equipment.[24]

Despite these problems Admiralty work continued to be profitable. In contrast to the period before the First World War, when rising costs had an adverse effect on the profitability of naval contracts,[25] profit margins on Admiralty contracts in the years leading up to the outbreak of the Second World War tended to become better rather than worse as war approached. The improvement was most noticeable in the case of Denny's. As is shown in table 10.3, the contribution to overheads and profit from the firm's destroyer contracts rose steadily from 7.9% of invoice price on two 'E' class destroyers completed in 1934 to 31.5% of invoice price on the 'J' and 'K' class destroyers completed in 1939:

**Table 10.3.** Destroyer Contracts Completed by Denny's 1934–1939

| YEAR COMPLETED | CLASS | BATCH SIZE | INVOICE PRICE | CONTRIBUTION TO OVERHEADS AND PROFIT | |
| --- | --- | --- | --- | --- | --- |
| | | | £ | £ | % |
| 1934 | 'E' | 2 | 495,433 | 39,109 | 7.9 |
| 1936 | 'H' | 2 | 508,616 | 72,315 | 14.2 |
| 1938 | 'TRIBALS' | 2 | 718,340 | 150,127 | 20.9 |
| 1939 | 'J'&'K' | 2 | 802,598 | 252,653 | 31.5 |

(Source: Author's figures based on detail abstracted from *UGD 3.* See Peebles, **thesis**, Appendix FVII)

While there is no evidence of a comparable improvement in the profitability of Admiralty contracts undertaken by Clyde yards which had been more regularly employed in warshipbuilding since the end of the war, there is no evidence either of any significant contraction in profit margins. On the contrary, apart from the orders for the engines of Dockyard-built cruisers, all of the Admiralty contracts undertaken by Clydebank, Fairfield and Scott's in 1935 and 1936 yielded contributions to overheads and profit of between 21.5% and 30.1% of invoice price, and Fairfield's records show that contracts undertaken in 1937 were more rather than less profitable than their immediate predecessors. The cruiser HMS PHOEBE, the destroyers HMS JUNO and HMS KELVIN and the battleship

HMS HOWE yielded contributions to overheads and profit of 30.9%, 33.9%, 38.1% and 29.9% respectively.

In part the continuing profitability of Admiralty contracts in the face of rising costs of production may have reflected the astuteness of the warshipbuilders, but in a large measure it was attributable to the effectiveness of the Warshipbuilders Committee in regulating prices. By 1936-37, when rearmament began in earnest, collusion on prices had rendered the whole system of competitive tendering meaningless.[26] The Admiralty had to rely increasingly on comparisons with the cost of Dockyard-built ships as its only check on the reasonableness of contractors' prices, a procedure which proved hopelessly inadequate as a means of ensuring that the Admiralty was obtaining value for money. Apart from the limited range of warships still being built in the Royal Dockyards, their costs were subsequently shown to be much higher than those of private yards.[27] In 1941, following an investigation of selected contracts undertaken by private firms from 1936 onwards, the Admiralty sought recompense for having been overcharged[28] but, in view of the problems created by the lack of naval work in earlier years, the warshipbuilders could hardly be blamed for having made the most of their opportunity.

By 1939 the plentiful supply of profitable Admiralty orders had transformed the financial situation of the Clyde warshipbuilding industry and the firms involved in it.

For Fairfield the improved outlook for warshipbuilding came none too soon. In the year to 30th June 1935 the company managed to earn a trading profit before depreciation of £62,394, but the collapse of the Anchor Line in the summer of 1935 occasioned a major crisis in Fairfield's affairs. As was customary when a reputable customer required credit, Fairfield had drawn bills on the Anchor Line in part-payment for the liners TUSCANIA and TRANSYLVANIA built by the yard in the 1920s. Under normal circumstances all of these bills would have been redemmed by the customer as they fell due, but by 1930 the Anchor Line was in financial difficulty and Fairfield had been obliged to agree to a moratorium on outstanding bills amounting to £145,000.[29] These bills were still outstanding when the affairs of the Anchor Line were placed in the hands of a receiver in June 1935 and Fairfield, which had discounted the bills in the normal course of business, was faced with the problem of finding £145,000 to meet the claims of the billholders when the bills were formally dishonoured and returned to drawer. Fairfield's neighbour Alexander Stephen & Sons, which had also discounted Anchor Line bills in the 1920s,[30] was in a similar situation but, following the sale of its interest in the Steel Company of Scotland in 1934,[31] Stephen's had the means to meet its obligations. Fairfield, which remained chronically illiquid despite the improvement in its trading situation, did not, and 'as no part of the funds available at the Bank of England could be used to discharge these bills', a serious situation ensued.[32] Technically the Fairfield Shipbuilding and Engineering Co. Ltd. was insolvent. It was rescued from its predicament only by the intervention of the Lithgow brothers, who agreed to assume responsibility for the company's overdraft and to meet the claims of the billholders in full in return for being sold the controlling interest of 24,260 ordinary shares previously registered in the name of Sir Alexander Kennedy — presumably as the nominee of the Shipbuilding Investment Co. Ltd.[33]

It is doubtful whether the Lithgow brothers would have been prepared to mount such a rescue bid if rearmament had not been in the offing. As the chairman of National Shipbuilders Securities Ltd. which had been instrumental in closing down other major warshipbuilding yards which had found themselves in financial difficulties, Sir James Lithgow's personal involvement in the rescue of a bankrupt yard would have been controversial had the national interest not made a further reduction in warshipbuilding capacity undesirable. As a member of the Industrial Panel set up in January 1934 to assist the government's Principal Supply Officers' Committee in preparing contingency plans for rearmament,[34] Sir James Lithgow was privy to information which was not available to the general public. He knew that the Eleventh Annual Report of the Principal Supply Officers' Committee dated 7th January 1935 had cast doubt on the ability of the shrinking shipbuilding industry to meet all the demands which were likely to be made upon it in the event of war:

> Investigations have revealed that many of the shipyards on which reliance had been placed have now closed down and that the existing active building slip capacity is insufficient to meet the combined naval and mercantile marine programmes. It is however considered probable that for the near future at least sufficient of the shipyards now unused could be reopened to meet requirements provided the necessary skilled labour were available.[35]

Further, no one was in a better position to judge how the closure of Fairfield would be received in official circles, and it can safely be assumed that he did not act without the government's tacit blessing if not at its behest.

Whatever the motives which prompted the Lithgow brothers to intervene, their purchase of Fairfield proved to be a sound investment.[36] When they took over, dividends on the company's preference shares were five years in arrears, the firm owed the Bank of Scotland £295,034[37] and, after providing for the losses on the Anchor Line bills, the balance of unused reserves and undistributed profits amounted to only £96,694. Less than four years later, in June 1939, bank borrowings had all been repaid, provision had been made for the elimination of the arrears of preference dividends and, while no dividend had yet been declared on the ordinary shares, reserves and undistributed profits amounted to £544,897.

The improvement in Fairfield's situation was gradual. At the Annual General Meeting held on 27th November 1935 the company's chairman, Sir Alexander Kennedy, spoke of a 'slight improvement' in demand which 'raised hopes of an early return to days of prosperity'[38] but, apart from a recent order for the 9,400 ton Gloucester class cruiser HMS LIVERPOOL, the firm had no work on hand due to be completed after June 1936. At the time of the Lithgow takeover early in November 1935, the firm's entire order book had comprised only the two 'G' class destroyers ordered as long before as April 1934, the 11,660 ton motorship DERBYSHIRE ordered by Bibby Brothers in September 1934 and the 449 ton

Clyde pleasure steamer MARCHIONESS OF GRAHAM ordered in September 1935. Apart from HMS LIVERPOOL, the only new order received in the interval was for the 314 ton pleasure steamer ST. SILIO. A year later evidence of recovery was more substantial. The firm was able to report a trading profit before depreciation of £74,196 for the year to 30th June 1936, and the order book had benefited from the receipt of orders for the 1,959 ton Tribal class destroyers HMS GURKHA and HMS MAORI, the 11,137 ton passenger and cargo liners CIRCASSIA and CELICIA for the reconstructed Anchor Line and the 642 ton paddle steamers JUNO and JUPITER for L.M.S., an order intake worth in all £1,828,352. As the chairman reported at the 1936 Annual General Meeting:

> The present position of the Shipbuilding Industry and the outlook for the next few years are encouraging ... The revival is due to the renewed confidence of shipowners in the future of Shipping as evidenced by the activities of the home market and the placing of many contracts for new vessels, assisted by the recent decision of the National Government to restore the Navy to its former high standard of efficiency.[39]

From then until the outbreak of war in 1939, Fairfield enjoyed a growing measure of prosperity. Apart from the twin-screw motor troopship DEVONSHIRE ordered by Bibby Brothers in June 1937, the firm took no further merchant orders, but from November 1936 onwards Fairfield's resources were increasingly given over to meeting the growing demand for naval work as the pace of rearmament quickened. Between December 1936 and June 1937, Fairfield was awarded the contracts for the 5,600 ton Dido class cruiser HMS PHOEBE, two 1,760 ton destroyers — HMS JUNO and HMS KELVIN — and the 36,727 ton King George V class battleship HMS HOWE as well as being asked to supply a new set of engines and boilers for the old battleship HMS QUEEN ELIZABETH. Further orders, for the 23,450 ton Implacable class aircraft carrier HMS IMPLACABLE and for two 'N' class destroyers, HMS NAPIER and HMS NESTOR, followed in October 1938 and May 1939 respectively. None of the orders received after November 1936 was completed by June 1939, but from 1936–37 onwards the firm adopted the practice of taking profits on account of unfinished contracts. Trading profits before depreciation of £219,299 in 1936–37, £290,010 in 1937–38 and £751,882 in 1938–39 fully reflected the profitability of the growing volume of Admiralty work on hand.

Fairfield's recovery was not entirely due to Admiralty work. In contrast to the merchant orders on hand at the time of the Lithgow takeover, all of the merchant contracts undertaken by the firm from November 1935 until the outbreak of war were profitable.[40] In particular, the liners CIRCASSIA and CELICIA yielded net profits of £24,090 and £55,475 respectively and made a total contribution to overheads and profit of £196,198 or 19.9% of their combined invoice price. In addition, from 1935–36 onwards a rising volume of jobbing work made a useful contribution to overheads and profit. Nevertheless, the critical importance of Admiralty work is apparent from an analysis of all the contributions to overheads and profit in the three years to 30th June 1939 in Table 10.4:

Clydebank's experience was very similar to that of Fairfield. Following

**Table 10.4.** Fairfield: Contributions to Overheads and
Profit, 1st July 1936 to 30th June 1939

|  | £ | % |
|---|---|---|
| ADMIRALTY CONTRACTS | 1,530,276 | 75.8 |
| MERCHANT CONTRACTS | 318,763 | 15.8 |
| JOBBING WORK | 170,352 | 8.4 |
|  | 2,019,391 | 100.0 |

(Source: Details abstracted from *UCS 2/31/12*)[41]

resumption of work on the QUEEN MARY in April 1934 and the receipt of orders for the 9,100 ton Southampton class cruiser HMS SOUTHAMPTON in May 1934 and for the machinery of the Dockyard-built cruiser HMS BIRMINGHAM in December 1934, the yard earned a trading profit before depreciation of £29,254 in the year to 31st March 1935 but it remained desperately short of work. In February 1935, with only the cruiser HMS SOUTHAMPTON on the stocks, Sir Thomas Bell, nearing the end of his long career as Clydebank's managing director, reported that tanker orders were only available at prices which 'cannot possibly contain any charges' and, that while contracts were on offer for one or two refrigerated-cargo ships, the 'wild tendering' of Workman Clark and Harland & Wolff made their prices 'absurd'.[42] Nevertheless, fears of a serious shortage of skilled labour when demand picked up led Clydebank to accept orders for the 6,837 ton oil tanker COMANCHE from the Anglo-American Oil Co. and for the 11,063 ton cargo liners ESSEX and SUSSEX from P. & O., to provide employment for skilled ironworkers in the shipyard and skilled machinemen in the engine works.[43] None of these contracts was remunerative. The price of the COMANCHE failed to cover the costs of materials and labour by £12,331 and the £714,284 contract for the ESSEX and SUSSEX yielded only a contribution to overheads and profit of £32,099.

By the summer of 1936 Clydebank's situation was more encouraging. During the winter the yard had taken orders for two 1,370 ton 'I' class destroyers, HMS ICARUS and HMS ILEX, the 8,900 ton submarine depot-ship HMS MAIDSTONE and two destroyers for Argentina;[44] following a decision to take credit for £85,000 on account of the expected profit on the contract for the QUEEN MARY,[45] the yard was able to report a trading profit before depreciation of £204,924 for the year to 31st March 1936, and the state of the yard's merchant order book was transformed by the receipt of the order for the 85,000 ton Cunard liner QUEEN ELIZABETH in July 1936. By December 1936, with the new Cunarder on the stocks and a battleship order in the offing, the situation was so changed that inquiries from the Royal Mail Line, Shaw Savill & Albion and the Gracie Line of America were turned away on the grounds that the yard could not accommodate the building of a third large vessel.[46] From then until the outbreak of war in 1939 Clydebank too was increasingly given over to naval work. By the summer of 1937 work on hand included the 36,727 ton King George V class battleship HMS DUKE OF YORK, the 9,050 ton submarine depot-ship HMS FORTH and the 1,760 ton 'J' class destroyers HMS JACKAL and HMS JAVELIN. Orders for the 8,530 ton Fiji class cruiser HMS FIJI and for the 11,000 ton destroyer depot-ship HMS HECLA followed in 1937-38 and 1938-39 respectively, and the order for the 11,145 ton cargo liner SUFFOLK from the Federal Steam Navigation Co. in May 1938 was accepted only because the vessel could be delivered to the fitting-out basin in time for completion before the space was needed for HMS DUKE OF YORK.[47]

From 1936 onwards Clydebank increasingly assumed the character of a naval dockyard. The confidence which the naval authorities reposed in the yard was reflected in the regularity with which the Admiralty entrusted it with the building of lead ships of a class — the cruiser HMS SOUTHAMPTON in 1934, the depot ship HMS MAIDSTONE in 1935 and the cruiser HMS FIJI in 1937 — and there was the closest co-operation between the firm's management and the Admiralty in making maximum use of the yard's capacity for naval production. One aspect of the relationship was the early warning which Clydebank received of the impending order for the battleship. Though the official invitations to tender were not sent out until December 1936, space for a battleship was reserved at Clydebank as early as March 1936[48] and the firm was given verbal permission to commence work on HMS DUKE OF YORK in November 1936 on the strict understanding that this was 'to be kept as quiet as possible' until April 1937.[49] Another aspect of the relationship was the extent to which the Admiralty was prepared to co-operate in providing Clydebank with a steady flow of work. The order for the two 'J' class destroyers received in January 1937 was expressly designed to provide employment for Clydebank's dock engineers in the summer of 1938 pending the launch of larger warships.[50] In March 1937 it was reported that:

> In order to provide work for our framing squads until such time as more rapid progress is possible on the battleship, we have arranged with the Admiralty to proceed with a repeat Maidstone.[51]

In contrast to Fairfield, the upturn in naval demand was not fully reflected in Clydebank's trading results up to 1939 as the yard did not normally take profit on contracts until they were completed, and none of the contracts taken after April 1936 was finished by March 1939. Nevertheless Clydebank's trading profits before depreciation averaged £225,968 per annum in the three years to 31st March 1939. The link between the upturn in naval demand and the yard's renewed prosperity is apparent from an analysis of the contract profits credited to the profit and loss account between 1st April 1935 and 31st March 1939. Excluding the QUEEN MARY on which Clydebank earned a net profit of £155,414, merchant contracts resulted in net losses of £7,279 while naval contracts yielded net profits of £403,931.

Further, net profits alone do not do full justice to the importance of warshipbuilding to Clydebank in these years. In 1928 management consolidated the yard's overheads into two elements: one element — 'Power and Insurance' — included all those overheads which tended to fluctuate with the level of output —

electricity, gas, oil, coal, hydraulic and pneumatic power, national insurance, workmen's compensation insurance, the upkeep of tools etc; the other element — 'General Charges' — comprised all other overheads except depreciation, directors' fees and interest — effectively the yard's fixed overheads. By the mid-1930s it was standard practice to apportion the annual cost of 'Power and Insurance' among all contracts in progress in proportion to the direct labour costs incurred during the year but 'General Charges' were applied more selectively.[52] In the five years to 31st March 1939 merchant contracts bore their fair share of 'Power and Insurance', accounting for £250,469 out of the £470,855 charged to all contracts, but warship contracts accounted for £758,657 out of the total of £895,870 of 'General Charges' applied to all contracts, none of the latter having at that point been charged to the contract for the QUEEN ELIZABETH.[53] As a result the breakdown in Table 10.5 of the total contribution to overheads and profit at Clydebank in the three years to 31st March 1939 is strikingly similar to that of Fairfield in Table 10.4 above.

**Table 10.5.** Clydebank: Contributions to Overheads and Profit, 1st April 1936 to 31st March 1939

|  | £ | % |
| --- | --- | --- |
| ADMIRALTY CONTRACTS | 1,149,157 | 77.8 |
| MERCHANT CONTRACTS | 238,868 | 16.2 |
| JOBBING WORK | 89,035 | 6.0 |
|  | 1,477,050 | 100.0 |

(Source: Detail abstracted from *UCS 1/7/3, 4 & 6*)[54]

Of the other four firms, the improvement in Yarrow's trading performance was the least spectacular. The firm did not lack Admiralty orders. The orders for the destroyer flotilla leaders HMS FAULKNOR and HMS GRENVILLE and for the 2820 ton netlayer HMS PROTECTOR, received in 1932–33 and 1933–34 respectively, were followed by Admiralty orders for a further six destroyers, two escort vessels, two river gunboats and a patrol vessel between 1935–36 and 1938–39. However, since destroyers for Yugoslavia and Portugal and five sets of engines for destroyers built in Portugal[55] to Yarrow's design had helped keep the firm profitable in the period before Admiralty demand picked up, the effect of the rising volume of Admiralty work on hand was correspondingly muted. The company's earnings after depreciation increased from an average of £13,563 per annum in the five years to 30th June 1933 to an average of £36,084 per annum in the five years to 30th June 1938.

The growing prosperity associated with rearmament was more apparent in the case of Denny's. In the year to 31st December 1934, when the firm completed the 'E' class destroyers HMS ECHO and HMS ECLIPSE, it suffered a trading loss before depreciation of £52,519. The following year Denny's suffered a trading loss before depreciation of only £8,010. The improvement continued over the following three years with trading profits before depreciation rising from £16,587 in 1936 to £103,510 in 1937 and £135,531 in 1938. The favourable trend of profits was the product of rising activity and the increasing profitability of individual contracts. Both were attributable primarily to the revival in naval demand. The orders for the 1,340 ton 'H' class destroyers HMS HASTY and HMS HAVOCK and the 1,190 ton sloop HMS STORK received in 1934–35, as with the earlier order for the two 'E' class destroyers, did no more than make a useful contribution to overhead recovery, but up to 1936 the improvement in Denny's performance was almost wholly attributable to the higher level of activity. The annual overhead recovery account which had been £62,333 in deficit in 1934 was £8,471 in surplus by 1936. Similarly, from 1937 onwards, when the continuing improvement in Denny's trading situation reflected the profits being earned on individual contracts, the profitability of Admiralty contracts was critical. The contracts for the 1,959 ton Tribal class destroyers HMS ASHANTI and HMS BEDOUIN and the 1,250 ton sloop HMS AUCKLAND accounted for 75.7% of the profits earned on all contracts completed in 1938, and the contracts for the 1,760 ton 'J' and 'K' class destroyers HMS JAGUAR and HMS KANDAHAR and for the 580 ton patrol vessels HMS GUILLEMOT and HMS PINTAIL yielded net profits of £238,288 in 1939 when the company earned a trading profit before depreciation of £378,345.

Scott's had a similar experience with the important difference that the impact of the renewed demand for warships was reflected in the firm's accounts as early as the year to 31st December 1934, when a trading profit before depreciation of £105,383 was entirely due to the net profit of £70,196 earned on the 'E' class destroyers HMS ESCAPADE and HMS ESCORT laid down in 1933 and to £40,000 taken on account of the anticipated profit on the contract for the cruiser HMS GALATEA, which had also been laid down in 1933.[56] Over the next four years trading profits before depreciation averaged £151,022 per annum, and in the year to 31st December 1939 the company was to report a trading profit before depreciation of no less than £275,548. This period of prosperity, which had no parallel in the company's long history, was almost entirely due to the steady stream of Admiralty orders with which the firm was favoured from 1935 onwards. The 9,100 ton Southampton class cruiser HMS GLASGOW and the 1,340 ton 'H' class destroyers HMS HOSTILE and HMS HOTSPUR laid down in 1935 were followed by the 1959 ton Tribal class destroyers HMS MATABELE and HMS PUNJABI and the 1,520 ton Grampus class submarine HMS CACHELOT in 1936; the 5,600 ton Dido class cruiser HMS BONAVENTURE, the engines for the Dockyard-built cruiser HMS SIRIUS and the 1,090 ton Triton class submarines HMS TRIBUNE and HMS TARPON in 1937; the 11,000 ton Destroyer depot-ship HMS TYNE, the 1,920 ton 'L' class destroyers HMS LOOKOUT and HMS LOYAL and the 1,090 ton Triton class submarine HMS TUNA in 1938; and the 5,600 ton Dido class cruiser HMS SCYLLA in April 1939. None of the warships laid down after 1936 was completed by the end of 1939 but £288,850 on account of the profits on these uncompleted naval contracts contributed to the firm's profitability[57] and Scott's merchant business in these years counted for very little. From the beginning of 1935 to the outbreak of war in 1939, the firm's total intake of merchant work amounted to a single 9,700 ton ship for Alfred Holt,[58] which yielded Scott's a net profit of only £4,400, and four diesel-powered cargo/passenger ships for Elder Dempster,[59] three of which ended in losses. The total contribution to overheads and profit from all four ships amounted to only £56,913 on an invoiced price of £637,267. In consequence naval contracts accounted for no less than 93.4% of the total contribution to overheads and profit from all the work done on contracts in the five years to 31st December 1939.[60]

Alexander Stephen & Sons Ltd. was something of a special case in being a newcomer to warshipbuilding in peacetime. In common with the leading warshipbuilders, Stephen's had enjoyed a period of exceptional prosperity in the boom conditions which prevailed in merchant shipbuilding after the First World War. In the two years to 31st March 1921, ship-repairing added £234,869 to trading profits before depreciation of £343,209. After 1921 the firm's ship-repairing business dwindled but Stephen's still managed to earn trading profits before depreciation averaging £79,767 per annum over the next four years. The period of prosperity came to an end in 1925-26 when the yard finally exhausted its post-war order book by completing the 17,000 ton liner CALEDONIA for the Anchor Line. Following a trading profit before depreciation of £185,320 in the year to 31st March 1926, Stephen's suffered total trading losses of £81,660 over the next two years, largely because of a loss of £72,560 on two 11,400 ton tankers built for the Imperial Oil Co.[61] The company returned to profit in 1928-29 but trading profits before depreciation totalled only £73,829 over the next three years, the £985,388 contract for the 19,648 ton P. & O. liner VICEROY OF INDIA, completed in March 1929, yielding a net profit of only £1,049. Net profits of £179,288 on the contracts for the 14,300 ton P. & O. liners CARTHAGE and CORFU resulted in a trading profit before depreciation of £186,616 in 1931-32, but by March 1932 work in progress comprised only a sailing yacht and a small cargo ship[62] and the directors took a gloomy view of the prospects:

> Notwithstanding the substantial profit shown, the Directors regret that in view of the serious position existing; the certainty of a heavy loss in the current year and the future outlook for the industry, they cannot see their way to recommend the payment of a dividend even on the Preference Shares. They have no doubt it will be recognised that they have no option but to adopt this course at a time when the adequacy of the Company's liquid resources to see it through the depression cannot but be a matter of serious anxiety.[63]

The company's liquidity problems were eased by the sale of its shares in the Steel Company of Scotland to the Lithgow brothers for £151,875 in 1934-35,[65] but the directors' pessimism on the trading outlook was amply justified by the trading results. In the three years to 31st March 1935 Stephen's suffered trading losses before depreciation amounting to £155,548.

Against this background the directors, apparently at the instigation of Alexander Murray Stephen who became chairman in 1933, decided to seek a share of Admiralty contracts.[65] In the winter of 1933-34 the company secured the orders for the 1,350 ton 'G' class destroyers HMS GALLANT and HMS GRENADE. Contracts for the 510 ton patrol vessels HMS MALLARD and HMS PUFFIN followed in 1934-35 and the more important contracts for the Tribal class destroyers HMS ZULU and HMS SIKH were added to the order book in 1935-36. Stephen's, which had not built a warship since the end of the First World War, apparently found the work congenial and, following a report that work on HMS ZULU was well ahead of all other Tribal class destroyers in February 1937,[66] the firm was rewarded with a succession of major orders — the 5,600 ton Dido class cruiser HMS HERMIONE and the 8,530 ton Fiji class cruiser HMS KENYA in 1937-38 and the 8,530 ton Fiji class cruiser HMS CEYLON and the 2,650 ton minelayer HMS MANXMAN in 1938-39. None of these major contracts was completed by 31st March 1939, and it does not appear to have been Stephen's practice to take credit for profits before contracts were completed, but a net profit of £38,109 on the two 'G' class destroyers enabled the company to earn a trading profit before depreciation of £35,129 in 1935-36. Profits taken on the completion of the two patrol vessels and the two Tribal class destroyers were reflected in trading profits before depreciation of £22,952 in 1936-37, £99,378 in 1937-38 and £94,466 in 1938-39.

Stephen's was more successful than Scott's in striking a balance between merchant and naval work, and nineteen merchant ships aggregating 81,243 tons were launched from the yard in the five years 1934-1938 inclusive, but the incomplete data available suggest that naval contracts played the major part in the improvement in Stephen's trading performance. While the merchant output included the 16,033 ton P. & O. liner CANTON and a succession of nine refrigerated cargo ships for the Union Steamship Company of New Zealand, eleven of the twenty-one merchant contracts completed in the five years to 31st March 1939[67] resulted in losses and there was an overall loss of £36,901 on merchant work, the £779,532 contract for the liner CANTON yielding a net profit of only £6,664.

The revival in the demand for warships solved the Clyde warshipbuilders' financial difficulties. Of the four independent companies which had been in financial difficulties prior to the upturn in naval demand, Scott's was exceptional in being in a position to resume the payment of ordinary dividends as early as 1934. The other three — Fairfield, Stephen's and Denny's — took longer to recover. Each of them had to pay off arrears of preference dividends before they were able to declare a dividend on their ordinary shares. The speed with which they were able to do so depended on the magnitude of their financial problems. Denny's, whose preference dividend was only one year in arrears in 1935, cleared the backlog in 1936; Stephen's, which was five years in arrears by the time it resumed payment in 1936, paid off the backlog in 1937; Fairfield, which was also five years in arrear in 1935, felt unable to resume payment until 1937 and the whole of the backlog was not paid off until 1939. As Fairfield's chairman, Sir Alexander Kennedy, warned the company's Annual General Meeting in November 1936:

> Following the long unprecedented depression in the industry ... the cash resources of the Company must first be strengthened and the creditor position dealt with.[68]

With the payment of the arrears of preference dividend by Fairfield in 1939 the financial rehabilitation of the Clyde warshipbuilders was virtually complete. Typically, Fairfield, which owed its bankers £316,064 at 30th June 1935, had amassed a cash balance of £506,000 by 30th June 1939. While the company was not as comfortably placed as the cash balance suggested, since creditors included £78,475 for preference dividends and debenture interest unpaid and large tax bills were in the offing (provisions for taxation having amounted to £40,000 in 1937–38 and £350,000 in 1938–39), liquidity was no longer a problem. The other Clyde warshipbuilders were in a similar position. As is shown in table 10.6, in every case where the data are available, liquidity ratios (debtors + cash + short-term investments/creditors + tax liabilities + short-term borrowings) in 1938–39 were not only better than in 1934–35 but also significantly better than in 1913–14:

**Table 10.6.** Liquidity Ratios

| FIRM | 1913–14 | 1934–35 | 1938–39 |
|------|---------|---------|---------|
| FAIRFIELD | 0.29 | 0.14 | 0.81 |
| SCOTT'S | 0.08 | 1.07 | 1.50 |
| STEPHEN'S | 0.47 | 0.56 | 1.72 |

(Source: Calculations based on figures given in Peebles, **thesis**, Appendix E)

To some extent the improvement in liquidity was achieved at the expense of neglecting capital investment. Large sums were expended in refurbishing plant and facilities which had been allowed to fall into disrepair when trade was bad. Scott's which had spent only £4,882 on maintenance in 1932 was spending £58,344 by 1938;[69] Fairfield which had spent only £6,755 on the maintenance of plant and buildings in 1932–33 was spending £109,904 by 1938–39;[70] and Clydebank which was spending as little as £7,554 on the maintenance of property and the upkeep of machinery as late as 1933–34 was spending £64,119 on the same accounts by 1938–39.[71] Firms still remained reluctant to purchase new equipment or to modify their existing facilities except when it was absolutely necessary to do so. At Clydebank a proposal to spend £20,000 on new machines to expand the capacity of the engine works in February 1937 was approved only after a high-powered sub-committee comprising Sir Thomas Bell, Stephen Piggott and the engineering director, Sir Holberry Mensforth, had examined it and assured the board that the increase in capacity was 'essential'.[72] At Fairfield, when the board approved plans to spend £27,000 on equipping the yard to build its first aircraft carrier in November 1938, the secretary was instructed to

> bring before the Board after the completion of the Aircraft Carrier the question of considering the special writing off of any capital expenditure so incurred.[73]

The warshipbuilders' caution was reflected in the relatively modest increases in balance-sheet figures for net fixed assets. In the five years preceding the outbreak of war in 1939, net additions to fixed assets less provisions for depreciation amounted to only £31,661 at Clydebank, to £31,793 at Scott's, and to £75,179 at Stephen's. At Fairfield, where the management apparently decided to provide for additionald depreciation to compensate for the lack of any provision over the previous five years, provisions for depreciation exceeded net additions to fixed assets by £243,232.

While capital expenditure was higher in the five years to 1938–39 than it had been at any time since the end of the post-war boom, total expenditure on net additions to fixed assets at Clydebank, Fairfield and Scott's in the decade preceding the outbreak of the Second World War was markedly lower than it had been in the decade preceding the outbreak of the First World War. This could be attributed in part to the absence of any technical stimulus comparable to that provided by the introduction of the steam turbine and the advent of the dreadnought in the decade before the First World War. However, the absence of a major technical stimulus does not account entirely for the low level of capital expenditure. There is reason to doubt whether the quality of the productive capacity was being maintained when, as table 10.7 shows, expenditure on net additions to plant and machinery in the three biggest warshipbuilding yards was no greater in the decade 1929–39 than it had been a quarter of a century earlier when costs were very much lower:

**Table 10.7.** Net Additions to Plant & Machinery

|  | 1904–14 £'000 | 1929–39 £'000 |
|---|---|---|
| CLYDEBANK | 216.2 | 202.2 |
| FAIRFIELD | 110.5 | 108.0 |
| SCOTT'S | 157.5 | 126.9 |

(Source: Author's figures based on detail abstracted from *UCS 1*, *UCS 2* and *GD 319*. See Peebles, **thesis**, Appendix E)

The warshipbuilders' caution was understandable. Naval demand remained vulnerable to shifts in government policy: Britain's economic weakness limited the size of the navy which she could afford to maintain; the opposition Labour Party was averse to spending on armaments in principle. Further, the gradual recovery in merchant shipbuilding which accompanied the early stages of rearmament petered out by 1939. Even in January 1938, with rearmament in full swing and the demand for merchant ships relatively buoyant, only 63% of the total plant and berth capacity of the United Kingdom's shipbuilding industry was gainfully employed.[74] During 1938 the Clyde shipbuilders were reported to have received only one new merchant order for every four ships which were launched, and in December 1938 there was no sign of the decline being arrested.[75] A memorandum prepared on behalf of the Shipbuilding Conference in the winter of 1938–39, which noted the fall in the United Kingdom's share of world output from 60.5% in 1904 to 34% in 1938,[76] the reduction in the size of the British merchant fleet from 20,322,000 tons in 1930 to 17,675,000 tons in 1938 and the steady decline in the proportion of world tonnage owned by British firms from 41.1% in 1914 to 26.4% in 1938,[77] put rearmament in perspective. The demand for merchant ships was falling at an alarming rate, the stimulus provided by the rearmament programme was likely to be of short duration and:

> If the trade cycle takes a normal course, it is possible that the years 1939–42 will be a period of severe depression in merchant shipbuilding, and that such a condition will remain at the time of the completion of the warship programme.[78]

Against this background, the Clyde warshipbuilders had no reason to take an optimistic view of their own prospects. Rearmament had brought them renewed prosperity, but no-one expected the period of prosperity to outlast the rearmament programme. The outlook for merchant shipbuilding was bleak and the experience of the inter-war years had shown that, even when merchant work was relatively plentiful, it was rarely very profitable. In consequence, prudence dictated that the warshipbuilders should use their renewed prosperity to prepare themselves for a possible collapse in profits when rearmament ended. Improving liquidity rather than investing in fixed assets might not be in the best long-term interest of the Clyde warshipbuilders but it greatly improved their chances of survival.

In the quarter of a century preceding the outbreak of the First World War in 1914, warshipbuilding had been one of the fastest-growing sectors in an expanding Clydeside shipbuilding industry. It was symptomatic of the extent to which the situation had changed that, twenty-five years later, warshipbuilding could do little more than provide some of the leading shipyards on the Clyde with the means to survive another slump.

## NOTES

1. The Ten-Year Rule, introduced in 1919 as the basis on which the fighting services were instructed to frame their estimates for 1920–21 (see Chapter 7, note 7 above), had governed the preparation of all subsequent defence estimates. In July 1928, at the instigation of the then Chancellor of the Exchequer, Winston Churchill, the Committee of Imperial Defence laid it down that it was to be treated:

> as a standing assumption that at any given date there will be no major war for at least ten years from that date.

See Roskill, *Naval Policy between the Wars*, Vol. 1, p. 560.

2. *Ibid.*, Vol. 2, p. 150.

3. M. Howard, *The Continental Commitment: the Dilemma of British Defence Policy in the Era of Two World Wars* (London 1972: Penguin edition 1974), p. 99, quoting C.I.D. 255th Meeting, 22nd March 1932. Cabinet 19(32) Concln. 2.

4. Roskill, *Naval Policy between the Wars*, Vol. 2, p. 167.

5. Howard, *The Continental Commitment*, pp. 110–11.

6. Statement relating to Defence, 1st March, 1935, *Parliamentary Papers, 1934–35* [*Cmd4827*] *XIII 803*, p. 10.

7. C. L. Mowat, *Britain between the Wars, 1918-1940* (London 1955: University Paperback edition 1968), p. 553.

8. Statement relating to Defence, 3rd March 1936, *Parliamentary Papers, 1935-36* [*Cmd5107*] *XVI 839*, p. 4.

9. Britain went to great lengths to adhere to the letter of its treaty obligations. During 1936 the Admiralty discovered that, as a result of modifications, its Tribal destroyers were going to have a design weight in excess of the limit of 1,850 standard displacement tons laid down for destroyers under the London Naval Treaty. Since the treaty expired at the end of the year, it was suggested that there was no need to report the increase but this proposal did not meet with official approval and the design change was only approved after the Admiralty Solicitor had confirmed that there would be no contravention of the terms of the treaty if the change in design was not put into effect until after 31st December 1936. See March, *British Destroyers*, p. 333.

10. Statement relating to Defence, 16th February 1937, *Parliamentary Papers, 1936-37* [*Cmd5374*] *XVII 1123*, pp. 3 & 41.

11. Defence expenditure rose from £262 millions in 1936-37 to an estimated £528 millions in 1938-39, but, as late as March 1938 it was still official policy 'to avoid as far as possible interference with the requirements of private industry'. See Statement relating to Defence, 2nd March 1938, *Parliamentary Papers, 1937-38* [*Cmd5682*] *XVII 1143*, p. 4 and Statement relating to Defence, 15th February 1939, *Parliamentary Papers, 1938-39* [*Cmd5944*] *XXI 225*, pp. 4-5.

12. Roskill, *Naval Policy between the Wars*, Vol. 2, pp. 450-1.

13. As an economy measure, Pembroke and Rosyth Dockyards had been put on a care and maintenance basis in 1925. See Pembroke and Rosyth Dockyards: Savings to be effected by a Reduction to a Care and Maintenance Basis, *Parliamentary Papers, 1924-25* [*Cmd2554*] *XVIII 873*.

14. Between 1933 and 1937, Portsmouth and Devonport Dockyards undertook the extensive reconstruction of the old Queen Elizabeth class battleships HMS MALAYA, HMS WARSPITE, HMS VALIANT and HMS QUEEN ELIZABETH and of the Renown class battlecruisers HMS REPULSE and HMS RENOWN, three of the battleships being fitted with completely new engines. Each of these reconstructions took approximately three years to complete and the last of them, that of the battleship HMS QUEEN ELIZABETH, was not completed until 1940. See Conway's *All the World's Fighting Ships, 1921-1946*, pp. 7-9.

15. See Appendix D.

16. The basis of calculation is given in Chapter 6, note 40 above.

17. Full details of these orders are given in Appendix EIV.

18. Jones, *Shipbuilding in Britain*, p. 181.

19. Figures abstracted from *UCS 1/52/1-6*, kindly made available to the author by Professor R. H. Campbell.

20. *UCS 1/9/79*, 'Memorandum on Conditions now existing in the Shipbuilding Industry', Confidential Report to Members by the Shipbuilding Conference dated December 1938, p. 15.

21. *UCS 1/1/2*, Minutes of Board Meeting, 29th September 1937.

22. Ibid., 17th February 1938.

23. March, *British Destroyers*, p. 361.

24. *Ibid.*, p. 335.

25. See Chapter 6 above.

26. W. Ashworth, *Contracts and Finance*, in *United Kingdom Civil Series on the History of the Second World War* (London 1953), pp. 106-7.

27. *Ibid.*, p. 109, citing evidence given to the Public Accounts Committee of the House of Commons in 1943.

28. *Ibid.*, pp. 108-9.

29. *UCS 2/1/5*, Minutes of Board Meeting, 10th December 1930.

30. Stephen's had built the liners CALIFORNIA and CALEDONIAN (Yard Nos. 494–5) for the Anchor Line after the war. In this case the amount of the dishonoured bills, which had to be written off in the year to 31st March 1936, was £99,401. See *UCS 3/3/36*.

31. Stephen's had purchased 11,250 ordinary shares in the Steel Company of Scotland in 1920–21. By 1931–32 the investment, which cost Stephen's £345,871, had been written down to £11,250. In 1934–35 the shares were sold to the Lithgow brothers for £151,875. See *UCS 3/3/20–35*.

32. *UCS 2/1/6*, Minutes of Board Meeting, 13th November 1935.

33. *UCS 2/5/2*, Directors' Report on the Accounts for the Year to 30th June 1935, and *UCS 2/1/6*, Minutes of Board Meeting, 27th November 1935.

34. The Industrial Panel, consisting of Lord Weir, Sir Arthur Balfour and Sir James Lithgow, was set up 'to advise on the necessary steps to ensure ... the proper co-ordination with industry' in the preparation of plans for wartime production. See *UGD 49/35/31*.

35. *UGD 49/35/31*, 7th Annual Report of the Supply Board (PSO 450) included in 11th Annual Report of the Principal Supply Officers Committee (PSO 450; CID No. 1158-8), Report of No. III Supply Committee, p. 22.

36. *GD 320/2/3/7*, Kingston Investment Co.'s Register of Investments.

37. *UCS 2/1/6*, Minutes of Board Meeting, 13th November 1935.

38. Ibid., Minutes of Annual General Meeting, 27th November 1935.

39. Ibid., Minutes of Annual General Meeting, 16th November 1936.

40. Yard Nos. 657, 661–4 and 670.

41. Contributions to overheads and profit from all work *carried out* in the period, i.e. taking account of profits and overheads in opening and closing work-in-progress.

42. *UCS 1/5/33*, Board Paper, 27th February 1935.

43. Ibid.

44. SAN JUAN and SAN LUIS. Clydebank's order for two ships was in accord with an agreement between members of the Warshipbuilders Committee that no firm should tender for more than three of the six destroyers on offer. See *UCS 1/5/34*, Board Paper, 9th January 1936.

45. The decision to take credit for profit on the, as yet uncompleted, QUEEN MARY was taken with the deliberate intention of maximising profits in case rearmament resulted in the reintroduction of the wartime Excess Profits Duty which had been levied on all profits in excess of a notional standard based on the average profits earned in previous years. This possibility had apparently been discussed at a John Brown board meeting and the decision to take profit on the QUEEN MARY was made following a telephone conversation between Clydebank and Sheffield on 7th March 1936. See *UCS 1/7/4*, Memorandum of telephone conversation with Mr. Bridges, 8th April 1936.

John Brown's fears were not without foundation. Two weeks later, the Budget included provision for a National Defence Contribution on business profits graduated according to the growth of a firm's profits during recent years. In the event, following widespread protests from the City and business organisations, the proposed tax was withdrawn and replaced by a straight 5% tax on all business profits, but the danger had been real and it is clear that not everyone was taken by surprise as suggested by Mowat, *Britain between the Wars*, p. 571.

46. *UCS 1/1/2*, Minutes of Board Meeting, 3rd December 1936.

47. *UCS 1/5/36*, Board Paper, 3rd June 1938.

48. *UCS 1/5/34*, Board Paper, 7th March 1936.

49. Ibid., Board Paper, 27th November 1936.

50. *UCS 1/5/35*, Board Paper, 28th January 1937.

51. Ibid., Board Paper, 23rd March 1937.

52. Full details of the composition of the two classes of overhead and their application from 1931–32 onwards are to be found in the relevant annual accounts working papers. See *UCS 1/7/1–6*.

53. *UCS 1/7/3, 4 & 6.*

54. Contributions to overheads and profit from all work *carried out* in the period, i.e. taking account of profits and overheads in opening and closing work-in-progress.

55. Two of the five destroyers built in Portugal were sold to Colombia while under construction in 1933. See Conway's *All the World's Fighting Ships, 1921–1946*, p. 397.

56. Scott's made a regular practice of taking profits on account of uncompleted contracts, and the outcome of this particular contract amply justified their confidence. HMS GALATEA, completed in 1937, yielded a total net profit of £128,294.

57. The profit on account of uncompleted naval contracts at 31st December 1939 was made up as follows:

|  | £ |
|---|---|
| HMS TRIBUNE | 22,450 |
| HMS TYNE | 34,500 |
| HMS BONAVENTURE | 107,000 |
| HMS TARPON | 62,500 |
| HMS TUNA | 19,000 |
| HMS LOOKOUT | 6,900 |
| HMS LOYAL | 9,000 |
| HMS SCYLLA | 20,000 |
| HMS SIRIUS (ENGINES) | 7,500 |
|  | 288,850 |

(Source: *GD 319/5/1/51*)

58. Yard No. 571.

59. Yard Nos. 566–7 and 573–4.

60. Based on details abstracted from *GD 319/2/69–73* and taking account of profits and overheads in opening and closing work-in-progress.

61. Yard Nos. 517–18.

62. Yard Nos. 536–7.

63. *UGD 4/12/3*, Minutes of Annual General Meeting, 1st September 1932.

64. See note 31 above.

65. Carvel, *Stephens of Linthouse*, p. 129.

66. March, *British Destroyers*, p. 333.

67. Yard Nos. 538–43, 546, 549–51, 554–9 and 561–5.

68. *UCS 2/1/6*, Minutes of Annual General Meeting, 16th November 1936.

69. *GD 319/5/2/66 & 73.*

70. *UCS 2/31/11 & 12.*

71. *UCS 1/7/5 & 6.*

72. *UCS 1/1/2*, Minutes of Board Meeting, 17th February 1937.

73. *UCS 2/1/6*, Minutes of Board Meeting, 16th November 1938.

74. *UCS 1/9/79*, 'Memorandum on Conditions now existing in the Shipbuilding Industry', p. 7.

75. *The Glasgow Herald*, Annual Trade Review, 29th December 1938.

76. *UCS 1/9/79*, 'Memorandum on Conditions now existing in the Shipbuilding Industry', p. 8.

77. Ibid., p. 12.

78. Ibid., p. 17.

# 11
## *Conclusions*

While the Clyde warshipbuilders produced over 1.6 million tons of warships for the Royal Navy in the fifty years to 1939, more than 40% of all the warships laid down by the Admiralty in private shipyards, their achievements should not be exaggerated. They started with a number of advantages. Warshipbuilding suited their existing scale of operations, they had made a particular specialisation of producing first-class ships and high-powered engines, and all of the leading yards had previous experience of Admiralty work. Further, in the years following the Navy Defence Act in 1889, market conditions were exceptionally favourable. Demand was buoyant and modifications to the Admiralty procurement system reduced the risk of failure to a minimum. Despite these advantages, the performance of the Clyde warshipbuilders in the boom years before the First World War was flawed in a number of respects. First, as warshipbuilders, the Clyde yards displayed little more than technical competence in building warships to Admiralty specification. Only Yarrow's made a success of warship design. Most of the Clyde's output consisted of ships and engines designed by the Admiralty. Clydebank, in particular, experienced great difficulty in achieving design speeds in destroyers of its own design, and Scott's early work on submarines was based on Italian designs. Significantly, only Yarrow's succeeded in winning regular orders from foreign governments. Clydebank's success in obtaining overseas warship orders in the 1880s and 1890s was not maintained and, despite much effort, the major Clyde yards had little to show for their attempts to complete with Vickers and Armstrong's in export markets in the years before the First World War. Second, in the absence of overseas warship orders, all of the major yards drifted into a situation where they were inordinately dependent on Admiralty work, a specialised business in which the level of demand was largely dictated by political considerations. Warshipbuilding may not have been undertaken at the expense of merchant shipbuilding but, by 1914, what remained of the warshipbuilders' merchant businesses was largely domestic in origin, and the most profitable part of it depended on the loyalty of a few customers with whom yards had longstanding connections. When these customers switched their allegiance or went out of business, the warshipbuilders were unable to replace them. Third, narrowing profit margins and the inability of any of the major Clyde warshipbuilding yards to earn satisfactory profits when the demand for warships was at its height in the years before the outbreak of the First World War can be seen as symptomatic of a worrying decline in competitiveness which boded ill for the future.

Reservations regarding the performance of the Clyde warshipbuilders and the quality of their management do not detract from the importance of warship-building. Naval work was extraordinarily profitable. The high profits earned on Admiralty orders may have owed more to imperfections in the market and considerations of the national interest than to the efficiency of the warshipbuilders themselves but, as Table 11.1 shows, the years during and immediately after the First World War, when merchant work was available on a cost-plus basis, was virtually the only time between 1894 and 1936 when the profitability of merchant work came close to matching the profitability of naval work undertaken in the same yard at the same time:

**Table 11.1.** Profitability of Naval and Merchant Work Undertaken by Three Major Warshipbuilding Yards 1894–1936

| ORDERS TAKEN | CONTRIBUTION TO OVERHEADS AND PROFITS AS A PERCENTAGE OF INVOICE PRICE | | | | | |
| | CLYDEBANK | | FAIRFIELD | | SCOTT'S | |
| | NAVAL % | MERCHANT % | NAVAL % | MERCHANT % | NAVAL % | MERCHANT % |
|---|---|---|---|---|---|---|
| 1894–1898 | 23.5 | 13.7 | 19.3 | 13.6 | 27.9 | 16.6[a] |
| 1899–1903 | 29.9 | 14.4 | 28.6 | 16.0 | 19.4 | 11.6 |
| 1904–1908 | 23.3 | 13.6 | 20.7 | 14.7 | 11.1 | 11.2 |
| 1909–1914 | 15.6 | 4.1 | 14.1 | 10.0 | 23.8 | 21.8 |
| WAR YEARS | 22.5 | 21.9 | 23.0 | 25.1 | | 21.8 |
| 1919–1923[b] | | 16.6 | | 22.1 | | |
| 1924–1928 | 15.0 | 4.3 | 20.6 | 6.0 | 13.7 | 8.5 |
| 1929–1933 | 16.9 | 10.1 | 20.0 | 10.4 | 25.2 | 12.1 |
| 1934–1936 | 22.9 | 2.2 | 27.6 | 14.0 | 25.9 | 8.4 |

a: 1900–1903 only

b: including orders booked for post-war completion

(Source: author's figures based on details abstracted from *UCS 1, UCS 2* and *GD 319*. For details, see Peebles, **thesis**, Volume II, Appendix F)

Under these circumstances, the availability of profitable naval work had a critical bearing on the fortunes of the Clyde warshipbuilders both before the First World War and in the inter-war years. In the years before the First World War, when naval orders were plentiful, the warshipbuilders prospered. All of the firms which took advantage of the expansion in the demand for warships in the 1890s were in financial difficulties, but profitable naval contracts revived their fortunes. From then until the outbreak of the First World War in 1914, naval work constituted a major part of their output and accounted for most of their profits. By 1914 all of the warshipbuilders had expanded their capacity and provided expensive new facilities largely on the strength of the demand for warships, and the three biggest yards were owned by armaments manufacturers who were primarily interested in shipyards for their warshipbuilding capability. In the 1920s and early 1930s, when naval orders were in short supply, the warshipbuilders suffered. Arms limitation resulted in the collapse of the pre-war armaments industry, and the warshipbuilders were faced with the problem of finding profitable work for capacity designed for the building of warships and warship engines. This proved to be impossible, and the decline in the demand for warships was the primary cause of the severe financial difficulties in which the warshipbuilders found themselves when the onset of the world financial crisis in 1931 brought merchant shipbuilding to a standstill. A leavening of profitable naval contracts helped to keep most of the warshipbuilding yards on the Clyde going, but had rearmament not been in the offing, it is doubtful if many of them would have survived the ensuing crisis. As it was, all of the warshipbuilders owed their subsequent financial recovery to the revival in naval demand associated with rearmament.

Whether the warshipbuilders' dependence on naval work was altogether healthy may be questioned. Arguably it was symptomatic of their declining competitiveness. Certainly it left them vulnerable to any contraction in the demand for warships. In the long run it may have been fatal to their chances of survival when the long-term decline in Britain's economic power made it impossible for her to support what was still in 1939 the largest navy in the world. However, nothing in the warshipbuilders' experience between 1889 and 1939 suggests that they would have been better served by concentrating on merchant shipbuilding at that time. On the contrary, all the evidence points to the conclusion that between 1889 and 1939 a significant proportion of the Clyde's merchant output was produced in yards which survived only because they were able to combine merchant work with more profitable naval work.

Any account of the history of the Clyde shipbuilding industry must needs take account of the warshipbuilders' experience. They may be untypical of the majority of Clyde firms which confined themselves to lower classes of work, but collectively and individually they are too important to be ignored. For good or ill, warshipbuilding demonstrably played a major part in the history of the Clyde shipbuilding industry between 1889 and 1939.

# Bibliography

*UNPUBLISHED SOURCES*

Main class references only are given here: detailed references to the sources used within each class are to be found in the text.


1) UPPER CLYDE SHIPBUILDERS (Part of the holding of the Scottish Record Office):

*UCS 1*: John Brown & Co., Clydebank
(held in Glasgow University Archives)
*UCS 2*: The Fairfield Shipbuilding & Engineering Co. Ltd.
(held in Strathclyde Regional Archives)
*UCS 3*: Alexander Stephen & Sons Ltd.
(held in Glasgow University Archives)


2) OTHER SHIPBUILDING RECORDS AND PAPERS (all held in Glasgow University Archives)

*UGD 3*: William Denny & Brothers Ltd.
*UGD 4*: Alexander Stephen & Sons Ltd.
*UGD 49*: Lithgow papers.
*UGD 100*: William Beardmore & Co. Ltd.
*GD 319*: Scott's Shipbuilding & Engineering Co. Ltd.
*GD 320*: Lithgow Ltd.
*GU 4935*: Robert Napier & Sons papers.


3) UNPUBLISHED THESES

CORMACK, W. S. An economic history of shipbuilding and marine engineering with special reference to the West of Scotland, (Ph.D. thesis: Glasgow University 1931)
MORE, C. R. V. The Fairfield Shipbuilding and Engineering Co. Ltd., 1889–1914, (M.Litt. thesis: London School of Economics 1976)
PEEBLES, H. B. Warshipbuilding on the Clyde, 1889–1939: A Financial Study, (Ph.D. thesis: University of Stirling 1986)


*NEWSPAPERS, JOURNALS ETC.*

*Engineering*

*Fairplay*
*Hansard*
*The Daily Record*
*The Glasgow Herald*
*The Times*


PARLIAMENTARY PAPERS

1. Statements of the First Lord of the Admiralty explanatory of the Navy estimates for . . .

1890–91: 1890 [C5958] XLIV 347
1891–92: 1890–91 [C6279] LI 331
1894–95: 1894 [C7295] LIV 305
1902–03: 1902 [Cd950] LIX 307
1903–04: 1903 [Cd1478] XXXIX 305
1905–06: 1905 [Cd2402] XLVII 293
1909–10: 1909 [Cd4533] LIII 285
1929–30: 1929–30 [Cmd3506] XX 575


2. Statements relating to Defence Expenditure

First: March 1935: 1934–35 [Cmd4827] XIII 803
Second: March 1936: 1935–36 [Cmd5107] XVI 839
Third: February 1937: 1936–37 [Cmd5374] XVII 1123
Fourth: March 1938: 1937–38 [Cmd5682] XVII 1143
Fifth: February 1938: 1938–39 [Cmd5944] XXI 225


3. Others (in order of date of issue)

Report of the Committee appointed to inquire into the conditions under which contracts are invited for the building and repairing of ships of the Navy, including their engines, and into the mode in which repairs and refits of ships are effected in dockyards, with Evidence and Appendix (The Ravensworth Committee) 1884–85 [C4219] XIV 125

Report of the Committee appointed by the Admiralty to inquire into the system of purchase and contract in the Navy, with Minute of Lord George Hamilton: with Evidence and Appendix (The Forwood Committee) 1887 [C4987] XVI 531.

Proceedings of the Colonial Conference at London with Appendix. 1887 [C5091] LVI 1

Extracts from the Report of the Committee on the Naval Manoeuvres, 1888, with the Narrative of the Operations and the Rules laid down for conducting the same. 1889 [C5632] L 735

Report of the Committee appointed to inquire into the arrears of Shipbuilding, 1902 [Cd1055] LX 1.

Report of the Conference appointed to examine the Shops and Machinery at Woolwich Arsenal ... in order to consider whether any article not now made in the Ordnance Factories can appropriately be made there with this machinery: with proceedings of the Conference, Minutes of Evidence and Appendices. 1907 [Cd3514] XLIX 449

Evidence taken before the Fair Wages Committee with Index thereto. 1908 [Cd4423] XXXIV 607

First Interim Report of the Committee on National Expenditure (The Geddes Committee) 1922 [Cmd1581] IX 1

Statement of the First Lord of the Admiralty explanatory of the Naval Construction Programme for 1930. 1929-30 [Cmd3620] XX 697

## ARTICLES

ASHWORTH, W. 'Economic Aspects of Late Victorian Naval Administration', *Economic History Review*, Second Series Vol. XXII (1969)

BELLAMY, J. M. 'A Hull Shipbuilding Firm', *Business History*, Vol. VI (1964)

BILES, J. H. 'Fifty Years of Warship-building on the Clyde', *North East Coast Institution of Engineers and Shipbuilders Transactions*, Vol. XXVI (1908-09)

BUXTON, N. K. 'The Scottish Shipbuilding Industry between the Wars: A Comparative Study', *Business History*, Vol. X (1968)

CAMPBELL, R. H. 'Overhead Costs and Profitability: A Note of Some Uses of Business Records', *Scottish Industrial History*, Vol. I (1977)

IRVING, R. J. 'New Investments for Old? Some Investment Decisions of Sir W. G. Armstrong, Whitworth & Co. Ltd., 1900-1914', *Business History*, Vol. XVII (1975)

LANE, F. C. 'Tonnage, Medieval and Modern', *Economic History Review*, Second Series Vol. XVII (1964)

LYONS, H. 'The Admiralty and Private Industry', in *Technical Change and British Naval Policy, 1860-1939*, ed. B. Ranft (London 1977)

MARRINER, S. 'Company Financial Statements as Source Material for Business Historians', *Business History*, Vol. XXII (1980)

MORE, C. R. V. 'Armaments and Profits: The Case of Fairfield', *Business History*, Vol. XXIV (1982)

POLLARD, S. 'The Decline of Shipbuilding on the Thames', *Economic History Review*, Second Series Vol. III (1950)

SLAVEN, A. 'A Shipyard in Depression: John Browns of Clydebank, 1919-1938', *Business History* Vol. XIX (1977)

SLAVEN, A. 'Management Policy and the Eclipse of British Shipbuilding', in *European Shipbuilding: One Hundred Years of Change*, Proceedings of the Third Shipbuilding History Conference at the National Maritime Museum, Greenwich, 13-15 April 1983 (London 1983)

TREBILCOCK, C. 'Legends of the British Armaments Industry, 1890-1914', *Journal of Contemporary History*, Vol. V (1970)

## BOOKS

ASHWORTH, W. *Contracts and Finance*, in *United Kingdom Civil Series on History of the Second World War* (London 1953)

BACON, R. *From 1900 Onward* (London 1940)

BANBURY, P. *Shipbuilders of the Thames and Medway* (Newton Abbot 1971)

BARNABY, K. C. *One Hundred Years of Specialised Shipbuilding and Engineering* (London 1964)

BARNES, E. C. (Lady Yarrow) *Alfred Yarrow: His Life and Work* (London 1923)

BREMNER, D. *The Industries of Scotland* (Edinburgh 1869)

CAMPBELL, R. H. *Scotland since 1707: The Rise of an Industrial Society* (Oxford 1965: 1971 edition)

CAMPBELL, R. H. *The Rise and Fall of Scottish Industry, 1707-1939* (Edinburgh 1980)

CARVEL, J. L. *Stephens of Linthouse: A Record of Two Hundred Years of Shipbuilding, 1750-1950* (Glasgow 1951)

CHURCHILL, W. S. *Lord Randolph Churchill* (London 1907)

CLARKE, J. F. *Power on Land and Sea: One Hundred Years of Industrial Enterprise on Tyneside: A History of R. & W. Hawthorn Leslie* (London 1978)

CONWAY'S *All the World's Fighting Ships* (four volumes) (London 1979-1985)

CROCKER, M. P. *Observor's Directory of Royal Navy Submarines, 1901-1982* (London 1982)

*The Denny List*, compiler D. J. Lyon (London 1975)

DITTMAR, F. J. & COLLEDGE, J. F. *British Warships, 1914-1919* (London 1972)

DOLBY, J. *The Steel Navy: A History in Silhouette, 1860-1962* (London 1962)

DOUGAN, D. *The History of North East Shipbuilding* (London 1968)

d'EYNCOURT, Sir Eustace *A Shipbuilder's Yarn* (London 1948)

*The Fairfield Shipbuilding and Engineering Works* (London 1909)

GRANT, Sir Allan *Steel and Ships: The History of John Brown's* (London 1950)

GREEN, Edwin & MOSS, Michael *A Business of National Importance: The Royal Mail Shipping Group 1902-1937* (London 1982)

HAMILTON, Henry *The Industrial Revolution in Scotland* (Oxford 1932: reissued London 1966)

HOWARD, M. E. *The Continental Commitment: The Dilemma of British Defence Policy in the Era of the Two World Wars* (London 1972: Penguin edition 1974)

HUME, J. R. & MOSS, M. S. *Beardmore: The History of a Scottish Industrial Giant* (London 1979)

HYDE, F. E. *Shipping Enterprise and Management 1830-1939: Harrisons of Liverpool* (London 1967)

HYDE, F. E. *Cunard and the North Atlantic, 1840-1973: A History of Shipping and Financial Management* (London 1975)

JENKINS, R. H. *Asquith* (London 1964)

JONES, Leslie *Shipbuilding in Britain: Mainly between the Two Wars* (Cardiff 1957)

KIRBY, M. W. *The Decline of British Economic Power since 1870* (London 1981)

LEWIS, M. A. *The History of the British Navy* (Harmondsworth 1957: hardback edition 1959)

MAGNUS, Philip *Gladstone: A Biography* (London 1954)

MARCH, E. J. *British Destroyers: A History of Development 1892-1953* (London 1967)

MARDER, A. J. *The Anatomy of British Sea Power: A History of British Naval Policy in the Pre-Dreadnought Era, 1880-1905* (Norwood, Massachusetts 1941: reissued London 1964)

MARDER, A. J. *From the Dreadnought to Scapa Flow: The Royal Navy in the Fisher Era, 1904-1919* (five volumes) (London 1961-1970)

MARQUAND, D. *Ramsay Macdonald* (London 1977)

MARRINER, S. & HYDE, F. E. *The Senior John Samuel Swire 1825-1898: Management in Far Eastern Shipping Trades* (London 1967)

McCOY, D. R. *Coming of Age: The United States during the 1920's and 1930's* (Harmondsworth 1973)

MOSS, M. S. and HUME, J. R. *Workshop of the British Empire: Engineering and Shipbuilding in the West of Scotland* (London 1977)

MOWAT, C. L. *Britain between the Wars, 1918-*1940 (London 1955: University Paperback edition 1968)

NAPIER, James *Life of Robert Napier of West Shandon* (Edinburgh 1904)

PADFIELD, P. *The Great Naval Race* (London 1974)

PARKES, O. *British Battleships: 'Warrior' 1860 to 'Vanguard' 1950: A History of Design, Construction and Armament etc.* (London 1957)

PAYNE, P. L. *Colvilles and the Scottish Steel Industry* (Oxford 1979)

POLLARD, S. *The Development of the British Economy, 1914-1967* (London 1962: second edition London 1969)

POLLARD, S. & ROBERTSON, P. *The British Shipbuilding Industry, 1870-1914* (Cambridge, Mass. 1979)

POLLOCK, D. *The Shipbuilding Industry* (London 1905)

REID, J. M. *James Lithgow: Master of Work* (London 1964)

RICHMOND, H. *Statesmen and Seapower* (Oxford 1946)

ROSKILL, S. W. *Naval Policy between the Wars* (two volumes) (London 1968 & 1976)

SCOTT, J. D. *Vickers: A History* (London 1962)

SCOTT, W. R. & CUNNISON, J. *The Industries of the Clyde Valley during the War* (Oxford 1924)

Scott's Shipbuilding & Engineering Co. Ltd. *Two Centuries of Shipbuilding by Scotts at Greenock* (London 1906)

SHAY, R. B. *British Rearmament in the Thirties: Politics and Profits* (London 1977)

SHIELDS, J. *Clyde Built* (Glasgow 1949)

SLAVEN, A. *The Development of the West of Scotland 1750-1960* (London 1975)

*Survey of Metal Industries,* Part IV of a Survey of Industries issued by the Committee on Industry and Trade (HMSO 1928)

TREBILCOCK, C. *The Vickers Brothers: Armaments and Enterprise, 1854-1914* (London 1977)

WALKER, F. M. *Song of the Clyde: A History of Clyde Shipbuilding* (London 1984)

WHITE, C. *Victoria's Navy: The End of the Sailing Navy* (Ensworth, Hants 1981)

WHITE, C. *Victoria's Navy: The Heyday of Steam* (Ensworth, Hants. 1981)

WILKINSON, E. *The Town that was Murdered* (London 1939)

*Yarrow & Co. Ltd., 1865-1977* (Glasgow 1977)

# APPENDIX A
## OUTPUT OF CLYDE SHIPBUILDING INDUSTRY, 1889–1938

| YEAR | WARSHIPS | | MERCHANT SHIPS | | TOTAL | | CLYDE'S SHARE OF MERCHANT OUTPUT | |
|---|---|---|---|---|---|---|---|---|
| | NO. | TONS | NO. | TONS | NO. | TONS | U.K. % | WORLD % |
| 1889 | 4 | 6810 | 245 | 328391 | 249 | 335201 | | |
| 1890 | 3 | 9680 | 299 | 352488 | 302 | 362168 | | |
| 1891 | 4 | 14300 | 337 | 311177 | 341 | 325477 | | |
| 1892 | 3 | 22817 | 347 | 313597 | 350 | 336414 | 28.2 | 23.0 |
| 1893 | 0 | 0 | 253 | 280160 | 253 | 280160 | 33.4 | 27.2 |
| 1894 | 3 | 840 | 254 | 340045 | 257 | 340885 | 32.4 | 25.6 |
| 1895 | 16 | 42112 | 305 | 318040 | 321 | 360152 | 33.4 | 26.1 |
| 1896 | 9 | 24425 | 368 | 396416 | 377 | 420841 | 34.1 | 25.2 |
| 1897 | 8 | 13665 | 310 | 326372 | 318 | 340037 | 34.2 | 24.5 |
| 1898 | 8 | 41158 | 320 | 425674 | 328 | 466832 | 31.1 | 22.4 |
| 1899 | 5 | 40275 | 279 | 450799 | 284 | 491074 | 31.8 | 21.2 |
| 1900 | 5 | 13515 | 313 | 479094 | 318 | 492609 | 33.2 | 20.7 |
| 1901 | 6 | 60146 | 291 | 451844 | 297 | 511990 | 29.6 | 17.2 |
| 1902 | 3 | 29400 | 309 | 488870 | 312 | 518270 | 34.2 | 19.5 |
| 1903 | 5 | 64800 | 272 | 382069 | 277 | 446869 | 32.0 | 17.8 |
| 1904 | 3 | 16400 | 326 | 401470 | 329 | 417870 | 33.3 | 20.1 |
| 1905 | 1 | 13550 | n.a. | 526300 | n.a. | 539850 | 32.4 | 20.9 |
| 1906 | 1 | 15925 | n.a. | 582916 | n.a. | 598841 | 31.8 | 19.9 |
| 1907 | 3 | 35001 | 424 | 584918 | 427 | 619919 | 36.3 | 21.0 |
| 1908 | 11 | 3199 | 558 | 352387 | 569 | 355586 | 37.9 | 19.2 |
| 1909 | 11 | 16644 | 343 | 386543 | 354 | 403187 | 39.0 | 24.1 |
| 1910 | 19 | 42534 | 339 | 349858 | 358 | 392392 | 30.6 | 17.8 |
| 1911 | 16 | 75024 | 397 | 555559 | 413 | 630583 | 30.7 | 20.9 |
| 1912 | 16 | 51520 | 373 | 589009 | 389 | 640529 | 33.8 | 20.2 |
| 1913 | 17 | 64617 | 353 | 692359 | 370 | 756976 | 35.8 | 20.7 |
| 1914–1918 | Figures unavailable | | | | | | | |
| 1919 | 76 | 126275 | 346 | 520682 | 422 | 646957 | 32.1 | 7.3 |
| 1920 | 0 | 0 | 330 | 672438 | 330 | 672438 | 32.7 | 11.4 |
| 1921 | 0 | 0 | 249 | 511185 | 249 | 511185 | 33.2 | 11.7 |
| 1922 | 0 | 0 | 143 | 388481 | 143 | 388481 | 37.6 | 15.7 |
| 1923 | 0 | 0 | 122 | 175528 | 122 | 175528 | 27.1 | 10.6 |
| 1924 | 0 | 0 | 251 | 538021 | 251 | 538021 | 37.3 | 23.9 |
| 1925 | 0 | 0 | 280 | 523322 | 280 | 523322 | 48.2 | 23.8 |
| 1926 | 2 | 11210 | 171 | 276034 | 173 | 287244 | 43.1 | 16.4 |
| 1927 | 6 | 21182 | 268 | 442346 | 274 | 463528 | 36.0 | 19.3 |
| 1928 | 3 | 21540 | 238 | 583071 | 241 | 604611 | 40.3 | 21.6 |
| 1929 | 5 | 7740 | 229 | 558058 | 234 | 565798 | 36.6 | 19.9 |
| 1930 | 5 | 3280 | 243 | 526564 | 248 | 529844 | 35.6 | 18.2 |
| 1931 | 2 | 2754 | 97 | 149909 | 99 | 152663 | 29.8 | 9.3 |
| 1932 | 2 | 2880 | 28 | 63757 | 30 | 66637 | 33.9 | 8.8 |
| 1933 | 4 | 4510 | 27 | 51858. | 31 | 56368 | 38.9 | 10.6 |

APPENDIX A (*continued*)

| YEAR | WARSHIPS | | MERCHANT SHIPS | | TOTAL | | CLYDE'S SHARE OF MERCHANT OUTPUT | |
|------|------|------|------|------|------|------|------|------|
| | NO. | TONS | NO. | TONS | NO. | TONS | U.K. % | WORLD % |
| 1934 | 11 | 29596 | 56 | 238525 | 67 | 268121 | 51.8 | 24.6 |
| 1935 | 8 | 9113 | 66 | 162817 | 74 | 171930 | 32.6 | 12.5 |
| 1936 | 11 | 30491 | 94 | 296366 | 105 | 326857 | 34.6 | 13.9 |
| 1937 | 19 | 43167 | 93 | 337937 | 112 | 381104 | 36.6 | 12.5 |
| 1938 | 19 | 32015 | 98 | 411600 | 117 | 443615 | 39.9 | 13.5 |

(Source: based on figures abstracted from the Annual Trade Reviews published by *The Glasgow Herald*)

## APPENDIX B
## OUTPUT OF CLYDE WARSHIPBUILDERS, 1889–1938

| YEAR | WARSHIPS | | MERCHANT WORK | TOTAL | % CLYDE OUTPUT | | |
|------|------|------|------|------|------|------|------|
| | BRITISH TONS | FOREIGN TONS | TONS | TONS | WARSHIPS | MERCHANT | TOTAL |
| 1889 | 6810 | | 95502 | 102312 | 100.00 | 29.08 | 30.52 |
| 1890 | 7000 | 2680 | 80243 | 89923 | 100.00 | 22.59 | 24.83 |
| 1891 | 14300 | | 75193 | 89493 | 100.00 | 24.16 | 27.50 |
| 1892 | 22000 | 817 | 62798 | 85615 | 100.00 | 19.97 | ˙25.45 |
| 1893 | | | 77183 | 77183 | | 27.55 | 27.55 |
| 1894 | 840 | | 63760 | 64600 | 100.00 | 18.75 | 18.95 |
| 1895 | 40962 | 600 | 102133 | 143695 | 98.69 | 32.05 | 39.90 |
| 1896 | 23685 | 740 | 102669 | 127094 | 100.00 | 25.85 | 30.20 |
| 1897 | 12065 | 1600 | 73505 | 87170 | 100.00 | 22.41 | 25.64 |
| 1898 | 41158 | | 108704 | 149862 | 100.00 | 25.54 | 32.10 |
| 1899 | 25075 | 15200 | 110099 | 150374 | 100.00 | 23.63 | 30.62 |
| 1900 | 13515 | | 104023 | 117538 | 100.00 | 21.71 | 23.86 |
| 1901 | 60146 | | 104401 | 164547 | 100.00 | 23.11 | 32.14 |
| 1902 | 29400 | | 110476 | 139876 | 100.00 | 22.60 | 26.99 |
| 1903 | 64800 | | 101475 | 166275 | 100.00 | 26.56 | 37.21 |
| 1904 | 16400 | | 67353 | 83753 | 100.00 | 16.78 | 20.04 |
| 1905 | 13550 | | 114820 | 128370 | 100.00 | 21.82 | 23.78 |
| 1906 | 15925 | | 158521 | 174446 | 100.00 | 27.19 | 29.13 |
| 1907 | 35001 | | 124026 | 159027 | 100.00 | 21.20 | 25.65 |
| 1908 | 745 | 2454 | 69061 | 72260 | 100.00 | 19.46 | 20.32 |
| 1909 | 14404 | 2240 | 86358 | 103002 | 100.00 | 22.21 | 25.55 |
| 1910 | 41414 | 1120 | 40002 | 82536 | 100.00 | 11.40 | 21.03 |
| 1911 | 74000 | 244 | 147963 | 222207 | 98.96 | 26.62 | 35.24 |
| 1912 | 51395 | 125 | 136582 | 188102 | 100.00 | 23.18 | 29.37 |

APPENDIX B (*continued*)

| YEAR | WARSHIPS BRITISH TONS | FOREIGN TONS | MERCHANT WORK TONS | TOTAL TONS | % CLYDE OUTPUT WARSHIPS | MERCHANT | TOTAL |
|------|------|------|------|------|------|------|------|
| 1913 | 63917 | 700 | 219455 | 284072 | 100.00 | 31.66 | 37.53 |
| 1914–1918 | Figures unavailable | | | | | | |
| 1919 | 92464 | 180 | 80325 | 172969 | 73.37 | 15.42 | 26.74 |
| 1920 | | | 187475 | 187475 | | 27.88 | 27.88 |
| 1921 | | | 185149 | 185149 | | 36.22 | 36.22 |
| 1922 | | | 141446 | 141446 | | 36.41 | 36.41 |
| 1923 | | | 57083 | 57083 | | 32.52 | 32.52 |
| 1924 | | | 168731 | 168731 | | 31.36 | 31.36 |
| 1925 | | | 162706 | 162706 | | 31.09 | 31.09 |
| 1926 | 11210 | | 64958 | 76168 | 100.00 | 23.53 | 26.52 |
| 1927 | 21182 | | 128685 | 149867 | 100.00 | 29.09 | 32.33 |
| 1928 | 21540 | | 203870 | 225410 | 100.00 | 34.96 | 37.28 |
| 1929 | 7740 | | 122611 | 130351 | 100.00 | 21.97 | 23.04 |
| 1930 | 2980 | 300 | 177922 | 181202 | 100.00 | 33.77 | 34.20 |
| 1931 | 354 | 2400 | 73548 | 76302 | 100.00 | 48.29 | 49.98 |
| 1932 | 2880 | | 14016 | 16896 | 100.00 | 21.98 | 25.36 |
| 1933 | 1310 | 3200 | 8025 | 12535 | 100.00 | 14.58 | 22.24 |
| 1934 | 29596 | | 111316 | 140912 | 100.00 | 46.67 | 52.56 |
| 1935 | 8238 | | 22573 | 30811 | 90.40 | 13.86 | 17.92 |
| 1936 | 30491 | | 47306 | 77797 | 100.00 | 15.96 | 23.80 |
| 1937 | 37927 | 2750 | 64165 | 104842 | 94.23 | 18.83 | 27.51 |
| 1938 | 22975 | 2800 | 154063 | 179838 | 80.51 | 37.18 | 40.54 |

(Source: Series constructed by the author based on data abstracted from the Annual Trade Reviews published by The Glasgow Herald. For details see Peebles, thesis, Appendix D)

## APPENDIX C
### CLYDE'S SHARE OF ADMIRALTY WARSHIP ORDERS, 1859–1888

| LAID DOWN | WARSHIPS ORDERED | | | PRIVATE CONTRACTORS | | | | CLYDESIDE'S SHARE | | | |
| | | HULLS | ENGINES | | HULLS | | ENGINES | | HULLS | | ENGINES |
| | NO. | TONS | H.P. | NO. | TONS | NO. | H.P. | NO. | TONS | NO. | H.P. |
|---|---|---|---|---|---|---|---|---|---|---|---|
| 1859–1860 | 13 | 49348 | 26039 | 4 | 30607 | 13 | 26039 | 1 | 9250 | 5 | 4184 |
| 1860–1861 | 10 | 24130 | 12654 | 2 | 13420 | 10 | 12654 | 1 | 6710 | 5 | 6558 |
| 1861–1862 | 4 | 41903 | 25832 | 3 | 32074 | 4 | 25832 | | | | |
| 1862–1863 | 1 | 3687 | 2128 | 1 | 3687 | 1 | 2128 | | | | |
| 1863–1864 | 4 | 26804 | 22865 | | | 4 | 22865 | | | | |
| 1864–1865 | *7 | 12314 | 8729 | 5 | 9192 | 7 | 8729 | | | | |
| 1865–1866 | 6 | 19486 | 19337 | | | 6 | 19337 | | | 1 | 1464 |
| 1866–1867 | 5 | 26192 | 23289 | 1 | 7767 | 5 | 23289 | | | 1 | 1597 |
| 1867–1868 | 10 | 41980 | 36940 | 6 | 27534 | 10 | 36940 | 2 | 12020 | 2 | 6919 |
| 1868–1869 | 11 | 42180 | 31448 | 5 | 24126 | 11 | 31448 | 1 | 4331 | 1 | 3500 |
| 1869–1870 | 3 | 20379 | 15428 | | | 3 | 15428 | | | | |
| 1870–1871 | 9 | 40105 | 32171 | 4 | 13920 | 9 | 32171 | 1 | 3480 | 4 | 10790 |
| 1871–1872 | 1 | 5200 | 5640 | | | 1 | 5640 | | | | |
| 1872–1873 | 10 | 20807 | 21441 | 3 | 5340 | 10 | 21441 | | | | |
| 1873–1874 | 5 | 30030 | 23386 | | | 5 | 23386 | | | 2 | 10475 |
| 1874–1875 | 10 | 31763 | 29455 | 6 | 23583 | 10 | 29455 | 2 | 15103 | 3 | 10894 |
| 1875–1876 | 9 | 31275 | 36069 | 2 | 2260 | 9 | 36069 | 2 | 2260 | | |
| 1876–1877 | 9 | 25050 | 22990 | 6 | 14280 | 9 | 22990 | 6 | 14280 | 3 | 7163 |
| 1877–1878 | *7 | 31970 | 24788 | 4 | 28580 | 7 | 24788 | | | | |
| 1878–1879 | 6 | 17830 | 19636 | | | 6 | 19636 | | | 1 | 1020 |
| 1879–1880 | 7 | 23770 | 19998 | | | 7 | 19998 | | | | |
| 1880–1881 | 7 | 26660 | 30440 | 3 | 12900 | 7 | 30440 | 3 | 12900 | 3 | 16500 |
| 1881–1882 | 11 | 43250 | 44910 | 2 | 1850 | 11 | 44910 | | | | |
| 1882–1883 | 6 | 34860 | 37600 | 1 | 10600 | 5 | 36400 | | | | |
| 1883–1884 | 9 | 26540 | 29770 | 4 | 5900 | 9 | 29770 | 1 | 1580 | 1 | 2000 |
| 1884–1885 | 14 | 30750 | 36300 | 7 | 12200 | 14 | 36300 | 6 | 10620 | 6 | 15000 |
| 1885–1886 | 13 | 76820 | 73700 | 8 | 49490 | 13 | 73700 | 2 | 11200 | 3 | 16500 |
| 1886–1887 | 5 | 15308 | 17600 | | | 5 | 17600 | | | | |
| 1887–1888 | 7 | 16730 | 48570 | 2 | 5900 | 7 | 48570 | 2 | 5900 | 2 | 3570 |
| 1888–1889 | 27 | 58180 | 114700 | 11 | 26795 | 27 | 114700 | 2 | 5150 | 2 | 8000 |

\* including warships purchased while under construction.

IN ADDITION TO THE MAJOR WARSHIPS INCLUDED ABOVE THE ADMIRALTY ORDERED
LARGE NUMBERS OF SMALLER WARSHIPS. AT LEAST 84 OF THESE (AGGREGATING 47699
TONS) WERE BUILT BY PRIVATE CONTRACTORS. 18 SHIPS AGGREGATING 9380 TONS WERE
BUILT ON THE CLYDE.

(Source: Author's figures. See Peebles, thesis, Appendix A)

# APPENDIX D
## CLYDE'S SHARE OF ADMIRALTY WARSHIPBUILDING PROGRAMMES, 1889–1938

| PROGRAMME | WARSHIPS ORDERED | | | PRIVATE CONTRACTORS | | | | CLYDESIDE'S SHARE | | | |
|---|---|---|---|---|---|---|---|---|---|---|---|
| | HULLS | | ENGINES | HULLS | | ENGINES | | HULLS | | ENGINES | |
| | NO. | TONS | H.P. | NO. | TONS | NO. | H.P. | NO. | TONS | NO. | H.P. |
| 1889 (N.D.A.) | 70 | 335060 | 466000 | 32 | 157510 | 63 | 429000 | 8 | 42850 | 14 | 110000 |
| 1893–1894 | 59 | 102183 | 297150 | 54 | 41663 | 57 | 270350 | 9 | 16415 | 9 | 57300 |
| 1894–1895 | 23 | 141435 | 168800 | 16 | 65710 | 21 | 166000 | 5 | 37125 | 5 | 42000 |
| 1895–1896 | 31 | 78910 | 244500 | 24 | 40640 | 29 | 229500 | 6 | 23485 | 7 | 61200 |
| 1896–1897 | 37 | 146525 | 321750 | 32 | 93940 | 37 | 321750 | 10 | 40835 | 11 | 112800 |
| 1897–1898 | 24 | 118324 | 209600 | 16 | 66519 | 21 | 198200 | 6 | 37790 | 7 | 76900 |
| 1898–1899 | 28 | 205350 | 383800 | 20 | 126040 | 27 | 382400 | 5 | 41050 | 6 | 115500 |
| 1899–1900 | 6 | 46830 | 86000 | 4 | 19970 | 6 | 86000 | 2 | 19600 | 2 | 44000 |
| 1900–1901 | *36 | 104071 | 250000 | 25 | 43871 | 33 | 245800 | 6 | 30540 | 6 | 78200 |
| 1901–1902 | *23 | 124655 | 283400 | 20 | 92295 | 22 | 270900 | 5 | 59010 | 4 | 81000 |
| 1902–1903 | 26 | 92220 | 293100 | 24 | 63085 | 26 | 293100 | 3 | 21605 | 3 | 51000 |
| 1903–1904 | 34 | 117770 | 278150 | 30 | 56875 | 34 | 278150 | 1 | 13550 | 2 | 41000 |
| 1904–1905 | *18 | 102992 | 142500 | 15 | 59192 | 18 | 142500 | 1 | 15925 | 1 | 27000 |
| 1905–1906 | 33 | 82872 | 298800 | 32 | 64762 | 33 | 298800 | 2 | 34700 | 2 | 82000 |
| 1906–1907 | 24 | 63516 | 152200 | 20 | 25336 | 24 | 152200 | 3 | 755 | 4 | 35000 |
| 1907–1908 | 28 | 72612 | 221165 | 23 | 29612 | 28 | 221165 | 3 | 1526 | 5 | 66000 |
| 1908–1909 | 38 | 84613 | 433200 | 33 | 42503 | 38 | 433200 | 11 | 21936 | 13 | 241400 |
| 1909–1910 | *48 | 269078 | 834125 | 42 | 212700 | 48 | 834125 | 18 | 98870 | 18 | 337225 |
| 1910–1911 | 46 | 180751 | 706500 | 39 | 121151 | 46 | 706500 | 18 | 52879 | 17 | 352800 |
| 1911–1912 | 37 | 174635 | 833300 | 30 | 108991 | 38 | 833300 | 12 | 64666 | 14 | 379200 |
| 1912–1913 | 45 | 194620 | 1199200 | 37 | 129743 | 45 | 1199200 | 18 | 81938 | 19 | 644000 |
| 1913–1914 | 46 | 196642 | 1010450 | 35 | 119092 | 46 | 1010450 | 11 | 36431 | 12 | 264950 |
| WARTIME EMERGENCY PROGRAMMES | | | | | | | | | | | |
| 1914–1915 | *217 | 443598 | 3088050 | 210 | 432018 | 217 | 3088050 | 82 | 151013 | 79 | 1140200 |
| 1915–1916 | 130 | 280296 | 3397750 | 121 | 237441 | 130 | 3397750 | 66 | 95028 | 59 | 1387550 |
| 1916–1917 | *121 | 337395 | 2486080 | 118 | 334345 | 121 | 2486080 | 37 | 145510 | 37 | 1028040 |
| 1917–1918 | 144 | 247290 | 3421840 | 134 | 243070 | 144 | 3421840 | 70 | 102495 | 70 | 1725650 |
| 1918–1919 | 59 | 82330 | 1343280 | 59 | 82330 | 59 | 1343280 | 30 | 37925 | 30 | 684600 |
| CANCEL-LATIONS | -85 | -251655 | -2016240 | -81 | -249045 | -85 | -2016240 | -43 | -102300 | -43 | -1093200 |
| SLOOPS ETC. (NET) | 414 | 380439 | 891800 | 414 | 380439 | 414 | 891800 | 241 | 225266 | 241 | 512050 |
| TOTAL | 1000 | 1519693 | 12612560 | 975 | 1460598 | 1000 | 12612560 | 483 | 654937 | 473 | 5384890 |
| | | | | | | | | | | | |
| 1921–1922 | 1 | 2425 | 2400 | | | 1 | 2400 | | | | |
| 1922–1923 | 3 | 73783 | 130000 | 2 | 67043 | 3 | 130000 | | | | |
| 1923–1924 | 1 | 1311 | 1350 | | | 1 | 1350 | | | | |
| 1924–1925 | 7 | 51275 | 472500 | 4 | 22025 | 7 | 472500 | 2 | 10923 | 3 | 193000 |
| 1925–1926 | 14 | 89902 | 505440 | 12 | 70202 | 14 | 505440 | 7 | 30714 | 8 | 327240 |
| 1926–1927 | 9 | 37000 | 248340 | 7 | 25600 | 9 | 248340 | 3 | 12925 | 3 | 82780 |
| 1927–1928 | 18 | 31566 | 404810 | 16 | 21701 | 18 | 404810 | 4 | 5348 | 4 | 136000 |
| 1928–1929 | 20 | 26224 | 386680 | 17 | 22659 | 20 | 386680 | 2 | 2720 | 2 | 68000 |
| 1929–1930 | 15 | 24932 | 274130 | 7 | 8562 | 15 | 274130 | 1 | 372 | 1 | 2250 |
| 1930–1931 | 20 | 41025 | 553110 | 11 | 19715 | 20 | 553110 | 2 | 2750 | 5 | 112000 |
| 1931–1932 | 21 | 47756 | 554220 | 15 | 31351 | 21 | 554220 | 8 | 16226 | 10 | 264840 |
| 1932–1933 | 20 | 39720 | 548920 | 16 | 30090 | 20 | 548920 | 4 | 9490 | 5 | 246000 |
| 1933–1934 | 21 | 46655 | 550370 | 18 | 43155 | 21 | 550370 | 11 | 21865 | 11 | 268110 |
| 1934–1935 | 24 | 75425 | 724010 | 19 | 58405 | 24 | 724010 | 8 | 16670 | 9 | 296500 |
| 1935–1936 | 31 | 72812 | 899020 | 27 | 61112 | 31 | 899020 | 10 | 31177 | 11 | 441630 |
| 1936–1937 | 44 | 214935 | 1691655 | 39 | 200585 | 44 | 1691655 | 17 | 29065 | 16 | 552200 |
| 1937–1938 | 49 | 267020 | 1797600 | 45 | 255770 | 49 | 1797600 | 21 | 129944 | 23 | 828700 |
| 1938–1939 | 21 | 124140 | 883550 | 20 | 123050 | 21 | 883550 | 10 | 66080 | 10 | 385700 |

Note: excluding peacetime cancellations * including warships purchased while under construction.
(Source: Author's figures. See Peebles, thesis, Appendix A)

APPENDIX E
DETAILS OF WARSHIPS BUILT ON THE CLYDE, 1859-1939

I. DETAILS OF ADMIRALTY ORDERS FOR WARSHIPS, 1859-1888
II. DETAILS OF ADMIRALTY ORDERS FOR WARSHIPS, 1889-1914
III. DETAILS OF ADMIRALTY ORDERS FOR WARSHIPS, 1914-1919
IV. DETAILS OF ADMIRALTY ORDERS FOR WARSHIPS, 1920-1939
V. DETAILS OF WARSHIPS ORDERED BY FOREIGN POWERS, 1859-1939
VI. DISTRIBUTION OF WARSHIP ORDERS, 1859-1939

NOTES ON SOURCES ETC.

a. In assembling data on warships built between 1859 and 1939 reference was made to the following sources:
*BRITISH BATTLESHIPS* by Oscar Parkes (Seeley, Service & Co., 1966).
*BRITISH DESTROYERS* by E. J. Marsh (Seeley, Service & Co., 1966).
*BRITISH WARSHIPS 1914-1919* by F. J. Dittmar & J. F. Colledge (Allan, 1972)
*ALL THE WORLD'S FIGHTING SHIPS* published by the Conway Maritime Press
Volume 1 (1860-1905) 1979
Volume 2 (1906-1921) 1985
Volume 3 (1921-1946) 1980.
*OBSERVOR'S DIRECTORY OF ROYAL NAVY SUBMARINES 1901-1982* by M. P. Crocker (Frederick Warne (Publishers) Ltd. 1982)
The composition of annual shipbuilding programmes between 1892-1893 and 1938-1939 has been determined by reference to these same sources and to the relevant Navy Estimates.
b. Admiralty programmes include all warships built in the United Kingdom for the Royal Australian Navy, the Royal New Zealand Navy, the Royal Indian Navy and for any of Britain's overseas dependencies.
c. In using these statistics it should be borne in mind that the displacement tonnage of warships built from 1921 onwards is not strictly comparable with the displacement tonnage of warships built earlier. Under the terms of the Washington Treaty, standard displacement was defined as the displacement of a warship excluding fuel and reserve feed but otherwise fully armed and equipped and ready for sea. Up to 1921 the displacement of British warships quoted by the Navy List normally included approximately half-fuel as well as the ordinary supply of stores, water etc. Similarly, care should be taken in using figures relating to the horsepower of machinery. Different measures were used for different types of engine and all aggregations of horsepower relating to different sizes of warship are necessarily misleading.

# I. DETAILS OF ADMIRALTY ORDERS FOR WARSHIPS, 1859–1888

| YEAR & TYPE | CLASS | NAME | HULL TONS | ENGINES H.P. | LAID DOWN | LAUNCHED | COM-PLETED | BUILDER |
|---|---|---|---|---|---|---|---|---|
| **1859–1860** | | | | | | | | |
| BROADSIDE IRONCLAD (HULL ONLY) | Warrior | BLACK PRINCE | 9250 | | 5.59 | 12.60 | 10.61 | ROBERT NAPIER & SONS |
| WOODEN FRIGATE ENGINES | Immortalité | BRISTOL | | 2088 | 9.59 | 2.61 | 10.65 | ROBERT NAPIER & SONS |
| WOODEN SLOOP ENGINES | Rosario | ROSARIO | | 464 | 6.59 | 10.60 | | GREENOCK FOUNDRY |
| WOODEN SLOOP ENGINES | Rosario | RAPID | | 460 | 8.59 | 11.60 | | GREENOCK FOUNDRY |
| WOODEN SLOOP ENGINES | Rosario | PETEREL | | 478 | 12.59 | 11.60 | | GREENOCK FOUNDRY |
| WOODEN SLOOP ENGINES | Cameleon | CHANTICLEER | | 694 | 2.60 | 2.61 | | A & J INGLIS |
| **1860–1861** | | | | | | | | |
| BROADSIDE IRONCLAD | Hector | HECTOR | 6710 | 3260 | 3.61 | 9.62 | 2.64 | ROBERT NAPIER & SONS |
| WOODEN FRIGATE ENGINES | none | ENDYMION | | 1620 | 10.60 | 11.65 | 9.66 | ROBERT NAPIER & SONS |
| WOODEN SLOOP ENGINES | Rosario | AFRICA | | 530 | 12.60 | 2.62 | | GREENOCK FOUNDRY |
| WOODEN SLOOP ENGINES | Rosario | COLUMBINE | | 521 | 5.60 | 4.62 | | GREENOCK FOUNDRY |
| WOODEN SLOOP ENGINES | Rosario | ROYALIST | | 627 | 11.60 | 12.61 | | GREENOCK FOUNDRY |
| **1865–1866** | | | | | | | | |
| WOODEN SLOOP ENGINES | Amazon | DRYAD | | 1464 | | 9.66 | | ROBERT NAPIER & SONS |
| **1866–1867** | | | | | | | | |
| WOODEN CORVETTE ENGINES | Juno | THALIA | | 1597 | | .66 | 7.69 | ROBERT NAPIER & SONS |
| COMPOSITE GUN VESSEL | Beacon | HART | 603 | 580 | | | | J & G THOMSON |
| COMPOSITE GUN VESSEL | Beacon | MIDGE | 603 | 580 | | | | JOHN ELDER & CO. |
| COMPOSITE GUN VESSEL | Beacon | PERT | 603 | 580 | | | | REID & CO. |
| COMPOSITE GUN VESSEL | Beacon | ROCKET | 603 | 580 | | | | LONDON & GLASGOW |
| **1867–1868** | | | | | | | | |
| CENTRAL BATTERY IRONCLAD (HULL ONLY) | Audacious | AUDACIOUS | 6010 | | 6.67 | 2.69 | 9.70 | ROBERT NAPIER & SONS |
| CENTRAL BATTERY IRONCLAD | Audacious | INVINCIBLE | 6010 | 4830 | 6.67 | 5.69 | 10.70 | ROBERT NAPIER & SONS |
| WOODEN CORVETTE ENGINES | Eclipse | DANAE | | 2089 | | | | ROBERT NAPIER & SONS |
| **1868–1869** | | | | | | | | |
| TURRET RAM | Hotspur | HOTSPUR | 4331 | 3500 | 10.68 | 3.70 | 11.71 | ROBERT NAPIER & SONS |

| YEAR & TYPE | CLASS | NAME | HULL TONS | ENGINES H.P. | LAID DOWN | LAUNCHED | COM-PLETED | BUILDER |
|---|---|---|---|---|---|---|---|---|
| **1870–1871** | | | | | | | | |
| MONITOR (HULL ONLY) | Cyclops | HYDRA | 3480 | | 9.70 | 12.71 | 5.76 | ROBERT NAPIER & SONS |
| MONITOR ENGINES | Cyclops | HYDRA | | 1472 | 9.70 | 12.71 | 5.76 | JOHN ELDER & CO. |
| MONITOR ENGINES | Cyclops | CYCLOPS | | 1660 | 9.70 | 7.71 | 5.77 | JOHN ELDER & CO. |
| TURRET RAM ENGINES | Rupert | RUPERT | | 4630 | 6.70 | 3.72 | 7.74 | ROBERT NAPIER & SONS |
| WOODEN CORVETTE ENGINES | Eclipse | TENEDOS | | 3028 | 5.70 | 7.72 | | JOHN ELDER & CO. |
| FLATIRON GUNBOAT | Ant | BUSTARD | 254 | 260 | | | | ROBERT NAPIER & SONS |
| FLATIRON GUNBOAT | Ant | KITE | 254 | 260 | | | | ROBERT NAPIER & SONS |
| **1873–1874** | | | | | | | | |
| TURRET SHIP ENGINES | Inflexible | INFLEXIBLE | | 8407 | 2.74 | 4.76 | 10.81 | JOHN ELDER & CO. |
| WOODEN CORVETTE ENGINES | Amethyst | MODESTE | | 2068 | 5.73 | 1.74 | | ROBERT NAPIER & SONS |
| COMPOSITE GUN VESSEL | Arab | ARAB | 620 | 570 | | | | ROBERT NAPIER & SONS |
| COMPOSITE GUN VESSEL | Arab | LILY | 620 | 570 | | | | ROBERT NAPIER & SONS |
| **1874–1875** | | | | | | | | |
| ARMOURED CRUISER | Nelson | NELSON | 7473 | 6624 | 11.74 | 11.76 | 7.81 | JOHN ELDER & CO. |
| ARMOURED CRUISER (HULL ONLY) | Nelson | NORTHAMPTON | 7680 | | 10.74 | 11.76 | 12.78 | ROBERT NAPIER & SONS |
| COMPOSITE CORVETTE ENGINES | Emerald | OPAL | | 2100 | | 8.75 | 1.76 | ROBERT NAPIER & SONS |
| COMPOSITE CORVETTE ENGINES | Emerald | EMERALD | | 2170 | | 8.76 | 6.78 | J & G THOMSON |
| **1875–1876** | | | | | | | | |
| COMPOSITE SLOOP (HULL ONLY) | Osprey | WILD SWAN | 1130 | | | 1.76 | | ROBERT NAPIER & SONS |
| COMPOSITE SLOOP (HULL ONLY) | Osprey | PENGUIN | 1130 | | | 3.76 | | ROBERT NAPIER & SONS |
| COMPOSITE GUNBOAT | Forester | MOORHEN | 455 | 515 | | | | ROBERT NAPIER & SONS |
| COMPOSITE GUNBOAT | Forester | SHELDRAKE | 455 | 515 | | | | ROBERT NAPIER & SONS |
| COMPOSITE GUNBOAT | Forester | FIREBRAND | 455 | 515 | | | | J & G THOMSON |
| COMPOSITE GUNBOAT | Forester | FIREFLY | 455 | 515 | | | | J & G THOMSON |
| **1876–1877** | | | | | | | | |
| STEEL CORVETTE | Comus | COMUS | 2380 | 2450 | .76 | 4.78 | .78 | JOHN ELDER & CO. |
| STEEL CORVETTE | Comus | CARYSFORT | 2380 | 2403 | .76 | 9.78 | .79 | JOHN ELDER & CO. |
| STEEL CORVETTE | Comus | CHAMPION | 2380 | 2310 | .76 | 7.78 | .78 | JOHN ELDER & CO. |
| STEEL CORVETTE (HULL ONLY) | Comus | CLEOPATRA | 2380 | | .76 | 8.78 | .78 | JOHN ELDER & CO. |
| STEEL CORVETTE (HULL ONLY) | Comus | CONQUEST | 2380 | | .76 | 10.78 | .79 | JOHN ELDER & CO. |
| STEEL CORVETTE (HULL ONLY) | Comus | CURACAO | 2380 | | .76 | 4.78 | .78 | JOHN ELDER & CO. |

| YEAR & TYPE | CLASS | NAME | HULL TONS | ENGINES H.P. | LAID DOWN | LAUNCHED | COMPLETED | BUILDER |
|---|---|---|---|---|---|---|---|---|
| **1878–1879** | | | | | | | | |
| COMPOSITE SLOOP ENGINES | Doterel | MIRANDA | | 1020 | | 9.79 | .86 | ROBERT NAPIER & SONS |
| **1879–1880** | | | | | | | | |
| COMPOSITE GUN VESSEL | Algerine | RAMBLER | 835 | 810 | | | 5.85 | JOHN ELDER & CO. |
| COMPOSITE GUN VESSEL | Algerine | RANGER | 835 | 810 | | | 4.86 | JOHN ELDER & CO. |
| TORPEDO BOAT | | NO. 15 | 28 | 450 | | | | HANNA DONALD & WILSON |
| **1880–1881** | | | | | | | | |
| 2ND CLASS CRUISER | Leander | ARETHUSA | 4300 | 5500 | 6.80 | 12.82 | | ROBERT NAPIER & SONS |
| 2ND CLASS CRUISER | Leander | LEANDER | 4300 | 5500 | 6.80 | 10.82 | | ROBERT NAPIER & SONS |
| 2ND CLASS CRUISER | Leander | PHAETON | 4300 | 5500 | 6.80 | 2.83 | | ROBERT NAPIER & SONS |
| **1884–1885** | | | | | | | | |
| 3RD CLASS CRUISER | Scout | SCOUT | 1580 | 2000 | 1.84 | 7.85 | 8.85 | J & G THOMSON |
| 3RD CLASS CRUISER | Archer | ARCHER | 1770 | 2500 | 3.85 | 12.85 | 12.88 | J & G THOMSON |
| 3RD CLASS CRUISER | Archer | BRISK | 1770 | 2500 | 3.85 | 4.86 | 3.88 | J & G THOMSON |
| 3RD CLASS CRUISER | Archer | COSSACK | 1770 | 2500 | 3.85 | 6.86 | 1.89 | J & G THOMSON |
| 3RD CLASS CRUISER | Archer | MOHAWK | 1770 | 2500 | 3.85 | 2.86 | 12.90 | J & G THOMSON |
| 3RD CLASS CRUISER | Archer | PORPOISE | 1770 | 2500 | 3.85 | 5.86 | 2.88 | J & G THOMSON |
| 3RD CLASS CRUISER | Archer | TARTAR | 1770 | 2500 | 3.85 | 10.86 | 6.91 | J & G THOMSON |
| **1885–1886** | | | | | | | | |
| ARMOURED CRUISER | Orlando | AUSTRALIA | 5600 | 5500 | 4.85 | 11.86 | 10.88 | ROBERT NAPIER & SONS |
| ARMOURED CRUISER | Orlando | GALATEA | 5600 | 5500 | 4.85 | 3.87 | 3.89 | ROBERT NAPIER & SONS |
| ARMOURED CRUISER ENGINES | Orlando | AURORA | | 5500 | 2.86 | 10.87 | 7.89 | J & G THOMSON |
| **1887–1888** | | | | | | | | |
| 2ND CLASS CRUISER (HULL ONLY) | Medea | MARATHON | 2950 | | 8.87 | 8.88 | .89 | FAIRFIELD |
| 2ND CLASS CRUISER (HULL ONLY) | Medea | MAGICIENNE | 2950 | | 8.87 | 5.88 | .89 | FAIRFIELD |
| COMPOSITE SLOOP ENGINES | Nymphe | NYMPHE | | 2000 | 7.87 | 5.88 | 2.89 | GREENOCK FOUNDRY |
| COMPOSITE SLOOP ENGINES | Nymphe | DAPHNE | | 1570 | 6.87 | 5.88 | 5.89 | GREENOCK FOUNDRY |
| TORPEDO BOAT | Nymphe | NO. 101 | 92 | 1000 | | | | HANNA DONALD & WILSON |

*Warshipbuilding on the Clyde*

| YEAR & TYPE | CLASS | NAME | HULL TONS | ENGINES H.P. | LAID DOWN | LAUNCHED | COM-PLETED | BUILDER |
|---|---|---|---|---|---|---|---|---|
| **1888–1889** | | | | | | | | |
| 3RD CLASS CRUISER | Pearl | RINGAROOMA | 2575 | 4000 | 12.88 | 12.89 | 2.91 | J & G THOMSON |
| 3RD CLASS CRUISER | Pearl | TAURANGA | 2575 | 4000 | 12.88 | 10.89 | 1.91 | J & G THOMSON |
| COMPOSITE GUNBOAT (HULL ONLY) | Redbreast | SPARROW | 805 | | | .89 | | SCOTT & CO. |
| COMPOSITE GUNBOAT (HULL ONLY) | Redbreast | THRUSH | 805 | | | .89 | | SCOTT & CO. |
| COMPOSITE GUNBOAT ENGINES | Redbreast | SPARROW | | 1200 | | | | GREENOCK FOUNDRY |
| COMPOSITE GUNBOAT ENGINES | Redbreast | THRUSH | | 1200 | | | | GREENOCK FOUNDRY |

## II. DETAILS OF ADMIRALTY ORDERS FOR WARSHIPS, 1889–1914

| YEAR & TYPE | CLASS | NAME | HULL TONS | ENGINES H.P. | LAID DOWN | LAUNCHED | COM-PLETED | BUILDER |
|---|---|---|---|---|---|---|---|---|
| **1889 (NAVY DEFENCE ACT)** | | | | | | | | |
| BATTLESHIP | Royal Sovereign | RAMILLIES | 14150 | 9000 | 8.90 | 3.92 | 10.93 | CLYDEBANK |
| BATTLESHIP ENGINES | Centurion | CENTURION | | 9000 | 3.90 | 8.92 | 2.94 | GREENOCK FOUNDRY |
| BATTLESHIP ENGINES | Centurion | BARFLEUR | | 9000 | 10.90 | 8.92 | 6.94 | GREENOCK FOUNDRY |
| PROTECTED CRUISER | Edgar | GIBRALTAR | 7700 | 10000 | 12.89 | 4.92 | 11.94 | ROBERT NAPIER & SONS |
| PROTECTED CRUISER ENGINES | Edgar | EDGAR | | 10000 | 6.89 | 11.90 | 3.93 | FAIRFIELD |
| PROTECTED CRUISER ENGINES | Edgar | HAWKE | | 10000 | 6.89 | 3.91 | 5.93 | FAIRFIELD |
| 2ND CLASS CRUISER | Apollo | TERPSICHORE | 3400 | 7000 | 8.89 | 10.90 | 4.92 | CLYDEBANK |
| 2ND CLASS CRUISER | Apollo | THETIS | 3400 | 7000 | 10.89 | 12.90 | 4.92 | CLYDEBANK |
| 2ND CLASS CRUISER | Apollo | TRIBUNE | 3400 | 7000 | 12.89 | 2.91 | 5.92 | CLYDEBANK |
| 2ND CLASS CRUISER | Apollo | INDEFATIGABLE | 3600 | 7000 | 9.89 | 3.91 | 4.92 | LONDON & GLASGOW |
| 2ND CLASS CRUISER | Apollo | INTREPID | 3600 | 7000 | 9.89 | 6.91 | 11.92 | LONDON & GLASGOW |
| 2ND CLASS CRUISER | Apollo | IPHIGENIA | 3600 | 7000 | 3.90 | 11.91 | 5.93 | LONDON & GLASGOW |
| 2ND CLASS CRUISER ENGINES | Astraea | HERMIONE | | 7500 | 12.91 | 11.93 | 1.96 | CLYDEBANK |
| TORPEDO GUNBOAT ENGINES | Dryad | HAZARD | | 3500 | 4.93 | 11.93 | 7.94 | FAIRFIELD |
| **1893–1894** | | | | | | | | |
| PROTECTED CRUISER | Powerful | TERRIBLE | 14200 | 25000 | 3.94 | 7.95 | 6.97 | CLYDEBANK |
| DESTROYER | A | ROCKET | 280 | 4100 | 2.94 | 8.94 | 7.95 | CLYDEBANK |

| YEAR & TYPE | CLASS | NAME | HULL TONS | ENGINES H.P. | LAID DOWN | LAUNCHED | COMPLETED | BUILDER |
|---|---|---|---|---|---|---|---|---|
| 1893–1894 (*continued*) | | | | | | | | |
| DESTROYER | A | SURLY | 280 | 4100 | 2.94 | 11.94 | 7.95 | CLYDEBANK |
| DESTROYER | A | SHARK | 280 | 4100 | 2.94 | 9.94 | 7.95 | CLYDEBANK |
| DESTROYER | A | HANDY | 275 | 4000 | 6.94 | 3.95 | 10.95 | FAIRFIELD |
| DESTROYER | A | HART | 275 | 4000 | 6.94 | 3.95 | 1.96 | FAIRFIELD |
| DESTROYER | A | HUNTER | 275 | 4000 | 6.94 | 12.95 | 5.96 | FAIRFIELD |
| DESTROYER | A | FERVENT | 275 | 4000 | 3.94 | 3.95 | 6.00 | HANNA DONALD & WILSON |
| DESTROYER | A | ZEPHYR | 275 | 4000 | 4.94 | 5.95 | 7.01 | HANNA DONALD & WILSON |
| 1894–1895 | | | | | | | | |
| BATTLESHIP | Majestic | JUPITER | 14725 | 10000 | 4.94 | 11.95 | 5.97 | CLYDEBANK |
| 2ND CLASS CRUISER | Eclipse | DIANA | 5600 | 8000 | 8.94 | 12.95 | 6.97 | FAIRFIELD |
| 2ND CLASS CRUISER | Eclipse | VENUS | 5600 | 8000 | 6.94 | 9.95 | 11.97 | FAIRFIELD |
| 2ND CLASS CRUISER | Eclipse | DIDO | 5600 | 8000 | 8.94 | 3.96 | 5.98 | LONDON & GLASGOW |
| 2ND CLASS CRUISER | Eclipse | ISIS | 5600 | 8000 | 1.95 | 6.96 | 5.98 | LONDON & GLASGOW |
| 1895–1896 | | | | | | | | |
| PROTECTED CRUISER | Diadem | EUROPA | 11000 | 16500 | 1.96 | 3.97 | 11.99 | CLYDEBANK |
| PROTECTED CRUISER | Diadem | DIADEM | 11000 | 16500 | 1.96 | 10.96 | 7.98 | FAIRFIELD |
| 3RD CLASS CRUISER ENGINES | Pelorus | PELORUS | | 5000 | 5.95 | 12.96 | 3.97 | CLYDEBANK |
| DESTROYER | C | BRAZEN | 380 | 5800 | 10.95 | 7.96 | 7.00 | CLYDEBANK |
| DESTROYER | C | ELECTRA | 380 | 5800 | 10.95 | 7.96 | 7.00 | CLYDEBANK |
| DESTROYER | C | RECRUIT | 380 | 5800 | 10.95 | 8.96 | 10.00 | CLYDEBANK |
| DESTROYER | C | VULTURE | 345 | 5800 | 11.95 | 3.98 | 5.00 | CLYDEBANK |
| 1896–1897 | | | | | | | | |
| BATTLESHIP ENGINES | Canopus | CANOPUS | | 13500 | 1.97 | 10.97 | 12.99 | GREENOCK FOUNDRY |
| PROTECTED CRUISER | Diadem | ARIADNE | 11000 | 18000 | 10.96 | 4.98 | 6.02 | CLYDEBANK |
| PROTECTED CRUISER | Diadem | ARGONAUT | 11000 | 18000 | 11.96 | 1.98 | 4.00 | FAIRFIELD |
| 2ND CLASS CRUISER | Highflyer | HERMES | 5650 | 10000 | 4.97 | 4.98 | 10.99 | FAIRFIELD |
| 2ND CLASS CRUISER | Highflyer | HIGHFLYER | 5650 | 10000 | 6.97 | 6.98 | 12.99 | FAIRFIELD |
| 2ND CLASS CRUISER | Highflyer | HYACINTH | 5650 | 10000 | 1.97 | 10.98 | 9.00 | LONDON & GLASGOW |
| DESTROYER | B Special | ARAB | 470 | 8600 | 3.00 | 2.01 | 1.03 | CLYDEBANK |
| DESTROYER | C | KESTREL | 350 | 5800 | 9.96 | 3.98 | 4.00 | CLYDEBANK |

| YEAR & TYPE | CLASS | NAME | HULL TONS | ENGINES H.P. | LAID DOWN | LAUNCHED | COM-PLETED | BUILDER |
|---|---|---|---|---|---|---|---|---|
| **1896–1897** (*continued*) | | | | | | | | |
| DESTROYER | C | OSPREY | 355 | 6300 | 11.96 | 4.97 | 7.98 | FAIRFIELD |
| DESTROYER | C | FAIRY | 355 | 6300 | 11.96 | 5.97 | 8.98 | FAIRFIELD |
| DESTROYER | C | GIPSY | 355 | 6300 | 10.96 | 3.97 | 7.98 | FAIRFIELD |
| **1897–1898** | | | | | | | | |
| ARMOURED CRUISER | Cressy | SUTLEJ | 12000 | 21000 | 8.98 | 11.99 | 5.02 | CLYDEBANK |
| ARMOURED CRUISER | Cressy | CRESSY | 12000 | 21000 | 10.98 | 12.99 | 5.01 | FAIRFIELD |
| ARMOURED CRUISER | Cressy | ABOUKIR | 12000 | 21000 | 11.98 | 5.00 | 4.02 | FAIRFIELD |
| 3RD CLASS CRUISER ENGINES | Pelorus | PIONEER | | 5000 | 12.97 | 6.99 | 1.00 | FAIRFIELD |
| GUNBOAT | Bramble | DWARF | 710 | 1300 | 12.97 | .98 | .99 | LONDON & GLASGOW |
| GUNBOAT | Bramble | THISTLE | 710 | 1300 | 12.97 | .99 | 11.99 | LONDON & GLASGOW |
| DESTROYER | C | LEVEN | 370 | 6300 | 1.98 | 6.98 | 7.99 | FAIRFIELD |
| **1898–1899** | | | | | | | | |
| ARMOURED CRUISER | Cressy | BACCHANTE | 12000 | 21000 | 2.99 | 2.01 | 11.02 | CLYDEBANK |
| ARMOURED CRUISER | Drake | LEVIATHAN | 14150 | 30000 | 11.99 | 7.01 | 6.03 | CLYDEBANK |
| ARMOURED CRUISER | Drake | GOOD HOPE | 14150 | 30000 | 9.99 | 2.01 | 11.02 | FAIRFIELD |
| ARMOURED CRUISER ENGINES | Monmouth | ESSEX | | 22000 | 1.00 | 8.01 | 3.04 | CLYDEBANK |
| DESTROYER | C | OSTRICH | 375 | 6250 | 6.99 | 3.00 | 12.01 | FAIRFIELD |
| DESTROYER | C | FALCON | 375 | 6250 | 6.99 | 12.99 | 12.01 | FAIRFIELD |
| **1899–1900** | | | | | | | | |
| ARMOURED CRUISER | Monmouth | BEDFORD | 9800 | 22000 | 2.00 | 8.01 | 11.03 | FAIRFIELD |
| ARMOURED CRUISER | Monmouth | MONMOUTH | 9800 | 22000 | 8.99 | 11.01 | 12.03 | LONDON & GLASGOW |
| **1900–1901** | | | | | | | | |
| BATTLESHIP ENGINES | London | PRINCE OF WALES | | 15000 | 3.01 | 3.02 | 3.04 | SCOTT |
| ARMOURED CRUISER | Monmouth | DONEGAL | 9800 | 22000 | 2.01 | 9.02 | 11.03 | FAIRFIELD |
| ARMOURED CRUISER | Monmouth | CUMBERLAND | 9800 | 22000 | 2.01 | 12.02 | 12.04 | LONDON & GLASGOW |
| ARMOURED CRUISER (HULL ONLY) | Monmouth | BERWICK | 9800 | | 4.01 | 9.02 | 12.03 | BEARDMORE |
| DESTROYER (PURCHASED) | C | THORN | 380 | 6400 | | 3.00 | 6.01 | CLYDEBANK |
| DESTROYER (PURCHASED) | C | TIGER | 380 | 6400 | | 5.00 | 6.01 | CLYDEBANK |
| DESTROYER (PURCHASED) | C | VIGILANT | 380 | 6400 | | 8.00 | 6.01 | CLYDEBANK |

| YEAR & TYPE | CLASS | NAME | HULL TONS | ENGINES H.P. | LAID DOWN | LAUNCHED | COM-PLETED | BUILDER |
|---|---|---|---|---|---|---|---|---|
| **1901–1902** | | | | | | | | |
| BATTLESHIP | King Edward VII | COMMONWEALTH | 15610 | 18000 | 2.02 | 5.03 | 3.05 | FAIRFIELD |
| ARMOURED CRUISER | Devonshire | ANTRIM | 10850 | 21000 | 8.02 | 10.03 | 6.05 | CLYDEBANK |
| ARMOURED CRUISER | Devonshire | ARGYLL | 10850 | 21000 | 9.02 | 3.04 | 12.05 | SCOTT |
| ARMOURED CRUISER | Devonshire | ROXBURGH | 10850 | 21000 | 6.02 | 1.04 | 9.05 | LONDON & GLASGOW |
| ARMOURED CRUISER (HULL ONLY) | Devonshire | CARNARVON | 10850 | | 10.02 | 10.03 | 5.05 | BEARDMORE |
| **1902–1903** | | | | | | | | |
| BATTLESHIP | King Edward VII | HINDUSTAN | 15885 | 18000 | 10.02 | 12.03 | 7.05 | CLYDEBANK |
| 3RD CLASS CRUISER | Forward | FORWARD | 2860 | 16500 | 10.03 | 8.04 | 8.05 | FAIRFIELD |
| 3RD CLASS CRUISER | Forward | FORESIGHT | 2860 | 16500 | 10.03 | 10.04 | 9.05 | FAIRFIELD |
| **1903–1904** | | | | | | | | |
| BATTLESHIP ENGINES | King Edward VII | AFRICA | | 18000 | 1.04 | 5.05 | 11.06 | CLYDEBANK |
| ARMOURED CRUISER | Warrior | COCHRANE | 13550 | 23000 | 3.04 | 5.05 | 2.07 | FAIRFIELD |
| **1904–1905** | | | | | | | | |
| BATTLESHIP (HULL ONLY) | Lord Nelson | AGAMEMNON | 15925 | | 5.05 | 6.06 | 6.08 | BEARDMORE |
| ARMOURED CRUISER ENGINES | Minotaur | DEFENCE | | 27000 | 2.05 | 4.07 | 2.09 | SCOTT |
| **1905–1906** | | | | | | | | |
| BATTLECRUISER | Invincible | INFLEXIBLE | 17290 | 41000 | 2.06 | 6.07 | 10.08 | CLYDEBANK |
| BATTLECRUISER | Invincible | INDOMITABLE | 17410 | 41000 | 3.06 | 3.07 | 6.08 | FAIRFIELD |
| **1906–1907** | | | | | | | | |
| BATTLESHIP ENGINES | Bellerophon | BELLEROPHON | | 23000 | 12.06 | 7.07 | 2.09 | FAIRFIELD |
| TORPEDO BOAT | Cricket | NO. 17 | 251 | 4000 | 4.07 | 12.07 | 4.08 | DENNY |
| TORPEDO BOAT | Cricket | NO. 18 | 251 | 4000 | 4.07 | 2.08 | 6.08 | DENNY |
| TORPEDO BOAT | Cricket | NO. 23 | 253 | 4000 | 2.07 | 10.07 | 2.08 | YARROW |
| **1907–1908** | | | | | | | | |
| BATTLESHIP ENGINES | St. Vincent | ST. VINCENT | | 24500 | 12.07 | 9.08 | 5.10 | SCOTT |
| LIGHT CRUISER ENGINES | Boadicea | BOADICEA | | 18000 | 7.07 | 5.08 | 6.09 | CLYDEBANK |
| DESTROYER | Tribal | MAORI | 1026 | 15500 | 8.08 | 5.09 | 11.09 | DENNY |

| YEAR & TYPE | CLASS | NAME | HULL TONS | ENGINES H.P. | LAID DOWN | LAUNCHED | COMPLETED | BUILDER |
|---|---|---|---|---|---|---|---|---|
| **1907–1908** (*continued*) | | | | | | | | |
| TORPEDO BOAT | Cricket | NO. 29 | 250 | 4000 | 2.08 | 8.08 | 11.08 | DENNY |
| TORPEDO BOAT | Cricket | NO. 30 | 250 | 4000 | 2.08 | 9.08 | 1.09 | DENNY |
| **1908–1909** | | | | | | | | |
| BATTLECRUISER ENGINES | Indefatigable | INDEFATIGABLE | | 43000 | 2.09 | 10.09 | 2.11 | CLYDEBANK |
| PROTECTED CRUISER | Bristol | BRISTOL | 4800 | 22000 | 3.09 | 2.10 | 12.10 | CLYDEBANK |
| PROTECTED CRUISER | Bristol | GLASGOW | 4800 | 22000 | 3.09 | 9.09 | 9.10 | FAIRFIELD |
| PROTECTED CRUISER | Bristol | GLOUCESTER | 4800 | 22000 | 4.09 | 10.09 | 9.10 | BEARDMORE |
| LIGHT CRUISER ENGINES | Boadicea | BELLONA | | 18000 | 6.08 | 3.09 | 2.10 | FAIRFIELD |
| DESTROYER | Beagle | BEAGLE | 950 | 14300 | 3.09 | 10.09 | 6.10 | CLYDEBANK |
| DESTROYER | Beagle | BULLDOG | 952 | 14300 | 3.09 | 11.09 | 7.10 | CLYDEBANK |
| DESTROYER | Beagle | FOXHOUND | 953 | 14300 | 4.09 | 12.09 | 8.10 | CLYDEBANK |
| DESTROYER | Beagle | GRASSHOPPER | 923 | 14300 | 4.09 | 11.09 | 7.10 | FAIRFIELD |
| DESTROYER | Beagle | MOSQUITO | 925 | 14300 | 4.09 | 1.10 | 8.10 | FAIRFIELD |
| DESTROYER | Beagle | SCORPION | 916 | 14300 | 5.09 | 2.10 | 8.10 | FAIRFIELD |
| DESTROYER | Beagle | RATTLESNAKE | 942 | 14300 | 4.09 | 3.10 | 8.10 | LONDON & GLASGOW |
| DESTROYER | Beagle | PINCHER | 975 | 14300 | 5.09 | 3.10 | 9.10 | DENNY |
| **1909–1910** | | | | | | | | |
| BATTLESHIP | Colossus | COLOSSUS | 20225 | 25000 | 7.09 | 4.10 | 7.11 | SCOTT |
| BATTLESHIP | Orion | CONQUEROR | 22200 | 27000 | 4.10 | 5.11 | 11.12 | BEARDMORE |
| BATTLECRUISER | Indefatigable | AUSTRALIA | 18500 | 43000 | 6.10 | 10.11 | 6.13 | CLYDEBANK |
| BATTLECRUISER | Indefatigable | NEW ZEALAND | 18500 | 43000 | 6.10 | 7.11 | 11.12 | FAIRFIELD |
| LIGHT CRUISER | Weymouth | YARMOUTH | 5250 | 22000 | 1.10 | 4.11 | 4.12 | LONDON & GLASGOW |
| LIGHT CRUISER | Weymouth | FALMOUTH | 5250 | 22000 | 2.10 | 9.10 | 9.11 | BEARDMORE |
| DESTROYER | Acorn | ACORN | 765 | 13500 | 11.09 | 7.10 | 12.10 | CLYDEBANK |
| DESTROYER | Acorn | ALARM | 765 | 13500 | 2.10 | 8.10 | 3.11 | CLYDEBANK |
| DESTROYER | Acorn | BRISK | 780 | 13500 | 2.10 | 9.10 | 6.11 | CLYDEBANK |
| DESTROYER | Acorn | CAMELEON | 755 | 13500 | 6.09 | 6.10 | 12.10 | FAIRFIELD |
| DESTROYER | Acorn | COMET | 755 | 13500 | 1.10 | 6.10 | 1.11 | FAIRFIELD |
| DESTROYER | Acorn | GOLDFINCH | 755 | 13500 | 2.10 | 7.10 | 2.11 | FAIRFIELD |
| DESTROYER | Acorn | SHELDRAKE | 755 | 13500 | 1.10 | 1.11 | 5.11 | DENNY |
| DESTROYER | Acorn | STAUNCH | 755 | 13500 | 1.10 | 10.10 | 3.11 | DENNY |
| DESTROYER | Acorn | FURY | 760 | 13500 | 3.10 | 4.11 | 2.12 | A & J INGLIS |

| YEAR & TYPE | CLASS | NAME | HULL TONS | ENGINES H.P. | LAID DOWN | LAUNCHED | COMPLETED | BUILDER |
|---|---|---|---|---|---|---|---|---|
| **1909–1910** (*continued*) | | | | | | | | |
| DESTROYER | Acheron | PARAMATTA | 700 | 10600 | .09 | 2.10 | 8.10 | FAIRFIELD |
| DESTROYER | Acheron | WARREGO | 700 | 10900 | .09 | 4.11 | .11 | FAIRFIELD |
| DESTROYER | Acheron | YARA | 700 | 12225 | .09 | 4.10 | 8.10 | DENNY |
| **1910–1911** | | | | | | | | |
| BATTLESHIP | King George V | AJAX | 23000 | 27000 | 2.11 | 3.12 | 3.13 | SCOTT |
| BATTLECRUISER ENGINES | Queen Mary | QUEEN MARY | | 75000 | 3.11 | 3.12 | 9.13 | CLYDEBANK |
| LIGHT CRUISER | Chatham | SOUTHAMPTON | 5400 | 25000 | 4.11 | 5.12 | 11.12 | CLYDEBANK |
| LIGHT CRUISER | Chatham | DUBLIN | 5400 | 25000 | 1.11 | 11.11 | 3.13 | BEARDMORE |
| LIGHT CRUISER | Chatham | SYDNEY | 5400 | 25000 | 2.11 | 8.12 | 6.13 | LONDON & GLASGOW |
| DESTROYER | Acheron | HIND | 775 | 13500 | 11.10 | 7.11 | 11.11 | CLYDEBANK |
| DESTROYER | Acheron | HORNET | 775 | 13500 | 1.11 | 12.11 | 3.12 | CLYDEBANK |
| DESTROYER | Acheron | HYDRA | 775 | 13500 | 2.11 | 2.12 | 5.12 | CLYDEBANK |
| DESTROYER | Acheron | GOSHAWK | 760 | 13500 | 1.11 | 10.11 | 5.12 | BEARDMORE |
| DESTROYER | Acheron | DEFENDER | 762 | 13500 | 11.10 | 8.11 | 1.12 | DENNY |
| DESTROYER | Acheron | DRUID | 770 | 13500 | 11.10 | 12.11 | 3.12 | DENNY |
| DESTROYER (HULL ONLY) | Acheron | BEAVER | 810 | | 10.10 | 10.11 | 11.12 | DENNY |
| DESTROYER (HULL ONLY) | Acheron | BADGER | 800 | | 10.10 | 7.11 | 8.12 | DENNY |
| DESTROYER | Acheron | LURCHER | 765 | 20000 | 7.11 | 6.12 | 10.12 | YARROW |
| DESTROYER | Acheron | FIREDRAKE | 767 | 20000 | 7.11 | 4.12 | 9.12 | YARROW |
| DESTROYER | Acheron | OAK | 765 | 20000 | 7.11 | 6.12 | 11.12 | YARROW |
| DESTROYER | Acheron | ARCHER | 775 | 16000 | 9.10 | 10.11 | 3.12 | YARROW |
| DESTROYER | Acheron | ATTACK | 785 | 16000 | 9.10 | 12.11 | 5.12 | YARROW |
| SUBMARINE DEPOT-SHIP | Maidstone | MAIDSTONE | 3600 | 2800 | .11 | .12 | | SCOTT |
| **1911–1912** | | | | | | | | |
| BATTLESHIP | Iron Duke | BENBOW | 25000 | 29000 | 5.12 | 11.13 | 10.14 | BEARDMORE |
| BATTLECRUISER | Tiger | TIGER | 28430 | 108000 | 6.12 | 12.13 | 10.14 | CLYDEBANK |
| LIGHT CRUISER ENGINES | Chatham | LOWESTOFT | | 25000 | 7.12 | 4.13 | 4.14 | FAIRFIELD |
| LIGHT CRUISER ENGINES | Active | FEARLESS | | 18000 | 11.11 | 6.12 | 10.13 | BEARDMORE |
| DESTROYER | Acasta | ACASTA | 935 | 24500 | 12.11 | 9.12 | 11.12 | CLYDEBANK |
| DESTROYER | Acasta | ACHATES | 935 | 24500 | 1.12 | 11.12 | 3.13 | CLYDEBANK |
| DESTROYER | Acasta | AMBUSCADE | 935 | 24500 | 3.12 | 1.13 | 6.13 | CLYDEBANK |
| DESTROYER | Acasta | FORTUNE | 1000 | 25000 | 6.12 | 3.13 | 12.13 | FAIRFIELD |

| YEAR & TYPE | CLASS | NAME | HULL TONS | ENGINES H.P. | LAID DOWN | LAUNCHED | COMPLETED | BUILDER |
|---|---|---|---|---|---|---|---|---|
| **1911–1912** (*continued*) | | | | | | | | |
| DESTROYER | Acasta | ARDENT | 981 | 24000 | 10.12 | 9.13 | 2.14 | DENNY |
| DESTROYER | Acasta | MIDGE | 935 | 24500 | 4.12 | 5.13 | 3.14 | LONDON & GLASGOW |
| DESTROYER | Acasta | OWL | 935 | 24500 | 4.12 | 7.13 | 4.14 | LONDON & GLASGOW |
| DESTROYER | Acasta | LYNX | 935 | 24500 | 1.12 | 3.13 | 1.14 | LONDON & GLASGOW |
| DESTROYER DEPOT-SHIP | Woolwich | WOOLWICH | 3380 | 2600 | | .12 | | LONDON & GLASGOW |
| SUBMARINE | S | S.1 | 265 | 600 | | .14 | | SCOTT |
| **1912–1913** | | | | | | | | |
| BATTLESHIP | Queen Elizabeth | BARHAM | 27500 | 75000 | 2.13 | 10.14 | 10.15 | CLYDEBANK |
| BATTLESHIP | Queen Elizabeth | VALIANT | 27500 | 75000 | 1.13 | 11.14 | 2.16 | FAIRFIELD |
| LIGHT CRUISER | Arethusa | UNDAUNTED | 3750 | 40000 | 12.12 | 4.14 | 8.14 | FAIRFIELD |
| LIGHT CRUISER | Arethusa | GALATEA | 3750 | 40000 | 1.13 | 5.14 | 12.14 | BEARDMORE |
| LIGHT CRUISER | Arethusa | INCONSTANT | 3750 | 40000 | 4.13 | 7.14 | 1.15 | BEARDMORE |
| LIGHT CRUISER | Arethusa | ROYALIST | 3750 | 40000 | 6.13 | 1.15 | 3.15 | BEARDMORE |
| LIGHT CRUISER ENGINES | Arethusa | ARETHUSA | 995 | 40000 | 10.12 | 10.13 | 5.15 | FAIRFIELD |
| DESTROYER | Laforey | LAFOREY | 1003 | 24500 | 9.12 | 10.13 | 5.14 | FAIRFIELD |
| DESTROYER | Laforey | LAWFORD | 1003 | 24500 | 9.12 | 10.13 | 5.14 | FAIRFIELD |
| DESTROYER | Laforey | LYDIARD | 1003 | 24500 | 12.12 | 3.14 | 6.14 | FAIRFIELD |
| DESTROYER | Laforey | LOUIS | 996 | 24500 | 12.12 | 12.13 | 3.14 | FAIRFIELD |
| DESTROYER | Laforey | LLEWELYN | 996 | 24500 | 11.12 | 10.13 | 3.14 | BEARDMORE |
| DESTROYER | Laforey | LENNOX | 991 | 24500 | 11.12 | 3.14 | .14 | BEARDMORE |
| DESTROYER | Laforey | LOYAL | 991 | 24500 | 9.12 | 11.13 | 5.14 | DENNY |
| DESTROYER | Laforey | LEGION | 986 | 24500 | 9.12 | 2.14 | 7.14 | DENNY |
| DESTROYER | Laforey | LARK | 994 | 24500 | 6.12 | 5.13 | 11.13 | YARROW |
| DESTROYER | Laforey | LAVEROCK | 990 | 24500 | 7.12 | 11.13 | .14 | YARROW |
| DESTROYER | Laforey | LINNET | 990 | 24500 | 6.12 | 8.13 | 12.13 | YARROW |
| DESTROYER | Laforey | LANDRAIL | | 24500 | 7.12 | 2.14 | .14 | YARROW |
| **1913–1914** | | | | | | | | |
| BATTLESHIP | Revenge | RAMILLIES | 28000 | 40000 | 11.13 | 9.16 | 9.17 | BEARDMORE |
| LIGHT CRUISER ENGINES | Caroline | CONQUEST | | 40000 | 3.14 | 1.15 | 6.15 | SCOTT |
| DESTROYER FLOTILLA LEADER | Lightfoot | NIMROD | 1608 | 36000 | .14 | 4.15 | 8.15 | DENNY |
| DESTROYER | M | MILNE | 900 | 25000 | 12.13 | 10.14 | .15 | CLYDEBANK |
| DESTROYER | M | MOORSAM | 900 | 25000 | 1.14 | 12.14 | .15 | CLYDEBANK |

| YEAR & TYPE | CLASS | NAME | HULL TONS | ENGINES H.P. | LAID DOWN | LAUNCHED | COM-PLETED | BUILDER |
|---|---|---|---|---|---|---|---|---|
| 1913–1914 (*continued*) | | | | | | | | |
| DESTROYER | M | MORRIS | 900 | 25000 | 1.14 | 11.14 | .15 | CLYDEBANK |
| DESTROYER | M | MIRANDA | 895 | 23000 | 5.13 | 5.14 | 8.14 | YARROW |
| DESTROYER | M | MINOS | 883 | 23000 | 5.13 | 8.14 | 10.14 | YARROW |
| DESTROYER | M | MANLY | 883 | 23000 | 5.13 | .14 | 11.14 | YARROW |
| SUBMARINE | S | S.2 | 265 | 600 | .14 | .14 | | SCOTT |
| SUBMARINE | S | S.3 | 265 | 600 | .15 | .15 | | SCOTT |
| SUBMARINE | Swordfish | SWORDFISH | 932 | 3750 | .16 | .16 | | SCOTT |

III. DETAILS OF ADMIRALTY ORDERS FOR WARSHIPS, 1914–1919 (EXCLUDING SMALLER WARSHIPS DESIGNED FOR CONSTRUCTION IN NON SPECIALIST YARDS)

| YEAR & TYPE | CLASS | NAME | HULL TONS | ENGINES H.P. | LAID DOWN | LAUNCHED | COM-PLETED | BUILDER |
|---|---|---|---|---|---|---|---|---|
| 1914–1915 | | | | | | | | |
| BATTLECRUISER | Renown | REPULSE | 26500 | 112000 | 1.15 | 1.16 | 8.16 | CLYDEBANK |
| BATTLECRUISER | Renown | RENOWN | 26500 | 112000 | 1.15 | 3.16 | 9.16 | FAIRFIELD |
| CRUISER | Calliope | CANTERBURY | 3750 | 40000 | 12.14 | 12.15 | 5.16 | CLYDEBANK |
| MONITOR | 12-inch GUN | SIR JOHN MOORE | 5900 | 2300 | 1.15 | 5.15 | 7.15 | SCOTT |
| MONITOR | 12-inch GUN | PRINCE RUPERT | 5900 | 2300 | 1.15 | 5.15 | 7.15 | HAMILTON |
| MONITOR (HULL ONLY) | 12-inch GUN | PRINCE EUGENE | 5900 | | 2.15 | 7.15 | 9.15 | HARLAND & WOLFF (GOVAN) |
| MONITOR (HULL ONLY) | 14-inch GUN | RAGLAN | 6150 | | 12.14 | 4.15 | 6.15 | HARLAND & WOLFF (GOVAN) |
| DESTROYER | L | LOCHINVAR | 1003 | 24500 | | 10.15 | | BEARDMORE |
| DESTROYER | L | LASSOO | 1003 | 24500 | | 8.15 | 10.15 | BEARDMORE |
| DESTROYER | M | MARNE | 1025 | 25000 | | 5.15 | | CLYDEBANK |
| DESTROYER | M | MONS | 1025 | 25000 | | 5.15 | | CLYDEBANK |
| DESTROYER | M | MAMELUKE | 1025 | 25000 | | 8.15 | | CLYDEBANK |
| DESTROYER | M | OSSORY | 1025 | 25000 | | 10.15 | | CLYDEBANK |
| DESTROYER | M | NAPIER | 1025 | 25000 | | 11.16 | | CLYDEBANK |

**1914–1915** (*continued*)

| YEAR & TYPE | CLASS | NAME | HULL TONS | ENGINES H.P. | LAID DOWN | LAUNCHED | COM-PLETED | BUILDER |
|---|---|---|---|---|---|---|---|---|
| DESTROYER | M | NARBOROUGH | 1025 | 25000 | | 3.16 | | CLYDEBANK |
| DESTROYER | M | MANDATE | 1025 | 25000 | | 4.15 | 8.15 | FAIRFIELD |
| DESTROYER | M | MANNERS | 1025 | 25000 | | 6.15 | 9.15 | FAIRFIELD |
| DESTROYER | M | MINDFUL | 1025 | 25000 | | 8.15 | 11.15 | FAIRFIELD |
| DESTROYER | M | MISCHIEF | 1025 | 25000 | | 10.15 | 12.15 | FAIRFIELD |
| DESTROYER | M | ONSLAUGHT | 1025 | 25000 | | 12.15 | 2.16 | FAIRFIELD |
| DESTROYER | M | ONSLOW | 1025 | 25000 | | 2.16 | 4.16 | FAIRFIELD |
| DESTROYER | M | ORCADIA | 1025 | 25000 | | 7.16 | 9.16 | FAIRFIELD |
| DESTROYER | M | ORIANA | 1025 | 25000 | | 9.16 | 11.16 | FAIRFIELD |
| DESTROYER | M | OBSERVOR | 1025 | 25000 | | 5.16 | 6.16 | FAIRFIELD |
| DESTROYER | M | OFFA | 1025 | 25000 | | 6.16 | 7.16 | FAIRFIELD |
| DESTROYER | M | OBDURATE | 1025 | 25000 | | 1.16 | | SCOTT |
| DESTROYER | M | OBEDIENT | 1025 | 25000 | | 11.15 | | SCOTT |
| DESTROYER | M | PALADIN | 1025 | 25000 | | 3.16 | | SCOTT |
| DESTROYER | M | PARTHIAN | 1025 | 25000 | | 4.16 | | SCOTT |
| DESTROYER | M | MAENAD | 1025 | 25000 | | 8.15 | 11.15 | DENNY |
| DESTROYER | M | MARVEL | 1025 | 25000 | | 10.15 | 11.15 | DENNY |
| DESTROYER | M | NARWHAL | 1025 | 25000 | | 12.15 | 2.16 | DENNY |
| DESTROYER | M | NICATOR | 1025 | 25000 | | 2.16 | 4.16 | DENNY |
| DESTROYER (HULL ONLY) | M | MYSTIC | 1025 | 25000 | | 6.15 | 12.15 | DENNY |
| DESTROYER | Yarrow M | MOON | 896 | 23000 | | 4.15 | | YARROW |
| DESTROYER | Yarrow M | MORNING STAR | 896 | 23000 | | 6.15 | | YARROW |
| DESTROYER | Yarrow M | MOUNSEY | 896 | 23000 | | 9.15 | | YARROW |
| DESTROYER | Yarrow M | MUSKETEER | 896 | 23000 | | 11.15 | | YARROW |
| DESTROYER | Yarrow M | NERISSA | 896 | 23000 | | 2.16 | | YARROW |
| DESTROYER | M | NIZAM | 1025 | 25000 | | 4.16 | 6.16 | STEPHEN |
| DESTROYER | M | NOBLE | 1025 | 25000 | | 11.15 | 2.16 | STEPHEN |
| DESTROYER | M | NONPAREIL | 1025 | 25000 | | 5.16 | 6.16 | STEPHEN |
| DESTROYER | M | NOMAD | 1025 | 25000 | | 2.16 | 4.16 | STEPHEN |
| SUBMARINE | E | E.35 | 662 | 1600 | | .16 | | CLYDEBANK |
| SUBMARINE | E | E.36 | 662 | 1600 | | .16 | | CLYDEBANK |
| SUBMARINE | E | E.50 | 662 | 1600 | | .17 | | CLYDEBANK |
| SUBMARINE | E | E.37 | 662 | 1600 | | .16 | | FAIRFIELD |
| SUBMARINE | E | E.38 | 662 | 1600 | | .16 | | FAIRFIELD |

**1914-1915** (*continued*)

| YEAR & TYPE | CLASS | NAME | HULL TONS | ENGINES H.P. | LAID DOWN | LAUNCHED | COM-PLETED | BUILDER |
|---|---|---|---|---|---|---|---|---|
| SUBMARINE | E | E.47 | 662 | 1600 | | .16 | | FAIRFIELD |
| SUBMARINE | E | E.48 | 662 | 1600 | | .17 | | FAIRFIELD |
| SUBMARINE | E | E.25 | 662 | 1600 | | .15 | | BEARDMORE |
| SUBMARINE | E | E.26 | 662 | 1600 | | .16 | | BEARDMORE |
| SUBMARINE | E | E.53 | 662 | 1600 | | .16 | | BEARDMORE |
| SUBMARINE | E | E.54 | 662 | 1600 | | .17 | | BEARDMORE |
| SUBMARINE | E | E.31 | 662 | 1600 | | .16 | | SCOTT |
| SUBMARINE | E | E.51 | 662 | 1600 | | .16 | | SCOTT |
| SUBMARINE | E | E.52 | 662 | 1600 | | .17 | | DENNY |
| SUBMARINE | E | E.55 | 662 | 1600 | | .17 | | DENNY |
| SUBMARINE | E | E.56 | 662 | 1600 | | .17 | | DENNY |
| SUBMARINE | E | E.27 | 662 | 1600 | | .16 | | YARROW |
| SUBMARINE | G | G.14 | 700 | 1600 | | .16 | | SCOTT |
| RIVER GUNBOAT | Small China | BLACKFLY | 98 | 175 | | 4.16 | | YARROW |
| RIVER GUNBOAT | Small China | BUTTERFLY | 98 | 175 | | 7.15 | | YARROW |
| RIVER GUNBOAT | Small China | CADDISFLY | 98 | 175 | | 4.16 | | YARROW |
| RIVER GUNBOAT | Small China | CRANEFLY | 98 | 175 | | 8.15 | | YARROW |
| RIVER GUNBOAT | Small China | DRAGONFLY | 98 | 175 | | 7.15 | | YARROW |
| RIVER GUNBOAT | Small China | FIREFLY | 98 | 175 | | 7.15 | | YARROW |
| RIVER GUNBOAT | Small China | GADFLY | 98 | 175 | | 8.15 | | YARROW |
| RIVER GUNBOAT | Small China | GREYFLY | 98 | 175 | | 8.15 | | YARROW |
| RIVER GUNBOAT | Small China | GREENFLY | 98 | 175 | | 9.15 | | YARROW |
| RIVER GUNBOAT | Small China | HOVERFLY | 98 | 175 | | 4.16 | | YARROW |
| RIVER GUNBOAT | Small China | MAYFLY | 98 | 175 | | 8.15 | | YARROW |
| RIVER GUNBOAT | Small China | SAWFLY | 98 | 175 | | 8.15 | | YARROW |
| RIVER GUNBOAT (ENGINES BY YARROW) | Large China | APHIS | 645 | 2000 | | 9.15 | | AILSA |
| RIVER GUNBOAT (ENGINES BY YARROW) | Large China | BEE | 645 | 2000 | | 12.15 | | AILSA |
| RIVER GUNBOAT (ENGINES BY YARROW) | Large China | CICALA | 645 | 2000 | | 12.15 | | BARCLAY CURLE |
| RIVER GUNBOAT (ENGINES BY YARROW) | Large China | COCKCHAFER | 645 | 2000 | | 12.15 | | BARCLAY CURLE |
| RIVER GUNBOAT (ENGINES BY YARROW) | Large China | CRICKET | 645 | 2000 | | 12.15 | | BARCLAY CURLE |
| RIVER GUNBOAT (ENGINES BY YARROW) | Large China | GLOWWORM | 645 | 2000 | | 2.16 | | BARCLAY CURLE |
| RIVER GUNBOAT (ENGINES BY YARROW) | Large China | GNAT | 645 | 2000 | | 12.15 | | LOBNITZ |
| RIVER GUNBOAT (ENGINES BY YARROW) | Large China | LADYBIRD | 645 | 2000 | | 4.16 | | LOBNITZ |
| SUBMARINE DEPOT-SHIP (converted merchant ship) | | TITANIA | 5250 | 3200 | | .15 | | CLYDE SHIPBUILDING |

| YEAR & TYPE | CLASS | NAME | HULL TONS | ENGINES H.P. | LAID DOWN | LAUNCHED | COMPLETED | BUILDER |
|---|---|---|---|---|---|---|---|---|
| **1915-1916** | | | | | | | | |
| CRUISER | Ceres | CERES | 4190 | 40000 | 7.16 | 3.17 | 6.17 | CLYDEBANK |
| CRUISER | Ceres | CARDIFF | 4190 | 40000 | 7.16 | 4.17 | 7.17 | FAIRFIELD |
| CRUISER | Hawkins | RALEIGH | 9750 | 60000 | 10.16 | 8.19 | 7.19 | BEARDMORE* |
| CRUISER | Centaur | CARADOC | 4120 | 40000 | 2.16 | 12.16 | 6.17 | SCOTT |
| MONITOR (HULL ONLY) | Erebus | EREBUS | 8000 | | 10.15 | 6.16 | 9.16 | HARLAND & WOLFF (GOVAN) |
| DESTROYER FLOTILLA LEADER | Anzac | ANZAC | 1666 | 36000 | .16 | 1.17 | 4.17 | DENNY |
| DESTROYER | M | PENN | 1025 | 25000 | | 4.16 | | CLYDEBANK |
| DESTROYER | M | PEREGRINE | 1025 | 25000 | | 5.16 | | CLYDEBANK |
| DESTROYER | M | PHOEBE | 1025 | 25000 | | 11.16 | 1.17 | FAIRFIELD |
| DESTROYER | M | PHEASANT | 1025 | 25000 | | 10.16 | 11.16 | FAIRFIELD |
| DESTROYER | M | PELICAN | 1025 | 25000 | | 3.16 | | BEARDMORE |
| DESTROYER | M | PELLEW | 1025 | 25000 | | 5.16 | | BEARDMORE |
| DESTROYER | M | PLUCKY | 1025 | 25000 | | 7.16 | | SCOTT |
| DESTROYER | M | PORTIA | 1025 | 25000 | | 8.16 | | SCOTT |
| DESTROYER | M | PRINCE | 1025 | 25000 | | 7.16 | 9.16 | STEPHEN |
| DESTROYER | M | PYLADES | 1025 | 25000 | | 9.16 | 11.16 | STEPHEN |
| DESTROYER | M | PETARD | 1025 | 25000 | | 3.16 | 5.16 | DENNY |
| DESTROYER | M | PEYTON | 1025 | 25000 | | 5.16 | 6.16 | DENNY |
| DESTROYER | Yarrow M | RELENTLESS | 896 | 23000 | | 4.16 | 4.17 | YARROW |
| DESTROYER | Yarrow M | RIVAL | 896 | 23000 | | 6.16 | | YARROW |
| DESTROYER | R | ROMOLA | 1066 | 27000 | | 5.16 | | CLYDEBANK |
| DESTROYER | R | RESTLESS | 1066 | 27000 | | 8.16 | | CLYDEBANK |
| DESTROYER | R | RIGOROUS | 1066 | 27000 | | 9.16 | | CLYDEBANK |
| DESTROYER | R | ROWENA | 1066 | 27000 | | 7.16 | | CLYDEBANK |
| DESTROYER | R | SKATE | 1066 | 27000 | | 1.17 | | CLYDEBANK |
| DESTROYER | R | SIMOOM(1) | 1066 | 27000 | | 10.16 | 12.16 | CLYDEBANK |
| DESTROYER | R | TARPON | 1066 | 27000 | | 3.17 | | CLYDEBANK |
| DESTROYER | R | TELEMACHUS | 1066 | 27000 | | 4.17 | | CLYDEBANK |
| DESTROYER | R | TEMPEST | 1066 | 27000 | | 1.17 | 3.17 | FAIRFIELD |
| DESTROYER | R | SATYR | 1066 | 27000 | | 12.16 | | BEARDMORE |
| DESTROYER | R | SHARPSHOOTER | 1066 | 27000 | | 2.17 | | BEARDMORE |
| DESTROYER | R | TANCRED | 1066 | 27000 | | 6.17 | | BEARDMORE |
| DESTROYER | R | SCEPTRE | 1066 | 27000 | | 4.17 | 5.17 | STEPHEN |

**1915-1916 (*continued*)**

| YEAR & TYPE | CLASS | NAME | HULL TONS | ENGINES H.P. | LAID DOWN | LAUNCHED | COMPLETED | BUILDER |
|---|---|---|---|---|---|---|---|---|
| DESTROYER | R | STURGEON | 1066 | 27000 | | 1.17 | 2.17 | STEPHEN |
| DESTROYER | R | TORMENTOR | 1066 | 27000 | | 5.17 | 8.17 | STEPHEN |
| DESTROYER | R | TORNADO | 1066 | 27000 | | 8.17 | 10.17 | STEPHEN |
| DESTROYER (HULL ONLY) | R | SALMON | 1066 | | | 10.16 | | HARLAND & WOLFF (GOVAN) |
| DESTROYER (HULL ONLY) | R | SKILFUL | 1066 | | | 2.17 | | HARLAND & WOLFF (GOVAN) |
| DESTROYER (HULL ONLY) | R | SPRINGBOK | 1066 | | | 3.17 | | HARLAND & WOLFF (GOVAN) |
| DESTROYER (HULL ONLY) | R | SYLPH | 1066 | | | 11.16 | | HARLAND & WOLFF (GOVAN) |
| DESTROYER (HULL ONLY) | R | TENACIOUS | 1066 | | | 5.17 | | HARLAND & WOLFF (GOVAN) |
| DESTROYER (HULL ONLY) | R | TETRARCH | 1066 | | | 4.17 | | HARLAND & WOLFF (GOVAN) |
| DESTROYER | R | ROB ROY | 1066 | 27000 | | 8.16 | 12.16 | DENNY |
| DESTROYER | R | ROCKET | 1066 | 27000 | | 7.16 | 10.16 | DENNY |
| DESTROYER | R | REDGAUNTLET | 1066 | 27000 | | 11.16 | 2.17 | DENNY |
| DESTROYER | Yarrow R | STRONGBOW | 897 | 23000 | | 9.16 | 11.16 | YARROW |
| DESTROYER | Yarrow R | SURPRISE | 910 | 23000 | | 11.16 | 1.17 | YARROW |
| DESTROYER | Yarrow R | ULLSWATER | 923 | 23000 | | 8.17 | 9.17 | YARROW |
| DESTROYER | Yarrow R | SABRINA | 900 | 23000 | | 7.16 | | YARROW |
| DESTROYER | Yarrow R | SYBILLE | 900 | 23000 | | 2.17 | | YARROW |
| DESTROYER | Yarrow R | TRUCULENT | 900 | 23000 | | 3.17 | | YARROW |
| DESTROYER | Yarrow R | TYRANT | 900 | 23000 | | 5.17 | | YARROW |
| DESTROYER | Modified R | UNDINE | 1085 | 27000 | | 3.17 | 6.17 | FAIRFIELD |
| DESTROYER | Modified R | ULSTER | 1085 | 27000 | | 10.17 | | BEARDMORE |
| DESTROYER | Modified R | URSULA | 1085 | 27000 | | 8.17 | | SCOTT |
| DESTROYER | Modified R | TIRADE | 1085 | 27000 | | 4.17 | | SCOTT |
| SUBMARINE | K | K.13/22 | 1883 | 10000 | | .16 | | FAIRFIELD |
| SUBMARINE | K | K.14 | 1883 | 10000 | | .17 | | FAIRFIELD |
| SUBMARINE | K | K.15 | 1883 | 10000 | | .17 | | BEARDMORE |
| SUBMARINE | K | K.16 | 1883 | 10000 | | .17 | | SCOTT |
| RIVER GUNBOAT | Small China | SEDGEFLY | 98 | 175 | | 9.16 | | YARROW |

| YEAR & TYPE | CLASS | NAME | HULL TONS | ENGINES H.P. | LAID DOWN | LAUNCHED | COMPLETED | BUILDER |
|---|---|---|---|---|---|---|---|---|
| **1915–1916** (*continued*) | | | | | | | | |
| RIVER GUNBOAT | Small China | SNAKEFLY | 98 | 175 | | 9.16 | | YARROW |
| RIVER GUNBOAT | Small China | STONEFLY | 98 | 175 | | 9.16 | | YARROW |
| RIVER GUNBOAT | Small China | WATERFLY | 98 | 175 | | 9.16 | | YARROW |
| SUBMARINE DEPOT-SHIP | | PLATYPUS | 3476 | 2650 | | .16 | | CLYDEBANK |
| DEPOT-SHIP | | SCOTSTOUN | 300 | 200 | | | | YARROW |
| **1916–1917** | | | | | | | | |
| BATTLECRUISER | Hood | HOOD | 41200 | 144000 | 9.16 | 8.18 | 3.20 | CLYDEBANK |
| BATTLECRUISER (CANCELLED) | Hood | RODNEY | 41200 | 144000 | | | | FAIRFIELD |
| AIRCRAFT CARRIER | Argus | ARGUS | 14450 | 20000 | 6.14 | 12.17 | 9.18 | BEARDMORE |
| AIRCRAFT CARRIER | Pegasus | PEGASUS | 3300 | 9500 | .14 | 6.17 | 8.17 | CLYDEBANK |
| AIRCRAFT CARRIER (Converted merchant ship) | | NAIRANA | 3070 | 6700 | .14 | 6.15 | 8.17 | DENNY |
| CRUISER | Danae | DRAGON | 4650 | 40000 | 1.17 | 12.17 | 8.18 | SCOTT |
| DESTROYER FLOTILLA LEADER | V | VALKYRIE | 1325 | 27000 | | 3.17 | 6.17 | DENNY |
| DESTROYER FLOTILLA LEADER | V | VALOROUS | 1325 | 27000 | | 5.17 | 8.17 | DENNY |
| DESTROYER | V | VANOC | 1300 | 27000 | | 6.17 | | CLYDEBANK |
| DESTROYER | V | VANQUISHER | 1300 | 27000 | | 8.17 | | CLYDEBANK |
| DESTROYER | W | WAKEFUL | 1300 | 27000 | | 10.17 | | CLYDEBANK |
| DESTROYER | W | WATCHMAN | 1300 | 27000 | | 12.17 | | CLYDEBANK |
| DESTROYER | V | VENDETTA | 1300 | 27000 | | 9.17 | | FAIRFIELD |
| DESTROYER | V | VENETIA | 1300 | 27000 | | 10.17 | | FAIRFIELD |
| DESTROYER | W | WALRUS | 1300 | 27000 | 2.17 | 12.17 | 12.18 | FAIRFIELD |
| DESTROYER | W | WOLFHOUND | 1300 | 27000 | 4.17 | 3.18 | | BEARDMORE |
| DESTROYER | V | VANCOUVER | 1300 | 27000 | | 12.17 | | BEARDMORE |
| DESTROYER | V | VANESSA | 1300 | 27000 | | 3.18 | | BEARDMORE |
| DESTROYER | V | VANITY | 1300 | 27000 | | 5.18 | | BEARDMORE |
| DESTROYER | W | WESTMINSTER | 1300 | 27000 | | 2.18 | | SCOTT |
| DESTROYER | W | WINDSOR | 1300 | 27000 | | 6.18 | | SCOTT |
| DESTROYER | V | VIDETTE | 1300 | 27000 | | 2.18 | 4.18 | STEPHEN |
| DESTROYER | V | VESPER | 1300 | 27000 | | 12.17 | 2.18 | STEPHEN |
| DESTROYER | V | VOYAGER | 1300 | 27000 | 5.17 | 6.18 | 6.18 | STEPHEN |
| DESTROYER | V | VENTUROUS | 1300 | 27000 | | 9.17 | 11.17 | DENNY |
| DESTROYER | V | VEHEMENT | 1300 | 27000 | | 7.17 | 10.17 | DENNY |
| DESTROYER | W | WALKER | 1300 | 27000 | 3.17 | 11.17 | 2.18 | DENNY |

**1916–1917** (*continued*)

| YEAR & TYPE | CLASS | NAME | HULL TONS | ENGINES H.P. | LAID DOWN | LAUNCHED | COM- PLETED | BUILDER |
|---|---|---|---|---|---|---|---|---|
| DESTROYER | W | WESTCOTT | 1300 | 27000 | 3.17 | 2.18 | 4.18 | DENNY |
| DESTROYER | V | VIVIEN | 1300 | 27000 | 1.17 | 2.18 | | YARROW |
| DESTROYER | V | VIVACIOUS | 1300 | 27000 | | 11.17 | | YARROW |
| SUBMARINE | L.1 | L.6 | 890 | 2400 | | .18 | | BEARDMORE |
| SUBMARINE | L.9 | L.15 | 895 | 2400 | | .18 | | FAIRFIELD |
| SUBMARINE | L.9 | L.16 | 895 | 2400 | | .18 | | FAIRFIELD |
| SUBMARINE | L.9 | L.9 | 895 | 2400 | | .18 | | DENNY |
| SUBMARINE | L.9 | L.10 | 895 | 2400 | | .18 | | DENNY |
| SUBMARINE | L.50 | L.55 | 960 | 1920 | | .18 | | FAIRFIELD |
| SUBMARINE | L.50 | L.54 | 960 | 1920 | | .19 | | DENNY* |

**1917–1918**

| YEAR & TYPE | CLASS | NAME | HULL TONS | ENGINES H.P. | LAID DOWN | LAUNCHED | COM- PLETED | BUILDER |
|---|---|---|---|---|---|---|---|---|
| CRUISER | Emerald | ENTERPRISE | 7600 | 80000 | 9.18 | 5.20 | 4.26 | CLYDEBANK* |
| CRUISER | Ceres | CARLISLE | 4190 | 40000 | 10.17 | 7.18 | 11.18 | FAIRFIELD |
| CRUISER | Ceres | COLOMBO | 4190 | 40000 | 12.17 | 12.18 | 6.19 | FAIRFIELD |
| CRUISER | Danae | DESPATCH | 4765 | 40000 | 7.18 | 9.19 | 6.22 | FAIRFIELD* |
| CRUISER (CANCELLED) | Emerald | EUPHRATES | 7600 | 80000 | | | | FAIRFIELD* |
| CRUISER (CANCELLED) | Danae | DARING | 4650 | 40000 | | | | BEARDMORE |
| CRUISER | Danae | DURBAN | 4650 | 40000 | 1.18 | 5.19 | 10.21 | SCOTT* |
| DESTROYER | S | SCIMITAR | 1075 | 27000 | 8.17 | 2.18 | | CLYDEBANK |
| DESTROYER | S | SCOTSMAN | 1075 | 27000 | 10.17 | 3.18 | | CLYDEBANK |
| DESTROYER | S | SCOUT | 1075 | 27000 | 10.17 | 4.18 | | CLYDEBANK |
| DESTROYER | S | SCYTHE | 1075 | 27000 | 1.18 | 5.18 | | CLYDEBANK |
| DESTROYER | S | SEABEAR | 1075 | 27000 | 12.17 | 7.18 | | CLYDEBANK |
| DESTROYER | S | SEAFIRE | 1075 | 27000 | 2.18 | 8.18 | | CLYDEBANK |
| DESTROYER | S | SEARCHER | 1075 | 27000 | 3.18 | 9.18 | | CLYDEBANK |
| DESTROYER | S | SEAWOLF | 1075 | 27000 | 4.18 | 11.18 | | CLYDEBANK |
| DESTROYER | S | SIMOOM(2) | 1075 | 27000 | 8.17 | 1.18 | | CLYDEBANK |
| DESTROYER | S | SIKH | 1075 | 27000 | 8.17 | 5.18 | 7.18 | FAIRFIELD |
| DESTROYER | S | SIRDAR | 1075 | 27000 | 8.17 | 7.18 | | FAIRFIELD |
| DESTROYER | S | SOMME | 1075 | 27000 | 11.17 | 9.18 | | FAIRFIELD |
| DESTROYER | S | SPEAR | 1075 | 27000 | 2.18 | 11.18 | | FAIRFIELD |
| DESTROYER | S | SPINDRIFT | 1075 | 27000 | 8.18 | 12.18 | | FAIRFIELD |
| DESTROYER | S | TACTICIAN | 1075 | 27000 | 11.17 | 8.18 | | BEARDMORE |

**1917–1918** (*continued*)

| YEAR & TYPE | CLASS | NAME | HULL TONS | ENGINES H.P. | LAID DOWN | LAUNCHED | COMPLETED | BUILDER |
|---|---|---|---|---|---|---|---|---|
| DESTROYER | S | TARA | 1075 | 27000 | 11.17 | 10.18 | | BEARDMORE |
| DESTROYER | S | TATTOO | 1075 | 27000 | 12.17 | 12.18 | | BEARDMORE |
| DESTROYER | S | TASMANIA | 1075 | 27000 | 12.17 | 11.18 | | BEARDMORE |
| DESTROYER | S | STRENUOUS | 1075 | 27000 | 3.18 | 11.18 | | SCOTT |
| DESTROYER | S | STRONGHOLD | 1075 | 27000 | 3.18 | 5.19 | | SCOTT |
| DESTROYER | S | STURDY | 1075 | 27000 | 4.18 | 6.19 | | SCOTT |
| DESTROYER | S | SWALLOW | 1075 | 27000 | 9.17 | 8.18 | | SCOTT |
| DESTROYER | S | SWORDSMAN | 1075 | 27000 | 10.17 | 12.18 | | SCOTT |
| DESTROYER | S | SABRE | 1075 | 27000 | 9.17 | 9.18 | 11.18 | STEPHEN |
| DESTROYER | S | SALADIN | 1075 | 27000 | 9.17 | 2.19 | 4.19 | STEPHEN |
| DESTROYER | S | SARDONYX | 1075 | 27000 | 3.18 | 5.19 | 7.19 | STEPHEN |
| DESTROYER (CANCELLED) | S | SATURN | 1075 | 27000 | | | | STEPHEN |
| DESTROYER (CANCELLED) | S | SYCAMORE | 1075 | 27000 | | | | STEPHEN |
| DESTROYER | S | SENATOR | 1075 | 27000 | 7.17 | 4.18 | 6.18 | DENNY |
| DESTROYER | S | SEPOY | 1075 | 27000 | 8.17 | 5.18 | 8.18 | DENNY |
| DESTROYER | S | SERAPH | 1075 | 27000 | 10.17 | 7.18 | 12.18 | DENNY |
| DESTROYER | S | SERAPIS | 1075 | 27000 | 12.17 | 9.18 | 3.19 | DENNY |
| DESTROYER | S | SERENE | 1075 | 27000 | 2.18 | 11.18 | 4.19 | DENNY |
| DESTROYER (HULL ONLY) | S | SESAME | 1075 | 27000 | 3.18 | 12.18 | 3.19 | DENNY |
| DESTROYER ENGINES | S | | | 27000 | 3.18 | 12.18 | 3.19 | CLYDEBANK |
| DESTROYER | Yarrow S | TOMOHAWK | 930 | 23000 | 7.17 | 5.18 | | YARROW |
| DESTROYER | Yarrow S | TORCH | 930 | 23000 | 6.17 | 3.18 | | YARROW |
| DESTROYER | Yarrow S | TRYPHON | 930 | 23000 | 8.17 | 6.18 | | YARROW |
| DESTROYER | Yarrow S | TUMULT | 930 | 23000 | 10.17 | 9.18 | | YARROW |
| DESTROYER | Yarrow S | TURQUOISE | 930 | 23000 | 11.17 | 11.18 | | YARROW |
| DESTROYER | Yarrow S | TUSCAN | 930 | 23000 | 12.17 | 3.19 | | YARROW |
| DESTROYER | Yarrow S | TYRIAN | 930 | 23000 | 4.18 | 7.19 | | YARROW |
| DESTROYER | Repeat W | VENOMOUS | 1325 | 27000 | 5.18 | 12.18 | | CLYDEBANK |
| DESTROYER | Repeat W | VERITY | 1325 | 27000 | 5.18 | 3.19 | | CLYDEBANK |
| DESTROYER | Repeat W | WANDERER | 1325 | 27000 | 8.18 | 5.19 | | FAIRFIELD |
| DESTROYER (CANCELLED) | Repeat W | WARREN | 1325 | 27000 | | | | FAIRFIELD |
| DESTROYER | Repeat W | VANSITTART | 1325 | 27000 | 7.18 | 4.19 | | BEARDMORE |
| DESTROYER (CANCELLED) | Repeat W | VANTAGE | 1325 | 27000 | | | | BEARDMORE |
| DESTROYER | Repeat W | VOLUNTEER | 1325 | 27000 | 4.18 | 4.19 | 10.19 | DENNY |

**1917–1918** (*continued*)

| YEAR & TYPE | CLASS | NAME | HULL TONS | ENGINES H.P. | LAID DOWN | LAUNCHED | COM-PLETED | BUILDER |
|---|---|---|---|---|---|---|---|---|
| DESTROYER (CANCELLED) | Repeat W | VOTARY | 1325 | 27000 | | | | DENNY |
| DESTROYER | Repeat W | WREN | 1325 | 27000 | 6.18 | 11.19 | | YARROW |
| DESTROYER (CANCELLED) | Repeat W | WYE | 1325 | 27000 | | | | YARROW |
| SUBMARINE | L.50 | L.56 | 960 | 1920 | | .19 | | FAIRFIELD |
| SUBMARINE (CANCELLED) | L.50 | L.57 | 960 | 1920 | | | | FAIRFIELD |
| SUBMARINE (CANCELLED) | L.50 | L.58 | 960 | 1920 | | | | FAIRFIELD |
| SUBMARINE (CANCELLED) | L.50 | L.59 | 960 | 1920 | | | | BEARDMORE |
| SUBMARINE | L.50 | L.69 | 960 | 1920 | | .18 | | BEARDMORE* |
| SUBMARINE | L.50 | L.71 | 960 | 1920 | | .19 | | SCOTT |
| SUBMARINE (CANCELLED) | L.50 | L.63 | 960 | 1920 | | | | SCOTT |
| SUBMARINE (CANCELLED) | L.50 | L.73 | 960 | 1920 | | | | DENNY |
| SUBMARINE | H | H.47 | 440 | 480 | | .18 | | BEARDMORE |
| SUBMARINE | H | H.48 | 440 | 480 | | .19 | | BEARDMORE |
| SUBMARINE | H | H.49 | 440 | 480 | | .19 | | BEARDMORE |
| SUBMARINE | H | H.50 | 440 | 480 | | .19 | | BEARDMORE |
| **1918–1919** | | | | | | | | |
| DESTROYER | Repeat W | VETERAN | 1325 | 27000 | 8.18 | 4.19 | | CLYDEBANK |
| DESTROYER (CANCELLED) | Repeat W | VIGO | 1325 | 27000 | | | | CLYDEBANK |
| DESTROYER (CANCELLED) | Repeat W | VIRULENT | 1325 | 27000 | | | | CLYDEBANK |
| DESTROYER (CANCELLED) | Repeat W | VOLAGE | 1325 | 27000 | | | | CLYDEBANK |
| DESTROYER (CANCELLED) | Repeat W | VOLCANO | 1325 | 27000 | | | | CLYDEBANK |
| DESTROYER (CANCELLED) | Repeat W | WISTFUL | 1325 | 27000 | | | | CLYDEBANK |
| DESTROYER (CANCELLED) | Repeat W | WATSON | 1325 | 27000 | | | | FAIRFIELD |
| DESTROYER (CANCELLED) | Repeat W | WAVE | 1325 | 27000 | | | | FAIRFIELD |
| DESTROYER (CANCELLED) | Repeat W | WEASEL | 1325 | 27000 | | | | FAIRFIELD |
| DESTROYER (CANCELLED) | Repeat W | WHITEBEAR | 1325 | 27000 | | | | FAIRFIELD |
| DESTROYER (CANCELLED) | Repeat W | VASHON | 1325 | 27000 | | | | BEARDMORE |
| DESTROYER (CANCELLED) | Repeat W | VENGEFUL | 1325 | 27000 | | | | BEARDMORE |
| DESTROYER (CANCELLED) | Repeat W | WHEELER | 1325 | 27000 | | | | SCOTT |
| DESTROYER (CANCELLED) | Repeat W | WHELP | 1325 | 27000 | | | | SCOTT |
| DESTROYER (CANCELLED) | Repeat W | WHIPPET | 1325 | 27000 | | | | SCOTT |
| DESTROYER (CANCELLED) | Repeat W | WHIP | 1325 | 27000 | | | | SCOTT |

* Completed in Royal Dockyards

1918-1919 (*continued*)

| YEAR & TYPE | CLASS | NAME | HULL TONS | ENGINES H.P. | LAID DOWN | LAUNCHED | COMPLETED | BUILDER |
|---|---|---|---|---|---|---|---|---|
| DESTROYER (CANCELLED) | Repeat W | WAGER | 1325 | 27000 | | | | DENNY |
| DESTROYER (CANCELLED) | Repeat W | WAKE | 1325 | 27000 | | | | DENNY |
| DESTROYER (CANCELLED) | Repeat W | WALDEGRAVE | 1325 | 27000 | | | | DENNY |
| DESTROYER (CANCELLED) | Repeat W | WALTON | 1325 | 27000 | | | | DENNY |
| DESTROYER (CANCELLED) | Repeat W | WHITTAKER | 1325 | 27000 | | | | DENNY |
| DESTROYER (CANCELLED) | Repeat W | YEOMAN | 1325 | 27000 | | | | YARROW |
| DESTROYER (CANCELLED) | Repeat W | ZEALOUS | 1325 | 27000 | | | | YARROW |
| DESTROYER (CANCELLED) | Repeat W | ZEBRA | 1325 | 27000 | | | | YARROW |
| DESTROYER (CANCELLED) | Repeat W | ZODIAC | 1325 | 27000 | | | | YARROW |
| SUBMARINE (CANCELLED) | L.50 | L.62 | 960 | 1920 | | | | FAIRFIELD |
| SUBMARINE (CANCELLED) | L.50 | L.70 | 960 | 1920 | | | | BEARDMORE |
| SUBMARINE (CANCELLED) | L.50 | L.64 | 960 | 1920 | | | | SCOTT |
| SUBMARINE (CANCELLED) | L.50 | L.72 | 960 | 1920 | | | | SCOTT |
| SUBMARINE (CANCELLED) | L.50 | L.74 | 960 | 1920 | | | | DENNY |
| SLOOP | 24 Class | CLIVE | 2100 | 1700 | | 12.19 | | BEARDMORE |
| SLOOP | 24 Class | LAWRENCE | 1259 | 1900 | | 7.19 | | BEARDMORE |

## IV. DETAILS OF ADMIRALTY ORDERS FOR WARSHIPS, 1920–1939

| YEAR & TYPE | CLASS | NAME | HULL TONS | ENGINES H.P. | LAID DOWN | LAUNCHED | COMPLETED | BUILDER |
|---|---|---|---|---|---|---|---|---|
| **1914-1915** | | | | | | | | |
| CRUISER | Kent | BERWICK | 9750 | 80000 | 9.24 | 3.26 | 2.28 | FAIRFIELD |
| CRUISER ENGINES | Kent | CORNWALL | | 80000 | 10.24 | 3.26 | 5.28 | BEARDMORE |
| DESTROYER | Ambuscade | AMBUSCADE | 1173 | 33000 | 12.24 | 1.26 | .27 | YARROW |
| **1925-1926** | | | | | | | | |
| CRUISER | Kent | AUSTRALIA | 9870 | 80000 | 8.25 | 3.27 | 4.28 | CLYDEBANK |
| CRUISER | Kent | CANBERRA | 9870 | 80000 | 9.25 | 5.27 | 7.28 | CLYDEBANK |
| CRUISER | London | SHROPSHIRE | 9830 | 80000 | 2.27 | 7.28 | 9.29 | BEARDMORE |

| YEAR & TYPE | CLASS | NAME | HULL TONS | ENGINES H.P. | LAID DOWN | LAUNCHED | COM-PLETED | BUILDER |
|---|---|---|---|---|---|---|---|---|
| 1925–1926 (*continued*) | | | | | | | | |
| CRUISER ENGINES | London | LONDON | | 80000 | 2.26 | 9.27 | 1.29 | FAIRFIELD |
| RIVER GUNBOAT | Peterel | GANNET | 310 | 2250 | 3.26 | .27 | .27 | YARROW |
| RIVER GUNBOAT | Peterel | PETEREL | 310 | 2250 | 3.26 | .27 | .27 | YARROW |
| RIVER GUNBOAT | Tern | SEAMEW | 262 | 1370 | 4.26 | .27 | .27 | YARROW |
| RIVER GUNBOAT | Tern | TERN | 262 | 1370 | 4.26 | .27 | .27 | YARROW |
| 1926–1927 | | | | | | | | |
| CRUISER | Norfolk | NORFOLK | 9975 | 80000 | 7.27 | 12.28 | 4.30 | FAIRFIELD |
| SUBMARINE | Odin | OLYMPUS | 1475 | 1390 | 4.27 | 12.28 | .30 | BEARDMORE |
| SUBMARINE | Odin | ORPHEUS | 1475 | 1390 | 4.27 | 2.29 | .30 | BEARDMORE |
| 1927–1928 | | | | | | | | |
| DESTROYER | A | ACASTA | 1337 | 34000 | 8.28 | 8.29 | .30 | CLYDEBANK |
| DESTROYER | A | ACHATES | 1337 | 34000 | 9.28 | 10.29 | .30 | CLYDEBANK |
| DESTROYER | A | ANTHONY | 1337 | 34000 | 7.28 | 4.29 | .30 | SCOTT |
| DESTROYER | A | ARDENT | 1337 | 34000 | 8.28 | 6.29 | .30 | SCOTT |
| 1928–1929 | | | | | | | | |
| DESTROYER | B | BASILISK | 1360 | 34000 | 8.29 | 8.30 | .31 | CLYDEBANK |
| DESTROYER | B | BEAGLE | 1360 | 34000 | 8.29 | 9.30 | .31 | CLYDEBANK |
| 1929–1930 | | | | | | | | |
| RIVER GUNBOAT | Falcon | FALCON | 372 | 2250 | 4.3 | .31 | .31 | YARROW |
| 1930–1931 | | | | | | | | |
| DESTROYER | D | DAINTY | 1375 | 36000 | 6.31 | 6.32 | 1.33 | FAIRFIELD |
| DESTROYER | D | DELIGHT | 1375 | 36000 | 4.31 | 5.32 | 1.33 | FAIRFIELD |
| DESTROYER ENGINES | D | DUNCAN | | 36000 | 9.31 | 7.32 | .33 | BEARDMORE |
| SLOOP ENGINES | Shoreham | MILFORD | | 2000 | 9.31 | 6.32 | .32 | YARROW |
| SLOOP ENGINES | Shoreham | WESTON | | 2000 | 9.31 | 7.32 | .33 | YARROW |
| 1931–1932 | | | | | | | | |
| CRUISER ENGINES | Perth | AMPHION | | 72000 | 6.33 | 7.34 | 7.36 | BEARDMORE |
| DESTROYER | E | ESCAPADE | 1405 | 36000 | 3.33 | 1.34 | .34 | SCOTT |
| DESTROYER | E | ESCORT | 1405 | 36000 | 3.33 | 3.34 | .34 | SCOTT |
| DESTROYER | E | ECHO | 1405 | 36000 | 3.33 | 2.34 | 10.34 | DENNY |

| YEAR & TYPE | CLASS | NAME | HULL TONS | ENGINES H.P. | LAID DOWN | LAUNCHED | COM-PLETED | BUILDER |
|---|---|---|---|---|---|---|---|---|
| **1931–1932** (*continued*) | | | | | | | | |
| DESTROYER | E | ECLIPSE | 1405 | 36000 | 3.33 | 3.34 | 11.34 | DENNY |
| DESTROYER ENGINES | E | EXMOUTH | | 38000 | 5.33 | 1.34 | .34 | FAIRFIELD |
| MINESWEEPER | Halcyon | HALCYON | 815 | 1770 | 3.33 | .33 | .34 | CLYDEBANK |
| MINESWEEPER | Halcyon | SKIPJACK | 815 | 1770 | 4.33 | .34 | .34 | CLYDEBANK |
| RIVER GUNBOAT | Robin | ROBIN | 226 | 800 | 4.33 | .33 | .34 | YARROW |
| DESTROYER DEPOT-SHIP | Woolwich | WOOLWICH | 8750 | 6500 | 5.33 | .34 | 6.35 | FAIRFIELD |
| **1932–1933** | | | | | | | | |
| CRUISER | Arethusa | GALATEA | 5220 | 64000 | 6.33 | 8.34 | 8.35 | SCOTT |
| CRUISER ENGINES | Perth | APOLLO | | 72000 | 8.33 | 10.34 | 1.36 | BEARDMORE |
| DESTROYER FLOTILLA LEADER | F | FAULKNOR | 1460 | 38000 | 7.33 | 6.34 | .35 | YARROW |
| DESTROYER | F | FOXHOUND | 1405 | 36000 | 8.33 | 8.34 | .35 | CLYDEBANK |
| DESTROYER | F | FORTUNE | 1405 | 36000 | 7.33 | 10.34 | .35 | CLYDEBANK |
| **1933–1934** | | | | | | | | |
| CRUISER | Southampton | SOUTHAMPTON | 9100 | 75000 | 11.34 | 3.36 | 3.37 | CLYDEBANK |
| DESTROYER FLOTILLA LEADER | G | GRENVILLE | 1465 | 38000 | 9.34 | 8.35 | 7.36 | YARROW |
| DESTROYER | G | GARLAND | 1350 | 34000 | 8.34 | 10.35 | 3.36 | FAIRFIELD |
| DESTROYER | G | GIPSY | 1350 | 34000 | 9.34 | 11.35 | 3.36 | FAIRFIELD |
| DESTROYER | G | GALLANT | 1350 | 34000 | 9.34 | 9.35 | 1.36 | STEPHEN |
| DESTROYER | G | GRENADE | 1350 | 34000 | 10.34 | 11.35 | 3.36 | STEPHEN |
| SUBMARINE | Shark | SEAWOLF | 670 | 1440 | 5.34 | 11.35 | .36 | SCOTT |
| SLOOP | Bittern | ENCHANTRESS | 1085 | 3300 | 4.34 | 12.34 | .35 | CLYDEBANK |
| PATROL VESSEL | Kingfisher | KINGFISHER | 510 | 3600 | 6.34 | .35 | .35 | FAIRFIELD |
| MINESWEEPER | Halcyon | SPEEDWELL | 815 | 1770 | 6.34 | .35 | .35 | HAMILTON |
| NETLAYER | Protector | PROTECTOR | 2820 | 9000 | 8.35 | .36 | .37 | YARROW |
| **1934–1935** | | | | | | | | |
| CRUISER | Southampton | GLASGOW | 9100 | 75000 | 4.35 | 6.36 | 9.37 | SCOTT |
| CRUISER ENGINES | Southampton | BIRMINGHAM | | 75000 | 7.35 | 9.36 | 11.37 | CLYDEBANK |
| DESTROYER | H | HOSTILE | 1340 | 34000 | 2.35 | 1.36 | .36 | SCOTT |
| DESTROYER | H | HOTSPUR | 1340 | 34000 | 2.35 | 3.36 | .36 | SCOTT |
| DESTROYER | H | HASTY | 1340 | 34000 | 4.35 | 5.36 | 11.36 | DENNY |
| DESTROYER | H | HAVOCK | 1340 | 34000 | 5.35 | 7.36 | 1.37 | DENNY |
| SLOOP | Bittern | STORK | 1190 | 3300 | 6.35 | 4.36 | 9.36 | DENNY |

| YEAR & TYPE | CLASS | NAME | HULL TONS | ENGINES H.P. | LAID DOWN | LAUNCHED | COMPLETED | BUILDER |
|---|---|---|---|---|---|---|---|---|
| 1934–1935 (*continued*) | | | | | | | | |
| PATROL VESSEL | Kingfisher | MALLARD | 510 | 3600 | 6.35 | .36 | 6.36 | STEPHEN |
| PATROL VESSEL | Kingfisher | PUFFIN | 510 | 3600 | 6.35 | .36 | 7.36 | STEPHEN |
| 1935–1936 | | | | | | | | |
| CRUISER | Gloucester | LIVERPOOL | 9400 | 82500 | 2.36 | 3.37 | 11.38 | FAIRFIELD |
| CRUISER ENGINES | Gloucester | GLOUCESTER | | 82500 | 9.36 | 10.37 | 1.39 | SCOTT |
| DESTROYER | I | ICARUS | 1370 | 34000 | 3.36 | 11.36 | .37 | CLYDEBANK |
| DESTROYER | I | ILEX | 1370 | 34000 | 3.36 | 1.37 | .37 | CLYDEBANK |
| DESTROYER | I | ISIS | 1370 | 34000 | 2.36 | 11.36 | .37 | YARROW |
| DESTROYER | I | IVANHOE | 1370 | 34000 | 2.36 | 2.37 | .37 | YARROW |
| DESTROYER | Tribal | GURKHA | 1959 | 44000 | 7.36 | 7.37 | 11.38 | FAIRFIELD |
| DESTROYER | Tribal | MAORI | 1959 | 44000 | 7.36 | 9.37 | 11.38 | FAIRFIELD |
| DESTROYER | Tribal | ZULU | 1959 | 44000 | 8.36 | 9.37 | 3.38 | STEPHEN |
| SUBMARINE | Grampus | CACHALOT | 1520 | 1630 | 5.36 | 12.37 | .38 | SCOTT |
| SUBMARINE DEPOT-SHIP | Maidstone | MAIDSTONE | 8900 | 7000 | 8.36 | .37 | .38 | CLYDEBANK |
| 1936–1937 | | | | | | | | |
| CRUISER | Dido | PHOEBE | 5600 | 62000 | 9.37 | 3.39 | 9.40 | FAIRFIELD |
| CRUISER ENGINES | Dido | SIRIUS | | 62000 | 4.38 | 9.40 | 5.42 | SCOTT |
| DESTROYER | Tribal | MATABELE | 1959 | 44000 | 10.36 | 10.37 | .39 | SCOTT |
| DESTROYER | Tribal | PUNJABI | 1959 | 44000 | 10.36 | 12.37 | .39 | SCOTT |
| DESTROYER | Tribal | SIKH | 1959 | 44000 | 9.36 | 12.37 | 7.38 | STEPHEN |
| DESTROYER | Tribal | ASHANTI | 1959 | 44000 | 11.36 | 11.37 | 12.38 | DENNY |
| DESTROYER | Tribal | BEDOUIN | 1959 | 44000 | 1.37 | 12.37 | 3.39 | DENNY |
| DESTROYER | J | JACKAL | 1760 | 40000 | 9.37 | 10.38 | .39 | CLYDEBANK |
| DESTROYER | J | JAVELIN | 1760 | 40000 | 11.37 | 12.38 | .39 | CLYDEBANK |
| DESTROYER | J | JUNO | 1760 | 40000 | 10.37 | 12.38 | 8.39 | FAIRFIELD |
| DESTROYER | J | JAGUAR | 1760 | 40000 | 11.37 | 11.38 | 9.39 | DENNY |
| DESTROYER | J | JUPITER | 1760 | 40000 | 9.37 | 10.38 | .39 | YARROW |
| SUBMARINE | Triton | TRIBUNE | 1090 | 1450 | 2.37 | 12.38 | .38 | SCOTT |
| PATROL VESSEL | Kingfisher | WIDGEON | 530 | 3600 | 3.37 | .38 | .38 | YARROW |
| MINELAYER | Plover | PLOVER | 805 | 1400 | 10.36 | 6.37 | 9.37 | DENNY |
| MINESWEEPER (HULL ONLY) | Halcyon | GOSSAMER | 815 | 1750 | 11.36 | .37 | .38 | HAMILTON |
| MINESWEEPER (HULL ONLY) | Halcyon | JASON | 815 | | 12.36 | .37 | .38 | AILSA |
| MINESWEEPER (HULL ONLY) | Halcyon | FRANKLIN | 815 | | 12.36 | .37 | .38 | AILSA |

| YEAR & TYPE | CLASS | NAME | HULL TONS | ENGINES H.P. | LAID DOWN | LAUNCHED | COM-PLETED | BUILDER |
|---|---|---|---|---|---|---|---|---|
| **1937–1938** | | | | | | | | |
| BATTLESHIP | King George V | DUKE OF YORK | 36727 | 110000 | 5.37 | 2.40 | 11.41 | CLYDEBANK |
| BATTLESHIP | King George V | HOWE | 36727 | 110000 | 6.37 | 4.40 | 8.42 | FAIRFIELD |
| CRUISER | Fiji | FIJI | 8530 | 72500 | 3.38 | 5.39 | 5.40 | CLYDEBANK |
| CRUISER | Dido | BONAVENTURE | 5600 | 62000 | 8.37 | 4.39 | 5.40 | SCOTT |
| CRUISER | Dido | HERMIONE | 5600 | 62000 | 10.37 | 5.39 | 3.41 | STEPHEN |
| CRUISER | Fiji | KENYA | 8530 | 72500 | 6.38 | 8.39 | 9.40 | STEPHEN |
| DESTROYER | K | KELVIN | 1760 | 40000 | 10.37 | 1.39 | 11.39 | FAIRFIELD |
| DESTROYER | K | KANDAHAR | 1760 | 40000 | 1.38 | 3.39 | 10.39 | DENNY |
| DESTROYER | K | KIPLING | 1760 | 40000 | 10.37 | 1.39 | 1.40 | YARROW |
| DESTROYER | L | LOOKOUT | 1920 | 48000 | 11.38 | 11.40 | | SCOTT |
| DESTROYER | L | LOYAL | 1920 | 48000 | 11.38 | 9.41 | | SCOTT |
| DESTROYER | L | LAFOREY | 1920 | 48000 | .38 | 2.41 | | YARROW |
| DESTROYER | L | LANCE | 1920 | 48000 | .38 | 11.40 | | YARROW |
| SUBMARINE | Triton | TARPON | 1090 | 1450 | 10.37 | 10.39 | | SCOTT |
| SUBMARINE | Triton | TUNA | 1090 | 1450 | 6.38 | 5.40 | | SCOTT |
| SLOOP | Egret | AUCKLAND | 1250 | 3600 | 6.37 | 6.38 | 11.38 | DENNY |
| PATROL VESSEL | Sheerwater | GUILLEMOT | 580 | 3600 | 8.38 | 7.39 | 10.39 | DENNY |
| PATROL VESSEL | Sheerwater | PINTAIL | 580 | 3600 | 8.38 | 8.39 | 11.39 | DENNY |
| MINESWEEPER | Halcyon | SPEEDY | 815 | 1750 | 12.37 | .38 | | HAMILTON |
| MINSWEEPER | Halcyon | SPHINX | 815 | 1750 | 1.38 | .39 | | HAMILTON |
| MINESWEEPER ENGINES | Halcyon | BRAMBLE | | 1750 | 11.37 | | | BARCLAY CURLE |
| MINESWEEPER ENGINES | Halcyon | BRITTOMART | | 1750 | 1.38 | | | BARCLAY CURLE |
| SUBMARINE DEPOT-SHIP | Maidstone | FORTH | 9050 | 7000 | 6.37 | .38 | | CLYDEBANK |
| **1938–1939** | | | | | | | | |
| AIRCRAFT CARRIER | Implacable | IMPLACABLE | 23450 | 148000 | 2.39 | 12.42 | 8.44 | FAIRFIELD |
| CRUISER | Dido | SCYLLA | 5600 | 62000 | 4.39 | 7.40 | 6.42 | SCOTT |
| CRUISER | Fiji | CEYLON | 8530 | 72500 | 4.39 | 7.42 | 7.43 | STEPHEN |
| ESCORT VESSEL | Black Swan | BLACK SWAN | 1300 | 4300 | 6.38 | 7.39 | | YARROW |
| ESCORT VESSEL | Black Swan | FLAMINGO | 1300 | 4300 | 5.38 | 4.39 | | YARROW |
| MINELAYER | Abdiel | MANXMAN | 2650 | 72000 | 3.39 | 9.40 | 6.41 | STEPHEN |
| RIVER GUNBOAT | Dragonfly | LOCUST | 625 | 3800 | 11.38 | .39 | .40 | YARROW |
| RIVER GUNBOAT | Dragonfly | MOSQUITO | 625 | 3800 | 12.38 | .39 | .40 | YARROW |
| DESTROYER DEPOT-SHIP | Tyne | HECKLA | 11000 | 7500 | 1.39 | .40 | | CLYDEBANK |
| DESTROYER DEPOT-SHIP | Tyne | TYNE | 11000 | 7500 | 7.38 | .40 | | SCOTT |

## V. DETAILS OF WARSHIPS ORDERED BY FOREIGN POWERS, 1859–1939

| LAUNCHED | TYPE | NAME | FOREIGN POWER | HULL TONS | ENGINES H.P. | BUILDER |
|---|---|---|---|---|---|---|
| 1863 | TURRET SHIP | ROLFE KRAKE | DENMARK | 1320 | 750 | ROBERT NAPIER & SONS |
| 1864 | BROADSIDE IRONCLAD | OSMANIEH | TURKEY | 6400 | 3735 | ROBERT NAPIER & SONS |
| 1865 | BROADSIDE IRONCLAD | ABDUL AZIZ | TURKEY | 6400 | 3735 | ROBERT NAPIER & SONS |
| 1865 | BROADSIDE IRONCLAD | ORKANIEH | TURKEY | 6400 | 3735 | ROBERT NAPIER & SONS |
| 1865 | CORVETTE | TORNADO (EX PAMPERO) | SPAIN (EX CONFEDERACY) | 2090 | 435 | J & G THOMSON |
| 1868 | TURRET RAM | BUFFEL | HOLLAND | 2284 | 2000 | ROBERT NAPIER & SONS |
| 1868 | MONITOR | TIJGER | HOLLAND | 1427 | 680 | ROBERT NAPIER & SONS |
| 1868 | GUNBOAT | KWANG TUNG | CHINA | 439 | 255 | DENNY |
| 1868 | GUNBOAT | SHANG TUNG | CHINA | 439 | 255 | DENNY |
| 1886 | TORPEDO GUNBOAT | DESTRUCTOR | SPAIN | 348 | 3784 | J & G THOMSON |
| 1886 | TORPEDO BOAT | VIBORG | RUSSIA | 166 | 1300 | J & G THOMSON |
| 1887 | PROTECTED CRUISER | REINA REGENTE | SPAIN | 4725 | 11500 | J & G THOMSON |
| 1890 | ARMOURED CRUISER | CHIYODA | JAPAN | 2400 | 5600 | CLYDEBANK |
| 1892 | GUNBOAT | BORNEO | HOLLAND | 787 | 1040 | CLYDEBANK |
| 1892 | GUNBOAT | RESTAURACION | SAN DOMINGO | 1000 | ? | ROBERT NAPIER & SONS |
| 1894 | GUNBOAT | INDEPENDENCIA | SAN DOMINGO | 322 | ? | ROBERT NAPIER & SONS |
| 1895 | GUNBOAT | HERMAN CORIES | SPAIN | 295 | ? | CLYDEBANK |
| 1895 | GUNBOAT | PIZARRO | SPAIN | 295 | ? | CLYDEBANK |
| 1895 | GUNBOAT | VASCO NUNEZ DE BALBOA | SPAIN | 295 | ? | CLYDEBANK |
| 1896 | GUNBOAT | DIEGO VELAZQUEZ | SPAIN | 250 | ? | CLYDEBANK |
| 1896 | GUNBOAT | PONCE DE LEON | SPAIN | 250 | ? | CLYDEBANK |
| 1896 | GUNBOAT | ALVARADO | SPAIN | 200 | ? | CLYDEBANK |
| 1896 | GUNBOAT | SANDOVAL | SPAIN | 200 | ? | CLYDEBANK |
| 1896 | DESTROYER | FUROR | SPAIN | 370 | 6000 | CLYDEBANK |
| 1396 | DESTROYER | TERROR | SPAIN | 370 | 6000 | CLYDEBANK |
| 1897 | DESTROYER | AUDAZ | SPAIN | 400 | 7500 | CLYDEBANK |
| 1897 | DESTROYER | OSADO | SPAIN | 400 | 7500 | CLYDEBANK |
| 1897 | DESTROYER | PLUTON | SPAIN | 400 | 7500 | CLYDEBANK |
| 1897 | DESTROYER | PROSPERINE | SPAIN | 400 | 7500 | CLYDEBANK |
| 1899 | BATTLESHIP | ASAHI | JAPAN | 15200 | 15000 | CLYDEBANK |

| LAUNCHED | TYPE | NAME | FOREIGN POWER | HULL TONS | ENGINES H.P. | BUILDER |
|---|---|---|---|---|---|---|
| 1908 | DESTROYER | PARA | BRAZIL | 560 | 8000 | YARROW |
| 1908 | DESTROYER | PIAUI | BRAZIL | 560 | 8000 | YARROW |
| 1908 | DESTROYER | AMAZONAS | BRAZIL | 560 | 8000 | YARROW |
| 1909 | DESTROYER | MATO GROSSO | BRAZIL | 560 | 8000 | YARROW |
| 1909 | DESTROYER | RIO GRANDE DO NORTE | BRAZIL | 560 | 8000 | YARROW |
| 1909 | DESTROYER | PARAIBO | BRAZIL | 560 | 8000 | YARROW |
| 1909 | DESTROYER | ALAGAOS | BRAZIL | 560 | 8000 | YARROW |
| 1909 | DESTROYER | SANTA CATHARINA | BRAZIL | 560 | 8000 | YARROW |
| 1909 | RIVER GUNBOAT | MACAO | PORTUGAL | 133 | 250 | YARROW |
| 1910 | DESTROYER | PARANA | BRAZIL | 560 | 8000 | YARROW |
| 1910 | DESTROYER | SERGIPE | BRAZIL | 560 | 8000 | YARROW |
| 1911 | TORPEDO BOAT | SORRIDEREN | DENMARK | 240 | 5000 | YARROW |
| 1914 | DESTROYER * | MELPOMENE (EX SAMOS) | GREECE | 1007 | 25000 | FAIRFIELD |
| 1915 | DESTROYER * | MELAMPUS (EX CHIOS) | GREECE | 1007 | 25000 | FAIRFIELD |
| 1915 | DESTROYER * | MEDEA (EX KRITI) | GREECE | 1040 | 25000 | CLYDEBANK |
| 1915 | DESTROYER * | MEDUSA (EX LESVOS) | GREECE | 1040 | 25000 | CLYDEBANK |
| 1915 | DESTROYER | URAKAZE | JAPAN | 907 | 22000 | YARROW |
| 1916 | DESTROYER | AUDACE (EX KAWAKAZE) | ITALY (EX JAPAN) | 922 | 22000 | YARROW |
| 1916 | SLOOP | ALDEBARAN | FRANCE | 1250 | 2000 | BARCLAY CURLE |
| 1916 | SLOOP | ALGOL | FRANCE | 1250 | 2000 | BARCLAY CURLE |
| 1916 | SLOOP | CASSIOPEE | FRANCE | 1250 | 2000 | BARCLAY CURLE |
| 1916 | SLOOP | REGULUS | FRANCE | 1250 | 2000 | BARCLAY CURLE |
| 1916 | SLOOP | ALTAIR | FRANCE | 1250 | 2000 | HAMILTON |
| 1916 | SLOOP | ANTARES | FRANCE | 1250 | 2000 | HAMILTON |
| 1916 | SLOOP | BELLATRIX | FRANCE | 1250 | 2000 | HENDERSON |
| 1916 | SLOOP | RIGEL | FRANCE | 1250 | 2000 | HENDERSON |
| 1918 | RIVER GUNBOAT | TETE | PORTUGAL | 100 | ? | YARROW |
| 1930 | GUNBOAT | BARRANQUILLA | COLOMBIA | 142 | ? | YARROW |
| 1930 | GUNBOAT | CARTAGENA | COLOMBIA | 142 | ? | YARROW |
| 1930 | GUNBOAT | SANTA MARIA | COLOMBIA | 142 | ? | YARROW |
| 1931 | DESTROYER | DUBROVNIK | YUGOSLAVIA | 1880 | 48000 | YARROW |
| 1933 | DESTROYER | LIMA | PORTUGAL | 1219 | 33000 | YARROW |

* TAKEN OVER BY THE ADMIRALTY WHILE UNDER CONSTRUCTION

| LAUNCHED | TYPE | NAME | FOREIGN POWER | HULL TONS | ENGINES H.P. | BUILDER |
|---|---|---|---|---|---|---|
| 1933 | DESTROYER | VOUGA | PORTUGAL | 1219 | 33000 | YARROW |
| 1937 | DESTROYER | SAN JUAN | ARGENTINA | 1375 | 34000 | CLYDEBANK |
| 1937 | DESTROYER | SAN LUIS | ARGENTINA | 1375 | 34000 | CLYDEBANK |
| 1938 | DESTROYER | VASILEFS GEORGIOS | GREECE | 1350 | 34000 | YARROW |
| 1938 | DESTROYER | VASILISSA OLGA | GREECE | 1350 | 34000 | YARROW |
| 1941 | DESTROYER | DEMIRHISAR | TURKEY | 1360 | 34000 | DENNY |
| 1941 | DESTROYER | SULTANHISAR | TURKEY | 1360 | 34000 | DENNY |

## VI. DISTRIBUTION OF WARSHIP ORDERS, 1859–1939 (EXCLUDING ORDERS CANCELLED BEFORE COMPLETION)

| YARD | ADMIRALTY ORDERS | | | | | | | | | | | | | | | | FOREIGN ORDERS 1859–1939 | |
|---|---|---|---|---|---|---|---|---|---|---|---|---|---|---|---|---|---|---|
| | 1859–1888 | | | | 1889–1914 | | | | WAR YEARS* | | | | 1920–1939 | | | | | |
| | No. | HULL TONS | ENGINES No. | H.P. | No. | HULL TONS | ENGINES No. | H.P. | No. | HULL TONS | ENGINES No. | H.P. | No. | HULL TONS | ENGINES No. | H.P. | No. | HULL TONS |
| ROBERT NAPIER & SONS | 20 | 72439 | 23 | 60456 | 1 | 7700 | 1 | 10000 | | | | | | | | | 8 | 25553 |
| BEARDMORE'S | | | | | 15 | 141227 | 13 | 365500 | 29 | 50205 | 29 | 481540 | 3 | 12780 | 8 | 344450 | 24 | 34671 |
| CLYDEBANK | 12 | 18863 | 14 | 34280 | 43 | 258215 | 50 | 1035300 | 42 | 137580 | 43 | 1307950 | 21 | 120226 | 22 | 876840 | 2 | 2014 |
| FAIRFIELD | 12 | 29926 | 11 | 28554 | 42 | 223283 | 50 | 893600 | 39 | 79410 | 39 | 931040 | 16 | 117050 | 18 | 998600 | | |
| SCOTT'S | 2 | 1610 | 10 | 9050 | 8 | 59402 | 15 | 219350 | 24 | 40482 | 24 | 532020 | 20 | 57902 | 22 | 814420 | | |
| LONDON & GLASGOW | 1 | 603 | 1 | 580 | 18 | 77297 | 18 | 252000 | 9 | 26446 | | | | | | | | |
| HARLAND & WOLFF (GOVAN) | | | | | | | | | 16 | 17539 | 16 | 420000 | 10 | 32948 | 10 | 442200 | | |
| STEPHEN'S | | | | | 17 | 12926 | 15 | 221025 | 31 | 35470 | 29 | 608590 | 13 | 17333 | 13 | 323500 | 4 | 3598 |
| DENNY'S | | | | | 13 | 10731 | 13 | 263000 | 42 | 26229 | 50 | 586200 | 21 | 23140 | 23 | 396090 | 23 | 15346 |
| YARROW'S ** | | | | | 3 | 1310 | 3 | 21500 | 10 | 16310 | 2 | 5500 | 6 | 4890 | 5 | 8750 | 8 | 10000 |
| OTHERS | 3 | 723 | 4 | 2724 | | | | | | | | | | | | | | |
| TOTAL | 50 | 124164 | 63 | 135644 | 160 | 792091 | 178 | 3281275 | 242 | 429671 | 232 | 4872840 | 110 | 386269 | 121 | 4204850 | 69 | 91182 |

*Excluding small warships expressly designed to be built in non-specialist yards, and warships under construction for foreign powers taken over by the Admiralty on the outbreak of war.

**From the date of Yarrow's move to the Clyde only.

# Index